CRUEL OPTIMISM

Duke University Press   Durham and London   2011

Lauren Berlant   **CRUEL OPTIMISM**

© 2011 Duke University Press

All rights reserved

Printed in the United States of America on acid-free paper ∞

Designed by Amy Ruth Buchanan

Typeset in Quadraat by Tseng Information Systems, Inc.

Library of Congress Cataloging-in-Publication Data appear
on the last printed page of this book.

An earlier version of chapter 4 appeared as "Two Girls,
Fat and Thin," in *Regarding Sedgwick*, ed. Stephen M. Barber
and David L. Clark. © Routledge, 2002.

CONTENTS

Acknowledgments vii

Introduction: Affect in the Present 1

ONE Cruel Optimism 23

TWO Intuitionists: History and the Affective Event 51

THREE Slow Death (Obesity, Sovereignty, Lateral Agency) 95

FOUR Two Girls, Fat and Thin 121

FIVE Nearly Utopian, Nearly Normal:
Post-Fordist Affect in La Promesse and Rosetta 161

SIX After the Good Life, an Impasse:
Time Out, Human Resources, and the Precarious Present 191

SEVEN On the Desire for the Political 223

Note on the Cover Image: If Body: Riva and Zora in Middle Age 265

Notes 269

Bibliography 303

Index 327

ACKNOWLEDGMENTS

The project that became *Cruel Optimism* began when I was a Leverhulme fellow at Lancaster University for a number of years, in conversation (now for over a decade) with the wonderful and brilliant crew of Bev Skeggs, Sarah Franklin, Sara Ahmed, Celia Lury, Jackie Stacey, Imogen Tyler, and the much-grieved Paul Fletcher. Speaking of grieving, it was during a conversation with Bill Readings about Lyotard that I first saw optimism as the thing that keeps the event open, for better or ill. Thanks to Roger Rouse for continuing to brainstorm with my aleatory thoughts about aleatoriness and my transnational thoughts about capital. Thanks to Ian Horswill for collaborating with me on everything related to anxiety and happiness, including all those long talks about politics, neuropsychology, and attachment (and Puck). Lee Edelman, one of the Press readers of the manuscript, did an extremely close and improving reading of the thing. I was already grateful for his friendship and collaboration; to have been able to work with his notes was a real gift, and I am almost abject with admiration. The other Press reader also read brilliantly and transferentially in the best sense, and I hope notes her/his substantial impact on the revisions.

To Ken Wissoker and Rachel Furnari, I can't thank you enough for all of your help and labor, including continuing to push me to get things done well, and for being so alive to the ambit of the work. I also greatly appreciate the calming, clarifying, and creative labor of the volume's editor, G. Neal McTighe, and its inspired designer, Amy Ruth Buchanan. More than thanks go to Riva Lehrer for permitting me to display and engage *If Body: Riva and Zora in Middle Age*. Other props go to the people who read and talked substantively with me about this project: Dipesh Chakrabarty, Tom Mitchell, Claire Pentecost, Mandy Berry, Dana Luciano, Amelia Jones, Kris Cohen, and Katie Stewart. And so much thanks to the broader Public Feelings/Feel Tank cohort for providing such a generous, flint-edged, thoughtful context for working things through and feeling things out: Sam Baker, Ann Cvetkovich, Lisa Duggan, Ruthie Gilmore, Debbie Gould, Vanalyne Green, Neville Hoad, Miranda Joseph, Heather Love, Fred Moten, José Muñoz, Amy Partridge, Mary Patten, Matthias Regan, Sandy Soto, Katie Stewart, Rebecca Zorach. *Cruel Optimism* is a Public Feelings project.

I dedicate this book to Katie Stewart, a stunning thinker, a fearless writer, a seriously critical-generous interlocutor, and one of those friends whom philosophers imagine when they dilate on the word "friend."

A relation of cruel optimism exists when something you desire is actually an obstacle to your flourishing. It might involve food, or a kind of love; it might be a fantasy of the good life, or a political project. It might rest on something simpler, too, like a new habit that promises to induce in you an improved way of being. These kinds of optimistic relation are not inherently cruel. They become cruel only when the object that draws your attachment actively impedes the aim that brought you to it initially.

All attachment is optimistic, if we describe optimism as the force that moves you out of yourself and into the world in order to bring closer the satisfying *something* that you cannot generate on your own but sense in the wake of a person, a way of life, an object, project, concept, or scene. But optimism might not *feel* optimistic. Because optimism is ambitious, at any moment it might feel like anything, including nothing: dread, anxiety, hunger, curiosity, the whole gamut from the sly neutrality of browsing the aisles to excitement at the prospect of "the change that's gonna come." Or, the change that is *not* going to come: one of optimism's ordinary pleasures is to induce conventionality, that place where appetites find a shape in the predictable comforts of the good-life genres that a person or a world has seen fit to formulate. But optimism doesn't just manifest an aim to become stupid or simple—often the risk of attachment taken in its throes manifests an intelligence beyond rational calculation.

Whatever the *experience* of optimism is in particular, then, the *affective structure* of an optimistic attachment involves a sustaining inclination to return to the scene of fantasy that enables you to expect that this time, nearness to this thing will help you or a world to become different in just the right way. But, again, optimism is cruel when the object/scene that ignites a sense of possibility actually makes it impossible to attain the expansive transformation for which a person or a people risks striving; and, doubly, it is cruel insofar as the very pleasures of being inside a relation have become sustaining regardless of the content of the relation, such that a person or a world finds itself bound to a situation of profound threat that is, at the same time, profoundly confirming.

This book considers relations of cruel optimism ranging from objects or scenes of romantic love and upward mobility to the desire for the political itself. At the center of the project, though, is that moral-intimate-economic thing called "the good life." Why do people stay attached to conventional good-life fantasies—say, of enduring reciprocity in couples, families, political systems, institutions, markets, and at work—when the evidence of their instability, fragility, and dear cost abounds? Fantasy is the means by which people hoard idealizing theories and tableaux about how they and the world "add up to something." What happens when those fantasies start to fray—depression, dissociation, pragmatism, cynicism, optimism, activism, or an incoherent mash?

Readers of my national sentimentality trilogy—*The Anatomy of National Fantasy, The Female Complaint*, and *The Queen of America Goes to Washington City*—will recognize these questions as central to its investigation of U.S. aesthetics, erotics, and politics over the last two centuries. These works look at the affective components of citizenship and the public sphere, focusing in particular on how intimate publics work in proximity to normative modes of love and the law. *Cruel Optimism* expands the concerns of that work transnationally and temporally, extending them to the contemporary moment. The archive of this project, straddling the United States and contemporary Europe, looks at precarious bodies, subjectivity, and fantasy in terms of citizenship, race, labor, class (dis)location, sexuality, and health. These cases are linked in relation to the retraction, during the last three decades, of the social democratic promise of the post–Second World War period in the United States and Europe.

Cruel Optimism does not cover the entire second half of the twentieth century into the twenty-first, though; nor is it a thorough exposé of the state's withdrawal from the uneven expansion of economic opportunity, social norms, and legal rights that motored so much postwar optimism for democratic access to the good life.[1] Instead, taking up mass media, literature, television, film, and video that appeared between 1990 and the present, it seeks out the historical sensorium that has developed belatedly since the fantasmatic part of the optimism about structural transformation realized less and less traction in the world. The fantasies that are fraying include, particularly, upward mobility, job security, political and social equality, and lively, durable intimacy. The set of dissolving assurances also includes meritocracy, the sense that liberal-capitalist society will reliably provide opportunities for individuals to carve out relations of reciprocity that seem fair and that foster life as a project of adding up to something and constructing cushions for enjoyment. The book is about what happens to fantasies of the good life when the ordinary becomes a landfill for overwhelming and impending crises of life-building and expectation whose sheer volume so threatens what it has meant to "have a life" that adjustment seems like an accomplishment. It tracks the emergence of a precarious public sphere, an intimate public of subjects who circulate scenarios of economic and intimate contingency and trade paradigms for how best to live on, considering.[2] Each chapter tells a story about the dissolution of optimistic objects/scenarios that had once held the space open for the good-life fantasy, and tracks dramas of adjustment to the transformation of what had seemed foundational into those binding kinds of optimistic relation we call "cruel."

But how can it be said that aesthetically mediated affective responses exemplify a shared *historical* sense? What follows sketches out the kinds of general conceptual shifts this book seeks to make in casting that question.

The historical sense with which *Cruel Optimism* is most concerned involves conceiving of a contemporary moment from within that moment. One of this book's central claims is that the present is perceived, first, affectively: the present is what makes itself present to us before it becomes anything else, such as an orchestrated collective event or an epoch on which we can look back. (Chapter 2, "Intuitionists," describes this way of thinking about "the affective present" in Marxist critical theory.) If the present is not at first an object but a mediated affect, it is also a thing that is sensed and under constant revision, a temporal genre whose conventions emerge from the personal and public filtering of the situations and events that are happening in an extended now whose very parameters (when did "the present" begin?) are also always there for debate.[3]

Discussions about the contours and contents of the shared historical present are therefore always profoundly political ones, insofar as they are about what forces should be considered responsible and what crises urgent in our adjudication of survival strategies and conceptions of a better life than what the metric of survival can supply. Focus on the present isn't invariably shallow presentism, or "the narcissism of the now," therefore — but even when it is, it involves anxiety about how to assess various knowledges and intuitions about what's happening and how to eke out a sense of what follows from those assessments.[4] This book pays a lot of attention to different styles of managing simultaneous, incoherent narratives of what's going on and what seems possible and blocked in personal/collective life. We understand nothing about impasses of the political without having an account of the production of the present.

Accordingly, *Cruel Optimism* has a broad interest in amassing genres of historical duration that mark the unfolding activity of the contemporary moment. This book's main genre for tracking the sense of the present is the "impasse." (See especially chapter 6, "After the Good Life," for an elaboration of this concept.) Usually an "impasse" designates a time of dithering from which someone or some situation cannot move forward. In this book's adaptation, the impasse is a stretch of time in which one moves around with a sense that the world is at once intensely present and enigmatic, such that the activity of living demands both a wandering absorptive awareness and a hypervigilance that collects material that might help to clarify things, maintain one's sea legs, and coordinate the standard melodramatic crises with those processes that have not yet found their genre of event.[5] Speaking of cruel optimism, it may be that, for many now, living in an impasse would be an aspiration, as the traditional infrastructures for reproducing life—at work, in intimacy, politically—are crumbling at a threatening pace. The holding pattern implied in "impasse" suggests a temporary housing. This leads us to the other sense of "impasse" that moves throughout the book: impassivity. *Cruel Optimism* pays a lot of attention to diverse class, racial, sexual, and gendered styles of composure. What Jacques Rancière calls "the distribution of the sensible" appears here not only in the class-based positioning of sensibility, but also in gestural economies that register norms of self-management that differ according to what kinds of confidence people have enjoyed about the entitlements of their social location. The way the body slows down what's going down helps to clarify the relation of living on to ongoing crisis and loss.

In addition to temporal genres of the stretched-out present, the book develops aesthetic ones for describing the activity of being reflexive about a contemporary historicity as one lives it. Many genres of the emerging event appear throughout the book, such as the situation, the episode, the interruption, the aside, the conversation, the travelogue, and the happening. For example, throughout I define the genre *situation* in terms of the situation comedy or the police procedural. The police conventionally say: "We have a situation here." A situation is a state of things in which *something* that will perhaps matter is unfolding amid the usual activity of life. It is a state of animated and animating suspension that forces itself on consciousness, that produces a sense of the emergence of something in the present that may become an event. This definition of situation resonates with the concept's appearance in Alain Badiou's work with the "event," but for Badiou the event is a drama that shocks being into radically open situations—the event constitutes the potential for a scene of ethical sociality.[6] (People can't have fidelity to a "situation" because they don't know what it is or how to be in it: and so, if one follows Badiou's idiom, the event is that element in the situation that elaborates the potential good in a radical break, and the antisovereign effect of the situation that undoes the subject and general sureties threatens ethical action.) Brian Massumi takes a similarly structural but more dialectical view, attending to the relation of the situation to the event by prioritizing "event" as that which *governs* the situation. But Massumi is also quite interested in the sense I value, seeing the situation as a genre of unforeclosed experience.[7]

In any case, the situation's state of animated suspension provides a way of thinking about some conventions with which we develop a historical sense of the present affectively as immanence, emanation, atmosphere, or emergence. *Perturbation* is Deleuze's word for disturbances in the atmosphere that constitute situations whose shape can only be forged by continuous reaction and transversal movement, releasing subjects from the normativity of intuition and making them available for alternative ordinaries.[8] The situation is therefore a genre of social time and practice in which a relation of persons and worlds is sensed to be changing but the rules for habitation and the genres of storytelling about it are unstable, in chaos. Chapter 5, "Nearly Utopian, Nearly Normal," argues that the precarious public sphere has generated a new popular variation, the "situation tragedy." In the situation comedy, the subject whose world is not *too* destabilized by a "situation" that arises performs a slapstick maladjustment that turns out absurdly and laughably, without destroying very much. In the situation tragedy, the subject's world is fragile beyond repair, one gesture away from losing all access to sustaining its fantasies: the situation threatens utter, abject unraveling. In the artwork or in response to other scenes, when an apprehending sensorium senses a potentially significant threat to the ordinary's ongoing atmosphere, it sparks the rhythms of situation tragedy, with its menacing new realism.

Yet while sometimes situations organize into world-shifting events or threaten the present with their devastating latency, mostly they do not. How do we learn to process x happening as an emerging event, and how do the conventional genres of event potentially foreclose the possibility of the event taking shape otherwise, as genres y and z, which might hover as possibilities but end up being bracketed and stored somewhere until repetitions call them back, if ever? This kind of attention to the becoming-event of something involves questions about ideology, normativity, affective adjustment, improvisation, and the conversion of singular to general or exemplary experience. This set of processes—the becoming historical of the affective event and the improvisation of genre amid pervasive uncertainty—organizes *Cruel Optimism*.

Thus rather than tracking the "waning of affect" as the mark of the present, I track the waning of genre, and in particular older realist genres (in which I include melodrama) whose conventions of relating fantasy to ordinary life and whose depictions of the good life now appear to mark archaic expectations about having and building a life.[9] Genres provide an affective expectation of the experience of watching something unfold, whether that thing is in life or in art. The waning of genre frames different kinds of potential openings within and beyond the impasse of adjustment that constant crisis creates. This project draws particularly from Giorgio Agamben's analysis of the class-related production of characteristic gestures that the cinema collects as they become archaic.[10] It also emerges from a long engagement with Raymond Williams's incitement to think about the present as a process of emergence.[11] In the present from which I am writing about the present, conventions of reciprocity that ground how to live and imagine life are becoming undone in ways that force the gestures of ordinary improvisation within daily life into a greater explicitness affectively and aesthetically. Cinema and other recording forms not only archive what is being lost but track what happens in the time that we inhabit before new forms make it possible to relocate within conventions the fantasy of sovereign life unfolding from actions.

Throughout, to manifest the unbinding of subjects from their economic and intimate optimism, *Cruel Optimism* depicts the work of new genres, such as the situation tragedy (in relation to melodrama and situation comedy), and an emergent aesthetics, such as in the cinema of precarity, in which attention to a pervasive contemporary social precariousness marks a relation to older traditions of neorealism, while speaking as well to the new social movements that have organized under the rubrics of "precarity" and the "precarious." These new aesthetic forms, I argue, emerge during the 1990s to register a shift in how the older state-liberal-capitalist fantasies shape adjustments to the structural pressures of crisis and loss that are wearing out the power of the good life's traditional fantasy bribe without wearing out the need for a good life.[12] Along with locating the historically specific dynamics of its governing situation, each chapter tracks specific styles of the unraveling of normative social convention in relation to genre.

Implied in what precedes this is a claim that, across diverse geopolitical and biopolitical locations, the present moment increasingly imposes itself on consciousness as a moment in extended crisis, with one happening piling on another. The genre of crisis is itself a heightening interpretive genre, rhetorically turning an ongoing condition into an intensified situation in which extensive threats to survival are said to dominate the reproduction of life. At the same time, as chapter 3, "Slow Death," argues, the genre of crisis can distort something structural and ongoing within ordinariness into something that seems shocking and exceptional.

This brings us to the book's second aim in relation to developing ways to attend to the sensual registers of mass crisis as they impact the historical sense of the present. Everyday life theory is one conventional framework for comprehending the contemporary world for which analysts of the historical present seek to provide new kinds of entry. But *Cruel Optimism* moves away from a recapitulation of everyday life theory as a vehicle for deriving an aesthetics of precarity from its archive in the contemporary United States and Europe. The Euro-modernist concern with the *shock* of urban anomie and mass society developed a rich sense of the sensorium of the early last century. This sense was exemplified by the milling crowd and the compensatory consciousness and practice of the flaneur and the flaneuse, whose modes of scanning and collecting the present are said to have relieved them of crisis, emancipated them from the private, but kept them mentally distant from the too-closeness of the world. But everyday life theory no longer describes how most people live. The short version of this argument is that the vast majority of the world's population now lives in cities and has access to mass culture via multiple technologies, and is therefore not under the same pressure to unlearn and adapt that their forebears might well have been. At the same time, as Nigel Thrift has argued, the reflexive scanning that provided relief for the flaneuse and the flaneur no longer does, but rather exemplifies the mass sensorium engendered by problems of survival that are public and that induce a variety of collective affective responses to the shapelessness of the present that constant threat wreaks.

In league with books like Thrift's *Non-Representational Theory*, Marc Augé's *Non-Places: Essays on Supermodernity*, Michael Taussig's *The Nervous System*, and Kathleen Stewart's *Ordinary Affects*, *Cruel Optimism* turns toward thinking about the ordinary as an impasse shaped by crisis in which people find themselves developing skills for adjusting to newly proliferating pressures to scramble for modes of living on. Observable lived relations in this work always have a backstory and induce a poetic of immanent world making. In this sense these scholars' mode of engaging the activity of affect articulates processes that are not ordinarily in academic conversation: history, phenomenology, trust in the potential exemplarity of any episode, and the ongoing work of storytelling (including criticism) in the making and mediation of worlds.

Instead of the vision of the everyday *organized* by capitalism that we find in Lefebvre and de Certeau, among others, I am interested in the overwhelming ordinary that is *disorganized* by it, and by many other forces besides. This is a matter of a different emphasis, not of a theoretical negation: the rhythms of ordinary existence in the present—Lefebvre's *dressage* as a model for subjectivity in general—scramble the distinction between forced adaptation, plea-surable variation, and threatening dissolution of life-confirming norms.[13] This ordinary is an intersecting space where many forces and histories cir-culate and become "ready to hand" in the ordinary, as Stanley Cavell would put it, for inventing new rhythms for living, rhythms that could, at any time, congeal into norms, forms, and institutions.[14] Each chapter enters the ordinary from the vantage point of ongoing crisis, and the book as a whole tracks the "crisis ordinary" from multiple vantage points along many differ-ent vectors of privilege.

The key here is not to see what happens to aesthetically mediated char-acters as equivalent to what happens to people but to see that in the affec-tive scenarios of these works and discourses we can discern claims about the situation of contemporary life.[15] At times I use terms like "neoliberal" or "transnational" as heuristics for pointing to a set of delocalized processes that have played a huge role in transforming postwar political and economic norms of reciprocity and meritocracy since the 1970s. But I am not claim-ing that they constitute a world-homogenizing system whose forces are played out to the same effect, or affect, everywhere. The differences matter, as do the continuities. My method is to read patterns of adjustment in spe-cific aesthetic and social contexts to derive what's collective about specific modes of sensual activity toward and beyond survival. Each chapter focuses on dynamic relations of hypervigilance, unreliable agency, and dissipated subjectivity under contemporary capitalism; but what "capitalism" means varies a lot, as each case makes its own singular claim for staging the general forces that dominate the production of the historical sensorium that's busy making sense of and staying attached to whatever there is to work with, for life.

This leads me to the book's final conceptual aim. I have described its de-parture from modernist models of cognitive overload in the urban every-day, in order to engage a broader range of physical and aesthetic genres that mediate pressures of the present moment on the subject's sensorium. Cruel Optimism argues, therefore, for moving away from the discourse of trauma—from Caruth to Agamben—when describing what happens to persons and populations as an effect of catastrophic impacts.[16] Why does that follow? Given trauma's primary location in describing severe transformations of physical health and life, it might be surprising to think about trauma as a genre for viewing the historical present. But in critical theory and mass society generally, "trauma" has become the primary genre of the last eighty years for describing the historical present as the scene of an exception that has just shattered some ongoing, uneventful ordinary life that was supposed just to keep going on and with respect to which people felt solid and confident. This book thinks about the ordinary as a zone of convergence of many histories, where people manage the incoherence of lives that proceed in the face of threats to the good life they imagine. Catastrophic forces take shape in this zone and become events within history as it is lived. But trauma theory conventionally focuses on exceptional shock and data loss in the memory and experience of catastrophe, implicitly suggesting that subjects ordinarily archive the intensities neatly and efficiently with an eye toward easy access.

A traumatic event is simply an event that has the capacity to induce trauma. My claim is that most such happenings that force people to adapt to an unfolding change are better described by a notion of systemic crisis or "crisis ordinariness" and followed out with an eye to seeing how the affective impact takes form, becomes mediated. Crisis is not exceptional to history or consciousness but a process embedded in the ordinary that unfolds in stories about navigating what's overwhelming. Each chapter narrates why a logic of adjustment within the historical scene makes more sense than a claim that merges the intense with the exceptional and the extraordinary. The extraordinary always turns out to be an amplification of something in the works, a labile boundary at best, not a slammed-door departure. In the impasse induced by crisis, being treads water; mainly, it does not drown. Even those whom you would think of as defeated are living beings figuring out how to stay attached to life from within it, and to protect what optimism they have for that, at least. Marcuse's prophetic description of postwar U.S. society charts it out: while people comfort themselves with stories about beating the system or being defeated by it, they "continue the struggle for existence in painful, costly and obsolete forms."[17]

I believe that these conceptual distinctions matter to how we view the ongoing activity of precariousness in the present, and each case points to how that mattering might open up the scenes we have delegated to the logic of trauma, with its fundamentally ahistoricizing logic. But some readers might respond to the questions I ask above by thinking that I'm overcomplicating things. They would call the fragilities and unpredictability of living the good-life fantasy and its systemic failures "bad luck" amid the general pattern of upward mobility, reliable intimacy, and political satisfaction that has graced liberal political/economic worlds since the end of the Second World

War. They might see collectively experienced disasters as a convergence of accidents in an imperfect system, and they wouldn't be wrong about that, either; there's a lot of contingency involved in localizing any process in a life, a scene, or an event. They might take the sense of trauma as equal to its claim to exceptionality. They might think that precarity is existential; they might argue that the focus on structural induction oversystematizes the world.

To this set of objections I would say that the current recession congeals decades of class bifurcation, downward mobility, and environmental, political, and social brittleness that have increased progressively since the Reagan era. The intensification of these processes, which reshapes conventions of racial, gendered, sexual, economic, and nation-based subordination, has also increased the probability that structural contingency will create manifest crisis situations in ordinary existence for more kinds of people.

One might also point out critically that this book's archive, which spans conventionally empirical and aesthetic kinds of knowledge, makes big claims on the backs of small objects about how people live now: claims derived from a variety of materials but from neither its own ethnography nor data from diaries, letters, or other primary materials of social history and autobiography. True enough! This book is not offering sociologically empirical cases about who beats the system and who succumbs to its systemic stresses, although it draws widely from an interdisciplinary body of secondary material on these matters. It is a book about the attrition of a fantasy, a collectively invested form of life, the good life. As that fantasy has become more fantasmatic, with less and less relation to how people can live — as the blueprint has faded — its attrition manifests itself in an emerging set of aesthetic conventions that make a claim to affective realism derived from embodied, affective rhythms of survival. I generate exemplary cases of adjustment to the loss of this fantasy of sustenance through the engaged construction of an archive of the impasse or transitional moment, and inquire into what thriving might entail amid a mounting sense of contingency. I don't, however, claim to be being comprehensive about all of the ways that an adjustment between life and fantasy can or has occurred amid the spreading anxiety about what's happened, happening, and potentially next in the relation of singular lives and translocal capitalist worlds. Cruel Optimism gives a name to a personal and collective kind of relation and sets its elaboration in a historical moment that is as transnational as the circulation of capital, state liberalism, and the heterofamilial, upwardly mobile good-life fantasy have become.

As my previous work on the case study makes explicit, I am extremely interested in generalization: how the singular becomes delaminated from its location in someone's story or some locale's irreducibly local history and circulated as evidence of something shared. This is part of my method, to track the becoming general of singular things, and to give those things materiality by tracking their resonances across many scenes, including the ones made by nonverbal but still linguistic activities, like gestures. Aesthetics is not only the place where we rehabituate our sensorium by taking in new material and becoming more refined in relation to it. But it provides metrics for understanding how we pace and space our encounters with things, how we manage the too closeness of the world and also the desire to have an impact on it that has some relation to its impact on us.

The chapters that follow were written slowly, over the same seven-year period during which I began to teach courses on affect theory. They do not advance any orthodoxy about how the evidence and intelligence of affect should be derived—neurological, psychoanalytic, schizoanalytic, historical, or normative.[18] They derive their concepts and genres of the sensorium of the present from patterns that mediate social forces and become exemplary of a scene of sociality. When it helps to go metatheoretical, to explain how a certain tradition of thought illuminates some particular style of activity within the stretched-out present moment, the essays detail that analytic too.

For example, during the writing of this book other discussions of hope, optimism, and happiness emerged within affect and queer theory. This is not the place to write a review essay about the relation of *Cruel Optimism* to these projects, but a few words are in order methodologically. Michael Snediker's beautiful and incisive *Queer Optimism*, which claims proleptic solidarity with this project, does share many presuppositions about the ways that optimism might manifest itself in affects, like shame, with which we do not normally associate the optimistic. We are also both interested in affective activity that makes beings bound to the present rather than to futures. But there are significant differences. His project conceptualizes queer optimism more than optimism as such (see Winnicott and Leibniz for that): he frames queer optimism as a reflexive site for meditations on the worldly conditions that would deserve optimism. Therefore his book is also drawn repeatedly to equating the optimism of attachment with the feeling of optimism itself, and optimism with happiness, feeling good, and the optimism about optimism. In this we diverge. His book's main interlocutor would be Sara Ahmed's *The Promise of Happiness*: like Snediker, she is not really working on affect, but emotion; unlike him, she is skeptical about optimism, at least in its appearance in contemporary regimes of compelled, often dissent-repressive, happiness. She is also more positive about its others, such as grumpiness and melancholy.

Cruel Optimism is a more formalist work than either of these projects. Here, optimism manifests in attachments and the desire to sustain them: attachment is a *structure* of relationality. But the experience of affect and emotion that attaches to those relations is as extremely varied as the contexts of life in which they emerge. An optimistic attachment is invested in one's own or the world's continuity, but might *feel* any number of ways, from the romantic to the fatalistic to the numb to the nothing. I therefore make no claims about what specific experiential modes of emotional reflexivity, if any, are especially queer, cool, resistant, revolutionary, or not. I am seeking out the conditions under which certain attachments to what counts as life come to make sense or no longer make sense, yet remain powerful as they work against the flourishing of particular and collective beings. Nonetheless, I could have had none of these thoughts about the multiple modes of attachment, endurance, and attunement to the world and to the contemporary world of spreading precarity and normative dissolution without a training in multiple critical theories of what Adorno calls the "it could have been otherwise" of *commitment*: queer theory, psychoanalysis, deconstruction, antiracist theory, subaltern studies, and other radical ethnographic historiographies of the present (anthropological, sociological, and journalistic) that derive concepts from tracking patterns, following out the coming-into-form of activity.

This book's argument about optimism more closely resonates with the arguments about hope made by Anna Potamianou, in *Hope: A Shield in the Economy of Borderline States*, and José Esteban Muñoz, in *Cruising Utopia*—with the important caveat that both works are future-oriented. Muñoz sees hope as pointing from the past's unfinished business to a future beyond the present to sustain the (queer) subject within it—he explicitly frames the present as a prison;[19] Potamianou too mainly sees hope (in "borderline" patients) as a stuckness within a relation to futurity that constitutes a problematic defense against the contingencies of the present. In both Muñoz's and Potamianou's cases the present is more or less a problem to be solved by hope's temporal projection. There is also a component of passivity in much of Potamianou's case material: hope often involves waiting for something specific to happen, although she recognizes that it can sometimes bind people to a genuinely, actively lived life as well. In this book optimism is not a map of pathology but a social relation involving attachments that organize the present. It is an orientation toward the pleasure that is bound up in the activity of world-making, which may be hooked on futures, or not. Like Potamianou, I am looking at the complexity of being bound to life. Even when it turns out to involve a cruel relation, it would be wrong to see optimism's negativity as a symptom of an error, a perversion, damage, or a dark truth: optimism is, instead, a scene of negotiated sustenance that makes life bearable as it presents itself ambivalently, unevenly, incoherently.

In contrast, Ghassan Hage's wonderful *Against Paranoid Nationalism* tracks the "availability, the circulation, and the exchange of hope" in Australian national culture, looking at unequal access to the affect as itself an emotional map of what it means to belong in the historical moment contemporary to its operation.[20] In work like this there is not much distinction between what he calls hope and what I call optimism. However, in his acute analysis of the class politics of worry (about internal others, like immigrants) versus care (a relation of general social dependency seen as an ethical and political obligation) the central actor is the state, and specific expectations of state agency within a neoliberal capitalist regime are what's at stake. While, in this book, optimism about the good life that I am tracking is related to crises in state participation in the economic and legal life of social actors and populations (see chapter 7), it usually takes other routes, through zones of labor, neighborhood, and intimacy that constitute the more immediate and manipulable material of good-life fantasy.

The suffusion of the ordinary with fantasy is what justifies this project's attempt to produce a materialist context for affect theory. On the face of it, affect theory has no place in the work of literary, or any, history. Gilles Deleuze writes, after all, that affects act in the nervous system not of persons but of worlds;[21] Brian Massumi represents the nervous system as so autonomous that affective *acts* cannot be intended, in contrast to affective *facts* that political entities can manipulate to foreclose future capacities for consciousness.[22] Positing the subject of history mainly as reactive and recessive, this sensorial construction of the historical field has engendered quite a bit of suspicion. Slavoj Žižek, for one, suspects that a Deleuzian politics, or something like a politics of affect, is an oxymoron or worse, a bourgeois mode of sensational self-involvement masquerading as a radically ungovernable activity of being.[23] Does this mean that to talk about the activity of affect historically or in political terms is mainly to be mired narcissistically, hysterically, or passively in the present? Massumi and Teresa Brennan—writing from a Lacanian tradition—argue, as I do, that affective atmospheres are shared, not solitary, and that bodies are continuously busy judging their environments and responding to the atmospheres in which they find themselves.[24] This refraction of Raymond Williams's concept of the "structure of feeling" suggests that, whatever one argues about the subject as sovereign agent of history, affective responses may be said significantly to exemplify shared *historical* time.[25]

What follows in this book moves with these critical traditions to demonstrate the contours of and potentiality in addressing the affective component of historical consciousness, especially when the problem at hand is apprehending the historical present. It observes forces of subjectivity laced through with structural causality, but tries to avoid the closures of symptomatic reading that would turn the objects of cruel optimism into bad and oppressive things and the subjects of cruel optimism into emblematic symptoms of economic, political, and cultural inequity. So, for example, I suggested that critics interested in the ways structural forces materialize locally often turn the heuristic "neoliberalism" into a world-homogenizing sovereign with coherent intentions that produces subjects who serve its interests, such that their singular actions only *seem* personal, effective, and freely intentional, while really being effects of powerful, impersonal forces.[26] Yet, at the same time, they posit a singularity so radical that, if persons are not fully sovereign, they are nonetheless caught up in navigating and reconstruing the world that cannot fully saturate them. This dialectical description does not describe well the messy dynamics of attachment, self-continuity, and the reproduction of life that are the material scenes of living on in the present, though, and this is where conceptualizing affectivity works illuminatingly. Likewise, I have described how, in gathering up scenes of affective adjustment to material that mediates the ongoing present across the recent, the now, and the next, *Cruel Optimism* tracks the fraying relation between post–Second World War state/economic practices and certain postwar fantasies of the good life endemic to liberal, social democratic, or relatively wealthy regions. But what a "region" or "locale" is varies: sometimes cities, sometimes nations, sometimes a transnational zone made by migratory patterns or capital flow, sometimes a bedroom, sometimes what is in someone's head.

Affect enters the description of the dissolution of these good-life fantasies not as a symptom of any mode of production's or ideology's damaging imprint on dignity, resilience, desire, or optimism. Its strength as a site of potential elucidation comes from the ways it registers the conditions of life that move across persons and worlds, play out in lived time, and energize attachments. As André Green argues, affect is a metapsychological category spanning what's internal and external to subjectivity. But it is more than this too. Its activity saturates the corporeal, intimate, and political performances of adjustment that make a shared atmosphere something palpable and, in its patterning, releases to view a poetics, a theory-in-practice of how a world works.

Affect's saturation of form can communicate the conditions under which a historical moment appears as a visceral moment, assessing the way a thing that is happening finds its genre, which is the same as finding its event. So in addition to the unlikely possibility of deriving the state of structural historical relations from patterns of affective response, I am claiming that the aesthetic or formal rendition of affective experience provides evidence of historical processes. How is it possible for affective traces in the aesthetic to provide evidence of anything, and not to amount simply to a record of writerly/readerly cleverness or ideology as such?

The following two chapters constitute one unit in answer to that question. The book proceeds then to enter the scene of neoliberal restructuring within the ordinary and tracks the fantasmatic, affective, and physical adjustments that organize each chapter's staging of survival in the impasse of the present, which includes telling stories that ask whether cruel optimism is better than none at all.

Chapter 1, "Cruel Optimism," introduces a model for encountering scenes where object loss appears to entail the loss of an entire world and therefore a loss of confidence about how to live on, even at the microlevel of bodily comportment. It pursues conceptually the question of how people maintain their binding to modes of life that threaten their well-being, and to do this it recasts the object of desire not as a thing (or even a relation) but as a cluster of promises magnetized by a thing that appears as an object but is really a scene in the psychoanalytic sense. This shift has two main purposes. One is to clarify how being incoherent in relation to desire does not impede the subject's capacity to live on, but might actually, at the same time, protect it. The other is to track what we learn about impediments to personal and social change from some attachments that become foundations for optimism even when they are damaging. The chapter looks at three scenes of object/

world loss, and tracks the relation between the loss of a singular thing (i.e., a way of being in the world in relation to objects) and the state of optimism as such. Works by John Ashbery ("Untitled"), Charles Johnson ("Exchange Value"), and Geoff Ryman (*Was*) play out the attachment to objects/worlds in the face of their failure and reveal the importance of taking into account the impact of sexual, racial, and class privilege on who can bear the loss of a way of (being in) life.

Chapter 2, "Intuitionists," takes the affective-aesthetic work that remediates subjectivity in "Cruel Optimism" and extends it to the historical field. Here subjectivity is represented by the category of "intuition." Intuition works as a kind of archiving mechanism for the affects that are expressed in habituated and spontaneous behavior that appears to manage the ongoing present. In this work "the ongoing present" is a place where pasts are spatialized among many elsewheres that converge in the sensorium of the people feeling out the conditions of their historical scene. The present is overdetermined by way of anachronism. The ongoing present is also the zone of convergence of the economic and political activity we call "structural," insofar as it suffuses the ordinary with its normative demands for bodily and psychic organization. The chapter's scenes are taken from artworks embedded in collective crisis: Gregg Bordowitz's film *Habit* and Susan Sontag's "The Way We Live Now" organize the chapter's first segment. Both document the AIDS endemic as a crisis in the historical sensorium of the present. They catalogue the effect of the disease on the destruction of habit and consider the proliferation of domains in which habituation has to be reinvented, along with what it means to be in life itself. The second part engages an underengaged tradition of thought about affect derived from Marxist cultural theory; this section focuses on the aesthetic mediation of the historical present in the historical novel. The final segments engage historical novels of the present motored by two women protagonists deemed to have supersensitive intuition—*The Intuitionists* and *Pattern Recognition*. In these novels a catastrophe moves the intuitionist out of her comfort zone in a way that makes her reorganize racial and political memory and sensation into an ongoing present that has to be taken in, navigated, and then moved toward an opening that does not involve rehabituation, the invention of new normativities, or working through and beyond trauma. In contrast to chapter 1, where the protagonists who were structurally unprivileged were harmed by the loss of their intuitive assurance when their worlds suddenly transformed, the subjects of this chapter are not harmed but have optimism for reconstituting habits of flourishing in the wake of the loss of intuition's assurance.

Chapters 3 through 7 track the impact of neoliberal restructuring on fantasies of the good life in the contemporary world.

Chapter 3, "Slow Death," takes up the previous chapter's engagement with the activity of marking a historical present by casting it as a crisis. Specifically, it turns toward what has been called the "obesity epidemic." It challenges the presumption that subjectivity is either always, usually, or at best sovereign, and substitutes for the concept of sovereignty a model of agency without intention that it calls "lateral" agency, a mode of coasting consciousness within the ordinary that helps people survive the stress on their sensorium that comes from the difficulty of reproducing contemporary life.

Chapter 4, "Two Girls, Fat and Thin," is about the Mary Gaitskill novel, *Two Girls, Fat and Thin*, and also about the work of Eve Kosofsky Sedgwick. Its inclusion in this book derives from its focus on how subjects living amid crisis—personal trauma, social upheaval—seek relief from the compelled pseudosovereignty of personality through immersion in various appetites. Gaitskill's novel provides an archive of self-interruptive gestures that elaborate the food- and appetite-related meditation on lateral agency and interrupted sovereignty described in "Slow Death." It works within the conventional technicalities of subjectivity shaped by post-traumatic stress disorder but depicts subjects moving through life seeking a rest from the feedback loop of trauma and compensation that their histories seemed to dictate. The chapter's engagement with Sedgwick advances a desire to desubjectivize queerness and to see it in practices that feel out alternative routes for living without requiring personhood to be expressive of an internal orientation or a part of a political program advocating how to live.

Chapter 5, "Nearly Utopian, Nearly Normal: Post-Fordist Affect in *La Promesse* and *Rosetta*," takes up the previous chapter's closing question about whether there is any place for a subject to rest amid the chaos of intimate and economic upheaval. In this chapter that question gets played out in relation to kinship normativity (i.e., "the family"). As in the previous chapter, crisis circulates between singular personal stories and an overdetermined historical context. Here the crisis begins more in the world than in the subject. Given the centrality of children to analyses of globalization, migration, labor exploitation, post-Fordism, and the like, this piece uses two examples that focus on children (from the Dardenne brothers: *Rosetta* [1996] and *La*

Promesse [1999]) to develop a concept of post-Fordist affect. Post-Fordist affect here designates the sensorium making its way through a postindustrial present, the shrinkage of the welfare state, the expansion of grey (semiformal) economies, and the escalation of transnational migration, with its attendant rise in racism and political cynicism. The chapter asks why the exhaustion and corruption of families in the brittle economy produces, nonetheless, a desire in these children for the "normal" life, "the good life." It concludes with a meditation on the cruelty of normative optimism and the changing meanings of mobility in the global capitalist scene.

Chapter 6, "After the Good Life, an Impasse: *Time Out, Human Resources*, and the Precarious Present," is about the fraying of the fantasy of "the good life" specifically attached to labor, the family wage, and upward mobility. Its cases are two films by Laurent Cantet (*Ressources humaines/Human Resources* [1999] and *L'Emploi du temps/Time Out* [2001]); its broader project is to engage the new affective languages of the contemporary global economy in Europe and the United States—languages of anxiety, contingency, and precarity— that take up the space that sacrifice, upward mobility, and meritocracy used to occupy. What happens to optimism when futurity splinters as a prop for getting through life? What happens when an older ambivalence about security (the Weberian prison of disenchanted labor) meets a newer detachment from it (everything is contingent)? How does one understand the emergence of this as an objective and *sensed* crisis? Focusing on comportment and manners at the end of an era of social obligation and belonging, the chapter tracks a variety of crises across class, gender, race, and nation: no longer is precarity delegated to the poor or the *sans-papiers*.

Chapter 7, "On the Desire for the Political," has two foci. The big question the chapter asks is, "When is the desire for the political an instance of cruel optimism?" The archival context for pursuing this query involves the centrality of the sound(track) and voice to contemporary performances of political intimacy, authenticity, and resistance. Propped against the media "filter" of mainstream mass politics, the chapter looks at a variety of modernist-style and anarchist avant-garde artworks that aim to affect the contemporary political sensorium by refunctioning aural mediation. The art focuses on catastrophes that have bled into ordinary life and become part of the ongoing political field: Iraq (Cynthia Madansky's *The PSA Project*) and contemporary U.S./Euro surveillance society (the Surveillance Camera Players); AIDS (*Organize the Silence* by the sound activist group Ultra-Red); Katrina (*South of Ten*, a film by Liza Johnson); and public mourning scenes around

9/11 and the death of JFK Jr. (Slater Bradley). Bradley's and Johnson's works place particular emphasis on the juxtapolitical domain of social immediacy. In *The Female Complaint* I describe the juxtapolitical as a world-building project of an intimate public that organizes life without threading through dominant political institutions. These works open up questions about political art whose aim is not a refunctioning of the political but a lateral exploration of an elsewhere that is first perceptible as atmosphere. The chapter's final section turns to contemporary anarchist antineoliberal activism, and asks what kinds of opening away from cruel optimism we can read in its forms of detaching from the nation/state as optimistic object.

From one vantage point, then, *Cruel Optimism* is a kind of proprioceptive history, a way of thinking about represented norms of bodily adjustment as key to grasping the circulation of the present as a historical and affective sense. As Fredric Jameson would argue, the activity of living within and beyond normative activity gets embedded in form, but I am less interested in the foreclosures of form and more in the ways the activity of being historical *finds* its genre, which is the same as finding its event. Adjustments to the present are manifest not just in what we conventionally call genre, therefore, but in more explicitly active habits, styles, and modes of responsivity.[27] Tracking such adjustments will not reveal a collection of singularities. People's styles of response to crisis are powerfully related to the expectations of the world they had to reconfigure in the face of tattering formal and informal norms of social and institutional reciprocity. I refer here to statuses like class, race, nation, gender, and sexuality; I am interested in these as they operate amid the rich subjective lives of beings who navigate the world from many copresent arcs of history and experience. People born into unwelcoming worlds and unreliable environments have a different response to the new precarities than do people who presumed they would be protected. But it is not as though the normative affect management styles of any status saturate the whole of anyone's being, psychology, way of interacting with themselves and the world, or experience of the world as an affecting force.

Some say that the differences among traditional classes and populations are less important than emerging convergences and solidarities around singularity and precarity. I am interested in and skeptical about this view of political optimism, as I argue in chapter 6, "After the Good Life," and chapter 7, "On the Desire for the Political." The book attends to these variations of sensual situation and their attendant tensions in spaces as big as collective atmospheres of contingency and as small as the gesture a quivering lip makes when a person feels threatened with the loss of the conditions that have undergirded his good-life fantasy. And it looks at what it might mean politically that conflicting dreams of a reciprocal world to belong to remain a powerful binding motive to preserve normative habits of social reproduction. (See especially chapter 5, "Nearly Utopian, Nearly Normal.")

The problem of detaching from the normal applies to writing criticism as much as it does to any object that coordinates intensities of projection into the historical present. Each of the chapters to follow is uncomfortable in its shape and length: is each a too-short little book, an overlong case study, or good-enough porridge? In relating animating events to analytic generalization, I become progressively less clear about how best rhetorically to manage the problems they crystallize, and more certain of the need to invent new genres for the kinds of speculative work we call "theory." In the meantime, though, I hope you will find, in these scenarios of living on in the ordinary, where subjectivity is depicted as overwhelmed, forced to change, and yet also stuck, incitements toward your own analyses of the kinds of unraveled life to which Cruel Optimism points: impasses in zones of intimacy that hold out the often cruel promise of reciprocity and belonging to the people who seek them—who need them—in scenes of labor, of love, and of the political.

1. *Optimism and Its Objects*

All attachments are optimistic. When we talk about an object of desire, we are really talking about a cluster of promises we want someone or something to make to us and make possible for us. This cluster of promises could seem embedded in a person, a thing, an institution, a text, a norm, a bunch of cells, smells, a good idea—whatever. To phrase "the object of desire" as a cluster of promises is to allow us to encounter what's incoherent or enigmatic in our attachments, not as confirmation of our irrationality but as an explanation of our sense of *our endurance in the object*, insofar as proximity to the object means proximity to the cluster of things that the object promises, some of which may be clear to us and good for us while others, not so much. Thus attachments do not all *feel* optimistic: one might dread, for example, returning to a scene of hunger, or longing, or the slapstick reiteration of a lover's or parent's predictable distortions. But being drawn to return to the scene where the object hovers in its potentialities is the operation of optimism as an affective form. In optimism, the subject leans toward promises contained within the present moment of the encounter with her object.[1]

In the introduction I described "cruel optimism" as a relation of attachment to compromised conditions of possibility whose realization is discovered either to be impossible, sheer fantasy, or *too* possible, and toxic. What's cruel about these attachments, and not merely inconvenient or tragic, is that the subjects who have x in their lives might not well endure the loss of their object/scene of desire, even though its presence threatens their well-being, because whatever the *content* of the attachment is, the continuity of its form provides something of the continuity of the subject's sense of what it means to keep on living on and to look forward to being in the world. This phrase points to a condition different from that of melancholia, which is enacted in the subject's desire to temporize an experience of the loss of an object/ scene with which she has invested her ego continuity. Cruel optimism is the condition of maintaining an attachment to a significantly problematic object. One more thing: sometimes, the cruelty of an optimistic attachment is more easily perceived by an analyst who observes the cost of someone's or some group's attachment to x, since often persons and communities focus on some aspects of their relation to an object/world while disregarding others.[2] But if the cruelty of an attachment is experienced by someone/some group, even in a subtle fashion, the fear is that the loss of the promising object/scene itself will defeat the capacity to have any hope about anything. Often this fear of loss of a scene of optimism as such is unstated and only experienced in a sudden incapacity to manage startling situations, as we will see throughout this book.

One might point out that all objects/scenes of desire are problematic, in that investments in them and projections onto them are less about them than about what cluster of desires and affects we can manage to keep magnetized to them. I have indeed wondered whether all optimism is cruel, because the experience of loss of the conditions of its reproduction can be so breathtakingly bad, just as the threat of the loss of x in the scope of one's attachment drives can feel like a threat to living on itself. But some scenes of optimism are clearly crueler than others: where cruel optimism operates, the very vitalizing or animating potency of an object/scene of desire contributes to the attrition of the very thriving that is supposed to be made possible in the work of attachment in the first place. This might point to something as banal as a scouring love, but it also opens out to obsessive appetites, working for a living, patriotism, all kinds of things. One makes affective bargains about the costliness of one's attachments, usually unconscious ones, most of which keep one in proximity to the scene of desire/attrition.

This means that a poetics of attachment always involves some splitting off of the *story* I can tell about wanting to be near *x* (as though *x* has autonomous qualities) from the *activity* of the emotional habitus I have constructed, as a function of having *x* in my life, in order to be able to project out my endurance in proximity to the complex of what *x* seems to offer and proffer. To understand cruel optimism, therefore, one must embark on an analysis of indirection, which provides a way to think about the strange temporalities of projection into an enabling object that is also disabling. I learned how to do this from reading Barbara Johnson's work on apostrophe and free indirect discourse. In her poetics of indirection, each of these two rhetorical modes is shaped by the ways a writing subjectivity conjures other ones so that, in a performance of fantasmatic intersubjectivity, the writer gains superhuman observational authority, enabling a performance of being that is made possible by the proximity of the object. Because this aesthetic process is something like what I am describing in the optimism of attachment, I'll describe a bit the shape of my transference with her thought.

In "Apostrophe, Animation, and Abortion," my key referent here, Johnson tracks the political consequences of apostrophe for what has become fetal personhood: a silent, affectively present but physically displaced interlocutor (a lover, a fetus) is animated in speech as distant enough for a conversation but close enough to be imaginable by the speaker in whose head the entire scene is happening.[3] But the condition of projected possibility, of a hearing that cannot take place in the terms of its enunciation ("you" are not here, "you" are eternally belated to the conversation with you that I am imagining) creates a fake present moment of intersubjectivity in which, nonetheless, a performance of address can take place. The present moment is made possible by the fantasy of you, laden with the *x* qualities I can project onto you, given your convenient absence. Apostrophe therefore appears to be a reaching out to a you, a direct movement from place *x* to place *y*, but it is actually a turning back, an animating of a receiver on behalf of the desire to make something happen *now* that realizes something *in the speaker*, makes the speaker more or differently possible, because she has admitted, in a sense, the importance of speaking for, as, and to, two—but only under the condition, and illusion, that the two are really (in) one.

Apostrophe is thus an indirect, unstable, physically impossible but phenomenologically vitalizing movement of rhetorical animation that permits subjects to suspend themselves in the optimism of a potential occupation of the same psychic space of others, the objects of desire who make you possible (by having some promising qualities, but also by not being there).[4] Later work, such as in "Muteness Envy," elaborates Johnson's description of the gendered rhetorical politics of this projection of voluble intersubjectivity.[5] The paradox remains that the lush submerging of one consciousness into another requires a double negation: of the speaker's boundaries, so s/he can grow bigger in rhetorical proximity to the object of desire; and of the spoken of, who is more or less a powerful mute placeholder providing an opportunity for the speaker's imagination of her/his/their flourishing.

Of course, existentially and psychoanalytically speaking, intersubjectivity is impossible. It is a wish, a desire, and a demand for an enduring sense of being with and in x and is related to that big knot that marks the indeterminate relation between a feeling of recognition and misrecognition. As chapter 4 argues at greater length, recognition is the misrecognition you can bear, a transaction that affirms you without, again, necessarily feeling good or being accurate (it might idealize, it might affirm your monstrosity, it might mirror your desire to be minimal enough to live under the radar, it might feel just right, and so on).[6] To elaborate the tragicomedy of intersubjective misrecognition as a kind of realism, Johnson's work on projection mines the projective, boundary-dissolving spaces of attachment to the object of address, who must be absent in order for the desiring subject of intersubjectivity to get some traction, to stabilize her proximity to the object/scene of promise.

When Johnson turns to free indirect discourse, with its circulation of merged and submerged observational subjectivity, the projection of the desire for intersubjectivity has even less pernicious outcomes.[7] In a narrator's partial-merging with a character's consciousness, say, free indirect discourse performs the impossibility of locating an observational intelligence in one or any body, and therefore forces the reader to transact a different, more open relation of unfolding to what she is reading, judging, being, and thinking she understands. In Johnson's work such a transformative transaction through reading/speaking "unfolds" the subject in a good way, despite whatever desires she may have not to become significantly different.[8] In this, her work predicted the aesthetics of subjective interpenetration more recently advanced by Tim Dean's Levinasian and Leo Bersani's psychoanalytic optimism about the cognitive-ethical decision to become transformed by a project of limited intersubjectivity, a letting in of the Other's being without any claim to knowledge of what the intimate Other is like.[9] Like Johnson's work on projection, their focus is on the optimism of attachment, and is often itself optimistic about the negations and extensions of personhood that forms of suspended intersubjectivity demand from the lover/reader.

What follows is not so buoyant: this chapter elaborates on and politicizes Freud's observation that "people never willingly abandon a libidinal position, not even, indeed, when a substitute is already beckoning to them."[10] Eve Sedgwick describes Melanie Klein's depressive position as an orientation toward inducing a circuit of repair for a broken relation to the world.[11] The *politically* depressed position exacerbates the classic posture by raising a problem of attachment style in relation to a conflict of aims. The political depressive might be cool, cynical, shut off, searingly rational, or averse, and yet, having adopted a mode that might be called detachment, may not really be detached at all, but navigating an ongoing and sustaining relation to the scene and circuit of optimism and disappointment. (The seeming detachment of rationality, for example, is not a detachment at all, but an emotional style associated normatively with a rhetorical practice.)

Then, there remains the question of the *direction* of the repair toward or away from reestablishing a relation to the political object/scene that has structured one's relation to strangers, power, and the infrastructures of belonging. So, too, remains the question of who can bear to lose the world (the "libidinal position"), what happens when the loss of what's not working is more unbearable than the having of it, and vice versa. *Cruel Optimism* attends to practices of self-interruption, self-suspension, and self-abeyance that indicate people's struggles to change, but not traumatically, the terms of value in which their life-making activity has been cast.[12]

Cruel optimism is, then, like all phrases, a deictic—a phrase that points to a proximate location. As an analytic lever, it is an incitement to inhabit and to track the affective attachment to what we call "the good life," which is for so many a bad life that wears out the subjects who nonetheless, and at the same time, find their conditions of possibility within it. This is not just a psychological state. The conditions of ordinary life in the contemporary world even of relative wealth, as in the United States, are conditions of the attrition or the wearing out of the subject, and the irony that the labor of reproducing life in the contemporary world is also the activity of being worn out by it has specific implications for thinking about the ordinariness of suffering, the violence of normativity, and the "technologies of patience" that enable a concept of the *later* to suspend questions about the cruelty of the *now*.[13] Cruel optimism is in this sense a concept pointing toward a mode of lived immanence, one that grows from a perception about the reasons people are not Bartleby, do not prefer to interfere with varieties of immiseration, but choose to ride the wave of the system of attachment that they are used to, to syncopate with it, or to be held in a relation of reciprocity, reconciliation, or resignation that does not mean defeat by it. Or perhaps they move toward the normative form to get numb with the consensual promise, and to misrecognize that promise as an achievement. Working from pieces by John Ashbery, Charles Johnson, and Geoff Ryman, this chapter traverses three episodes in which what constitutes the cruel bindings of cruel optimism is surprising and induces diverse dramas of adjustment to being postgenre, postnormative, and not knowing entirely how to live. In the middle of all that, we discover in the impasse a rhythm that people can enter into while they're dithering, tottering, bargaining, testing, or otherwise being worn out by the promises that they have attached to in this world.

II. *The Promise of the Object*

A recent, untitled poem by John Ashbery stages the most promising version of this scene of promises for us, foregrounding the Doppler effect of knowledge, phrasing as a kind of spatial lag the political economy of disavowal we drag around like a shadow, and yet providing an experience of liveness in the object that's not only livable, but at once *simplifying and revolutionary*—that bourgeois dream couplet:

> We were warned about spiders, and the
>   occasional famine.
> We drove downtown to see our
>   neighbors. None of them were home.
> We nestled in yards the municipality had
>   created,

reminisced about other, different places—
but were they? Hadn't we known it all
    before?

In vineyards where the bee's hymn
    drowns the monotony,
we slept for peace, joining in the great
    run.
He came up to me.
It was all as it had been,
except for the weight of the present,
that scuttled the pact we made with
    heaven.
In truth there was no cause for rejoicing,
nor need to turn around, either.
We were lost just by standing,
listening to the hum of the wires overhead.[14]

The opening frame is the scene of the American dream not realized, but al-most—or as Ashbery says in a contiguous poem, "Mirage control has sealed the borders/with light and the endless diffidence light begets."[15] Likewise, here, home and hymn *almost* rhyme; but we are restless, no one is home, nature threatens our sense of plenitude; and then there is what the speaker calls "the weight of the present" that makes our politics, therefore, quiet-ist, involving sleeping for peace, deflating the symbolic into the somatic. How long have people thought about the present as having weight, as being a thing disconnected from other things, as an obstacle to living? Every-thing in this poem is very general, and yet we can derive some contexts from within it—imagining, for example, the weight of the default space of the poem, as it instantiates something of the American dream, suburb-style. The people who maintain the appearance of manicured space are not agents in the poem's "we"; they are actors, though, they make noise. Their sounds are the sounds of suburban leisure, not the workers' leisure. We know noth-ing of where they came from, the noises of their day beyond work, and their play. We know nothing about what any of the bodies look like, either: this is practical subjectivity manifesting personhood in action and rhetorical re-fraction. We can speculate, though, that the unmarked speaking people are probably white and American while their servants are probably not, but the poem's idiom is so general and demographic so suppressed that its location in the normative iconicity of the unmarked forces realism into speculation.

This transition is part of its pedagogy of desire. These materialist concerns are not foregrounded in the poem's sense of its event or scene of prolific consciousness. It does not, however, violate the poem's aesthetic autonomy or singularity to think about the conditions of the production of autonomy in it. If anything, the explicit rhetoric of the neighbor shows it to be aware, after all, that the American dream does not allow a lot of time for curiosity about people it is not convenient or productive to have curiosity about. It is a space where the pleasure that one's neighbors give is in their proximity, their light availability to contact: in the American dream we see neighbors when we want to, when we're puttering outside or perhaps in a restaurant, and in any case the pleasure they provide is in their relative distance, their being parallel to, without being inside of, the narrator's "municipally" zoned property, where he hoards and enjoys his leisured pleasure, as though in a vineyard in the country, and where intrusions by the nosy neighbor, or superego, would interrupt his projections of happiness from the empire of the backyard.[16] The buzz of other people's labor in the vineyards is the condition of the privilege of being bored with life and three-quarters detached, absorbed in a process of circulating, in a vaguely lateral way.

In short, in this untitled poem, "we" have chosen to be deadened citizens, happy to be the color someone has placed inside of the lines: "we" would be tickled if, after all, "we" were those characters in Donald Barthelme's short story "I Bought a Little City" who live simply in a housing complex that, seen from the sky, reproduces the *Mona Lisa* for anyone with the time and money to inhabit a certain perspective. "We" live our lives as works of formal beauty, if not art: "we" live with a sense of slight excitement, composing ourselves patiently toward fulfilling the promise of living not too intensely the good life of what Slavoj Žižek might call a decaffeinated sublime.[17] There is nothing especially original or profound in Ashbery's send-up of suburban pleasures: the comforting sound and slightly dull rhythm of cliché performs exactly how much life one can bear to have there, and what it means to desire to move freely within the municipality, a manicured zone of what had been a fantasy.

Marx comments on the political economy of such a self-medicating and self-mediating subject orientation as an outcome of its relation to regimes of private property:

Private property has made us so stupid and one-sided that an object is only *ours* when we have it—when it exists for us as capital, or when it is directly possessed, eaten, drunk, worn, inhabited, etc.,—in short, when it is *used* by us. . . . In the place of all physical and mental senses there has therefore come the sheer estrangement of all these senses, into the sense of *having*. The human being had to be reduced to this absolute poverty in order that he might yield his inner wealth to the outer world. . . . The abolition of private property is therefore the complete ēmancipation of all human senses and qualities, but it is this emancipation precisely because these senses and attributes have become, subjectively and objectively, human. The eye has become a *human* eye, just as its *object* has become a social, human object—an object made by man for man. *The senses* have therefore become directly in their practice theoreticians. They relate themselves to the thing for the sake of the thing, but the thing itself is an *objective human* relation to itself and to man, [in practice I can relate myself to a thing humanly only if the thing relates itself humanly to the human being] and vice versa. Need or enjoyment have consequently lost its *egotistical* nature, and nature has lost its mere *utility* by use becoming *human* use.[18]

Marx's analysis of the senses resonates throughout Ashbery's poem. As Marx would predict, the "we" of this poem begins by owning what it sees and seeing what it owns, feeling nature as an impingement on his auto-referential world; but, then, "we" is haunted that its knowledge is a repetition of a something it can't quite remember, perhaps because, as subjects of productive and consumer capital, "we" were willing to have our memories rezoned by the constant tinkering required to maintain the machinery and appearance of dependable life. "We" were docile, compliant, good sports. "We" live in proximity to a desire now bound up in this version of the good life and can almost remember being alive in it, flooded by a sense of expectation that "we" knew was only pointed to by property and the dependable life we meant to make for it. Our cruel objects don't feel threatening, just tiring.

Our senses are not yet theoreticians because they are bound up by the rule, the map, the inherited fantasy, and the hum of worker bees that fertilize materially the life we're moving through. Then again, maybe we did not really want our senses to be theoreticians: because then we would see ourselves as an effect of an exchange with the world, beholden to it, useful for it, rather than sovereign, at the end of the day. What do we do for a living, after all? "We" seem to be folks of leisure, of the endless weekend, of our own exploitation off-screen, where a consumer's happy circulation in familiarity is almost all that matters: "Hadn't we known it all before?"

But despite the presenting face of it, as a poem voiced from within the community of faceless universal subjects of self-referentiality, the action of the poem is not bound up wholly in the vague attachment to an American dream that is actually lived as a series of missed encounters with disaster and human contact, cut to size in barely experienced episodes. The action of the poem is charted in the small movement between Home, Hymn, and Hum. Most importantly, there is an event that breaks up the undramatic self-hoarding of the collective life, and it is not the vacation in the vineyards that the relief of suburban unproductivity suggests.

Ashbery might be having a Christian thought, in the space between reverie and reverence: the bees seem to echo the famous passage from Sir Thomas Browne's *Religio Medici* that describes how the wisdom of bees is far in advance of what human reason understands about its condition.[19] Relatedly, with all the Miltonic and Eliotic resonance of the poem's tropes, he might be revising his relation to religious lyric.[20] We might even think that the point is to contrast the poem's wittily ironic and vaguely sacred meditations with its key present and fleshly event, that scene of gayness in America embodied in the phrase: "He came up to me." This moment recalls the sexual shock of Virginia Woolf's "Chloe liked Olivia."[21] He came up to me and broke my contract with heaven not to be gay. Queerness and religious affect open up a space of resonance and reverence here: life is at the best imaginable of impasses. Life has been interrupted and, as Badiou would say, seized by an event that demands fidelity.[22]

This event, however, also has impact *despite* the autobiographical. The poem closes by focusing on what happens when someone allows himself to continue to be changed by an event of being with the object, not in the semi-anonymous projected proximity of apostrophe or the we-did-this and we-did-that sociality of the first stanza and not in terms of a dramatics of an uncloseted sexual identity, indeed not in terms of biography at all. The aesthetic and sexual scenario induces a mode of impersonality that is fully felt and dispersed in relationality and in the world. The seismic shift takes place in yielding to the proximity of an intimacy undefined by talking, made by a gesture of approach that holds open a space between two people just standing there, linked newly.

This shift in registers, which relocates the speaker of the poem into a suspended place, might be understood in a Habermasean way. In *The Structural Transformation of the Public Sphere* Habermas talks about the public/private zoning of normative being in terms of a split within the man of modernity, who is a man of the house and a man of the market.[23] Habermas suggests that the problem of living capitalist modernity is in managing the relations between these spheres as a bourgeois and a subject of emotions. A bourgeois is someone who instrumentalizes his social relations in terms of the rules of the market, and who is zoned by the people who assign value to property as having value in proximity to his property and his being self-possessed. For the bourgeois there is property, there is home, and the man is a little leader in the home, and everyone recognizes his authority wherever he carries his propriety onto property. At the same time the man cultivates an image of himself as fundamentally shaped in transactions of feeling, not capital. The "*homme*" in the house who sees himself as effective in the world and an authority in all domains of activity is distinguished and made singular by participation in a community of love, among people who choose each other—who, one might say, can come up to each other. The poem says that "In truth there was no cause for rejoicing": there was no cause for rejoicing in truth, or objectivity. Instead, there is the expectation of intimacy. And lyric poetry.

The event of live intimacy there is in this poem, though, happens outside of the home and the municipality, in an unzoned locale. The event of the poem is the thing that happens when he comes up to me and reminds me that I am not the subject of a hymn but of a hum, the thing that resonates around me, which might be heaven or bees or labor or desire or electric wires, but whatever it is it involves getting lost in proximity to someone and in becoming lost there, in a lovely way. He and I together experience a hum not where "we" were but all around, and that hum is a temporizing, a hesitation in time that is not in time with the world of drives and driving; nor is it in a mapped space, but in a space that is lost. What intersubjectivity there is has no content but is made in the simultaneity of listening, a scene of subjective experience that can only be seen and not heard along with the poet and his "him." Their intimacy is visible and radically private, and mostly uncoded. Life among *les hommes* between home and hymn becomes interrupted by an um, an interruption of truth, where the meaning of "we" shifts to the people who are now lost but alive and unvanquished in their displacement.

It might be kind of thrilling to think about this poem as delineating a means of production of the impasse of the present that hasn't yet been absorbed in the bourgeois senses, but that takes one out to the space of sociality and into the world whose encounters absorb one into an unpredicted difference. Be open to the one who comes up to you. Be changed by an encounter. Become a poet of the episode, the elision, the ellipsis . . .

At the same time, it matters who speaks in this poem: a confident person. He finds possibility in a moment of suspension and requires neither the logic of the market to secure his value nor the intimate recognition of anything municipally normal or domestic to assure that he has boundaries. He can hold a nonspace without being meaningful. This does not seem to threaten him. Thus this instance of optimism might or might not be a part of cruel optimism: we don't know. The promise is everywhere, and the dissolution of the form of being that existed before the event is not cause for mourning or rejoicing: it is just a fact. Does the episodic nature of the interruption enable him, after the moment, to return to the suburbs refreshed? Will they go to a high-end café and buy some intensified coffee supercharged by sugar and milk? Will they go get otherwise stimulated? Will they become different in a way on which they can build a world? Is the couple a stand-in for the collective that can now be awake for peace rather than somnambulant? Does the aesthetic moment of the different autonomy they get when they exist together in reverie become not a condition for *detaching* from the market but the condition of living in it, so that they can think that who they *really are* are people who can be lost in a moment? Habermas would perhaps note that the fantasy of the lovers' worlding power enables the speaker to disavow how otherwise he is constituted as a man of property and the market. John Ricco might argue that the men's outsideness and outsiderness demonstrates the potential resource of gayness to make a queer antinormativity that does not look back to domesticity wishfully. It is impossible to say how deep the break is. By the end, the speaker thinks he *really* lives now, in a moment of suspension. He *really* is a lover, an intimate, no longer the user of gas and fertilizer and the delegator of labor to others. That was in another life, so it seems.

Or, perhaps we can read the scale of the shift in terms of the humming soundtrack. We hear the hum of the world, says Ashbery's optimist, and aspire to be in proximity to it. In melodrama, the soundtrack is the supreme genre of ineloquence, or eloquence beyond words: it's what tells you that you are really most at home in yourself when you are bathed by emotions you can always recognize, and that whatever dissonance you sense is not the real, but an accident that you have to clean up after, which will be more pleasant if you whistle while you work. The concept of "the soundtrack of our lives"—to cite a cliché that is also the ironic name of a great postpunk neopsychedelic band and a growing category of niche marketing—is powerful because it accompanies one as a portable hoard that expresses one's true inner taste and high value. It holds a place open for an optimistic rereading of the rhythms of living, and confirms everybody as a star. Your soundtrack is one place where you can be in love with yourself and express your fidelity to your own trueness in sublime conventionality, regardless of the particularity of the sounds. Our poem performs the situation of that potentially sustaining self-integration.

But that does not close the case of cruel optimism here, either, because the political context of the poem matters: it matters how much an instance of sentimental abstraction or emotional saturation costs, what labor fuels the shift from the concrete real to the soundtrack reel, and who's in control of the meaning of the shift, the pacing of the shift, and the consequences of detaching, even for a moment, from the consensual mirage. The political context that is mutely present does not trump the pleasures and openings either: what's irreconcilable measures the situation. Moving from home to hymn to hum, Ashbery's poem makes an interruptive stillness that's ineloquent and eloquent, meaningful and a placeholder for an unformed transitional experience. The soundtrack he hears is like lyric itself, comfortable with displacing realism about the material reproduction of life and the pain of intimacy and numbness to another time and space.

Moving from home to hum, to *homme* to um, an interruption: it sounds like punning, this Thoreauvian method of sounding out the space of a moment to measure its contours, to ask what is being stopped, who gets to do it, and what it would mean to be in this moment and then beyond it. It is always a risk to let someone in, to insist on a pacing different from the productivist pacing, say, of capitalist normativity. Of course "he" was not *my object*, my cluster of promises: "he" came up to *me*. Even if being the object is more secure than having one and risking disappointment, the poem stops before anyone gets too deep into the projecting and embedding. It's a poem about being open to an encounter that's potentially transformative, without having yet congealed into the couple form, a friendship, a quick sexual interlude, anything. It gestures toward being lost or suspended in a process of knowing nothing about how a scene of collaborative action will open up a space of potential liveness that is not a space on which anything can be built. In the space of lag between he and me something happens and the royal or sovereign we of the poem is no longer preoccupied. The encounter releases the speaker to lose himself in the um of a singular sociality whose politi-cal economy we are asking questions of. If its happiness is cruel, requiring someone else's or some class's expenditure, we'll never know: the substitu-tion of habituated indifference with a spreading pleasure might open up a wedge into an alternative ethics of living, or not. What happens next is the unfinished business of the poem: right now, the senses it stages are open to becoming theoreticians.

Sounding the poem for the meaning of the impasse it portrays in an event that displaces and dissolves ordinary life does not confirm that all lyric or episodic interruptions are even potentially a condition of possibility for imagining a radically resensualized post-neoliberal subject. But analytically this singular lyric opens up an opportunity to learn to pay attention to, have transference with, those moments of suspension in which the subject can no longer take his continuity in the material world and contemporary his-tory for granted, because he feels full of a *something* ineloquently promising, a something that reveals, at the same time, a trenchant *nothing* about the general conditions of optimism and cruel optimism. Attending to the het-erosonic and heterotemporal spaces within capital in which an event sus-pends ordinary time, sounds and senses can change, potentially, how we can understand what being historical means. Because Ashbery's speaker is confident, because he has the ballast of normative recognitions and modes of social belonging in the habit of his flesh, I believe, he can stand detach-ing from the promise of his habituated life and can thrive in the openness of desire to form, as heady as that might be. If it is to be any more than a story about his singularity, though, the new intersubjective scene of sense would have to be able to extend the moment to activity that would dissolve the legitimacy of the optimism embedded in the now displaced world, with its promising proprietary zones, scenes, scapes, and institutions. Otherwise this is not an event but an episode in an environment that can well absorb and even sanction a little spontaneous leisure.

III. *The Promise of Exchange Value*

Ashbery's speaker is very lucky that he gets to dissolve and thrive in the col-laborative unknowing initiated by the gesture, the encounter, and poten-tially the event that unbottle whatever it is that "he/me" can now rest in hearing. In Charles Johnson's "Exchange Value" a situation that might also have turned out that way does not. The way the story plays out what happens when a certain kind of person is defeated by being between one habituated life and another yet to be invented because something good turns out to be unbearable says something about why the phrase "political economy" must thread throughout our analysis of cruel and usual optimism. Why do some people have the chops for improvising the state of being unknowing while others run out of breath, not humming but hoarding?

As with Ashbery's lyric, this story begins with a meditation on neighbors and neighborhoods. "Exchange Value" takes place during the 1970s on the South Side of Chicago, around 49th Street.[24] The protagonists, eighteen-year-old Cooter and his older brother, Loftis, are poor and African American. They do not drive downtown regularly to see their friends, or frequent other neighborhoods regularly: they do not have cars. Home and the 'hood are spaces of localized, personalized practices of encountering, wandering, and scrounging. But here, the intimacy of proximity has nothing to do with anyone's lyric intersubjectivity, even though the story takes place in the meditative rhythms of Cooter's way of parsing a new situation. The subjects of "Exchange Value" are expressive and opaque, but with quite different valences than in our previous example.

The story opens onto a plot: two brothers concoct a plan to rob their possibly dead neighbor, Miss Bailey. Who is Miss Bailey? Nobody knows: she is a neighbor, so one does not need to know her; her job is to be around, to be a "character," which is what you call someone who performs a familiar set of actions around you but is not intimate with you. Miss Bailey dresses in cast-off men's clothes; like Cooter and Loftis, she eats free meals that she begs off of a local Creole restaurant; when Cooter gives her pocket change, she doesn't spend it, she puts it in her mouth and eats it. This is what Cooter knows about her, deducing nothing more about her from her actions. The story takes place because she's always around and then she isn't. Cooter and Loftis think that perhaps she's died and determine to get the first pickings.

This kind of behavior, this scavenging in other people's stuff, is not characteristic of Cooter, but it doesn't violate his fundamental relation to the world either. Compared to his brother, he's always been branded a loser. "Mama used to say it was Loftis, not me, who'd go places . . . . Loftis, he graduated fifth at DuSable High School, had two gigs and, like Papa, he be always wanting the things white people had out in Hyde Park, where Mama did daywork sometimes." The children's parents are both dead by this point in their lives: Papa from overwork and Mama because she was "big as a Frigidaire."[25] Having watched this, Cooter refuses to ride the wave of the American dream: remembering his parents "killing theyselves for chump change—a pitiful li'l bowl of porridge—I get to thinking that even if I ain't had all I wanted, maybe I've had, you know, all I'm ever gonna get" and so organizes his life through the lateral enjoyments of fantasy (29–30).[26] "I can't keep no job and sorta stay close to home, watching TV, or reading World's Finest comic books, or maybe just laying dead, listening to music, imagining I see faces or foreign places in water stains on the wallpaper" (29).

During the 1970s the World's Finest series paired Batman and Superman as a double crime-fighting team. But Cooter's fantasies aren't mimetic—they're aleatory and passive ways of inhabiting and making an environment in which attachments are not optimistically pointing toward a cluster of transcendent promises but toward something else, something bearable that holds off not just the imminence of loss but the loss that, inevitably, just happened. For Cooter fantasy isn't a plan. It calibrates nothing about how to live. It is the action of living for him, his way of passing time not trying to make something of himself in a system of exploitation and exchange. In the political economy of his world, that system does not produce rest or waste but slow death, the attrition of subjects by the situation in which capital determines value. In this story, that scene dedicates the worker's body to a deferred enjoyment that, if they're on the bottom of the class structure, they are not likely to be around to take pleasure in, as his parents' fate demonstrates.[27]

In contrast, Loftis's relation to fantasy is realist. He inherited his parents' optimism toward his life by being ambitious. But his strategies are strictly formal. He takes classes from Black Nationalists at the "Black People's Topographical Library," reads Esquire and The Black Scholar, and sews upscale labels onto his downscale clothes:[28] to him getting ahead is what counts, whether it is via power, labor, or the "hustle" (29). His opinion of Cooter is quite low, because the younger brother is dreamy and has no drive. Nonetheless, they decide to do the job together.

Miss Bailey's apartment is pitch dark and reeks of shit: a newspaper clipping from the Chicago Defender among the garbage reveals that her former employer, Henry Conners, had left her his entire estate, and that all of the years of scavenging and weirdness masked her possession of enormous wealth. It all makes sense in the dark. But when the light turns on, Cooter notes, "shapes come forward in the light and I thought for an instant like I'd slipped in space" (30). In this moment Cooter enters an impasse: his talent at making out foreign shapes becomes applied to his own life, which he can no longer occupy.

> Her living room, webbed in dust, be filled to the max with dollars of all denominations, stacks of stock in General Motors, Gulf Oil, and 3M company in old White Owl cigar boxes, battered purses, or bound in pink rubber bands. . . . [E]verything, like a world inside the world, you take it from me, so like picturebook scenes of plentifulness you could seal yourself off in here and settle forever. Loftis and me both drew breath suddenly. There be unopened cases of Jack Daniel's, three safes cemented to the floor, hundreds of matchbooks, unworn clothes, a fuel-burning stove, dozens of wedding rings, rubbish, World War II magazines, a carton of a hundred canned sardines, mink stoles, old rags, a birdcage, a bucket of silver dollars, thousands of books, paintings, quarters in tobacco cans, two pianos, glass jars of pennies, a set of bagpipes, an almost complete Model A Ford dappled with rust, and I swear, three sections of a dead tree. (30–31)

How do we understand this collection not only of things but of details? Cooter's verbal response is not to be a historian but a moralist: "A *tree* ain't normal" (31). But to my eye the story's main event, the scene of potential change, is somatic. Change is an impact lived on the body before anything is understood, and as such is simultaneously meaningful and ineloquent, engendering an atmosphere that they spend the rest of the story and their lives catching up to. It's like winning the lottery, getting a wash of money they haven't earned; being possessed by coming into possession of possessions, they are shocked into something impassive. This crack in the necessities of history makes Cooter's head get light— "My knees failed; then I did a Hollywood faint" (32); Loftis "pant[s] a little" and "for the first time . . . looked like he didn't know his next move" (31). Their bodies become suspended.

But if riches change history, they also make it possible for history to be something other than a zone of barely or badly imagined possibility. Loftis returns to crazy reason and puts the break on their adrenalin. He forces Cooter to catalogue everything. Eventually,

> that cranky old ninnyhammer's hoard adds up to $879,543 in cash, thirty-two bank books (some deposits be only $5), and me, I wasn't sure I was dreaming or what, but I suddenly flashed on this feeling, once we left her flat, that all the fears Loftis and me had about the future be gone, 'cause

Miss Bailey's property was the past—the power of that fellah Henry Conners trapped like a bottle spirit—which we could live off, so it was the future too, pure potential: can do. Loftis got to talking on about how that piano we pushed home be equal to a thousand bills, jim, which equals, say, a bad TEAC A-3340 tape deck, or a down payment on a deuce-and-a-quarter. Its value be (Loftis say) that of a universal standard of measure, relational, unreal as number, so that tape deck could turn, magically, into two gold lamé suits, a trip to Tijuana, or twenty-five blow jobs from a ho—we had $879,543 worth of wishes, if you can deal with that. Be like Miss Bailey's stuff is raw energy, and Loftis and me, like wizards, could transform her stuff into anything else at will. All we had to do, it seemed to me, was decide exactly what to exchange it for. (34–35)

Cooter's senses, awakened to the promises clustered around things, have truly become theoreticians. Exchange value is not identical to the price of things, but marks a determination of what else a thing can get exchanged for, as though money were not involved, exactly, in the mediations. Your coat for a piano. Your money for your life.

The scene of shocking wealth changes the terms of the meaning of life, of the reproduction of life, and of exchange itself. Loftis gets very quiet. Cooter grabs a bunch of money and goes downtown to spend it. But though downtown Chicago is just a few miles away, it is like a foreign country to Cooter: he does not speak its economic language. Theory aside, in practice Cooter doesn't have a clue what to do with the money and realizes sickeningly, right away, that money cannot make you feel like you belong if you are not already privileged to feel that way. He buys ugly, badly made, expensive clothes that shame him right away. He eats meat until he gets sick. He takes cabs everywhere. When he gets home, his brother's gone psychotic. Loftis has built an elaborate trap, a vault to protect the money. He yells at Cooter for spending, because the only power is in hoarding. Loftis says, "As soon as you buy something you lose the power to buy something" (36). He cannot protect himself from Miss Bailey's fate: "suffering that special Negro fear of using up what little we get in this life" (37); inheritance "put her through changes, she be spellbound, possessed by the promise of life, panicky about depletion, and locked now in the past because every purchase, you know, has to be a poor buy: a loss of life" (37–38).

Notice how frequently Johnson reverts to the word "life." Can a person on the bottom survive living "life" stripped of the illusion of indefinite endurance via whatever kinds of fantasmatic practices he's been able to cobble together? How quickly can one dispense with the old bargains between defense and desire, adapting to a regime whose rules provide no felt comfort? "Exchange Value" demonstrates the proximity of two kinds of cruel optimism: with little cultural or economic capital and bearing the history of a racial disinheritance from the norms of white supremacist power, you work yourself to death, or coast to nonexistence; or, with the ballast of capital, you hoard against death, deferring life, until you die. Cooter is the realist; he can see that there's no way out, now, no living as if not in a relation to death, which is figured in all of the potential loss that precedes it.

This story is exquisitely tender toward the surrealism of survival in the context of poverty so extreme that riches can only confirm insecurity. On either side of the capital divide, human creativity, energy, and agency are all bound up in bargaining, strategizing: it only begins with the mother at the sink predicting which of her sons has the sense to ride the rhythms of remuneration in the system; the parents dying before the kids are of age because of having had to scavenge for what Cooter scathingly calls "chump change"; Cooter choosing to live to feed his passivity and capacity for fantasy; and Loftis living amorally among a variety of styles for gaining upward mobility. Before the windfall they all manifest the improvisatory opportunism of people on the bottom who, having little to lose, and living in an economy of pleading, sharing, and hiding, will go for something if the occasion permits (29).

But the inheritance the sons engineer produces a sensorial break for them, and whereas the earlier modes of optimism included a community and a meanwhile that meant being somewhere and knowing people no matter what style of living-on one chose, the later modes almost force privacy, hoarding, becoming pure potential itself. The inheritance becomes the promise of the promise, of a technical optimism; it sutures them both to life lived without risk, in proximity to plenitude without enjoyment. For Loftis it destroys the pleasure of the stress of getting through the day because the scale of potential loss is too huge. Cooter is more passive: he'll fold himself in to his brother's crypt because that's who he is, a person who does not make spaces but navigates the available ones.

At the same time, the withdrawal of the brothers from even vague participation in a life made from scheming mimes another aspect of the logic of capital. We have seen that they have always been the subjects of cruel optimism and its modes of slow death, having inherited their parents' future-directed, life-building, do-it-so-your-kids-won't-have-to discipline of the respectable body and soul. Now, in this relation of life-building to life-expending, they induce new generational orientations toward exhaustion. From coasting to the activity of the hustle they embody styles of being that can seem anything from subcivilized and extralegal to entrepreneurial and ambitious, in the good sense. In this final logic, though, capitalist sensibility in "Exchange Value" manifests as crazy in the way that reason is crazy—not only crazy-dogged, crazy-compulsive, crazy-formalist, and crazy-habituated, but crazy from the activity of maintaining structural contradictions.

In this world the subject's confrontation with singularity is the most horrifying thing of all. Singularity is the part of one's sovereignty that cannot be handed off to a concept, object, or property. Under capitalism, money is power and if one has only surplus amounts of it, sovereignty is infinite and yet a weight that cannot be borne. Exchange value was supposed to leaven the subject through the handoff of value to another, who would return something in kind. The space of exchange would make breathing space, and breathing space is what the capitalist subject, in all of her ambition, is trying to attain—the good life, as in Ashbery's poem. But what usually gets returned in the exchange of desire embedded in things is merely, disappointingly, a brief episode, often with a thing as memento of the memory and not the actualization of desire. In "Exchange Value" the money form in particular reveals in-kind reciprocity as a mirage, the revelation of which destroys for the brothers, and Miss Bailey before them, the whole infrastructure of trust in the world that merges the credit with the affectional economy and keeps people attached to optimism of a particular kind.

If consumption promises satisfaction in substitution and then denies it because all objects are rest stops amid the process of remaining unsatisfied that counts for being alive under capitalism, in the impasse of desire, then hoarding seems like a solution to something. Hoarding controls the promise of value against expenditure, as it performs the enjoyment of an infinite present of holding pure potential. The end, then, is the story's tableau of the structural contradiction that shakes, stuns, and paralyzes its protagonists. Under capitalism, being in circulation denotes being in life, while an inexhaustible hoard denotes being in fantasy, which is itself a hoarding station against a threatening real, and therefore *seems* like a better aspirational realism. But in fantasy one is stuck with one's singular sovereignty in an inexhaustable nonrelationality. Therefore, an unquantifiable surplus of money—what any capitalist subject thought anyone would want—turns each brother into a walking contradiction, a being who has what everyone wants and yet who reveals that the want that had saturated the fantasy of the whole imaginable world is wanting, because sovereignty, while ideal, is a nightmarish burden, a psychotic loneliness, and just tainted.

This means that the object of cruel optimism here appears as the thing within any object to which one passes one's fantasy of sovereignty for safekeeping. In cruel optimism the subject or community turns its treasured attachments into safety-deposit objects that make it possible to bear sovereignty through its distribution, the energy of feeling relational, general, reciprocal, and accumulative. In circulation one becomes happy in an ordinary, often lovely, way, because the weight of being in the world is being distributed into space, time, noise, and other beings. When one's sovereignty is delivered back into one's hands, though, its formerly distributed weight becomes apparent, and the subject becomes stilled in a perverse mimesis of its enormity. In a relation of cruel optimism our activity is revealed as a vehicle for attaining a kind of passivity, as evidence of the desire to find forms in relation to which we can sustain a coasting sentience, in response to being too alive.

iv. *The Promise of Being Taught*

Even amid the racial mediations entrenched in capitalist inequalities in the United States, optimism involves thinking that in exchange one can achieve recognition. But, one must always ask, recognition of what? One's self-idealization, one's style of ambivalence, one's tender bits, or one's longing for the event of recognition itself? For Ashbery, recognition's exchange value takes him out of personality, that cluster of familiar repetitions. It is pure potentiality in the good sense and provides a lovely experience of realizing that the flurry of activity that stood in for making a life was an impasse now passed by and replaced by another, slower one, where he experiences hanging around, letting something or someone come in the way a sound comes, without being defensive. For the men who still feel like boys at the close of "Exchange Value" the affect attached to optimism is either panic or numbness, not humming. While, as defenses, these modes of vibrating near-paralysis are cognate to the modes of getting by that preceded Miss Bailey's death, those earlier styles of floating beneath value while having fantasies of it seem utopian compared to the crypt of shattered being that pecuniary optimism cruelly engenders.

It is striking that these moments of optimism, which mark a possibility that the habits of a history might *not* be reproduced, release an overwhelmingly negative force. One predicts such effects in traumatic scenes, but it is not usual to think about an optimistic event as having the same potential consequences. The conventional fantasy that a revolutionary lifting of being might happen in proximity to the new object/scene of promise would predict otherwise than that a person or a group might prefer, after all, to surf from episode to episode while leaning toward a cluster of vaguely phrased prospects. And yet: at a certain degree of abstraction both from trauma and optimism the sensual experience of self-dissolution, radically reshaped consciousness, new sensoria, and narrative rupture can look similar; the subject's grasping toward stabilizing form, too, in the face of dissolution, looks like classic compensation, in which the production of habits that signify predictability defends against losing emotional shape entirely.

I have suggested that the particular ways in which identity and desire are articulated and lived sensually within capitalist culture produce such counterintuitive overlaps. But it would be reductive to read the preceding as a claim that anyone's subjective transaction with the optimistic structure of value in capital *produces* the knotty entailments of cruel optimism as such. People *are* worn out by the activity of life-building, *especially* the poor and the nonnormative. But lives are singular; people make mistakes, are inconstant, cruel, and kind; and accidents happen. This essay's archive focuses on artworks that deliberately remediate singularities into cases of nonuniversal but general abstraction, providing narrative scenarios of how people learn to identify, manage, and maintain the hazy luminosity of their attachment to being *x* and having *x*, given that their attachments were promises and not possessions after all. Geoff Ryman's historical novel, *Was*, offers yet a different scenario for tracking the enduring charisma of the normative. Weaving highly subjective activities of fantasy-making through agrarian Kansas and the mass culture industry, *Was* uses four encounters with *The Wizard of Oz* to narrate the processes by which people hoard themselves in fear of dissolution and yet seek to dissolve their hoard in transformative experiences of attachment whose effects are frightening, exhilarating, the only thing that makes living worthwhile, and yet a threat to existence itself. *Was* provides a kind of limit case of cruel optimism, as its pursuit of the affective continuity of trauma and optimism in self-unfolding excitement is neither comic, nor tragic, nor melodramatic—but metaformal. Mining self-loss in episodes ranging from absorption in pretty things to crazy delusion, it thinks about genre as *defense*. *Was* validates fantasy as a life-sustaining defense against the attritions of ordinary violent history.

In this novel as in our other examples, the affective feeling of normativity is expressed in the sense that one ought to be dealt with gently by the world and to live happily with strangers and intimates without being torn and worn out by the labor of disappointment and the disappointment of labor. Here, though, evidence of the possibility of enduring that way in one's object/scene is not embedded in the couple form, the love plot, the family, fame, work, wealth, or property. Those are the sites of cruel optimism, scenes of conventional desire that stand manifestly in the way of the subject's thriving. Instead, the novel offers a two-step of saturation in mass fantasy and history as solutions to the problem of surviving the brutality of trauma *and* optimism in the ordinary world. It sees leaving the singular for the general through embracing a range of stranger intimacy as the best resource for thriving, but in at least one case, even those encounters endanger the subject who is so worn out by the work of surviving the bad life that all she has left, in a sense, are her defenses.

Was constructs a post-traumatic drama that is held together, in the end, by the governing consciousness of Bill Davison, a mental health worker, a white heterosexual Midwesterner whose only previous personal brush with trauma had been ambivalence toward his fiancée, but whose professional capacity to enter into the impasse with his patients, and to let their impasses into him, makes him the novel's optimistic remainder, a rich witness. The first traumatic story told is about the real Dorothy Gale, spelled Gael, partly, I imagine, to link up the girl who's transported to Oz on a strong breeze to someone in prison, and also to link her to the Gaelic part of Scotland, home of the historical novel, the genre whose affective and political conventions shape explicitly Ryman's meditation on experiences and memories whose traces are in archives, landscapes, and bodies scattered throughout Kansas, Canada, and the United States. Like Cooter, this Dorothy Gael uses whatever fantasy she can scrape together to survive her scene of hopeless historical embeddedness. But her process is not to drift vaguely but intensely, by way of multigeneric invention: dreams, fantasies, private plays, psychotic projection, aggressive quiet, lying, being a loud bully and a frank truth-teller. Dorothy's creativity makes a wall of post-traumatic noise, as she has been abandoned by her parents, raped and shamed by her Uncle Henry Gulch, shunned by children for being big, fat, and ineloquent. Part Two of *Was* tells the story of Judy Garland as the child Frances Gumm. On the *Wizard of Oz* set she plays Dorothy Gale as vaguely sexualized sweetheart, her breasts tightly bound so that she can remain a child and therefore have *her* childhood stolen from her. It is not stolen through rape but by parents bound up in their own fantasies of living through children in terms of money and fame (Gumm's mother) or sex (Gumm's father, whose object choice was young boys). The third story in *Was* is about a fictional gay man, a minor Hollywood actor named Jonathan, whose fame comes from being the monster in serial-killer movies titled *The Child Minder* and who, as the book begins, is offered a part in a touring *Wizard of Oz* company while he is entering AIDS dementia. All of these stories are about the cruelty of optimism revealed to people without control over the material conditions of their lives, or whose relation to fantasy is such that the perverse shuttling between fantasy and realism destroys, according to Ryman, people and the nation. I cannot do justice here to the singularities of what optimism makes possible and impossible in this entire book; instead, I want to focus on a scene that makes the whole book possible. In this scene Dorothy Gael encounters a substitute teacher, Frank Baum, in her rural Kansas elementary school.

"The children," writes Ryman, "knew the Substitute was not a real teacher because he was so soft."[29] "Substitute" derives from the word "succeed," and the sense of possibility around the changeover is deeply embedded in the word. A *Substitute* brings optimism if he hasn't yet been defeated—by life or by the students. He enters their lives as a new site for attachment, a de-dramatized possibility. He is by definition a placeholder, a space of abeyance, an aleatory event. His coming is not personal—he is not there for anyone in particular. The amount of affect released around him says something about the intensity of the children's available drive to be less dead, numb, neutralized, or crazy with habit; but it says nothing about what it would feel like to be in transit between the stale life and all its others, or whether that feeling would lead to something good.

Of course often students are cruel to substitutes, out of excitement at the unpredictable and out of not having fear or transference to make them docile or even desiring of a recognition that has no time to be built. But this substitute is special to Dorothy: he is an actor, like her parents; he teaches them Turkish and tells them about alternative histories lived right now and in the past (171). Dorothy fantasizes about Frank Baum not in a narrative way, but with a mixture of sheer pleasure and defense: "Frank, Frank, as her uncle put his hands on her" (169); then she berates herself for her "own unworthiness" (169) because she knows "how beautiful you are and I know how ugly I am and how you could never have anything to do with me" (174). She says his name, Frank, over and over: it "seemed to sum up everything that was missing from her life" (169). Yet face-to-face she cannot bear the feeling of relief from her life that the substitute's being near provides for her. She alternately bristles and melts at his deference, his undemanding kindness. She mocks him and disrupts class to drown out her tenderness, but obeys him when he asks her to leave the room to just write something, anything.

What she comes back with is a lie, a wish. Her dog, Toto, had been murdered by her aunt and uncle, who hated him and who had no food to spare for him. But the story she hands in to the substitute *is* a substitute: it is about how happy she and Toto are. It includes sentences about how they play together and how exuberant he is, running around yelping "like he is saying hello to everything" (174). Imaginary Toto sits on her lap, licks her hand, has a cold nose, sleeps on her lap, and eats food that Auntie Em gives her to give him. The essay suggests a successful life, a life where love circulates and extends its sympathies, rather than the life she actually lives, where "[i]t was as if they had all stood back-to-back, shouting 'love' at the tops of their lungs, but in the wrong direction, away from each other" (221). It carries traces of all of the good experience Dorothy has ever had. The essay closes this way: "I did not call him Toto. That is the name my mother gave him when she was alive. It is the same as mine" (175).

Toto, Dodo, Dorothy: the teacher sees that the child has opened up something in herself, let down a defense, and he is moved by the bravery of her admission of identification and attachment. But he makes the mistake of being mimetic in response, acting soft toward her in a way he might imagine that she seeks to be: " 'I'm very glad,' he murmured, 'that you have something to love as much as that little animal' " (175). Dorothy goes ballistic at this response and insults Baum, but goes on to blurt out all of the truths of her life, in public, in front of the other students. She talks nonstop about being raped and hungry all the time, about the murder of her dog, and about her ineloquence: "I can't say anything," she closes (176). That phrase means she can't do anything to change anything. From here she regresses to yelping and tries to dig a hole in the ground, to become the size she feels, and also to become, in a sense, an embodiment of the last thing she loved. After that, Dorothy goes crazy. She lives in a fantasy world of her own, wandering homeless and free, especially, of the capacity to reflect on loss in the modalities of realism, tragedy, or melodrama. To protect her last iota of optimism, she goes crazy.

In *Was* Baum goes on to write *The Wizard of Oz* as a gift of alternativity to the person who can't say or do anything to change her life materially, and who has taken in so much that one moment of relief from herself produces a permanent crack in the available genres of her survival. In "What is a Minor Literature?" Deleuze and Guattari exhort people to become minor in exactly that way, to deterritorialize from the normal by digging a hole in sense like a dog or a mole.[30] Creating an impasse, a space of internal displacement, in this view, shatters the normal hierarchies, clarities, tyrannies, and confusions of compliance with autonomous individuality. This strategy looks promising in the Ashbery poem. But in "Exchange Value," a moment of relief produces a psychotic defense against the risk of losing optimism. For Dorothy Gael, in *Was*, the optimism of attachment to another living being is itself the cruelest slap of all.

From this cluster we can understand a bit more of the magnetic attraction to cruel optimism. Any object of optimism promises to guarantee the endurance of something, the survival of something, the flourishing of something, and above all the protection of the desire that made this object or scene powerful enough to have magnetized an attachment to it. When these relations of proximity and approximate exchange happen, the hope is that what misses the mark and disappoints won't much threaten anything in the ongoing reproduction of life, but will allow zones of optimism a kind of compromised endurance. In these zones, the hope is that the labor of maintaining optimism will not be negated by the work of world-maintenance as such and will allow the flirtation with *some* good-life sweetness to continue. But so many of the normative and singular objects made available for investing in the world are themselves threats to both the energy and the fantasy of ongoingness, namely, that people/collectivities face daily the cruelty not just of potentially relinquishing their objects or changing their lives, but of losing the binding that fantasy itself has allowed to what's potentially there in the risky domains of the yet untested and unlived life. The texts we have looked at stage moments when life could become otherwise, in the good sense. A substantive change of heart, a sensorial shift, intersubjectivity, or transference with a new promising object does not generate on its own the better good life, though, and never without an equally threatening experience of loss—and neither can a single collaboration, whether of a couple, brothers, or in pedagogy. Fantasy is an opening and a defense. The vague expectations of normative optimism produce small self-interruptions as the heterotopias of sovereignty amid structural inequality, political depression, and other intimate disappointments. By staging the impasse in which breakdown does its work on suspending the rules and norms of the world, these works show us how to pay attention to the built and affective infrastructure of the ordinary, and how to encounter what happens when infrastructural stress produces a dramatic tableau. In scenarios of cruel optimism we are forced to suspend ordinary notions of repair and flourishing to ask whether the survival scenarios we attach to those affects weren't the problem in the first place. Knowing how to assess what's unraveling there is one way to measure the impasse of living in the overwhelmingly present moment.

I. *The Way We Live Now: Affect, Mediation, Ideology*

So far, we have focused on the conceptual component of cruel optimism, proposing that optimism is cruel when it takes shape as an affectively stunning double bind: a binding to fantasies that block the satisfactions they offer, and a binding to the promise of optimism as such that the fantasies have come to represent. Cruelty is the "hard" in a hard loss. It is apprehensible as an affective event in the form of a beat or a shift in the air that transmits the complexity and threat of relinquishing ties to what's difficult about the world. What remains, therefore, is to specify how the activity of affective attachment can be located formally in a historical, cultural, and political field in ways that clarify the process of knotty tethering to objects, scenes, and modes of life that generate so much overwhelming yet sustaining negation.

Any account of realism requires an account of affect, and any object/scene could come to belong to a realist genre—an anecdote, an uncanny sound, a dream, a pet, or a cookie.[1] What matters is the presence of a relation that invests an object/scene with the prospect of the world's continuity. At least since Althusser, ideology theory has been the place to which critical theory has gone for explanations of affective realism, of how people's desires become mediated through attachments to modes of life to which they rarely remember consenting, at least initially. It's still an ideological relation, whether these modes of life actually threaten well-being or provide a seemingly neutral, reliable framework for enduring in the world, or both. We assume our position as subjects in a world and therefore it is in us as a structuring condition for apprehending anything. Our epistemological self-attachment is all bound up with literacy in normativity, and their relation constitutes the commonsense measure of trust in the world's ongoingness and our competence at being humans. Our sense of reciprocity with the world as it appears, our sense of what a person should do and expect, our sense of who we are as a continuous scene of action, shape what becomes our visceral intuition about how to manage living.

As its title suggests, this chapter introduces "intuition" as the process of dynamic sensual data-gathering through which affect takes shape in forms whose job it is to make reliable sense of life. In *Matter and Memory*, Henri Bergson writes that intuition is the work of history translated through personal memory. At the same time, I would argue, the visceral response is a trained thing, not just autonomic activity. Intuition is where affect meets history, in all of its chaos, normative ideology, and embodied practices of discipline and invention.[2] This chapter develops, in scenes of shifting and adjustment, an account of how narratives involving the education of embodied intuition in a transforming world situation can be said to capture the drama of their historical present. Here, the affective work of memory is just one among many forces that together constitute what gets refracted as the present: memory and the past emerge in mediated zones of visceral presence distributed across scenes of epistemological and bodily activity. You forget when you learned to *use your inside voice*—it just seems like the default mode, even to write in it. But that is never the end of the story.

The story of how attachment to reproducing the intelligibility of the world nudges affective forces into line with normative realism is also the story of liberal subjectivity's fantasies of individual and collective sovereignty, the public and the private, the past's relation to the future, and the distribution of sensibilities that discipline the imaginary about what the good life is and how proper people act.[3] But the idiom that affect theory can provide encourages more than a focus on orthodoxies of institutions and practices. It can provide a way to assess the disciplines of normativity in relation to the disorganized and disorganizing processes of labor, longing, memory, fantasy, grief, acting out, and sheer psychic creativity through which people constantly (consciously, unconsciously, dynamically) renegotiate the terms of reciprocity that contour their historical situation.[4] The ordinary is, after all, a porous zone that absorbs lots of incoherence and contradiction, and people make their ways through it at once tipped over awkwardly, half-conscious, and confident about common sense. Laws, norms, and events shape imaginaries, but in the middle of the reproduction of life people make up modes of being and responding to the world that altogether constitute what gets called "visceral response" and intuitive intelligence.

Therefore, I would claim, affect theory is another phase in the history of ideology theory; the moment of the affective turn brings us back to the encounter of what is sensed with what is known and what has impact in a new but also recognizable way. To think about sensual matter that is elsewhere to sovereign consciousness but that has historical significance in domains of subjectivity requires following the course from what's singular—the subject's irreducible specificity—to the means by which the matter of the senses becomes general within a collectively lived situation. The training of intuition is the story of individual and collective biography. Catching this drift is not just a matter of coding affect into normative emotion. It enables us to formulate, without closing down, the investments and incoherence of political subjectivity and subjectification in relation to the world's disheveled but predictable dynamics.[5]

The next section of this chapter builds a thicker case for tracking intuition as the most acute mediator of the ways affect can take form in a crisis-intensified historical present. Here we focus on what habit does. Gregg Bordowitz's film Habit and Susan Sontag's "The Way We Live Now" recount the multiple threats presented by AIDS to derive, in the dérive, a case for the centrality of intuitive rehabituation for the subject/world's capacity to maintain itself amid an impossible, but no longer unlivable, situation. The section following locates intuition in the strand of Marxist aesthetic theory that focuses on the centrality of the affective sensorium to the sensing of the historical present. Then, the chapter asks what a historicism that takes seriously the form or aesthetics of the affective event might have to attend to, in relation to the institutions, events, and norms that are already deemed history's proper evidence, especially when that history is the history of the present.

Colson Whitehead's *The Intuitionist* and William Gibson's *Pattern Recognition* provide the chapter's final case material. These recent historical novels feature protagonists who sport super-sensitive intuitions that they have professionalized: they make a living off of their intuition. Catastrophes force their talents into both operation and crisis. Already hypervigilant, the protagonists then seek to relearn the present, and in so doing, shift their affective and political practices in relation to intuitions of the present and of the place of fantasy in it. Forced out of their comfort zones, they also abandon rehabituation and leap into the impasse of a postintuitive consciousness that refuses a return to the ordinary that had required them to dedicate their gifts to predictability. The aesthetic and political point seems to be, in all cases, that the drama of adjustment to a pervasive atmosphere of unexpected precarity makes certain situations exemplary laboratories for sensing contemporary life in new idioms of affective realism.

It is worth noting in advance that many analysts would call this chapter's material for modeling the historical present "post-traumatic." As I explained in the introduction, for the past few decades, trauma theory has provided the main way of periodizing any crisis-shaped historical present. I prefer tracking the work of affect as it shapes new ordinaries to the logic of exception that necessarily accompanies the work of trauma. My aim is to construct a mode of analysis of the historical present that moves us away from the dialectic of structure (what is systemic in the reproduction of the world), agency (what people do in everyday life), and the traumatic event of their disruption, and toward explaining crisis-shaped subjectivity amid the ongoingness of adjudication, adaptation, and improvisation. In what follows, all generality—what nations do, how power works, how persons manage the sensual work of the reproduction of life—derives from stories constituted by a collective catching up to what is already happening in ordinary worlds shaped in a crisis-defined and continuing now. The concept of the "we" is itself aesthetic evidence of the process in which affective response becomes form amid the uncertainties of the present whose norms are also fraying. Consciousness of that polyrhythmic activity transforms our intuitions about how trauma induces crises in understanding a present moment that is at once enigmatic and overpresent.

. . .

Gregg Bordowitz's film Habit (2001) is part of a body of work that enables him, as he says in the soundtrack, "to understand [his] own historical present." The singularity of this present, though, the thing that is "his own," includes attention to what is general, not singular, in him—an American, a white man, a Jew, a lover, a friend, an artist, a queer-identified person, and a person who is HIV positive. Bordowitz reveals the complexities of this situation autobiographically, but not just through monologue. The real work of the piece is in its soundscape and its landscape, both shared spaces. Habit derives the poetic of the historical present through the protagonist's own senses, through the reported stories of others, and through a multitude of sonic layerings. (For more on "ambient citizenship," see chapter 7, "On the Desire for the Political.")

So, what he calls "my own" history is a collective story whose generic shape is absorptive and experimental, like the lives people lead amid crisis. These stories include those of his partner, Claire Pentecost, who thinks about their disease-threatened future "every day" while reflecting that no couple can guarantee the future that it projects out into an indefinite stretch; his friend, Yvonne Rainer, whose ageing and aversion to the mirror compare with Bordowitz's demonstrable AIDS-related weight loss; and his friend, Zackie Achmat, who explains the way he lives with AIDS not in the everyday of the reproduction of domestic life or the attrition of the body, but as an activist who breaks international law to distribute life-extending drugs in South Africa. All of these activists/artists are public figures, but it's the dynamic of their intimacy, distance, and difference that focuses the story.

Achmat's poetic of living is organized around refusal: his refusal to take drugs to prolong his own life in a world that sees value only in the health of the wealthy, and his refusal to honor the capitalist apartheids that deny health to the nations and classes that right now can't afford to pay the market price. This contrasts with what we see of Bordowitz, who never talks directly about the monetary cost of his health. Almost affectless and in shadow, and in a kind of dry plainspokenness, he sits at a table and explains to the camera his daily self-maintenance routines, counting out his pills into a calendrical pillbox to show days and weeks as the near future on which he

1.1. Gregg Bordowitz

1.2. Yvonne Rainer

1.3. Zackie Achmat

must focus in order to have the bodily strength and mental clarity to imagine other times and spaces. His interlocutors have their own perspectives on the consciousness of finite life, their own techniques of tracking the countdown toward death in which the making of life in the bodily everyday transpires. Everyone's need for habitude is exemplary, but no one's habitude is exemplary.

That is, everyone lives the present intensely, from within a sense that their time, this time, is crisis time. Bordowitz extends this time to his audience. They might not be in the same crises biographically or physiologically, but all must inhabit the shared atmosphere of dehabituation and forced improvisation that an endemic and pandemic health crisis induces. Their solidarity around surviving this scene and staying attached to life involves gathering up diverse practices for adjusting to the singular and shared present. In a sense, Habit responds to an imperative to develop and to circulate as many idioms of the claim on life as can be imaginatively effective. Here, habit is an idiom of the claim on life.

There are others, too, in this film, other friends, colleagues, activists—other conversations about experimental modes of staying tethered to life. In the collection and collision of stories and voice-overs, Habit is foremost a conversation film, made with a quiet, patient camera. In general, conversation is a key genre of the present: when a conversation ends, its singular time ends, and then it becomes like all other episodes, something mainly forgotten, distorted, and half-remembered. But, providing the action of this film, conversation is a space of time that makes its own rules and boundaries, its own terms of being contemporary and of taking over what would otherwise seem the arrhythmic rule of crisis.

But that is not all conversation is: in a crisis, vital information-trading proliferates and demands conversation across many media. Informal networks of knowledge sharing are central to the endurance and vitality of any intimate public. AIDS especially produced an information revolution involving the democratic distribution of medical expertise to anyone interested, especially interested in taking expert knowledge and creating a vernacular for its broader circulation. It was a matter of life and death to become, literally, conversant. As Deborah Gould has shown in great detail, this process opened up a field where gossip and life teamed up for rethinking what constitutes life as such and the good life.[6]

This apprehension of conversation-for-life is the impulse that Susan Sontag mobilizes, too, in "The Way We Live Now," her story of the durable, enduring present of AIDS.[7] Her "we" is both singular and general—the crisis makes the people impacted by AIDS *kinds of people* who are not identical, nonetheless, to any biopolitical norm. The story is a conversation piece: that is all it is. The reader eavesdrops, participating as a lurker in the intimate public of the illness. The talk that circulates makes a claim and a world within the time of the historical present.

Specifically, the structure of the story is talk among friends connected to each other through their connection to one man—Stephen. The story places the reader on a "first name basis" with the figures talking, transforming the name into a medium for seeing life as a place that is intimate and affectively intense and yet general, dislocated, and sensually abstract. Stephen, whom the reader has never known when well, neither dies nor is cured in the story: he's in an impasse. But the conditions of his historical present change as his people report a shift between the death sentence of AIDS and the invention of the AIDS cocktail that turned fated life back into an ellipsis, a time marked by pill- and test-taking, and other things, the usual. The story is about the conversion of one event—a diagnosis—into a condition that is never fully realized in the echoing of an end.

Even if the story moved from diagnosis to death, knowing the sick one and his friends only by the referential performance time of their habits of affective manifestation, the reader would become distracted from the typical recover-or-not narrative of disease and absorbed in following the pattern of personality they emit by saying certain kinds of things habitually. Yet their voices are not crisply distinct either. We find all the friends in the middle of a desperately improvised pedagogic process, teaching each other ways to adapt to the new survival imperatives that include learning how to be chronically ill, how to be with a dying person, how to make a fold within that person's world, and how to identify with him without also dying or becoming ill.

> But you know you're not going to come down with the disease, Quentin said, to which Ellen replied, on her behalf, that is not the point, and possibly untrue, my gynecologist says that everyone is at risk, everyone who has a sexual life, because sexuality is a chain that links each of us to many others, unknown others, and now the great chain of being has become a chain of death as well. . . . But this isn't going to go on forever, Wesley said, it can't, they're bound to come up with something (they, they, muttered Stephen), but did you ever think, Greg said, that if some people

don't die, I mean even if they can keep them alive (they, they, muttered Kate), they continue to be carriers, and that means, if you have a conscience, that you can never make love, make love fully, as you'd been wont—wantonly, Ira said—to do. (19, 23)

With its movement of meaning back and forth across the progressing surface of the text, Sontag's brilliant Barthesianism can be read a number of ways. The stylistic decision to perform a mimetic reenactment of what the senses do when they're catching up to something might, for instance, enact the literalism of a modernist literary psychology that aspires to use free verse, streams of consciousness, and the representation of a flooding mentality as evidence of an autonomic explosion of sensations and reflections. But this is not a psychological work attempting to represent interiority as a universal fact about humans. In narrative and formal terms, Sontag's story focuses on the formal production of individual and group sensoria through talk's intimate mediation to represent the organization of a mode of production for survival. The story does narrate transformation—Stephen becomes more ill as time passes. But while so many sentences create a whiplash of authorship and referentiality in the way they shift speaker in the middle of phrases, the mode of surface response maintains a predictable form and pacing and remains in the suspended zone of affective and moral judgment that moves among love and gossip. They're in a race to jog in place, to not lose a step, or trip: to maintain—no, attain—composure. In this way "The Way We Live Now" remediates our intuitions about how intuition itself moves between the singular and the general. Survival in the present of an ordinary collective life suffused with a historic and historical crisis to which we are always catching up is *the way we live now*. The text enacts Harry Harootunian's claim that contemporary global crisis time is thick, "a new time marked by a boundless present."[8]

Through genres like this, refracting the present moment as a historical one, "The Way We Live Now" joins *Habit* in dissolving the distinction among and fetishization of memory, history, fantasy, and futurity as the grounds for determining the value of *having lived*. Thinking about life during lived time, everyone is figuring out the terms and genres for valuing *living*. No one imagines having expertise enough to have mastered the situation—just a commitment to cultivating better intuitive skills for moving around this extended, extensive time and space where the crisis of the present meets multiple crises of presence.

Habit is also a travelogue, another genre of the present. In Bordowitz's story of his ambient lives and actions as an activist, friend, lover, and collaborator qua conversationalist, his camera circles the globe, suturing scenes from Durban, South Africa, India, the UN, Chicago, a park, a basement, a laundry room, a bedroom, a dinner party, and a car. He thus interrupts his political and bodily depression and a default narrative of morbidity by creating a filmic pathocartography, a scenic route in an emotional map whose construction is a mode of self-maintenance on a "plane of immanence."[9] The world's infinite scenes of crisis and process jar with the brutal ongoingness of time, its many dashes and ellipses, but that is okay: preserving the potentiality for casual life is important in a crisis, and whoever shows up in the film is in a here and now, taking a look, having a listen, and sometimes talking.

Through that visual mapping he encounters a lot, not just friends. There are neighborhoods where strangers live and play as though without a care, but one never knows from the outside whether play is a forgettable moment or a life-saving interruption of anxious waiting. There are neighborhoods shaped by the chronically ill who self-organize against corporate privilege over human health, and whose politics induces a joy in excess of their instrumental aim. There is a global capitalist culture manifested in the absence of affordable medicine that tries to control how poor and sexually nonnormative people experience privacy (i.e., as having no safety net) and publicness (i.e., as a responsibility to state public health requirements and social conventions). There is the ordinary life luck—luck that is both made and an effect of inherited privilege—of some privileged subjects to have insurance and flexible work, which makes their survival exigencies somewhat more medical than economic. All of the struggles are political. There is an urgency to make work that makes worlds, that subtends art and politics for communicating the proliferating urgencies and techniques of survival. Along with that, the pulsations of the ordinary are felt across glances, in speeches, and in the camera's long take and distant position from the noise and the quiet of crisis.

Habit's camera and cutting are quiet and contemplative, unfolding the aesthetic present and summing up as form what they gather up, too, across the different moods associated with those different spaces. In this aesthetic rhythm across time and space the film manifests the collective nervous system that Michael Taussig describes, in which the subject's encounters with the world in which he circulates open up a modular narrative that stages the

2.1–2.2. Claire Pentecost and Gregg Bordowitz, Rituals of the Day (*Habit*, 2001)

forces transecting a scene without adding up to some big summation. Biography, psychology, law, mode of production, intentionality: all of these are in play, but no single logic provides assurance about the conditions of the endurance of the present.

Bordowitz's "habit" is thus neither the compulsion of addiction, nor an unreflexive knee-jerk movement of personality fascinated with its self-development, nor the self-exemplarity of bourgeois universalism. To the contrary, if bourgeois universalism ruled the affective history cobbled together here, there would be no need constantly to check in with strangers and intimates and to document the variety in different lives shaped by the same crisis — a crisis of history, body, and intuition about how we live now. Even Bordowitz manifests as both stranger and intimate to himself. This irreducible alterity, constant lag, and catching up within the ongoing present is what, I think, motivates the film's choice to begin with Pentecost's performance of yogic practice. She is seated on the floor, still, but the very work of cultivating a practice of stillness is evidence of the situation's constant pressure on the subject's aspirational adequacy to life and to living.

Ritual is yet another genre of the present. It evokes a tradition, and respects the place of tradition in the ongoing punctuation of time. It sutures different temporal arcs. It gestures toward therapy and redemption without narrating those ends. Most significantly, the ritual habit is another route to preserving banality, turning care of the self into a mode of ordinariness. Bordowitz often naps during the day: we watch him wake up disoriented, and we watch him get a grip. These naps, shot in shadow, do not feel sacred. You cannot tell if the naps are out of depression, self-preservation, bodily fatigue, or self-love. Probably the mood changes, and therefore so too does the event. So the ritual aspiration of *Habit* involves Bordowitz following himself and his entire community communicating how they are learning to submit to both the passivity and the activity of feeling forced to take on living as a practice, on the way to the deliberate mode becoming a habit, a comfortable gestural rhythm. The torpor of and need for banality points Bordowitz to another comforting and discomfiting affect of the contingent present. To be in crisis is not to have the privilege of the taken-for-granted: it is to bear an extended burden of vulnerability for an undetermined duration. To be in goes-without-saying ordinariness can only be an aspiration for those whose other option is to be overmastered by the moment of the event that began at a time that only retroactively leads one to diagnosis.

In so tracking his singular maps, schedules, intimacies, and estrangements, Bordowitz is trying to make a point about the political centrality of making genres for affective practice in relation to shaping the historical import of the present moment. His collection of encounters and maps of the precarious is not antithetical to the times, spaces, and built environments of the ordinary of the straight and healthy, but moves across them, revealing both distinct and indistinct meanings and management styles of being around the same spaces of intimacy and alterity, threat and safety, comfort and contingency. But it is not as though this is a serene adjustment. As chapter 3, "Slow Death," will argue at greater length, chronic illness is an illness of time. Bordowitz says that his body and his nature are his enemies; they represent the abrasions of time, a process of wearing out amid the activity of making life. He says that he wishes he could live in the performative present of active consciousness and not in the narrative rollout of corporeal decay. But the pressures of his situation force his gaze, voice, and ear to engender a particular kind of present: chronotypical, in care-of-the-self-shaped hours of the day; historical, as marked by institutional work and media-normative events; political, marked by collective consciousness, activity, and desire to change a structure; affective, an ongoing space of feeling things out, noticing mood's arcs and trails, and becoming habituated and alive to the intensities of a being passing through a phase that could be an impasse, or life itself.

There is nothing smooth about living in crisis, but the film performs the need to develop intuitions about managing that. Skidding across *Habit*'s final moments is an uneven electronic soundtrack that accompanies a car driving around at night in proximity to a *whatever, wherever*.[10] The time/space scenario of the present emerges fitfully, like the staticky, incoherent, hesitant violin and synthesizer samples that have no narrative genre. The historical present is only smooth when art or history take it over and make a priority among forms. *Habit*'s fundamental rough measure is the work of affective tendencies making their way toward form, toward intuition. Whatever one might say about history and memory tumbles together into an ordinariness that has not quite been achieved, nor rested in, but that comforts, somehow, because the camera keeps going into the familiar/unfamiliar spaces of the ongoing, drive-through present, marked by its jerky rhythm. Aspirations to habit do not here equal a kind of praxis that amounts to the equation of revolution with breaks, transcendence, or utopian vision, therefore. For amid crisis, without the scrolling out of the ordinary all energy would be sucked into the decisionism of a life lived minute to minute. Henri Lefevbre's *Rhythmanalysis* calls the mode of enacting life through habituated gestures that stretch the present out so that enjoyment is possible a kind of autopoetic, proprioceptive "dressage."[11] One might also think about coasting, cruising, or drifting in the mode of a slightly heightened, anxious seeking toward a habit. Habit produces a freedom for thought beyond immediacy. Bordowitz ends the film not quite comfortably there.

II. *Histories of the Present*

In the previous section, my aim was to introduce the scene of a historical present that becomes apprehensible as an affective urgency to remake intuitions for living through collecting presentist genres — conversation, pathocartography, ritual — that might someday achieve a habitual rhythm.[12] Here, figures move transversally across spaces, quickly and lingeringly, reflectively and in the flesh, projecting and sensing atmospheres and impacts to which they have to catch up and respond. Sometimes they unlearn, sometimes they repeat, sometimes they surprise themselves, often they just lean numbly or wonderingly toward the next potentiality. Occupying the long middle of a crisis, their ambitious pursuit of an understanding of the presenting situation produces a personal, political, and aesthetic ambit that pushes the on-going event into something that has not found its genre.

This very need to block the becoming-object of the event is what embeds the affective in the historical. When Foucault talks about eventilization, he refers to a need to move analytically beyond the moment when a happening moves into common sense, or a process congeals into an object-event that conceals its immanence, its potentially unfinished or enigmatic activity.[13] In these narrative histories of the present, a shift between knowing and un-certain intuitionisms enables us to think about being in history as a densely corporeal, experientially felt thing whose demands on survival skills map not the whole world in one moment but a way to think about the history of sensualized epistemologies in the atmosphere of a particular moment now (aesthetically) suspended in time.

But what's personal, local, and sensual about the perception of the his-torical present often produces skepticism about its historical actuality and exemplarity. Situated squarely within the mainstream tradition of Marxian cultural theory, even formidable critics like Harry Harootunian and Moishe Postone argue for seeing the present as an effect of historical forces that cannot be known fully by the presently living, who require scholarly and political education toward comprehending the structural and the systemic. Otherwise the present is cast as virtually ahistorical, fleeting, fantasmatic, or a space of symptomatic pseudoactivity. Žižek in particular casts the present as a space protected by disavowals that keep taking blows from the real that constantly shocks people about what determines their lives.[14]

It is easy to forget that cultural Marxism itself provided us with an ac-count of the matter of affect as key to reading the historical present. De-spite the frequent aspersions cast toward Marxist anticulturalism, Marxism has a long tradition of interlacing descriptions of the present across rela-tions of ownership and control, the reproduction of labor value, and vari-eties of subjected position with the affective components of labor-related subjectivity. It has not claimed that subjects feel *accurately* or objectively his-torical—this is why the concept of ideology had to be invented—but this tradition has offered multiple ways to engage the affective aspects of class antagonism, labor practices, and a communally generated class feeling that emerges from inhabiting a zone of lived structure.

Notably, theorists from Lukács to Jameson and Benedict Anderson, to name a few, have cast historicism via the historical novel as the aesthetic expression of an affective epistemology, an encounter with the historical present via the intensities of its tone, whether emergent, chaotic, or waning. Lukács constantly refers to the "feeling" and the aesthetic "tone" that gets at the heart of the experiential shape of a historical period.[15] Williams, by way of the "structure of feeling," points to "specifically affective elements of consciousness and relationships" and to "elements of impulse, restraint, and tone." The "structure of feeling" is a residue of common historical experience sensed but not spoken in a social formation, except as the heterogeneous but common practices of a historical moment would emanate them:[16] Williams wrote and interpreted all literary work in terms of the articulation of historical and bodily events. Anderson too uses the historical novel to describe what he calls the *feeling* of national modernity engendered aesthetically, notably in the Philippines, but generically, in the historical novel, too. Finally, Jameson, famously, marked the shift into postmodernism via the waning of affect in postmodern *culture*.

To Jameson, affect equates with "feeling or emotion, all subjectivity"; here, affect is not a technical term but a coarse measure of a shift from a norm of modernist care for the historical resonance in the represented object to a postmodern investment in flatness and surface. This shift denotes not a mere waning of affect in *images* as such; it marks, he claims, a departure in the general social imaginary from attachment to "the carnal reality of the human member" to a "virtual deconstruction of the very aesthetic of expression itself," an expression, he says, that no longer translates the inner pain of "the monad" to the world.[17] Presumably this inner pain is a rich and profound register of historical subjectification, and the melodramatic ethics of Jameson's preferred aesthetic casts the historical present as a theater of its expression.

The Political Unconscious had introduced a materialist practice of reading all work in the affective tradition of the historical novel: but affect is not an explicit problem in that book. It arises only when Jameson expands this epistemological and political project to the aestheticized, sensualized, and commodified postmodern world moment generally, at which point he mistakes the aspirationally flat affects of a small elite sector of the aesthetic public for the experience of a general population. Yet the liberal culture of true feeling was never so sentimentally present as in the growth of diaristic, autobiographical, personal-is-political, intensified artwork across so many aesthetic sectors of the same period he covers at the close of the twentieth century.

My main point, though, is that historians of the historical novel have long understood the genre as a locus of affective situations that not only generate exemplary aesthetic conventions but exemplify political and subjective formations local to a particular time and space. This means that the historical novel aimed to induce certain affects in the reader whose value sutured that reader to history and genealogy, producing a capacity to sense historical experience in an aesthetic feedback loop. As I have argued in *The Female Complaint*, all genres are distinguished by the affective contract they promise: by claiming that certain affects embed the historical in persons and persons in the historical in ways that only the aesthetic situation could really capture, the cultural Marxist take on the historical novel foregrounds affect not as the sign of ahistoricism, but as the very material of historical embeddedness.[18] Critics read these novels for the *sense* of the historical they provide: history is neither in footnotes, nor in the representation of historical figures or events, nor in style as such, as in the period piece, but in atmospheres (an aesthetic genre). This tradition of the novel points to something barely apprehensible in ordinary life and consciousness. It emerged from the space of time and practice that not only made people historical but made them feel responsive to and shaped by something historical in an atmosphere they've lived, whether in the flesh or through mediated inheritances of what is always bodily memory.

I have taken this excursion through the genre of the historical novel, therefore, for a few reasons. First, because for Scott and his heirs the *point* of the historical novel was a paradoxical one: to become embedded in the affective life of a past moment that might have been the run-up to the future that was now a present, and to create distances from the present moment of writing whose own shared contours one can only intuit. The purpose of the genre is, to borrow the terms of Valerie Rohy's brilliant analysis, to engender in an aesthetic field of historical signification a punctum that appears singularly ahistorical — affect — but which is, because of the detail it cuts across and unites, a relay through which the historical can be said to be sensed before it is redacted. Speaking experientially and analytically, Scott and those working in his tradition would argue that all historical moments are anachronistic.[19] But the feeling of being historical and the aesthetic experience of a space of time, seen as a historical sense, feeling, or tone, was something else. It pointed to a converging unity of experience in an ongoing moment that could later be called epochal but that at the time marked a shared nervous system that it was the novelist's project to put out there for readers.

This concept, of the affectivity of the historical present relayed by an aesthetic transmission, has not been central to the work of Americanists, who have been trained, for the last few decades, to posit historicism against formalism, aestheticism, and "theory," and who are trained to see every referent as a hyperlink to an untold history that can justify, if the archive is thick enough, a "reading" that must not stray too far from some version of the historical record. Anyone schooled in the work of genre will know that it is impossible to comprehend the terms of a cultural discussion among those who left traces without encountering what's affective (a literary convention, a sense held in collective memory about a "time") about the aesthetics of that translation. But too often we derive a sense of a time, place, and power through historical archives whose job it is to explain something aesthetic without thinking the aesthetic in the sensually affective terms that conventions of entextualizing always code, perform, and release. Thinking about genre historically bridges the historiography of an entexualized moment and the affectivity gathered up in the evidence that points to the animating situation.

Related to this aesthetic embeddedness in the affectivity of the present is the centrality of everyday life to the conceptualization of the ordinary I've been advancing here. To return to Jameson, an underheralded aspect of *The Political Unconscious* was the centrality of Deleuze's and Guattari's *Anti-Oedipus* to the working through of Jameson's three interpretive horizons, especially that of the synchronic, that relatively disrespected zone of distortion and singularity that I have been calling the historical present. Deleuze's and Guattari's aim, he writes, was to "reassert the specificity of the political content of everyday life" against master narrative methodological reductions of matter in the aesthetic scene, a method that they critiqued for being too enigmatic or pre-empirical.[20]

The reason the historical present has been disrespected, Jameson suggests, is that the sense of the present as a lived structure that bodies apprehend and that people respond to has often been cast as a scene in which duped or epistemologically limited subjects grope their ways toward survival, except in exceptional moments such as—and, here, Jameson cites Baudrillard's list—"the wildcat strike, terrorism, and death."[21] Of the current literature in this tradition, Harootunian has made the best recent case. In "Remembering the Historical Present," Harootunian argues that capitalism always blocks the development of a historical sense that can grasp the structural determinations that constitute the present, engendering a distorted apprehension of pastness and a devastating misrecognition of how contemporary forces work. But two events have especially distorted this condition. The failure of the socialist project and related imaginaries and 9/11 are said to have heightened the intensities that make "the present rhythms of consumption" that I have been locating in atmospheres of "survival" substitute for a rich consciousness of contemporary existence.[22] Harootunian narrates the importance of returning to the present and presentism a conception of the future that would expose the unstable histories of force that have converged in the emergent moment: without such a claim and a concept the subjects of capitalism will be doomed to think of themselves as merely inhabitants of a "thick" and nonporous present.

I am entirely in accord with Harootunian's demand that historians, including literary ones, produce as the present a sense of "noncontemporaneous contemporaneity," a history of the forces that bear on the everyday and interrupt its appearance of apparent homogeneity to reveal cracks in the local experience of life that can be mobilized toward alternative imaginaries. But his model of the thick present is of a kind that sees the modes of intelligence for getting by as cramped imaginaries without much shot at alternativity, an alternativity that he equates with the taking in of historicist genealogies of nationalism and globalization.

This disrespect for what's apprehensible in the ordinary seems off to me, as does the focus on futurity as the primary lubricant for counter-normative political consciousness. In the present moment, our understanding of ordinary life might indeed require different parameters than the paradigms offered by everyday life theory, where sensual impulses, skills, and developments are opposed to a historical sense and structural causality while being nonetheless formed by them.[23] Everyday life theory—from Simmel through to Benjamin, Lefebvre, and Nigel Thrift—has focused on something unprecedented in modernity, the new sensorium provided by the city for its new concentrated populations, which no longer lived in spaces where they were known, but in spaces they could never know and not usually be known in, anonymous spaces where new varieties of knowing and being known emerged from the improvisations forced by the new, modernist spatial rhythms. The city produced objects and scenes that created events and obstacles and forced fundamental changes in the new inhabitants' nervous systems so that they could process the ongoing work of the impact and intensity of the new infrastructure of the everyday. Everyday life theory thus ought properly to be seen as a framework for early twentieth century urbanization or for wherever the collective sensorium is shown to be shocked in ex-

tremis by rapid urbanization, mediatization, and remediation of the relation between strangers and intimates.

The Deleuzian strain in Jameson's work, which is now elaborated by theorists like Stewart and Massumi, would look differently at the contemporary everyday, as movements within the present demand different dramas of adjustment and sensual self-development from the capitalist modes of the past. The sensual idiom of this tradition of reading the historical through its affective resonance in a present encounter would have to redescribe the *something* developing within the geopolitical field that makes itself known as unstable, if not in crisis; in a regime of affective labor, structural relations of alienation are viscerally the opposite, saturating the sensorium while yet monetized, disciplinary, and exploitative. Given the multi- and trans-medial platforms that make contemporary political and intuitive disarray available to more people in diverse kinds of world, old structuralisms of the before and after are inadequate. What constitutes continuity amid the pressure of structural inconstancy? What is the good life when the world that was to have been delivered by upward mobility and collective uplift that national/ capitalism promised goes awry in front of one? What is life when the body cannot be relied on to keep up with the constant flux of new incitements and genres of the reliable, but must live on, maintaining footing, nonetheless? The historical novel of the present provides, as Massumi writes, "an expanded culture of empiricism," where the "self-activity of experience" provides a kind of "color-patch" of the collective moment.[24]

III. The Affectsphere and the Event

The Intuitionist and *Pattern Recognition* feature two citizens of a U.S. world where the grey iniquities of political, military, and economic practice saturate everything, while the public hegemons—politicians, community leaders, and the like—proclaim that the worst of political violence is exceptional or in the past. Yet negating through revelation the open secret of ordinary injustice does not make these conditions any more vulnerable to transformation than they were when they were occulted. The books' visions are dark about what better realism can do: they seek genre the way the subordinated seek justice, and are as likely to fail, too, if formal adequation is the goal and trauma is the dominant idiom of the historical present. Wandering through the New York Crystal Palace of 1853; the era of Jim Crow; the Cold War; the department store as modern fantasia and commodity design as postmodern art; the global culture of disseminated production and localized consumption; 9/11; and the militarization both of state sovereignty and of intellectual property rights, both novels push the traditionally empirical material of the historical novel into the register of utopias that won't wait, that demand a more robust place in the present than any heterotopic fold can offer. From our discussion of the historical novel we already know that this plane of transformed history is present and accessible through the aesthetics of the affectsphere.

The Intuitionist has its eye on a utopian future in which elevators will move beyond the "plodding, mundane" physical world as ordinary "citizens" now know it to create the technological context for new sensoria, movement, and space (254);[25] and Pattern Recognition spends pages speculating on "how we [already] look . . . to the future" in a way that induces an ethics of distributed presence, in the present (54, 57).[26] In these narrated archives, pasts are mutable and futures intuited; so the main attention is to the adaptation, adjustment, and excitation of the protagonists to the world through which they move and whose object status they remake through movement. Their biographies are not what matters, though. As their singular stories turn into exemplary ones, the focus is less on how historically stimulated affect is being transmitted to them across eras and spaces than on what this affect's organization of force and desire reveals for living on generally.

The main focus is on what events in the historical present do to the competence of persons: in that, these novels are not unusual. But their protagonists are unusual: ordinary women with supersensitive capacities for apprehension. Theirs is not the supersensorium associated with "women's intuition," though, with its claim to have special access to the affectsphere's unstated intimate truths. Instead, the protagonists have sensitive intuiting systems attuned to structural causality, as accessed through a particular kind of machinic value: in The Intuitionist, Lila Mae Watson inspects the health of elevators; in Pattern Recognition, Cayce Pollard can read the potential power of any commoditized logo. But traumatic events push the protagonists out of their intuitive zones of professional authority. Forces transforming the historical present force them, and their readers, not into new confirming stabilizations of being, nor into profoundly dissociated states, but into sensually porous intuitive quandaries that stand in for the drive to not repeat the past in the making of contemporary history. Life in the impasse turns from threat to aim. To enter experience without eventilizing it will mean knowing something is afoot without forcing prediction into being, as though it would be possible to place one's affect on a kind of confident cruise control. The literary figures grow something like that: a historically capacious, neointuitive sense of becoming-present.

. . .

Shortly after The Intuitionist opens, Lila Mae Watson leans against an elevator wall. Lila Mae inspects elevators. The narrative sets the stage for the multiple anomalies that converge in this scene. She is African American in a profession that is white supremacist, a woman in a profession that is otherwise all male. It is around 1964; most professions are still segregated. The city she lives in, implicitly New York City, has just recovered from a race riot, but things are simmeringly quiet now, in the everyday. That is, they are quiet if one's index for apprehending the historical is the conventional event and the perspective of the structurally privileged. But Lila Mae is an Intuitionist. In this novel, Intuitionism is, foremost, a school of thought advanced by elevator inspectors. It advocates that inspectors take on the sensual perspective of the object they investigate to read the state of the object's health: Lila Mae's epistemology, that is, is an aesthetic relation.[27] Intuitionists read the state of the elevator by pressing their bodies to the elevator wall as it moves. The Empiricists are the Intuitionists' rivals. The empirically-minded engineers are a school of thought rather than feeling; they examine machinery for its engineered state rather than claiming to know its potential performance through affective gestalts. Here is Lila Mae at work:

> As the elevator at 125 Walker reaches the fifth floor landing, an orange octagon cartwheels into her mind's frame. It hops up and down, incongruous with the annular aggression of the red spike. Cubes and parallelograms emerge around the eighth floor, but they're satisfied with halfhearted little jigs and don't disrupt the proceedings like the mischievous orange octagon. The octagon ricochets into the foreground, famished for attention. She knows what it is. The triad of helical buffers recedes farther from her, ten stories down the dusty and dark floor of the well. No need to continue. Just before she opens her eyes she tries to think of what the super's expression must be. She doesn't come close. (6)

James Fulton, the original theorist of Intuitionism, calls these "excreted chemicals, understood by the soul's receptors . . . *true speech*" (87) (italics mine).

At the same time, Lila Mae's nervous system has developed other intuiting gifts that register her place in the human world, although her most powerful reciprocal relations are with things that enclose: elevators, books, and what's in her head. The narrator comments that, as she moves toward the elevators she's about to inspect, Lila Mae negotiates the city landscape by feeling its atmospheres too: like Bordowitz, she knows the street maps but what counts is the affectsphere, organized by the sensory pressures of the biopolitical. There is, she senses, a "zero-point" of collective kinetic life, "a locus of metropolitan disaffection" situated in the heart of the city (4). That zero-point, a collective affective habit and norm of the city, is where history in the novel first reveals itself shaping the affective ordinary. The farther she gets from it the more precisely she can "predict just how much suspicion, curiosity, and anger she will rouse in her cases" because she is African American, female, poised, reserved, and a little scary in her stark underperformance of the normative social pleasures and rhythms.

It is not only that, in contrast to Lila Mae, most elevator inspectors are white men who drink lustily and enjoy their union's patriarchal pecking order.[28] It is that, as she moves farther from the zero-point, Lila Mae knows that she will be transacting affective exchanges that do not congeal into events. She knows that she will do nothing to incite the perturbation her body makes in the racist and misogynist world, because she's turned her face into a mask that refuses to play the game of "equality-staring" or incited response that shoots through the nervous system of transracial (and here, sexual) contact in the era of white and male supremacy.[29] Virtually her entire cluster of relations takes place as a communication across nervous systems. Lila Mae *knows* hardly anyone. Although she's "been a practicing solipsist since before she could walk," minimalism is now a strategy of survival (235). She is safe flying under the radar: anonymity can provide a kind of proprioceptive freedom amid the performance demands of structural privilege.

Lila Mae's freedom not to react is helped a lot by the fact that, as the narrator says, she "is never wrong" about elevators or social threat (9, 197). The reader is instructed to trust her perceptions, and the novel contains numerous scenes in which nothing much happens apart from her sensing and sifting some witnessed action. She sits in the dark corner of a bar apprehending; looks around a room, wondering; waits for traffic to move, speculating; stays quiet while she's being home-invaded and kidnapped, always taking the time that her composure requires. Aleatory being is where she lives, except in those few moments of professional performance where, focused, she feels the elevator's health in the affects her body releases once pressed against the vertically moving wall. This is to say that she has developed her intuition into two registers, the machinic and the social. Each reaches regularly its own peaks of demand on her affective intelligence.

There is a lot of demand on her acuity, too. The entire world of this novel takes place in the register of crisis, as structural antagonism plays itself out both within relations of rule and between managers and the managed. Affective crisis wears out individuals and spreads across days and myriad lives until publics see themselves constituted in their precarity and in whatever enclaves and pleasures they can produce amid threat. Sometimes the register of racial, class, and political formation focuses the crisis, shaping relations among the city, the region, and the nation, all of which are impersonal but *felt* personally. Sometimes crisis rolls in as anxious gestures of control over things, people, comportment, and value by corporate, union, and mafia capitalist institutions that cloak their vulnerability with proactive dynamics that require violence and secrecy. Things feel random when they are not, and things feel systemic when accidents actually happen. What threatens might therefore be political where the power stakes are palpable, or entirely fantasmatic—the difference does not make much difference in the encounter with what might happen and what does happen. Lila Mae registers all of this. From the perspective of the problem of managing her existence as such, *The Intuitionist* maintains fidelity to the historical novel's mission to transmit what it felt like to live on in proximity to a suffused violence so systemic and intensity-magnetizing that it is a relief when an event expresses it. At the same time, and crucially, the narrator notes that a catastrophe is just "what happens when you subtract what happens all the time" (230). So the work of the novel is to put catastrophe back into the ordinary, which is where its protagonist has no choice but to live. It refuses the exceptionality of the traumatic event, even when that event appears to have its own aesthetic structure, but catastrophe has to involve the unraveling of form and the suffusion of effects throughout the historical field.

In *The Intuitionist*, amid the atmospheres that keep the material of crisis pulsating throughout the surface of existence, there is such an event: a major elevator crash. The event looks entirely political: the Intuitionists and the Empiricists are in the middle of an election for control over the mob-ridden Elevator Guild, and it looks like an act of terrorist sabotage by one side to undermine the other's credibility and aura of competence. But the crash turns out to be at least two kinds of red herring. It allows for a staged political crisis in the historical present in which everyone plays their parts so that the resolution seems to have moved something rather than reiterated the fundamental structural domination of the colluding classes over the populations at whose pleasure they serve. It also reveals paradoxes on paradoxes about how different antagonisms internal to political, economic, and industrial power shape the everyday.

Lila Mae thinks the Empiricists did it to the building and to her, because she had been the evaluator of that elevator the day before, when she checked out the Fanny Briggs building. Fanny Briggs was a famous escaped slave: Lila Mae had studied her as a child (11–12). As the only female African American inspector, she knows she got the gig for symbolic reasons, for the building is supposed symbolically to embody a United States that supports racial uplift. Only in catastrophe does the building bearing the name of an escaped slave become symbolically apt, however. As the elevator that escapes its gears, it serves to expose the machinery of white supremacy at the heart not only of politics, corporate ideology, and the modern city but, as we will see, of its very engineering.

Lila Mae first senses the catastrophe as a message to her: sure that she has read the elevator correctly, she hears it calling out to her to clear her name and to reveal corrupted truths. The detective plot she initiates opens up new "contracts" between Lila and her world and does reveal multiple crises in the kinds of knowledge that make will reign in the elevator public, the political sphere, and for Lila Mae: most importantly, it sends Lila Mae into a detective mode that leads to the destruction of her intuition (166).

Her journey reveals slowly a secretly racialized map of twentieth-century capitalism, seen as a utopian technology gone haywire. It turns out that James Fulton, having migrated from the U.S. South to the North and from socially African American to passing as white, made up Intuitionism as a joke on the engineers that oppressed him and his like. Then Fulton came to believe his own joke. In *The Intuitionist* jokes are usually forms of racial and sexual aggression against the duped and the dominated, the pleasure of the Alpha. But here the joke's very power opens up a counterfactual and counterphysical world. Fulton extended it into a story about uplift that violated racial norm and natural law. He invents, in code, a "black box" whose blackness provides multiple keys to a new gravity. He writes: "There is another world beyond this one" (62). This sentence sounds like it is about the future but the point, in the novel, is spatial. Theorizing opens up the present to a lived alternativity in the present.

This axiom, from Fulton's journals, was the key phrase in his tome *Theoretical Elevators*. Reading it in class induced in Lila Mae a "conversion experience" from Empiricism to Intuitionism (59). The phrase about the "other world" reshaped her viscera, moving her intuitions away from technical empiricism toward a concrete epistemo-sensual utopianism. The novel then tracks her being jolted out of her habituated viscerality a second time, after the elevator crash. Its affective historicism slyly imitates the noir novel's structure of associated intensities: be cynical and professional, get too interested in a problem, find evidence of corruption and make people pay, produce near-vigilante justice, and meanwhile in the opening to attention not just to the built world but to the evidence of motive, become a sucker for love and a victim of all the things that do not change even if the case gets successfully closed. All of this happens to Lila Mae. It turns out that the thugs who pursue Lila Mae *and* the people who protect her are not all that they seem. They are all corporate agents hot for the information about Fulton that they think she has: because they find her name in Fulton's notes, they figure that she has the plans for the black box whose engineering would potentially destroy the world of their hoarded power, their historical present. Fulton merely saw her studying late into the night at the Institute for Vertical Transport, and left in his papers a marginal question about who she was.

Most thugs act like thugs; it is their pleasure to dispense with manners. But one of the elevator corporations sends Raymond Coombes, or "Natchez," to seduce her into wanting to turn her knowledge into an intimate exchange. He does this both by appealing to her sexually and by "disclosing" that he is secretly Fulton's nephew, a race man who wants to protect his uncle's legacy. Lila Mae has no skills for intuiting desire: she believes him and begins to transform her practices of visceral response, suddenly acting coy, thinking about clothes, and strategizing the minor intimate secrecies. Then she gets the jolt of revelation. After, late in the book, someone tells her the *true* story of her contemporary life and she discovers Natchez's true status and motive, Lila Mae reverts to Intuitionist strategies: be intimate with the world of things and be alienated from the world of capital and love, the world of false reciprocity. But in the meanwhile that is the intensified moment of crisis, the ground of her intuition shifts. As she takes on the project of extending Fulton's utopian vision, her speculative realism about the relation of things to forces performs the place for a world beyond, yet within, this one.

Cayce Pollard, the protagonist of William Gibson's *Pattern Recognition*, is an intuitive like Lila Mae, and has likewise turned her intuition into a career. To be more precise, she is a "sensitive," "allergic" to commoditized icons, like the Michelin Bibendum or the Tommy Hilfiger logo. We see her go "sideways," falling apart at the force of the commoditized sign: the encounter is not pretty. As her psyche "swells" in the face of an out-of-tune logo, her being experiences an "avalanche" of affects, a resonance that produces the bitter intense sensation like "biting down hard on a piece of foil" (17). This sensually mixed metaphor performs the intensities that "crash" onto her, disrupting the safety and estrangement of her constant "soul lag," such that it is all she can do to ride the wave of the moment, a moment that is neither absent nor saturated with being. The effect of "critical event stress" (354) manifests the career and careening of what Stewart calls "Speculation, curiosity, and the concrete . . . the forces that come into view as habit or shock, resonance or impact. *Something* throws itself together in a moment as an event and a sensation; a something both animated and inhabitable."[30] The language Gibson's narrator uses for Cayce's sensorium is not solely the language of dissolution, therefore. In her attunement she thrives in an attenuated way.

Cayce is postepistemological in a world "more post-geographic than multinational," a world where she "has no way of knowing how she knows" what's powerful (12). Yet she is not debilitated by this condition. Moreover, the very authenticity of her powerful nonsovereignty makes people want to hire her, to shape their products according to her nervous system (6, 8). She markets her nerves as a freelancer: the freelancer is one of the sovereign figures of neoliberalism, the person on contract, who makes short-term deals for limited obligation and thrives through the hustle over the long haul. She prefers entrepreneurial precarity to the too closeness of the world, and the book is structured around her migration from one place to another, a becoming found in becoming lost that is like giving "herself to the dream" (309).

But as for Lila Mae, in this regard Cayce is an extreme of exemplarity, not exceptionality. This is broadly telegraphed in her name's marriage of the visionary Edgar Cayce and the American Israeli spy Jonathan Pollard, but the novel's embedding of Cayce's capacities in the intuitive ordinary is extensive. In *Pattern Recognition* everyone is on the make to monetize affect and intimacy: advertising, filmmaking, viral marketing, recycling trash into desirable kitsch are just some of the relevant activities shaping global economic and political relations. Hubertus Bigend, head of Blue Ant, the advertising firm with which she is presently contracted, tells her that the present is the empire of the amygdala, the epoch of the limbic system that "culture tricks us into recognizing . . . as all of consciousness" (69). Cayce is the empress of the amygdala.

But while Cayce has a singular talent for reading the trademark's potential power, the value of her talent derives from the fact that she exemplifies the *general* nervous system. The novel foregrounds a number of cognate aesthetic forms for organizing affective intelligence: in particular, steganography, a practice of watermarking or distributing information by concealing it throughout other signification (74–76), and apophenia, "the spontaneous perception of connections and meaningfulness in unrelated things" (115). Sometimes, Cayce has to remind herself, there are actual coincidences. But in the novel that is rarely so: the nervous system is always intuiting the incessant communication across beings and things that have being, and tracking their traversal across infinite points on the grid of encounter. Thus whatever potentiality exists in *Pattern Recognition* is not about pasts or futures. This version of the detective novel exploded into the historical novel's seminar on affect produces alternative presents, not—as critics have argued—to point to a utopian ahistoricism (Blattberg), an immanent future (Jameson, Wegner), or the negation of the capitalist, commodified present (almost everyone). People follow their intuitions about what they don't know and so change the shape of the present, which is not fleeting at all, but a zone of action in a space marked by its experiments in transitioning. As with *The Intuitionist*, this is a drama of adjustment: of intuitive retraining in becoming-present to the present defined by its intensified sentience. Otherwise the world endures manifestly without guarantees. The potentiality of the deal that could always sour is also the primary scene of optimism, and the potential for achieving genuine human reciprocity is always held out as the seduction to become further invested in the normativity of the techno-political game.

Amid this process-oriented subjective self-extension, Cayce, like Lila Mae, encounters a trauma, a situation that has become stuck in the event. And, as Lila Mae's elevator crash just organizes and foregrounds a racial and gendered situation as a crisis within the ordinary, so too the situation of unstable affect ballasted by "psychological prophylaxis" (46) that Cayce has been living has been brought to focus by publicly mediated trauma. *Pattern Recognition* is organized by the relation between two such happenings: the Twin Towers destruction of 9/11/01 and the sudden emergence on the Web of footage of a kiss that comes to magnetize an intimate public. Yet 9/11 is Cayce's individual trauma and is not the event that shapes the novel's narrative. That role is taken up by the footage, which "has a way of cutting across boundaries, transgressing the accustomed order of things" (20).

The kiss footage that structures Cayce's world journey is located on the website F:F:F, Fetish Footage Forum, where fans all over the world debate whether a slowly emerging collection of film frames that seem to stage a heterosexual kiss are a narrative or something nonteleological, a work in progress. The trifling yet life-shaping dramas of fan culture echo the parodic political debates in *The Intuitionist*. Here the Progressivists dispute theories and concepts with the Completists, one group claiming that the film is unfolding without a plan, the other believing that a completed object is being released puzzle piece by puzzle piece. Bankrolled by Blue Ant's desire to possess or employ the imaginary for worldmaking that has induced the magnetic "marketing" or distribution of the footage, Cayce flies all over the world to solve the mystery of the film of the lovers, which is also the mystery of contemporary intimacy in relation to life narrative itself. In this, as Deleuze and Guattari write, "the organization of power is the unity of desire and the economic infrastructure."[31] Her only resources are the familial skills she inherits: from her father, a spy, she learns methods of secrecy, security, and code-breaking detection; and from her mother, a psychic who hears voices from another world through a kind of electronic static, she learns how to turn voices into messages that chart the present.

Having inherited incommensurable ways of knowing the unknowable, she travels to Tokyo, Russia, and London; to trailer parks, apartments, restaurants, cafés, markets, and hotels; and takes the subway, the train, the sidewalk, and the plane. But if, when Bordowitz does this, he's producing new habits, when Cayce does this she is unlearning old ones. Formerly focused, insomniac, and hypervigilant, she learns to "table all intentionality" and to wander (256). The film, and everything, turns out to be "a work in progress," which is different from a progress narrative. Yet Cayce is no modernist flaneuse, even when she is acting as one: the aleatory collection of experience is a monetized *style*, not a mode of being, in the contemporary moment of *Pattern Recognition*. You might say that the work of the plot is to enable Cayce to radicalize the wandering of the flaneuse: she genuinely detaches from the defense of a cosmopolitan intuitional style so that she might actually attach to particular persons and wander with them. Feeling, in the end, what she has only been able to sense throughout, she notes "the recent weirdness of her life shift beneath her, rearranging itself according to a new paradigm of history. Not a comfortable sensation" (340). If Lila Mae gives up the project of staying in synch with any being that distracts from her utopian orientation, Cayce gives up distinguishing the past from the present so that the present can become open. *Pattern Recognition* ends with Cayce in bed with Parkaboy, the one attachment she's made from the F:F:F. fansite who turns out to be willing to be inconvenienced for her, and in bodily synch they float away from the hustle of contemporary life-making that constitutes the usual intuitive self-education about the impasse of the present.

iv. The Falling Man and the Screaming Man: Anonymity and Trauma

I have made a series of claims about the ways that affect has had a privileged place in the construction of the experience and redaction of the historical present. One involves an aesthetic claim about the centrality of affect to the mediation of the present of any historical moment.[32] A second claim has been that navigating the question of affect is related but not identical to many discussions of unconscious attachment in proximity to the theory of ideology, as evidenced in the centrality of intuition to the exemplary novelistic representation of historical transition. In these novels, and in this essay, intuition is the contact zone between the affects and their historical contexts of activity, a zone of inference that, as it encounters the social, will always shift according to the construction of evidence and explanation. By being located so explicitly in the nervous system, while remaining more vernacular than technical about it, *The Intuitionist* and *Pattern Recognition* archive numerous ways of articulating intuitions of the present, engaging genres and modes of detection like empiricism, intuitionism, completism, progressivism, looking around, and checking things out in order to clarify the question of how to live with, catch up to, respond to, extend, interfere with, or mind the gap in the present moment that one lives singularly but in a shared way too.

In these novels' conception of the contemporaneous moment, however, the present is dramatically articulated in the vernacular of trauma. The traumatic happening intensifies the nervous system of worlds and focuses persons on the sense that what's going on in front of them is history in the making. Using this aesthetic device of periodization, both novels open up what *The Intuitionist* calls the "panoply of trajectories" in a given space of time. The trauma produces *something* in the air without that thing having to be more concrete than a sense of the uncanny—free-floating anxiety in the room, negativity on the street, a scenario seeming to unfold within the ordinary without clear margins, even when a happening is also specific. I use "happening" rather than event, as the Preface argues, because the narratives track the becoming-event of the happening, spending most of their time in situation genres within the impasse that crisis creates, so that the resonances and implications can be written out fully in their overdetermination. So even when some *thing* has happened, even in those cases where there's a consensually recognized event, there is no *a priori* consequence, habit, or style of resonance that intensifies the ordinary in a particular way. However one views the physical and neurophysiological qualities that a medical person might call "trauma," when encountered, the event called traumatic turns out mainly to be one genre of explanation for the situation of being without genre.

Cultural theorists do not usually think of trauma through the affective conventions of genre. Nor do they think about trauma as a style of responding to a happening, a style of mediating it into event. Nor, as genre, has it been recognized as having induced a periodizing norm for writing about the history of the present, at least since the U.S. 1950s. There are a number of reasons for this set of neglects. The main one is related to the authority of Cathy Caruth's model in humanities work on trauma, which represents trauma through a symptom's blockage of full subjective experience, performing, marking, and foreclosing the exposure to self-shattering loss.[33] From this perspective, we have allowed the traumatic event to be self-evident both in its autopoesis (we know it when we know it) and in its denial of self-mastery (we know that we cannot possess a trauma, but are possessed by it).

Relatedly and somewhat paradoxically, the literature on the traumatic event has been dominated by a consensus that trauma detaches the subject from the historical present, sentencing its subjects to a terrifying suffusion of the past into something stuck in the subject that stands out ahistorically from the ordinary.[34] But the temporal whiplash of the concept *Nachträglichkeit* is far more complex. As an affective concept, it bridges: a sense of belatedness from having to catch up to the event; a sense of the double-take in relation to what happened in the event (through the genre of the *après-coup*, a second event that reanimates a prior moment as having been traumatic); a sense of being saturated by it in the present, even as a structure of dissociation; a sense of being hollowed out by the pressures of overdetermination; a sense of being frozen out of the future (now defined by the past); and, because ordinary life does go on, a sense of the present that makes no sense with the rest of it, merging hyperconsciousness with the kind of self-interruptive or self-forgetting action that we have seen both in ordinary habituated and supersensory intuition. Living trauma as whiplash, treading water, being stuck, drifting among symptoms, and self-forgetting, which is different from amnesia: this mess of temporalization points to what Caruth also claims, which is that around trauma there is always a surplus of signification.[35] My claim here is that "trauma" best describes one or two styles among many for managing being overwhelmed.[36] Trauma, after all, does not make experiencing the historical present impossible but possible: not in the sense that one still has a conventional biography to tell that relates and provides a foundation for self-possessed identity, but in the sense that as trauma shatters the biostory that was a foundation for what gets taken for granted about life's historical self-continuity, it transforms the the work of survival without much of a normative plot or guarantees. Caruth would also claim that the too-closeness of the event does not bar but floods experience, memory, knowledge, and practices of habituation, *all of which are different modes of retention*, with their own conventions of distortion—for example, management, mediation, genre. But flooding does not always feel like flooding, just as the affective structure of any relation can manifest as a range of emotions. I might be flooded and feel numb, overwhelmed, teary, angry, detached, capacious, sleepy, or *whatever*, for those things that we call traumatic events do not always induce traumatic responses. Adam Phillips talks about the symptom as something half-remembered, half-forgotten, a thing caught in the throat of memory, incompletely metabolized.[37] Often the emotions vary, while the affective structure remains. Second, as life goes on, habituation does too. The subject of the traumatizing event is opened to a new habitation of history.

The utility of thinking about "crisis ordinariness" as that which is incited by the traumatic event is in its focus on the spreading of symbolizations and other inexpressive but life-extending actions throughout the ordinary and its situations of living on. A history of any contemporaneous moment, whether traumatic or not, involves gathering up this kind of matter and the reflections on it that mark its force, and tracking the dynamics of blockage and expression involved in its circulation. Sometimes trauma does present as an event already concluded. But what makes something available to genres of the event are the intensities of a situation that spreads into modes, habits, or genres of being.

Demonstrating how an object relation of optimism might snap into cruelty and back out again, our two novels provide many genres for apprehending the diffusion of trauma through the ordinary. *Pattern Recognition* calls the moments in the impasse of the historical present in which one responds to a heightened intensity in the atmosphere without knowing what kind of affective world it denotes "soul-lack" and "soul-delay" (35). For Cayce, lack is existential but lived as a displacement in time: jet lag, a gnawing information lag, situation lag, a temporal expression of a sense of being out of control over the conditions of living, and yet continuing to live. It would be easy to misread these situations of being somewhere specific as not anxious, ordinary in the forgettable sense: Cayce smells the monomers in a refrigerator, senses the tone of mannequins, yellow walls, and café décor, notices that foreign things taste different, and, when she's tired, finds that what feels like neutrality actually means that she's mildly depressed in "her present loneliness." Aloneness is different from loneliness, but neither is melodramatic; they're stripped down like Cayce's de-labeled clothes toward a numbed realism that is what it is, organized by pattern recognition, which is different from event or even thought and more like taking stock (24). The sense of how to live the situation of her present is to adapt, adjust, to take in things that happen in moments, for a moment. Even her obsession with the Fetish Footage Forum involves a kind of mild addiction, a slight excitation, the self-perturbation of being a fan, nothing that would disturb the mode of mediated circulation that she's embraced as her existence.

Everything is approximate: "familiar as a friend's living room" (3), "a second home" (65), "almost" monochrome, tender, soothing (3, 50, 55). It's the rhythm of an almost de-eventilized life. Before Cayce is sent on her mission to find the source of the footage, she returns to F:F:F almost casually: "There will be much to catch up on, taking it from the top, getting the drift of things." (38). Most people she meets emit these affects too, of getting in the drift: they're all from somewhere else, mildly or intensively on the make, but mainly making contact, seeking a rhythm, finding a place, and poking around. "She likes Pilates because it isn't, in the way she thinks about yoga, meditative. You have to keep your eyes open . . . and pay attention" (6).

Thus it is worth it for us to slow down to absorb her process of slowing down, maintaining balance. Here, a random event, as her eyes graze a room:

> On the wall to her left is a triptych by a Japanese artist whose name she forgets, three four-by-eight panels of plywood hung side by side. On these have been silkscreened in layers, logos and big-eyed manga girls, but each successive layer of paint has been sanded to ghostly translucency, varnished, then overlaid with others, which have in turn been sanded, varnished. . . . The result for Cayce being very soft, deep, almost soothing, but with the uneasy hallucinatory suggestion of panic about to break through. (55)

Nothing comes of this, except for information about the circulation of affect in the moment of the novel's temporal present. What does it say about her nervous system that it senses the aura of panic around a softness whose status as *consequence*, an effect of an operation, is simultaneously as intensely perceived as the images themselves? It is not just that Cayce has been falling apart since childhood at the sight of the grossest trademarks: "Some people ingest a single peanut and their head swells like a basketball. When it happens to Cayce, it's her psyche. . . . A glance to the right and the avalanche lets go" (17). It is also that forever she has lived in the worlds of her mother's psychic paranormality and her father's CIA agent paranoia, an environment that provided skills and methods for maintaining modes of security that allowed for her some "[p]sychological prophylaxis . . . [to] get on with ordinary business. Maintain morale" (45–46). It even provided her with phrases to interrupt her affects when they overintensified, to make herself possible where she's impossible: "He took a duck in the face at two hundred and fifty knots . . . would allay the onset of the panic she invariably felt upon seeing the worst of her triggers" (34).

But 9/11 changes all that, as it triggers and reshapes her sensorium. For the first fourteen chapters she can refer to it only in unspecific fragments, nothing narrative. Her nemesis, the industrial spy Dorotea, asks:

> "How was the winter, then, in New York?"
> "Cold," Cayce says.
> "And sad? Is it still sad?"
> Cayce says nothing. (13)

Chapter 15, "Singularity," finally allows Cayce to "unforget her father's absence" (134) and its destruction of her "interiority." Singularity: the concept bridges what's absolutely ungeneralizable about the subject and the place where the space-time continuum folds in on itself and becomes a black hole—trauma. This chapter lists everything Cayce absorbed and sensed eventlessly on the morning whose details did not feel that they mattered until suddenly they marked the last moment she felt that she had a default world, a default environment that was ongoing, a default foundation for her ordinariness. This is what 9/11 changed. It did not change her basic mode of intuitiveness; she was already the aleatory being that she continued to be. Among the things she remembers having sensed and encountered that morning are: noises in the city, the style of a staircase, a dried petal falling in a store showcase window, someone's unzipped fly, CNN, and the crash of the second plane into the World Trade Center. Her sensorium had collected these as a history of impacts held in reserve, and later she thinks that "she must have seen people jumping, falling" but she has no memory of it (137).

This all gets shifted from affective suspension to transaction after the fact, once Cayce has worked through her plot (in all the senses) and found her mirror-world, traumatic double-doppelganger in the Wolkov sisters, who are manufacturing and distributing the images from Russia. These artists of the kiss clip have also lost their parents to political violence. Their film, of a romantic kiss, is the doppelganger to this novel too, as it might well refer to their parents' approach to each other, the moment before the sisters' own origin, and the fantasy that, when people come together in desire, things are simple, and simplifying. After encountering them Cayce is able to channel her own parents. Like her mother listening to voices of beings lost in the ether, Cayce hears her father's voice transmit in the electrified atmosphere of the global present. Her superhuman capacity saves her from being poisoned. In the end, the reweaving of her parents into her interiority amounts to Cayce's reachievement of sensory confidence. This time her sense of things is autonomic, postintuitive.

So the chapters before the narrative of trauma register a person we recognize, who flows conveniently through the world making light contact with it, and only gradually reveal her as shell-shocked, in multiple ways. Yet the very things that might be symptoms of shock trauma are also readable as style: managerially folded within her self-protective habit of wearing clothes without labels, she drinks café coffee, sleeps in strange places, and allows herself extensive folds of pleasure in the Film Fetish Forum and the street bazaar.

The phrase Gibson uses for the trauma of 9/11, its transformation of

Cayce's aloneness into something negative, a defense, is "deeply personal insult" (137). In medical language, an insult is that which causes bodily damage. "Insult" echoes the shift within trauma from a physical hit to an affective event resonating within the sensorium. But is catastrophe only a personal insult that turns her toward a style of defensive impersonality? At some point Cayce allows that the liminality of being wounded resonates with an existential problem, the randomness of threat and the unpredict-ability of harm, death, or just not mattering to the conditions of one's own existence (34). There is no place sufficiently under the radar to avoid the in-sult that the world is not organized around your sovereignty. She walks by an accident,

> [a]nd for an instant she sees that unconscious, unmarked face, its lower half obscured by the transparent mask, the evening's rain falling on closed eyes. And knows that this stranger may now inhabit the most limi-nal place of all, poised perhaps on the brink of nonexistence, or about to enter some existence unimagined. She cannot see what hit him, or what he might have hit. Or else the street itself had risen up, to smite him. It is not only these things we must fear that do that, she reminds herself. (54)

This kind of episode, of noting, reflecting, adjusting, and understanding that "worrying about problems doesn't help solve them" (92), of feeling freed from defense by the inevitability of randomness, enables Cayce even-tually to release herself from her defenses. She does this by taking on other people's (Bigend's and Parkaboy's) projects, and in the same gesture return-ing herself to desire by pursuing the one fun thing in her life, the one re-maining consensual, affectional, quasi-intimate site of play, the footage. The detective novel then morphs into a romance, the friendliness with Parkaboy turns in the end into a lovers' vacation, and the bad impasse of the traumatic present into a good impasse. Meanwhile, the impasse of the present that is controlled structurally by transnational capital with all its force of direct and indirect violence and coercion—that hasn't changed. But, still, she does not know about the falling man.

The falling man is an enigma from 9/11 who has generated other novels and documentaries about the horror of anonymous death.[38] He remains a noted but de-eventilized affect site here, a figure of a crisis in knowledge, and a figure of what is not mimetic in trauma, the scene of a happening that has no intuition to magnetize and mobilize it. He's suspended in the sensorium without hitting a nerve. He's an object that might yet become a *something* in another intensified present or another sensorium, but that meanwhile falls without landing in the suspended imaginary of the impasse, producing a shared affectsphere, a structure of feeling, a punctum in the historical present without becoming event in any narrative sense.

The spacing of life in contemporaneous time is a suspension of the need to know *what* the connections are before one expresses assurance *that* the connections *exist* when different impacts appear to be neighbors to each other, proximate in the singular suspension of an experience that is also a shared suspension of a historical field where the "now" is always present, always elsewhere, tipped "sideways" (17). It dissolves the relation of the personal to the impersonal, the passive to the active. "'I know,'" Cayce says, "and that is really all she can say, so she just sits there, wondering what she might have set in motion, where it might go, and why" (112). To set something in motion is different from knowing or acting on something: thus the poetics of rhythm and resonance. Life can turn then toward the mode of what Anne-Lise François has called "recessive action," an orientation toward active rest that can be a resource for living on without projecting false futures and pasts into the faux-sovereign world of events.[39]

Recasting the traumatic event into an ordinary intensity suggests an entirely different model of the ways post-traumatic history and memory *repersonalize* the subject. Fred Moten might call the novel's episodic form a "cut" structure, a kind of anaclisis or propping that reshapes the resonant relations among things, including persons.[40] Citing Derrida, Gayatri Spivak would call the process "teleopoiesis," in its "finding proof in unlikely places," proof where the idea of proving is absurd.[41] In teleopoiesis a communication addresses a distant other: it is like *receiving* what appeared to be apostrophe. This is the beginning of attachment's open temporality whether or not trauma forced open a new route: a new route makes possible new genres of reciprocity. These models point to a long migrating trail of actions bouncing off of various points on a chronologically heterogeneous grid, where the encounter is defined as an incitement to judge and to remake the meanings of closeness and distance.

Pattern Recognition's affectsphere expresses something else, too—a different relation of anonymity to being known and knowing than one would have predicted on the modernist grid. There's a shared sense among strangers that the default gesture of the present is to haggle, to debate over value. Cayce meets a man on the street, and because he is alive, he's on the hustle. Cayce's acquaintance Voytek talks strangers up to support his "scaffolding";

his sister is a cool hunter who pretends to have casual conversations about products; when Cayce meets Hobbs, her living contact with the CIA, it sets in motion haggling over barter. The processual value management of the haggle and the barter is related to the other major spatial practice of the novel: everyone curates. Curating is like cultivating, but it's not about natural development; rather, it's about collecting phenomena for the purpose of their gaining value. Everything is instrumental, and the rhetoric is that of trading: yet this version of instrumentality is optimistic, not reified in the old ways, because the penetration of the intuition by encounters with objects, people, and scenarios actually creates a sense of solidarity and recognition, based on a sense of the collective desire to survive what might have otherwise seemed like the fate of traumatic inscription.

The historicist atmospherics of intuition in *The Intuitionist* track many of the same patterns of intuitive exchange as those of *Pattern Recognition*, yet project some different motives for and models of how to historicize the shape of the protagonist's affective aim amid the intensified infrastructural threats that shape ordinary life. For the African American subjects who organize the plot of the novel, U.S. cities are not part of a localized global world as in *Pattern Recognition*, but they are effects of a displaced affect. They turn out to be utopian inventions of people who are very "country" (236). Both Fulton and Lila Mae have migrated from the South, come up North for anonymity. They love anonymity: they imagine the utopian city as a place where people live on top of each other but "do not speak. Nobody knows anybody's business. Nobody knows where you came from" (134). They also imagine the anonymity of cities as the solution to the problem of the *intimacy* of racism in the U.S. South (27): the atmosphere of Fulton's childhood is shaped by his very origin, his mother raped by her employer, his sister having to keep both of them together, all in an atmosphere where the truths were whispered and the children relegated to hypervigilant observation of the mother's states of being, added to which were the thick proprioceptive dances of everyday racism in the South, where at any moment the proximity of whites and blacks could erupt into a catastrophe or the tyrannical ritual of manners.

With the rape saturating the everyday ordinary of disrupted affect that Fulton experiences as the default sense of disruption in his life (135), he also experiences, via his light skin, "this peculiar thing": an "old colored man steps aside to let him buy his candy. . . . It takes him a long time to figure out what happened. Long after he has finished the sweet candy. What he figures out is sour" (136). Lila Mae's father, Marvin, too is buffeted by the not traumatic but ordinary insults of supremacist intimacy, affronted by racist elevator inspectors and ignored by the white customers who sense him more than see him as a part of the machinery that engineers the free flow (vertical ascent) of their privilege. Cities are where you go to become anonymous, to *not* have impact or to be a perturbation; where you go to control the pacing of a de-eventilized, dedramatized world, to be able to measure your way of existing through the negotiation of more space than anyone needs.

Thus while Cayce's traumatized intuition helps her to circulate freely throughout professional and personal life, Lila Mae's intuitionism grows from a compartmentalizing defense.

> She thinks, what passing for white does not account for: the person who knows your secret skin, the one you encounter at that unexpected time on that quite ordinary street. What Intuitionism does not account for: the catastrophic accident the elevator encounters at that unexpected moment on that quite ordinary ascent, the one who will reveal the device for what it truly is. The colored man passing for white and the innocent elevator must rely on luck, the convenience of empty streets and strangers who know nothing, dread the chance encounter with the one who knows who they are. The one who knows their weakness. (231)

In *The Intuitionist*, dread is the main crisis-affect of the African American subject who wants to pass through white supremacist space. Her position is precarious "everywhere she goes in this city, for that matter, but she's trained dread to keep invisible in its ubiquity, like fire hydrants and gum trod into black sidewalk spackle. Makeshift weapons include shoes, keys and broken bottles. Pool cues if they're handy" (24). Supremacist space is crisis space embedded in the ordinary as the "lots of other stuff going on, dirty water and more land beyond that dirty water . . . a crop of weedy smokestacks, lots of stuff, 360 degrees to choose from and the generous illusion of choice" that marks the skyline (17). Dread fears the event, too, because it's only going to be confirming of the time one suffers as the historical present. Dread looks forward to rest from even the possibility of the event. "This is the true result of gathering integration: the replacement of sure violence with deferred sure violence" (23).

"Not much progress in this traffic" (12). But after the catastrophic elevator crash, Lila Mae traces and reshapes the pathogeography of what is happening in the world and to her. She forces progress to happen amid the ordinariness—she is so focused on trying to *force* the traffic to progress that she almost gets into a car accident—at first only to save her reputation, which is the only protection she has had in the racist, misogynist, nonanonymous world of elevator inspection. Later the aim changes because her entire epistemological foundation, her entire sensorium, is threatened and shaken by the information about Intuitionism she gleans—both its radical post-empiricism, its basis in Fulton's "joke" that wreaks a passive-aggressive revenge, and the race history it occults. To do this she must violate the profound anonymity she had sought. This traumatic opening, though, is also an opening to desire, toward bodily perturbation, to risk, and to dreaming. Her prior sense of being precarious joined geographical displacement with structural racism—but this convergence had nothing on what was to follow (23–24): namely, sexuality, not love, just the faintest impulse of desire that could mess up everything she'd built into her intuitions about remaining composed enough to live. The mistakes she makes become situations that might unfold to produce revolutionary change. In the interim, at first, she does "not have a plan, which is unlike her," and she experiences the affect of "anxious and aimless cogitation," destabilizing, flooding, and dissipating intensities that are seeking an object to give them shape (150). But then "scenarios, as they will, unfold" (148).

To desire to be available to know the whole thing means to desire to be open to knowing anything. As in *Pattern Recognition*, this means that Lila Mae must suspend her defenses, develop her affective skills, seek out conversation, listen hard, solicit and cajole, be pushy and, what's hardest, receptive. This is a very different sovereignty style than she manifests in the pretraumatic world. In the end, she makes a couple of sorts—with Fulton. She hears his voice the way Cayce hears her father's, telepathically. Hiding from thugs in a dancehall, "She asks her partner, who is not her [dancing] partner now but someone who is dead and will not answer except in what remains of him, his words, 'Why did you do it?' 'You'll understand'" (216). This coupled form reveals the extent of the transformation of Lila Mae's intuition: she has experienced the need of a lover, but rediscovers that live humans are unreadable and unreliable, even if you press your body to theirs, as in the slow dance or sex. But if no one living can be trusted for that, one can find it intellectually: the logic of apostrophe reemerges here too, in the imagined rhetorical intimacy of two souls theorizing as one. Lila Mae "has always considered herself an atheist, not realizing she had a religion. Anyone can start a religion. They just need the need of others" (241). In *The Intuitionist* it is as though the distorted intimacies of white supremacy make singular love and intimate sociality impossible. But theoretical love beyond the pale is *necessary*, the only sensorium through which the subordinated ones might re-engineer the world. There is no revolutionary love, no culminating love, no interpersonal relief among the living. The utopian, postpragmatic uplift of the race that Fulton opens up gives Lila Mae a more profound connection to life, one that as yet has no physics, no method, no habits through which to engineer genuine flourishing, apart from what she invents for it in the continuing affectively saturated present of writing.

At one point in the middle of this catastrophe-induced crisis, Lila Mae is kidnapped. Thugs, agents of industrial espionage, take her to a place where the mob tortures people, along with sitting around cracking jokes and talking about old times. We have visited this casualized place of torture previously in the novel. Urich, the other investigative journalist, was also kidnapped and taken there. He was tortured because he had uncovered the existence of the utopian black box that Fulton conjured, the box whose engineering would mean the end of corporate hegemony and cities as we know them, and the elevator interests borrow the mob to make sure all that potential for change goes away. They take Urich to a torture chamber. This place remakes the historical present violently by forcing the tortured to dismantle his sensorium, his investigative habit of feeling out time. The torture chamber reeks of the temporally polymorphous intensity of trauma. Later we witness another torture, of someone anonymous even to us except as the effect of a cause:

> There were no windows and they took his watch so he had no idea how long he had been down there. Long enough to have been nicknamed the Screaming Man, long enough for him to have earned the sobriquet a dozen times over. He screamed the first time when the large man without eyes broke the first of his fingers. He screamed a couple times after that, and things just flowed from there. . . . They chained him to the cot that stank of piss and vomit and other murky fluids the human body can be counted on to expel from time to time. Pus. The mattress bore tattoos, dark amorphous stains that corresponded to where different body parts fell on the mattress, a brown cloud around the right knee, some murk congealed near the groin. He screamed when he saw the mattress, and screamed more as they chained him to the bed and he saw his limbs and parts positioned over previous guests' secretions. . . . The blood from his

wounds (plural) sprayed the cinderblock wall and dried and eventually became indistinguishable from the dried blood from the others before him. (95)

Even the men in the vicinity of him are said to be more changed by this event than he appears to be: these men, "normally of imperturbable heart, experienced a new unease" and plot serious life changes (97). Lila Mae encounters the Screaming Man on the way to a room near the torture chamber. But again this episode, of the revelation of someone's total anonymity, has no consequence in the plot of the novel. Lila Mae has seen him and yet he had no impact on her. She does not remember him at all. When she'd encountered him on the stairs "he screamed" but no response by her is recorded and later, the narrator comments, in her name, "She wants the man to stop screaming" (105).

In both of these novels, it is as though the most sublime threat of all to the sensorium that must make an ordinariness out of what could be shattering trauma is the revelation that, in the singular present that is the zone of an ongoing life, one has only been loaned a name and biography and personality and meaningfulness, and that that loan could be recalled not just by death but by the cruel forces of life, which include randomness but which are much more predictable, systematic, and world-saturating than that too. This is especially shattering to Lila Mae when the lender is a principle of randomness or luck (the forces of unanticipated catastrophe) that cannot be prevented by professional competence, but it is shattering enough when the lender is whoever embodies the structural forces of "deferred violence." Sovereign anonymity as a defense against wanting to be able to need or make a claim on the world and people in it produces a livable impasse for both protagonists. But in the end, facing the death of the illusion that their personality and history are grounds rather than habits multiplies histories, intensifies affects across the spectrum of negativity and positivity, creates scenes and confuses dreaming with living: it demands a deft improvisatory renaturalization of the evidence of ongoingness that constitutes the default historical present, the now of being in the world.

This haste to batten down the historical present is revelatory. In the two novels the traumatic event always produces something technical, without content: a sense of out-of-synchness with the world that is reproduced in the protagonist. These singular figures, embedded in a semipublic life by virtue of their professionalization of their sensual singularity, become accidentally an event in the (novelized) world. This perturbation of the world and their lives becomes recuperated in the novels' summary moves toward a new intuitivism that is at peace with being in the impasse of the present. This is to say, paradoxically, that their early senses of being out of synch are actually mimetic and harmonious, as they represent a point of synchronicity between the peripatetic Intuitionist and the traumatized world that feels its way into an ongoing crisis, that has to start "recalibrating [the] imagination" of what rules govern the ordinary rhythms of it (*The Intuitionist*, 221). The catastrophe produces a *sense* of catastrophe, but this means that the protagonist has not split off absolutely from the world but instead has become more deeply embedded in it, maintaining the tightness of some sutures while loosening others. Under the pressure of survival they improvise, they realize that their habits of personality can be unlearned and reconfigured. Recalibrating the intuition requires for them a new psychogeography that remediates their singularity and their place in history—the ongoing present—and portends what's imminent and immanent (love, theory) without following them through to materialize any potential transformation in the conditions of that history. Transformation is always in the language of the aftertime; what the novels want is to provide the sensorium for a reconceptualized present.

Indeed I have described that, in both novels, crisis within the ordinary incites research projects, going to the library, to the Internet, and to other humans, to find out something not in the idiom of pasts and futures or about the past's presence as *revenant* or living for the future but about the present's ongoing condition. In their styles of resolving the perturbed intuitions of their protagonists and their historical presents, though, these are optimistic novels. Written for the middle- and highbrow audiences of literary fiction, they believe that "healing" is humane and that we know what it would feel like. It would feel like someone and some world had become unstuck, less systematically violent, and less predictably disappointing and alienating. It would look something like a moving through the event and its symptoms toward a sense of freedom that would feel lighter than the sense of an unfree, faux-sovereign defensiveness that saturated both the pre- and post-traumatic histories in which the protagonists lived.

Lila Mae ends up more Intuitionist than ever, after losing her faith for a moment; Cayce resolves her father's death, mourns this or the last century, and gets a boyfriend. Their suspension of a sensorium organized around the ongoing desperation of bad precarity shifts into an aleatory intuition of a better precarity that feels like openness. The novels thus resolve multiple scenarios of crisis and catastrophe in entirely irrational ways. The diminution of loneliness into openness stands for the solution to the crisis that was much bigger than that.

There are always screaming men and falling men: one does not much witness them, they live offscreen. But the protagonists are them, too, that is, people who live on in unstable and shattered ordinaries and who are building a new nervous system around them no longer based on foreclosure but in the optimism of learning from one's precarity. People develop worlds for their new intuitions, habits of ordinariness, and genres of affect management in recognition of the unfinished business of the historical moment they are living on in, where they live the rhythm of the habit called personality that can never quite settle into a shape. *Habit* even imagines a kind of intuitionist *politics*, a politics that refuses conventions and refuses to succumb to the lure of a continuous genealogy. Trauma forces its subjects not into mere stuckness but into crisis mode, where they develop some broad, enduring intuitions about the way we live in a now that's emerging without unfolding, and imagining a historicism from within a discontinuous present and ways of being that were never sovereign.

(Obesity, Sovereignty, Lateral Agency)

1. *Slow Death and the Sovereign*

The phrase *slow death* refers to the physical wearing out of a population in a way that points to its deterioration as a defining condition of its experience and historical existence. The general emphasis of the phrase extends the focus of the last two chapters on the phenomenon of collective physical and psychic attenuation from the effects of global/national regimes of capitalist structural subordination and governmentality. It takes as its point of departure David Harvey's polemical observation, in *Spaces of Hope*, that under capitalism sickness is defined as the inability to work. This powerful observation about the rationalization of health is an important part of the story, but it is not the whole story either.[1] Through the space opened up by this concept, I offer up a development in the ways we conceptualize contemporary historical experience, especially where that experience is simultaneously at an extreme and in a zone of ordinariness, where life building and the attrition of human life are indistinguishable, and where it is hard to distinguish modes of incoherence, distractedness, and habituation from deliberate and deliberative activity, as they are all involved in the reproduction of predictable life.

The shift I propose reframes the ways we think about normativity in relation to sovereignty. It emphasizes in particular a nonmimetic relation between political and personal or practical sovereignty. From Carl Schmitt to Giorgio Agamben and Georges Bataille to Achille Mbembe, the current discussion of sovereignty as a condition of and blockage to justice recapitulates the widespread contemporary projection of sovereignty onto events of decision-making. Mbembe is exemplary: "To exercise sovereignty is to exercise control over mortality and to define life as the deployment and manifestation of power."[2] Phrased as such, the sovereignty concept has a few problems that are related but nonidentical. For one thing, the image of control it denotes derives from an archaic tradition of theologically-based royal or state privilege, and while that form of sovereignty continues to have a limited relevance (in clemency proceedings, for example), it masks in a discourse of "control" the wide variety of processes and procedures involved historically in the administration of law and of bodies, even during periods when sovereign rulers exerted their wills by fiat.[3] Additionally, in casting death as a fact separate from the administration of life processes, this version of the sovereignty concept has provided an alibi for normative ways of keeping separate the productive procedures of governmentality and the violence of the state, when, as I will argue, the procedures of managing collective life include a variety of inducements for managing life's wearing out, which only sometimes amalgamates death to an act or event. Third, sovereignty described as the foundation of individual autonomy (represented and secured, for some, by the General Will) overidentifies the similarity of self-control to this fantasy of sovereign performativity and state control over geographical boundaries.[4] It thereby affords a militaristic and melodramatic view of individual agency by casting the human as most fully itself when assuming the spectacular posture of performative action. This mimetic concept of sovereignty also legitimates as something objective the individual's affective *sense* of autonomy. Finally, in linking and inflating consciousness, intention, and decision or event, it has provided an alibi for hygienic governmentality and justified moralizing against inconvenient human activity. Even Bataille's radically alternate version of sovereignty—as an ecstatic departure from a strong notion of intentionality and agency—reproduces personhood as a monadic affective drama of self-expansion, just this time a drama of heterogeneity rather than subjective overorganization.[5]

While Mbembe's definition renders life and mortality as transparent, Foucault argues that the relation of sovereignty to biopower involves a significant recasting of what those referents mean, even before the apparition of decision-making is raised. It would seem at first that the most variable term is *life*. Foucault's phrasing is precise. Sovereignty "is not the right to put people to death or to grant them life. Nor is it the right to allow people to live or to leave them to die. It is the right to take life or let live."[6] Life is the *a priori*; sovereign agency signifies the power to *permit* any given life to endure, or not. But biopower, he argues, which does not substitute for but reshapes sovereignty, is the power to *make* something live or to let it die, the power to regularize life, the authority to *force* living not just to happen but to endure and appear in particular ways. The difference between sovereign agency under a regime of sovereignty and under a regime of biopower, then, can be thought of as a distinction between individual life and collective living on, where living increasingly becomes a scene of the administration, discipline, and recalibration of what constitutes health.

The relative passivity of letting die in the context of shaping living does change as the decision and the event of agency in proximity to life and mortality evolve different norms and institutions, though. Foucault focuses on biopower's attempt to manage what he calls "endemics," which, unlike epidemics, are "permanent factors . . . [that] sapped the population's strength, shortened the working week," and "cost money." In this shift Foucault dissolves the attention to scenes of *control* over individual life and death under sovereign regimes and refocuses on the dispersed *management* of the putatively biological threat posed by certain populations to the reproduction of the normatively framed general good life of a society.[7] Slow death occupies the temporalities of the endemic.

Because of these convolutions and variations sovereignty is an inadequate concept. Sovereignty, after all, is a fantasy misrecognized as an objective state: an aspirational position of personal and institutional self-legitimating performativity and an affective sense of control in relation to the fantasy of that position's offer of security and efficacy. But it is inadequate for talking about agency outside of the power of the King's decree or other acts in proximity to certain performances of law, like executions and pardons. It is also a distorting description of the political, affective, and psychological conditions in which the ordinary subjects of democratic/capitalist power take up positions as agents. These states might best be redefined as only partially (that is to say fantasmatically or not) sovereign.

But some may want to continue using the concept because of the history of investment in it as a marker for the liberal sense of personal autonomy and freedom, or because of its association with democracy and with the legal protection of the body politic and subgroups within it.[8] To take a page from Ernesto Laclau's and Paul Gilroy's strategic defenses of universality, one might argue legitimately that renouncing a popular or civil society politics of sovereign persons and publics in self-relation and relation to the state would cede to the groups who benefit from inequality the privilege to define the procedures of sovereign representation, authority, and conceptualization of the human in a self-ratifying way.[9] (Of course this is also an argument against the ways sovereignty discourse organizes political contestation, as it gives vast credence to claims that an affectively perceived threat to autonomy is a threat to justice itself.) I am persuaded enough by these kinds of reservations not to push for a wholesale exorcism of sovereignty's spirit by a dramatic act of taxonomic substitution; legal and normative ghosts have precedential power, after all. But, even if we cede sovereignty to perpetuity as a fantasy that sustains liberty's normative political idiom, we need better ways to talk about a more capacious range of activity oriented toward the reproduction of ordinary life: from the burdens of contemporary compelled will that fuel everyday employment and household pressures, for example, to the pleasures of spreading-out activities like sex or eating, aleatory modes of self-abeyance that do not occupy time, decision, or consequentiality in anything like the sovereign registers of autonomous self-assertion.

Practical sovereignty would be better understood not to take the mimetic or referred shape of state or individual sovereignty but a shape made by mediating conditions of zoning, labor, consumption, and governmentality, as well as unconscious and explicit desires not to be an inflated ego deploying power and manifesting intention. This chapter, then, looks at the complexly articulated relations between pragmatic (life-making) and accretive (life-building) activity and tracks their relation to the attrition of the subject. It focuses on what's vague and gestural about the subject and episodic about the event. It presumes nothing about the meaning of decision or the impact of an act. Without attending to the varieties of constraint and unconscious-ness that condition ordinary activity, we persist in an attachment to a fantasy that in the truly lived life emotions are always heightened and expressed in modes of effective agency that ought justly to be and are ultimately conse-quential or performatively sovereign. In this habit of representing the inten-tional subject, a manifest lack of self-cultivating attention can easily become recast as irresponsibility, shallowness, resistance, refusal, or incapacity; and habit itself can begin to look overmeaningful, such that addiction, re-action formation, conventional gesture clusters, or just being different can be read as heroic placeholders for resistance to something, affirmation of something, or a world-transformative desire. I am not saying that any given response or evidence of sentience is not these things, but one should not take for granted, either, that subjects are always involved, universally and in full throttle, in projects of self-extension that seek to lock in the will-have-been of future anteriority.[10] Self-continuity and self-extension are different things. Another way to say this might be that lives are not novels—or maybe they are, as no critic has ever accounted for all the acts and details in a novel either.

Through the space opened by slow death, then, I seek to recast some tax-onomies of causality, subjectivity, and life-making embedded in normative notions of agency. More particularly, I suggest that to counter the moral science of biopolitics, which links the political administration of life to a melodrama of the care of the monadic self, we need to think about agency and personhood not only in inflated terms but also as an activity exercised within spaces of ordinariness that does not always or even usually follow the literalizing logic of visible effectuality, bourgeois dramatics, and lifelong accumulation or self-fashioning.

The first part of this chapter emphasizes questions of sovereignty in the time and space of ordinary living and then unfolds tactically into an un-heroizable case, the so-called obesity or "globesity" phenomenon that is said to be sweeping the United States and the parts of the world affected by U.S.-style consumer practices.[11] This so-called epidemic has been seen as a shaming sickness of sovereignty, a predicament of privilege and of poverty, a crisis of choosing and anti-will,[12] and an endemic disease of development and underdevelopment. It engenders strong data, florid prose, and sensa-tional spectacles that I have no intention of reducing to their proper analyti-cal and affective scale.[13] I recast this situation within a zone of temporality marked by ongoingness, getting by, and living on, where structural inequalities are dispersed and the pacing of experience is uneven and often mediated by way of phenomena that are not prone to capture by a consciousness organized by archives of memorable impact.

Here the kind of interruptive agency that we have witnessed in the past two chapters aspires to detach from a condition of exhausted practical sovereignty or actually to diminish being meaningful. Melodramas of the overwhelmed can obscure the motives and temporalities of these aspects of living. This recasting of sovereignty provides an alternative way of talking about phrases like "self-medication," which we use to imagine what someone is doing when they are becoming dissipated, and not acting in a life-building way—the way that liberal subjects and happy people are supposed to. The chapter closes with a meditation on lateral agency, speculating about subjectivity and self-interruption. It argues that in the scene of slow death, a condition of being worn out by the activity of reproducing life, agency can be an activity of maintenance, not making; fantasy, without grandiosity; sentience without full intentionality; inconsistency, without shattering; and embodying, alongside embodiment.

II. *Conceiving the Genre of the Case*

Slow death prospers not in traumatic events, as discrete time-framed phenomena like military encounters and genocides can appear to do, but in temporally labile environments whose qualities and whose contours in time and space are often identified with the presentness of ordinariness itself, that domain of living on in which everyday activity; memory, needs, and desires; and diverse temporalities and horizons of the taken-for-granted are brought into proximity and lived through.[14] Just as I have been distinguishing "happening" from "event" throughout the book in order to attend to affective mediation, here I distinguish "environment" from "event." One motive for this is to describe the historical present as a back-formation from practices that create a perceptible scene, an atmosphere that can be returned to.[15] In this way there is no need to foreground space and scale as important mediators of the present in absolute contrast to time. Teresa Brennan defines these punctuated atmospheres through the psychic, temporal, physical, legal, rhetorical, and institutionally normative procedures that govern them.[16] A materialism of the atmosphere points to something more solid, like "environment."

An event is a genre calibrated according to its intensities and kinds of impact.[17] Environment denotes a scene in which structural conditions are suffused through a variety of mediations, such as predictable repetitions and other spatial practices that might well go under the radar or, in any case, not take up the form of event. An environment can absorb how time ordinarily passes, how forgettable most events are, and overall, how people's ordinary perseverations fluctuate in patterns of undramatic attachment and identification.[18] In an ordinary environment, most of what we call events are not of the scale of memorable impact but rather are *episodes*, that is, occasions that frame experience while not changing much of anything.

But at stake in making out the scene of slow death are more than establishing the episodic nature of most events and the absorptive function of most environments.[19] In "Intuitionists," I described problems with the translation of all transformative impacts into the inflated rhetoric and genre of trauma, and there I suggested that a concept like "crisis ordinariness" better keeps open the problem of the forms heightened threat can take as it is managed in the context of living. Without the ballast of ordinariness to distribute our analyses of "structure" as a suffusion of practices throughout the social, crisis rhetoric itself can assume a similar kind of inflation. Often when scholars and activists apprehend the phenomenon of slow death in long-term conditions of privation, they choose to misrepresent the duration and scale of the situation by calling a crisis that which is a fact of life and has been a defining fact of life for a given population that lives that crisis in ordinary time. Of course this deployment of crisis is often explicitly and intentionally a redefinitional tactic, an inflationary, distorting, or misdirecting gesture that aspires to make an environmental phenomenon appear suddenly as an event, because as a structural or predictable condition it has not engendered the kinds of historic action we associate with the heroic agency a crisis implicitly calls for.

Meanwhile, having been made rhetorically radiant with attention, compassion, analysis, and sometimes reparation, the population wearing out in the space of ordinariness becomes a figure saturated with emotion that is said to have been generated by a lack of or need for the responsibility of the still seemingly sovereign privileged classes. This is why, to turn ordinary life into crisis, social justice activists often engage in the actuarial imaginary of biopolitics; what seem like cool facts of suffering become hot weapons in arguments about agency and urgency that extend from imperiled bodies.[20] Even as this rhetoric often makes bizarre intimacies between unthinkable harshness and the ordinary work of living, it becomes a way of talking about what forms of catastrophe a world is comfortable with or even interested in perpetuating. Yet since catastrophe means change, crisis rhetoric belies the constitutive point that slow death—or the structurally induced attrition of persons keyed to their membership in certain populations—is neither a state of exception nor the opposite, mere banality, but a domain where an upsetting scene of living is revealed to be interwoven with ordinary life after all, like ants discovered scurrying under a thoughtlessly lifted rock.[21] The very out-of-scaleness of the sensationalist rhetoric around crisis within the ordinary measures the structural intractability of a problem the world can live with, which just looks like crisis and catastrophe when attached to freshly exemplary bodies. While death is usually deemed an event in contrast to life's extensivity, in this domain dying and the ordinary reproduction of life are coextensive, opening to a genealogy of a contemporary way of being that is not just contemporary or solely located in the United States, but takes on specific shapes in this time and space.

In the contemporary U.S. context, obesity figures as the freshest case of slow-death crisis-scandal management. Its origin is not in the work of social justice advocates calling for compassion to extort political transformation—although a vast number of lay authorities and diet hobbyists have developed such voices on the Internet. But the main public discussion comes from the collaboration of insurance companies, public health departments, and corporate PR offices. If this chapter were a living organism, its footnotes would expand daily with a diet of crisis and response headlines from mainstream and professional papers, journals, newspapers, and magazines.[22] The first time I presented this chapter as a talk, morning headlines heralded a crisis for Kraft Foods, whose profit was depressed by a fall in the rate of increase in Oreo sales stemmed only by gains in the equally unhealthy breakfast pseudo–health bar market; then news came of a hastily written "cheeseburger bill" introduced in the U.S. House of Representatives to protect companies from litigation stemming from charges that corporate food produced obesity-inducing addiction (this bill was passed, finally, as the "Personal Responsibility in Food Consumption Act of 2005");[23] the third time, I was greeted by an AOL headline, "Would You Like a Serving of Obesity with That?," which linked to an article about a voluntary trend toward putting nutrition labels on the menus of franchise restaurants (a trend now codified in law).[24]

The pedagogical project of turning eating into medicine and its effects into a health crisis has also been taken up by the Obama administration;

Michelle Obama's signature activist "issue" is childhood obesity.[25] The Obama administration has recently intensified the contradictions in this classically sentimental project. The "Partnership for a Healthier America" creates a collaborative context among antagonistic interests from academia, corporate capitalism, and public health institutions and foundations on behalf of the nation's children. Their role is, of course, just advisory.

In short, every day more and more advice circulates from more locations about how better to get the fat (the substance and the people) under control. It would be easy and not false to talk about this as an orchestrated surreality made to sell drugs, services, and newspapers, and to justify particular new governmental and medical oversight of the populations whose appetites are out of control (a conventional view of the masses, subalterns, the sexually identified, and so on).[26] We learned most recently from AIDS, after all, that the epidemic concept is not a neutral description; it's inevitably part of an argument about classification, causality, responsibility, degeneracy, and the imaginable and pragmatic logics of cure.

But that there are debates over what constitutes health and care and responsibility for them does not mean that there is no problem. So what is our object, our scene, our case? The following description mobilizes the catalogue as a genre, aiming toward clustering disparate explanations of the phenomenon; this is the state of analytic improvisation our case requires even from bio-related and social scientists, as analysis cannot help but cross over dissimilar domains of bodily, subjective, and institutional practice. How does it matter, for example, that overweight, obesity, morbid obesity, and a mass tendency, in industrialized spaces, toward physically unhealthy bodily practices amass a weirdly compounded scene of a system and persons gone awry? The case is not a thing but a cluster of factors that looks solid only at a certain distance.

While for insurance purposes obesity has been deemed an illness, the rest of the literature calls it something else: a "chronic condition," etymologically a disease of time, and vernacularly a condition that can never be cured, only managed. The transaction between persons and the ethics, politics, and economics of management or administration makes this phenomenon exemplary as a scene for playing out structural antagonisms. For example, mass overweight is deemed an international phenomenon of the United Kingdom and the United States, and progressively other intensively commoditized places.[27] In the U.S. it is deemed a national epidemic because it serves institutional interests of profit and control, while taxing local healthcare systems; at the same time, the medical literature sees the patterns of overweight in terms of the global circulation of unhealthy commodities. Meanwhile the United Nations has taken it on as a global political problem. Likewise, in the United States, in an era of intense antistate sentiment, making weight trends into an epidemic has provided an opportunity for liberals to reinvigorate the image of the state as a reparative resource and the corporation as an entity with social and economic responsibilities to citizens. At the same time, of course, conservatives tend to call all state health initiatives, including this one, "nanny state" or socialist activity.[28] Yet, simultaneously, these problems of reimagining public health and recalibrating health insurance conjoin habits and styles of intervention that focus on how to recharacterize, moralize about, and reimagine agency among consumers, especially the relatively poor and young. Serious and opportunistic social change agents alike flail away at the obesity endemic by amplifying moral and political urgencies in any and every possible register.

In addition to this congeries of concerns, another story pulsates without making headlines, a story older and more complex than could be effected by the eradication of this symptom: the damage to bodies made in spaces of production and in the rest of life. The obesity epidemic is also a way of talking about the destruction of life, bodies, imaginaries, and environments by and under contemporary regimes of capital. "Capitalism" here stands in for the relations between capitalists and workers and capitalists and consumers amid the shifting character of capitalist strategies, and the net effect of the interaction of those strategies on already vulnerable populations, which include people of color, children, and the aged but more broadly, too, the economically crunched. Capitalism points to a variety of phenomena related to the physical experience of production and consumption throughout a life cycle, the privatization of schools and public metropolitan spaces, and the pushing out of the political from concepts of publicness, now saturated by the logic and activity of markets. It also involves the more normative and informal (but not unpredictable) modes of social capital that have so much to do with the shaping of managed and imagined health.[29]

Many of the players in this discussion are genuinely worried about the diminishing quality of life in the United States, especially for poor and young people. However, the rhetoric of policy requires that one subscribe to a model of institutional and individual agency that frames the adjustment as a dramatic act (is eating a disease of the will or an addiction or compulsion?

And what should *we* do *now*?). Long-term problems of embodiment within capitalism, in the zoning of the everyday, the work of getting through it, and the obstacles to physical and mental flourishing, are less successfully addressed in the temporalities of crisis and require other frames for elaborating contexts of doing, being, and thriving.

How else, then, to understand the intersection of the long history of poor people's shorter lives and the particular conditions of contemporary speed-up? What does it mean to consider the ethics of longevity when, in an unequal health and labor system, the poor and less poor are less likely to live long enough to enjoy the good life whose promise is a fantasy bribe that justifies so much exploitation? How do we think about labor and consumer-related subjectivities in the same moment, since, in my view, one cannot talk about scandals of the appetite—along with food, there's sex, smoking, shopping, and drinking as sites of moral disapprobation, social policy, and self-medication—without talking about the temporality of the workday, the debt cycle, and consumer practice and fantasy? Finally, what does it mean that African Americans and Latinos and Latinas are especially bearing this body burden along with the symbolic negativity long attached to it, so much so that one physician, a member of the Black Women's Health Network, observes that the "most lethal weapon" against Black people in the contemporary United States is the fork?[30]

Frequently, when such mass patterns are recognized at all, they are strategically dramatized in contradictory ways: in paranoid fashion, as the effects of an enemy institution's intentionally inhuman relation to consumers and clients (corporate capitalism, physicians, insurance companies, and so on); as the unintended consequences of capitalist innovation; or as the shameful toxic habits of individuals who, not knowing or not caring, and having financial resources, undermine their own health one bad decision at a time. As the concept of biopower indicates, there is no good reason to adopt a strictly paranoid style. While employers frequently neglect the health of their workplaces and sacrifice laboring bodies to profit, it's rare (but not unheard of) that corporate or individual sovereigns act deliberately to harm consuming bodies—that's *usually* collateral damage. We also know that people are neither dupes to the interests of power as such nor gods of their own intention, unless they are merely hedonistic or compulsive.[31] Biopower operates when a hegemonic bloc organizes the reproduction of life in ways that allow political crises to be cast as conditions of specific bodies and their competence at maintaining health or other conditions of social belonging; thus this bloc gets to judge the problematic body's subjects, whose agency is deemed to be fundamentally destructive. Apartheid-like structures from zoning to shaming are wielded against these populations, who come to represent embodied liabilities to social prosperity of one sort or another. Health itself can then be seen as a side effect of successful normativity, and people's desires and fantasies are solicited to line up with that pleasant condition. But, again, to call embodiment *biopolitical* is only to begin a discussion, not to end it.

III. *Obesity's Actuarial Rhetoric*

This case commonly referred to as "the obesity epidemic" burdens the working classes of the contemporary United States, the United Kingdom, and increasingly all countries in which there is significant participation in the global processed-food regime. Scientific and journalistic studies recite the phrases in scandalized disbelief: "The number of extremely obese American adults—those who are at least 100 pounds overweight" or who have a BMI of fifty or above "has quadrupled since the 1980s" and "works out to about 1 in every 50 adults."[32] Likewise, the slightly less obese percentages (a BMI of forty to fifty) grew to one in forty; and the percentage of ordinary overweight grew to one in five. By 2010 those percentages and measurements of the obese were old hat, and researchers were relieved to see that the rate of increase had not continued: "In 2007–2008, the prevalence of obesity was 32.2% among adult men and 35.5% among adult women. The increases in the prevalence of obesity previously observed do not appear to be continuing at the same rate over the past 10 years, particularly for women and possibly for men." These statistics do not include the merely very overweight.

The situation requires no hyperbole. For the first time in the history of the world there are as many overfed as underfed people and, also for the first time in the history of the world, the overfed are no longer only the wealthiest and the underfed no longer the poor and starving.[33] All Americans, the absolute and relatively well off and the poor, are getting fatter. I will go on to argue, though, that between unequal access to health care, the cramped conditions of everyday life, and the endemically unhealthy workplace, it is most notably the bodies of U.S. working-class and subproletarian populations that fray slowly from the pressure of obesity on their organs and skeletons. Meanwhile U.S. and corporate food policy continues to emaciate drastically the land and the bodies of our food producers to the south, in Mexico and South America, as well as in Africa and rural China.[34]

These inversions are more than an irony or a paradox. Each is distinguished by its own trajectory of slow death. Mass emaciation and obesity are mirror symptoms of the malnourishment of the poor throughout the contemporary world. But how does the recognition of the contours of a case organize our imagination for responding to it? We understand the need to get food to the underfed poor, and quickly, for that is what they would do if they had the means of production in their own hands. As for the overfed, owning the means of production might well produce more overfeeding, more exercise of agency toward death and not health, and certainly not against power. Unless one wants to see being overweight as a protest against hegemonic notions of health and wealth there is nothing promising, heroic, or critical about this development.[35]

In the context of this singular mix of privilege and negativity, the overweight populations of industrialized societies thus challenge any cultural-historical analysis rooted in notions of sovereignty or its denial. Aversion to fatness increases along with fatness. Aversion to fatness is aesthetic and health-related; it imbues the word *cost* with psychological, social, and economic inflections. The history of this dynamic anxiety begins with the Cold War.

Although concern about the decline of physical health and the increase in weight of Americans has been a public topic since the turn of the twentieth century, it became a state and federal topic during the Cold War when Sputnik and the rise of product plenitude in the United States combined to create anxiety about the weaknesses of America's children.[36] While Sputnik helped launch an era of massive federal funding of public education, the component of Cold War readiness related to health produced more symbolic than economic responses: inspirational gestures from state entities like Kennedy's President's Council on Fitness, whose intention to whip up strong national bodies has led to programs like "America on the Move," Health Secretary Tommy Thompson's 2003 collaboration with Dr. Joyce Brothers and local pharmacies and health clubs to provide free testing to determine health plans for any participating citizen, and inspirational slogans to encourage youths to exercise.[37] But the national discourse about weight's relation to collective well-being entered its current stage of intensified concern when, in 2001, the Surgeon General David Satcher produced a report calling obesity an epidemic, claiming it caused "$117 billion in health care costs and lost wages and killed 300,000 people a year."[38] Other numbers go as high as 240 billion, a figure that does not include the $33 billion spent yearly on weight-loss products and diet regimes.[39]

For a change, this health crisis was phrased not simply on behalf of children and the national future but also in terms of the next few decades of increasingly infirm adult bodily experience. Specters were raised of multiple generations of obese members of the same households unable to care well for themselves or each other, let alone to participate in the labor economy.[40] In the initial justification for action by an administration dedicated to shrinking the domestic government as a resource for the socially, physically, or economically disabled, we get images of stressed-out overworked bodies responding biologically by hoarding even healthy food in the body's fat stores. This physiology of stress translates into increasing anxieties about the health care costs that businesses have to face.

Of course the reduced fate of the body under regimes of the production of value for others has long been a topic of discussion. David Harvey, summarizing Marx, details extensively the costs of

> harnessing basic human powers of cooperation/collaboration; the skilling, deskilling, and reskilling of the powers of labor in accord with technological requirements; acculturation to routinization of tasks; enclosure within strict spatiotemporal rhythms of regulated (and sometimes spatially confined) activities; frequent subordinations of bodily rhythms and desires as "an appendage of the machine"; socialization into long hours of concentrated labor at variable but often increasing intensity. . . . [A]nd, last but not least, the production of variability, fluidity, and flexibility of labor powers able to respond to those rapid revolutions in production processes so typical of capitalist development.

This cyborgian regime makes "the recognition of variation of labor and hence of the fitness of the worker for the maximum number of different kinds of labor into a question of life and death,'" Marx writes.[41] Thus the destruction of bodies by capital isn't just a "crisis" of judgment in the affective present but an ethico-political condition of long standing that seems to emerge as a new formation in the phrase "obesity epidemic." At the same time this "epidemic" marks a limit, not in the public, state, or corporate conscience about whether or how extensively the working body should be sacrificed to profit, but to what kinds of sacrifice best serve the reproduction of labor power and the consumer economy. Thus partly at issue in the obesity crisis is the definition of adequate food, and the conflicting models of health. Is health a biological condition, the availability for work, or a scene of longevity? Compassion and corporatism collaborate in these particular epidemics of the failing will and body as long as concern for the health of profits "balances" concerns for the health of persons.

These particular facts that cluster around obesity echo other epidemiologic crisis pronouncements by the federally supported health apparatus, such as the designation of National Depression Screening Day (in 1991), which established its claim on crisis consciousness explicitly based on the costs of human mental suffering not just to humans but to "productivity" at work, business profits, insurance, health care providers, and the state.[42] The disease becomes an epidemic and a problem when it interferes with reigning notions of what labor should cost: the disease is now too expensive, which is why privatized health care and business-oriented programs of education are the usual means of diminishing the cost of the symptom. The popular initiatives around depression are linked with the national obesity initiative for other reasons, too. Depression Day stakes out a public interest in getting persons to feel better by changing their behaviors and therefore to be more reliable to themselves, their families, and their bosses. To do so the invested partner provides pedagogical resources for those who need them, and advocates in state and federal legislatures for resources to that end. Antidepression and anti-obesity initiatives both seek to orchestrate a translocal, collective environment for personal social change, involving families, friends, teachers, colleagues, and medical professionals.

In other words, in both cases medicalization did not just mean privatization: and, for that matter, privatization itself is a rerouting of the relations of governmental, corporate, and personal responsibility rather than, as it often seems to be, the ejection of the state from oversight of the public good in deference to corporations. The Clinton, Bush, and Obama administrations responded to the adipose-related national health crisis within the norms of the social contract forged during the period of welfare state liberalism of the 1960s. (This is why the obesity initiative has outraged conservative pundits and groups, which recognize accurately the centrality of a nonsovereignty-based notion of personal agency in the explicit state and state-related discourse of crisis and cure.)[43] Yet the neoliberal shift within the entitlement activity of the state is evident in many of the policy formulations adjacent to the specifically ameliorative programs that have been developed. The Bush administration continued to support a statement issued in 1996 by the United States at the World Food Summit, which declared that "the right to adequate food is 'a goal or aspiration' but not an international obligation of governments."[44] The overdetermination of the problem/scene continues to obscure the political debate about which bodies are accountable for the dire situation.

The depression and obesity epidemics also share an attachment to explanations from genetic factors as they affect the public discussion of responsibility. These factors too not only confuse mainstream analyses of personal and corporate responsibility, intention, and cure but make questions of causality effectively moot. What does it imply genetically that around 60 percent of American adults and 20 percent of U.S. children are overweight to obese and that one out of every three children born during or after the year 2000 will be afflicted with an obesity-related disorder such as diabetes mellitus or type 2 diabetes?[45] As Kelly Brownell and Katherine Battle Horgen argue, if over sixty percent of the American people are overweight or obese, the other forty percent are not; as far back as 1995 the Institute of Medicine was releasing studies "saying that the environment, and not genetics, was responsible for increasing obesity."[46] The explanation from genetic predisposition often attempts to deshame individuals for their body size/mental state and to release them from paralyzing burdens of responsibility for it. But explanation from genetics gives a misleading shape to this amorphous phenomenon, obscuring other impersonal factors that might be contributing to the increase in bad American health.

Apart from the genetic solution, other structural or impersonal conditions or etiologies have been assembled. I can only gesture toward these here: urban development; longer working days; an increase in temporary and part-time labor with increasingly more workers working more than one job or juggling work and family in a way that relegates exercise to a leisure time people barely have; the refocusing of the food industry as the immediate gratifier for energy for service-sector workers of the working classes and the professional managerial class, both of which increasingly eat fast food at lunch, live off of vending machines, multitask while eating, work during lunch and the coffee break, and so on; the expansion of fast-food availability and of snack culture generally, of frozen food franchising, and of microwaves at work and at home; and finally the increasing percentage of the U.S. household budget spent in restaurants rather than for food to be eaten at home.[47] As Marion Nestle and Michael Jacobsen observe, "Americans spend about half of their food budget and consume about one-third of their daily energy on meals and drinks consumed outside the home. . . . About 170,000 fast-food restaurants and three million soft drink vending machines help ensure that Americans are not more than a few steps from immediate sources of relatively non-nutritious foods."[48] Moreover, when low-fat versions of these kinds of food are made available, people tend to purchase double what they ordinarily would to provide that full-fat feeling.

The reference to zoning above reminds us that countless local, state, and federal regulations and programs contribute to the U.S. fat count. Decisions on behalf of sustaining the attraction of capital to particular tax bases and the shaping of regulations favoring that attraction have had significant effects on the increase in obesity, especially in the inner city. Fast-food outlets, like other franchises, are a highly valued part of empowerment-zone developments; schools are not penalized but rewarded for their increasing reliance on creative corporate "partnerships" with fast-food and soda franchises and the like, since these partnerships compensate for the enormous cuts in the percentages of spending on education most states have realized, even during the growth in collective wealth of the Clinton era. Now those partnerships are being redirected toward monetizing better health. One federal program aimed at teaching nutrition to children is sponsored by Gatorade, another by Kellogg. At the same time as the high-fat, high-fructose world of cheap pleasure food becomes the ordinary American's frequent lunch and dinner, schools have cut back severely on physical education programs and adults work at desks or do errands in cars when they otherwise might walk. The U.S. Department of Health and Human Services has argued that ten minutes of extra walking during the day would solve the obesity crisis, but it also claims that this is difficult to schedule given the time constraints faced by workers with families, commutes, or multiple jobs.[49]

Lest one feel conspiratorial about it, what becomes clear as one reads the history of agricultural policy and the development of tax and zoning codes is that they have diminished the health of the U.S. wage and low-salaried worker mainly through indirect means. The chapter subtitled "Where the Calories Come From," opening Greg Critser's *Fat Land: How Americans Became the Fattest People in the World*, begins with the words "Earl Butz" and tells a tragicomic story about the politically driven promotion of fructose over sucrose and palm oil over soy oil during the Nixon administration's crisis over inflation in the early 1970s.[50] No one who was making these decisions meant to do anything to harm individuals' or a working-class population's bodies; the aim was to control international markets, bankrupt struggling southern and Pacific Rim production communities, and drive food prices down, a paradoxical aid to the poor who were about to be harmed by the food to come. No one meant to fatten up the world population scarily. Nonetheless, Critser reports that Congressional testimony to these eventualities was provided and promptly disregarded by politicians and bureaucrats. The unintentional effect of this shift was the inculcation in children of a taste for salt, sugar, and fat and, after the 1980s, the spread of cheap fast food in supersized containers that lowered the per-unit profit margin for, say, McDonald's, but actually increased sales.

During the twentieth century the per capita consumption of sugar products increased nearly 100 percent, mostly after 1970. Fat consumption has increased at a much slower rate, but with the increasing inactivity of children and adults and the lack of exercise habits as part of the habits of living, consumption has had a more profound effect on bodily well-being. Researchers have shown that these particular molecular modes of sweetness and fat are metabolized with particular inefficiency and toxic effect by the human body, and since they produce more fat storage and food cravings, the phrase *supply and demand* could easily be rephrased as *supply and manufactured need.*[51]

These figures would suggest that most Americans increasingly eat quickly and badly, often away from home. Researchers and pundits emphasize the class and racial dimensions of this expansion. But a Google image search on *obesity* calls up countless images of fat statues and of large white people in standard "before" postures; often they advertise diet schemes and, most notably, bariatric surgery. Generally, these advertising images mean to be iconic or universal, each relatively deracinated from any historical environment. Given their significant Internet presence, these images are helping drive one of the fastest growing areas of U.S. medical practice: the varieties of stomach stapling. No doubt this quasi classicism too is a strategy for de-shaming obesity.

Nonetheless, there is a more complicated genealogy of the aversion to fat, which has to do with the specter of downward mobility for most of the U.S. working population. For the large part of this century the default image of the obese was of white people—the aged and the Southern—just as the usual image of the poor was also white, appearing as an iconically emaciated rural person or an urban immigrant. Both trends shifted in the 1970s, when poverty became associated with debates over the welfare state and representations of the poor became disproportionately African American.[52] To the extent that emaciation in the United States remains coded as white and weight excess coded as black, the so-called crisis of obesity continues to juggle the symbolic burden of class signified through the elision of whiteness from the racial marking of poverty: these markings, at minimum, not only shape particular aversions to the people of excess (already negated as both too much and too little for ordinary social membership) but also the topic of excess as a general issue of public health. One way around this racialization of obesity has been the obfuscation of distinctions among the merely overweight, the obese, and the morbidly obese in the crisis rhetoric of care. Still, the phrase *morbidly obese* seems so frequently to raise the African American specter in ways that reinforce the image of African Americans as a population already saturated by death and available for mourning, compelled by appetites rather than by strategies of sovereign agency toward class mobility. People of color generally stand in, in the discourse of obesity, for the entire culture of U.S. nonelites. The word *culture* here is no accident; as food practices seem more cultural, obesity can seem less related to the conditions of labor, schooling, and zoning that construct the endemic environment of the "epidemic's" emergence.

This symptom of unhealth does characterize, disproportionately, the bodily propensities of working-class and subproletarian Americans of all races and regions, and especially people of color. At the same time, the numbers of poor Americans reporting going without meals, requiring emergency food assistance, or experiencing fairly constant hunger has also increased dramatically, especially since the shrinkage of food programs for the poor in the late 1990s.[53] Yet the vast majority of the morbidly or very obese are also close to or beneath the poverty line.

The populations of people of color—Native Americans, African Americans, and Hispanics, especially Mexican Americans—are characterized by a significantly higher percentage of obesity than Anglo or Asian populations. By the year 2000, 68 percent of African American adult women were overweight or obese; today, their children are likely to be as well.[54] The bodily consequences of this increase in obesity are catastrophic for those children, and not only for their "self-esteem." They now suffer the wearing diseases of old age. High blood pressure and diabetes are especially catastrophic, as these portend early heart disease, liver and pancreatic failure, strokes and aneurysms, as well as blindness and circulation problems. Circulation problems lead to arthritis and other difficulties in movement, along with amputation. Arguments persist as to whether these effects mean that obesity itself kills or whether, instead, it produces effects of "comorbidity," exacerbating other bodily ailments.[55]

But why be picky? The bodies of the U.S. waged workers will be more fatigued, in more pain, less capable of ordinary breathing and working, and die earlier than the average for higher-income workers, who are also getting fatter, but at a slower rate and with relatively more opportunity for exercise.[56] Apart from working-class and subproletarian white women, who are more successful in mobilizing bourgeois beauty norms for economic success in the service-sector economy, these overweight and obese poor will find it harder to get and keep jobs, remain healthy meanwhile, and afford health care for the ensuing diseases.[57] They will become progressively more sedentary not just from the increasing passivity of the more sedentary kinds of service-sector work, not just from working more jobs more unevenly, not just because of television, and not just because there are fewer and fewer public spaces in which it is safe and pleasurable to walk but because it is harder to move, period. They will live the decay of their organs and bodies more explicitly, painfully, and overwhelmingly than ever before; and it has become statistically clear that between stress and comorbidity they will die at ages younger than their grandparents and parents.[58] As one African American essayist describes the ongoing familial and cultural lure of the actually existing American four food groups (i.e., sugar, fat, salt, and caffeine), we see that morbidity, the embodiment toward death as a way of life, marks out slow death as what there is of the good life for the vast majority of American workers.[59]

IV. *From Distributed Causality to Interruptive Agency*

This analysis thinks about agency and causality as dispersed environmental mechanisms at the personal as well as the institutional level, and so far has been demonstrating the overdetermination of environments that create the dramatic consequences of endemic overweight. Yet it is not sufficient to argue that the habitus inculcated at work and school—in the contexts of speed-up in the production sector and, in the public sector, privatization, defunding, and zoning—is "responsible" for obesity any more than it is sufficient to argue that an epidemic of the diseased will is throttling productivity and longevity in the U.S. workforce. At the other end of the disintegrating circuit we have the agency of the medicalized subject who can be lectured at, shamed, and exhorted to diet, to put the family on a diet, to eat at home, and to exercise. For many reasons these exhortations go unheard. Epidemiologists suggest that the lower one is on the socioeconomic scale, the less open one is to yet another shaming or even quasi-criminalizing lecture about diet from an institutional professional, even when she's acting like a normative "mom," a First Lady; expertise has so often been used shamingly to confirm the social negativity of dominated populations that even good advice is appropriately viewed with suspicion.[60] But more than an image of a historically and politically explicable decision to resist compliance is required to understand the spread of contemporary unhealthy weight.

To engage this phenomenon fully, the image of obesity seen as a biopolitical event needs to be separated from eating as a phenomenological act, and from food as a space of expressivity as well as nourishment. The recalcitrance of obesity as a problem has led scholars to think about eating as an activity motivated by stress, as a desire for self-medication, as a pleasure, and as a cultural norm, but it has made them think less clearly about eating as an exercise that violates any definition of sovereign identity.[61] My focus here will be on seeing eating as a kind of self-medication through self-interruption. Mariana Valverde argues that self-medication isn't merely a weakness of those with diseases of the will.[62] It is often a fitting response to a stressful environment, like a family. It is also often part of being in a community, or any space of belonging organized through promises of comfort. The pleasures might be personal (if one is a regular somewhere) or anonymous (if one is merely somewhere). Relaxing in these locations can be a temporal, episodic thing, but whatever it is, it extends being in the world enjoyably and, usually, undramatically.[63] The conviviality of consumption from this perspective marks duration: a different definition of "slow food," a concept and a movement that recognizes in a practice of ordinary inefficiency a way to counter the speeds with which capitalist activity destroys its environments while at the same time it makes living possible and produces contexts for thriving, merely living, and wearing out for the people making life within them.[64] Food is one of the few spaces of controllable, reliable pleasure people have. Additionally, unlike alcohol or other drugs, food is necessary to existence, part of the care of the self, the reproduction of life. But how do we articulate those urgencies of necessity and pleasure with the structural conditions of existence that militate against the flourishing of workers and consumers? The forms of spreading pleasure I've just been describing are also folded into the activity of doing what's necessary to lubricate the body's movement through capitalized time's shortened circuit—

not only speed-up at work but the contexts where making a life involves getting through the day, the week, and the month. Time organized by the near future of the paying of bills and the management of children coexists with the feeling of well-being a meal can provide. And although one might imagine that the knowledge of the unhealthiness would make parents force themselves and their children into a different food regime, ethnographies of working-class families argue that economic threats to the family's continuity and the parents' sense of well-being tend to produce insular households in which food is one of the few stress relievers and one of the few sites of clear continuity between children and parents.[65] Moreover in scenes of economic struggle kids take on parental stress and seek to find comfort where the parents do as well, even as they cultivate small generational differences. So in the sociality of eating the complexity of maintaining dependency identifications can be simplified, providing ordinary and repeatable scenes of happiness, if not health.

This is the material context for so many. Working life exhausts practical sovereignty, the exercise of the will as one faces the scene of the contingencies of survival. At the same time that one builds a life the pressures of its reproduction can be exhausting. Eating can be seen as a form of ballast against wearing out, but also as a counter-dissipation, in that, like other small pleasures, it can produce an experience of self-abeyance, of floating sideways. In this view it is not synonymous with resistant agency in the tactical or effectual sense, as it is not always or usually dedicated singly to self-negation or self-extension. Eating amid the work of the reproduction of contemporary life is best seen as activity releasing the subject into self-suspension.

I am not asking to replace a notion of cognitive will with a notion of involuntary or unconscious activity. In the model I am articulating here, the body and a life are not only projects, but also sites of episodic intermission from personality, the burden of whose reproduction is part of the drag of practical sovereignty, of the obligation to be reliable. Most of what we do, after all, involves not being purposive but inhabiting agency differently in small vacations from the will itself, which is so often spent from the pressures of coordinating one's pacing with the working day, including times of preparation and recovery from it. These pleasures can be seen as interrupting the liberal and capitalist subject called to consciousness, intentionality, and effective will. Interruption and self-extension are not opposites, of course; that is my point. But the other point is that in the scene of slow death—where mental and physical health might actually be conflicting aims, even internally conflicting—the activity of riding a different wave of spreading out or shifting in the everyday also reveals confusions about what it means to have a life. Is it to have health? To love, to have been loved? To have felt sovereign? To achieve a state or a sense of worked-toward enjoyment? Is "having a life" now the process to which one gets resigned, after dreaming of the good life, or not even dreaming? Is "life" as the scene of reliable pleasures located largely in those experiences of coasting, with all that's implied in that phrase, the shifting, diffuse, sensual space between pleasure and numbness?

I am focusing here on the way the attrition of the subject of capital articulates survival with slow death. Impassivity and other politically depressed relations of alienation, coolness, detachment, or distraction, especially in subordinated populations, can be read as affective forms of engagement with the environment of slow death, much as the violence of battered women has had to be reunderstood as a kind of destruction toward survival.[66] But what I am offering here is also slightly different. In this scene, activity toward reproducing life is neither identical to making it or oneself *better* nor a mimetic response to the structural conditions of a collective failure to thrive, nor just a mini-vacation from being responsible—such activity is also directed toward making a less-bad experience. It's a relief, a reprieve, not a repair. While these kinds of acts are not all unconscious—eating involves many kinds of self-understanding, especially in a culture of shaming and self-consciousness around the moral mirror choosing pleasures so often provides—they are often consciously and unconsciously not toward imagining the long haul, for example.

The structural position of the overwhelmed life intensifies this foreshortening of consciousness and fantasy. Under a regime of crisis ordinariness, life feels truncated, more like desperate doggy paddling than like a magnificent swim out to the horizon. Eating adds up to something, many things: maybe the good life, but usually a sense of well-being that spreads out for a moment, not a projection toward a future. Paradoxically, of course, at least during this phase of capital, there is less of a future when one eats without an orientation toward it.

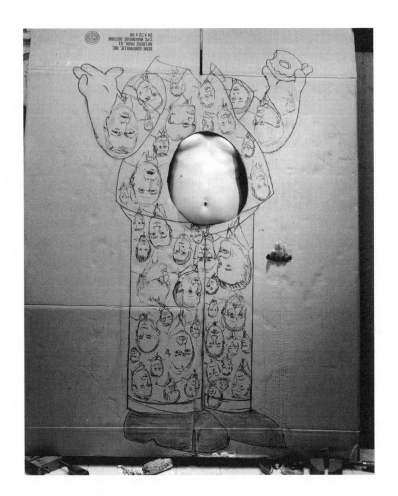

3. Claire Pentecost, "Appetites/Sovereignty" (2007)

Slow death is not primarily a gloss on the lives of quiet desperation that Thoreau attributed to men in capitalist society, although the phrase *soul killing* has been used often enough to describe the attritions of bourgeois sociality that one might say something about the many sacrifices people make to remain in proximity to mirages of sovereignty. Nor is it in the melodramatic idiom that Baudrillard uses when he refers to "slow death" as the double execution of the capitalist subject by the sacrificial violence of being in labor and an always-increasing seduction to consumer overexcitement.[67] Nor is the phrase an existential way of talking about living as such, on the way to dying. Nonetheless, even this list of rejected exempla suggests something important about the space of slow death that shapes our particular biopolitical phase; mainly, people do live in it, just not very well.

For ordinary workers this attrition of life or pacing of death where the everyday evolves within complex processes of globalization, law, and state regulation is an old story in a new era.[68] Likewise the world continues to pulsate with counterexploitive activity, in a variety of anarchist, cooperative, anticapitalist, and radical antiwork experiments. People are increasingly using the time they do not have—what with the exigencies of the reproduction of life—to refuse to maintain the vampirism of profit extraction that exhausts the body and saturates the infrastructure of even the most benign and impulsive everyday pleasures.[69] But for most, potentiality within the overwhelming present is less well symbolized by energizing images of sustainable life and less guaranteed by the glorious promise of bodily longevity and social security than it is expressed in regimes of exhausted practical sovereignty, lateral agency, and, sometimes, counterabsorption in episodic refreshment, for example in sex, or spacing out, or food that is not for thought.

1. *When You Wish Upon A Star*

History hurts, but not only. It also engenders optimism in response to the oppressive presence of what dominates or is taken for granted. Political emotions are responses to prospects for change: fidelity to those responses is optimistic, even if the affects are dark. It is usual to think of critical theory as dark, not as an optimistic genre, not only because, traditionally, it's suspicious: but also since it creates so much exhausting anxiety about the value of even the "thinkiest" thought.[1] But the compulsion to repeat optimism, which is another definition of desire, is a condition of possibility that also risks having to survive, once again, disappointment and depression, the protracted sense that nothing will change and that no-one, especially oneself, is teachable after all. All that work for what? Love isn't the half of it.

To be teachable is to be open for change. It is a tendency. It is to turn toward the story of what we have said in terms of phrases we haven't yet noticed.[2] Eve Sedgwick's work has changed sexuality's history and destiny. She is a referent, and there is a professional field with a jargon and things, and articles and books that summarize it. For me, though, the luck of encountering her grandiosity, her belief that it is a good to disseminate the intelligent force of an attachment to a thing, a thought, a sensation, is of unsurpassable consequence. In the pleasure/knowledge economy of her work, the force of attachment has more righteousness than anything intelligibly or objectively "true": she enables the refusal of cramped necessity by way of a poetics of misrecognition.

Misrecognition (*méconnaissance*) describes the psychic process by which fantasy recalibrates what we encounter so that we can imagine that something or someone can fulfill our desire: its operation is central to the state of cruel optimism. To misrecognize is not to err, but to project qualities onto something so that we can love, hate, and manipulate it for having those qualities—which it might or might not have.[3] A poetics of misrecognition may seem to risk collapsing the critical analysis of fantasy into fantasy itself. Maybe so, but such a risk is unavoidable. Fantasy is what manages the ambivalence and itinerancy of attachment. It provides representations to make the subject appear intelligible to herself and to others throughout the career of desire's unruly attentiveness. That is, fantasy parses ambivalence in such a way that the subject is not defeated by it.

To track fantasy across the scene of the subject in history, in this view, is to take seriously the magical thinking, or formalism, involved in seeing selves and worlds as continuous.[4] This is a theory of being, and it is also a theory of reading. As any reader of her work on Henry James would attest, Sedgwick's mode of reading is to deshame fantasmatic attachment so as to encounter its operations as knowledge.[5] For example, we may feel the violence of history as something "it" does to "us," but Sedgwick argues that the stories we tell about how subjectivity takes shape must also represent our involvement with the pain and error, the bad memory and mental lag, that also shape our desire's perverse, twisted, or, if you prefer, indirect routes toward pleasure and survival. To admit your surprising attachments, to trace your transformation over the course of a long (life) sentence, is sentience—that's what I've learned. The pain of paying attention pays me back in the form of eloquence: a sound pleasure.

Yet for a long time now, Sedgwick argues, skepticism has been deemed the only ethical position for the intellectual to take with respect to the subject's ordinary attachments. Even Adorno, the great belittler of popular pleasures, can be aghast at the ease with which intellectuals shit on people who hold to a dream.[6] Dreams are seen as easy optimism, while failures seem complex. Sedgwick writes against the hermeneutics of suspicion on the grounds that it always finds the mirages and failures for which it looks: she finds critics overdedicated to a self-confirming scene of disappointment.[7] In this view the disappointed critic mistakes his act of negation for a performance of his seriousness; perhaps he also elevates his thought by disdaining anything that emanates a scent of therapy, reparation, or utopianism.

How does one go about defetishizing negation while remaining critical? Begin with Freud's dictum that there is no negative in the unconscious. Sedgwick seeks to read every word the subject writes (she believes in the author) to establish the avowed and disavowed patterns of his or her desire, and then understands those repetitions in terms of a story about sexuality that does not exist yet as a convention or an identity. That aim is what makes her writing so optimistic. In it the persistence of sexually anomalous attachment figures as the social potential of queerness, in which what counts is not one's "object choice" as such but rather one's sustaining attachments, which are only sometimes also one's social relations. In this way repetition, heavily marked as a process of reading and rereading, has a reparative effect on the subject of an unwieldy sexuality. The queer tendency of this method is to put one's attachments back into play and into pleasure, into knowledge, into worlds. It is to admit that they matter. In Sedgwick's work desire's self-elaboration enables an aesthetic that is organized neither by the sublime nor the beautiful, the dramatic nor the banal, but by something vibratingly quiet. This would also be the erotic tonality struck by what she calls "reparative criticism," her antidote to the hermeneutics of suspicion. Set against the practice of deconstructing truth forms that she locates in the literary theory of the 1970s, Sedgwick's reparative criticism aims to sustain the unfinished and perhaps unthought thoughts about desire that are otherwise defeated by the roar of conventionality or heteronormative culture.[8] Any writer's task, in this view, would be to track desire's itinerary, not on behalf of confirming its hidden or suppressed Truths or Harms but to elaborate its variety of attachments as sexuality, as lived life, and, most importantly, as an unfinished history that confounds the hurts and the pleasures.

I love the idea of reparative reading insofar as it is a practice of meticulous curiosity. But I also resist idealizing, even implicitly, any program of better thought or reading. How would we know when the "repair" we intend is not another form of narcissism or smothering will? Just because we sense it to be so? Those of us who think for a living are too well-positioned to characterize certain virtuous acts of thought as dramatically powerful and right, whether effective or futile; we are set up to overestimate the proper clarity and destiny of an idea's effects and appropriate affects. As I argued in "Slow Death," such dramas can produce strange distortions in the ways we stage agency as a mode of heroic authorship, and vice versa: such dramas of inflation distract attention from the hesitancy and recessiveness in ordinary being. The distinction I'm making here is about an attitude toward what thinking (as *écriture*, as potentiality) can do. I'm suggesting that the overvaluation of reparative thought is both an occupational hazard and part of a larger overvaluation of a certain mode of virtuously intentional, self-reflective personhood.

Elaine Hadley tells the long history of the liberal elevation of cultivated self-reflection starting from its congealing image in John Stuart Mill's *Autobiography*. Mill, she argues, posits an identity between thought and interiority, such that his version of the ethical subject takes on the shape of the intellectual who cultivates his self-awareness—that is, his awareness of himself as a self.[9] More recently, there was a seemingly antithetical moment—call it '68—when a program of history from the subject opposed the proprietary clarities of institutional and bodily truth claims even, or even especially, in liberal capitalist/democratic contexts that elevate mental abstraction over bodily labor.[10] In this anti-Oedipal moment the subject's amalgam of knowledges—thoughts and practices—became a generative ground for refiguring the normatively social, especially in the domains of socialist and sexual politics. Bodies were elevated as, in a sense, smarter and more knowing than minds, although ultimately the distinction heads toward exhaustion.

We are still in that epoch and need still to be, and yet there can be an uncanny confluence between the ideal of liberal abstraction or inner-directedness and the antiliberal orientation toward the subject's affective knowingness that we find in identity politics and, as previously argued, a certain kind of self-confirming affect theory. Like Eve, I desire to angle knowledge toward and from the places where it is (and we are) impossible.

But individuality—that monument of liberal fantasy, that site of commodity fetishism, that project of certain psychoanalytic desires, that sign of cultural and national modernity—is to me a contrary form, a form already interrupted by inconstancy that has a hard time bearing it. There is an orientation toward interiority in much queer theory that brings me up short and makes me wonder: must the project of queerness start "inside" of the subject and spread out from there?

This distinction is not an opposition. Here is a biographical way of showing it, though in writing this way I am working against my own inclination. Eve's public stories about becoming possible—in *Fat Art, Thin Art*; *Tendencies*; and *A Dialogue on Love*—recount a crowded world of loving family and friends in which she thrives partly by living in the fold of her internal counternarrative.[11] My story, if I wrote it, would locate its optimism in a crowded scene too, but mine was dominated by a general environment not of thriving but of disappointment, contempt, and threat. I salvaged my capacity to attach to persons by reconceiving of both their violence and their love as impersonal. *This isn't about me.* This has had some unpleasant effects, as you might imagine. But it was also a way to protect my optimism. Selves seemed like ruthless personalizers. In contrast, to think of the world as organized around the impersonality of the structures and practices that conventionalize desire, intimacy, and even one's own personhood was to realize how uninevitable the experience of being personal, of having personality, is. Out of this happy thought came an orientation toward fidelity to inclinations of all sorts, including those intellectual and political.

Attachments are made not by will, after all, but by an intelligence after which we are always running. (It's not just "Hey, you!" but "Wait up!")[12] This lagging and sagging relation to attachment threatens to make us feel vertiginous and formless, except that normative conventions and our own creative repetitions are there along the way to help quell the panic we might feel at the prospect of becoming exhausted or dead before we can make sense of ourselves.[13] In other words, the anxiety of formlessness—whose potentiality follows us everywhere—makes us awfully teachable, for a minute. To the degree that the conventional forms of the social direct us to recognize only some of our attachments as the core of who we are and what we belong to, one's relation to attachment is impersonal. To belong to the normal world is to misrecognize only certain modes of intelligibility as expressing one's true self. It brings out my queerness to think of living not only as self-extension but also as a process that interferes with the drama of the self. You will note that I am talking about impersonality not as the opposite of the personal—say, as "structure" or "power"—but as one of its conditions.

In this sense my world operates according to a proximate, but different, fantasy of disappointment, optimism, aversion, and attachment than the one I attribute to Eve. I think of how I met the girl. We are both shy—who isn't? She gave a paper, and we talked about it. Years later, I gave one, and she listened to it. She wrote another book, and I read it. There were meetings in airports and hotel dining rooms. We took walks, talked. Once, by accident, we took a small plane together. Reading is one place where the impersonality of intimacy can be transacted without harm to anyone; writing and paper-giving are others. There is no romance of the impersonal, no love plot for it. But there can be optimism, a space across which to move.

Stupid optimism is the most disappointing thing of all. By "stupid" I mean the faith that adjustment to certain forms or practices of living and thinking—for example, the prospect of class mobility, the romantic narrative, normalcy, nationality, or a better sexual identity—will secure one's happiness. Achieving conventionality, as we will see, is not the same as achieving security. Here is a stupidity of mine: "History is what hurts," that motto of The Political Unconscious, is a phrase that I love.[14] It resonates as truth; it performs a truth-effect in me. But because it is in the genre of the maxim, I have never tried to understand it. That is one project of this essay.

II. Did Somebody Say Wish?

In the previous section, bodies and sexualities were in the wings. Eve and I both wrote about fat because we identified as fat, rightly or wrongly. She: "I used to have a superstition that/ there was this use to being fat: no one I loved could come to harm/ enfolded in my touch."[15] Me, writing about someone else, of course: "for him, it is a narrative in which the very compulsion to desire specific things . . . forces him to risk insatiability, a constant inadequacy to one's own desire."[16] My claim is that our relations to these modes of embodiment register our proximate approaches to the incorporative and impersonal strategies of queer/utopian thought.

Mary Gaitskill's novel, Two Girls, Fat and Thin, tells a story that approaches encapsulating these dialectical impulses. All of her books try to make sense of the relation between painful history and the painful optimism of traumatized subjects trying to survive within that history, since they cannot put it behind them.[17] Trauma can never be let go of: it holds you. It locates you at the knot that joins the personal and the impersonal, specifying *you* at the moment you have the least control over your own destiny and meaning. You become like a small animal that, when picked up, never stops moving its legs.

In *Two Girls, Fat and Thin*, Dorothy Never and Justine Shade—shades of *The Wizard of Oz*, *Pale Fire*, and *Justine*—come in contact because of their common interest in Anna Granite, an Ayn Rand–like figure. Like Rand, Granite intoxicates her audience with the promise that identification with one's sexual and intellectual power can produce happiness and fulfillment, achieving a victory over the deadening normal world.[18] Justine Shade has decided to write an article on Anna Granite and the people who follow her for *Urban Vision*, a hip paper like the *Village Voice*. She has learned of Granite at her day job in a doctor's office, where the promise they make to cure bodies in pain appears to her a false but necessary way to forestall despair. When a young patient with heart disease tells her about Granite, the philosophy strikes Justine as both stupid and powerful.

Dorothy Never had once been a Granite acolyte, liberated by the thought of living and promoting the beauty of destructive passion. The two girls meet when Dorothy responds to an index card that Justine has posted on a laundromat wall asking for information about Granite. At the time of their meeting, neither Justine nor Dorothy has had a good conversation with anyone in many years: each has long ago drawn a "cloak" around herself (112, 158, 173) that acts as an "invisible shield" or "square of definition" (128, 129). Yet from the moment of their initial phone call they resonate with each other, a resonance that they take personally but that has, in a sense, nothing to do with anything substantive about each other, except insofar as each woman functions formally as an enigmatic opportunity for something transformative. This resonance to one side of the material is what Deleuze calls a "percept"; fidelity to its potentiality is what Badiou calls an event; and it is also the opportunity misrecognition affords for an optimism that allows curiosity. "I invented possible scenarios daily," Dorothy recalls, "growing more and more excited by the impending intellectual adventure" (17). They convert into disembodied, vocal actors in each other's fantasy world: Dorothy is "lulled by the expressionless, melancholy quality" of Justine's voice (16), while Dorothy's "voice . . . stroked Justine on the inside of her skull in a way that both repelled and attracted her" (23). There is an attachment, yet the interlocutor factors in it not as a known being, or a biographical human-with-subjectivity, but as a formal point of attachment, an opening toward something beyond individuality, surfacing from the rhythms of encounter and relation. This paradox of the impersonality of attachment—that it circumvents the personal and the historical on the way to enumerating their relation—organizes the women's mutual attraction/aversion throughout the novel. They feel taken over by it at the same time as they are taken up in it.

During the studied formalism of their interview, they find themselves overwhelmed by a compulsion to historicize, to narrate their lives to each other, and yet the exchange of personal narrative does not necessarily amount to an intimate exchange of something personal. In part, this is a banal effect of the situation, as one role of the contemporary journalist is to foment exemplary therapeutic confessional storytelling. Any number of times in the novel the girls tell their life stories to a stranger who exchanges his or her own for it: such is the strange sociability of contemporary trauma talk. But the girls' mutual attachment goes well beyond convention. Each woman becomes a "strange world" into which the other "unwittingly pitched" herself (11, 17). Each woman's usual practice is to solicit, to listen, and not to narrate. They both register ambivalence and embarrassment toward the need they feel to tell each other something, which is not at all their usual practice.

Dorothy's fierce desire to tell Justine about her childhood turns into an aversion to Justine for animating this wish to be released from her life of self-containment, a life in which she has hoarded her knowledge and made her body into a grotesque shield (39). Obesity and ugliness create a force field around her, seeming to neutralize what, in those "gatherings of the normally proportioned," might come from others—curiosity or attachment (169). In this way she is protected from saying what she knows, just as she is protected from the world's demand to know what she knows. "I preferred the elegance of distance," she notes (226). One might say that she shows, rather than tells. Yet she is also like a sadistic Sleeping Beauty, aggressively waiting for an opportunity to trust someone. On meeting Justine, Dorothy begins to detach from her own defenses, but not from her own pleasures. Her mode of enfleshment stays the same, but she follows the trail of the voice, and she's not sure why.

Justine's response to Dorothy is at first like Dorothy's to her—a desire to tell a hard story to a stranger to whom she feels averse, followed by confusion about that impulse lived as ambivalence toward the person who animates it. Far more impersonal than Dorothy, Justine has a slower emotional metabolism (yet Dorothy is the fat one, Justine the thin), but eventually she returns to Dorothy, sensing that Dorothy knows something that Justine cannot bear to know on her own. This meeting and return frame the book. Meanwhile, the body of the novel narrates the whole life stories of Justine and Dorothy, which they never fully tell each other. We witness them growing up paralyzed by fear and at the same time launching into madnesses of thinking, reading, eating, masturbating, attaching, and fucking. A traumatic frenzy of interiority and impersonality constitutes a scene of being and embodiment that they both control and control not a whit. If she wants a good life, what's a girl, or two girls, to do? When does the doing matter?

This question takes shape generically through the novel's proximity to the case study. Each girl knows she's a case, in many senses—it's no accident that Justine works for a doctor and Dorothy for a law firm. This proximity to the case is repeated aesthetically as well. Until the very end of the novel, each chapter has its own narrative voice, which is to say that it assigns each case its own norm of expertise. Dorothy tells her own story in the first person, while the narrator talks about Justine as "she." Each girl's mode of representation performs her relation to impersonality and self-cultivation, but not in a mimetic way. That is, Dorothy details how protecting her vigilant subjectivity requires strategies of social impersonality, while Justine's narrator tenderly registers the formation of Justine's dissociated intimacies. Yet their distinct lives mesh thematically in a hundred ways too, as though there were a certain generic rhythm to the traumatic tableau: peripatetic nuclear families, miserable fathers and mothers, childhood sexual abuse, never the right tone of voice or body. When the two girls are in their childhood families, they don't notice this that much. Their mothers give them enemas, their fathers overvalue them, whatever: they love whatever they can (mis)recognize as love. Distortion is the shape love takes.

Here is some of the case study content: a doctor friend of Justine's doctor-father repeatedly and painfully masturbates her at the age of five. The awful "clawing" feeling of this event confirms something overwhelming that she already knows without knowing it about the too intense emotional enclosure of her family: it involves them-against-the-world with an intensity of hermeticism that holds her close, but impersonally so. Justine participates in the economy of familial love by being "good": pretty and smart and submissive to parental aggression. At the same time she cultivates school as an alternative public for her badness. At seven, she gets a neighbor friend to tie her up and whip her; at eleven, she and her friends torture a fat and ugly girl with the nickname "Emotional"; at twelve, she rapes a playmate with a toothbrush, masturbating to the memory later (99, 109–11). Later, the playmate asks for more, and Justine refuses her. During high school she develops a secret trashy wardrobe in which she can fit in with the popular girls who are marked by being *knowing*. They produce hierarchies of social value by trafficking in stereotype and mockery; they compete among themselves sexually to have the most "adult" experience.

In short, school is a world in which intimacies are always betrayed. But to Justine its viciousness offers a kind of confirming relief, for the explicit rule of cruelty feels truer to her than the familial amalgam of aggressive intimacy. She enters into adolescent heterosexuality by enacting the ambivalence of this scene repeatedly, but with herself as top and bottom, men being merely the instruments of violent relief from her "goodness." Perhaps her most telling act is to design a plot to lose her virginity violently at home. The scene to which she lures an indifferent boy is the rough floor of the family "rec room," and its purpose is both to enact a fantasy of sexual surrender and to remain interesting to her closest female friend, Watley. The unpleasant hardness of the unfeeling fuck confirms something ruthless in Justine, and yet it marks her vulnerability too. After pretending that the experience was good high drama, she confides in her friend that it wasn't. Watley drops her and uses the story as capital to diminish Justine socially. Vulnerability makes you worthless: survival depends on producing forms of hardened identity and closeting the soft remainders. On realizing that she has been outed as a sexual failure, Justine "walked with her arms around her middle feeling loneliness and humiliation coupled with the sensation that she was, at this moment, absolutely herself" (156). At the moment of that holding thought she is having, perhaps, the best sex of her life.

Dorothy also grows up in a white suburb with an angry father and a passive-aggressive mother, both of whom comment constantly on their daughter, whose value shifts according to the tempestuous parental mood. As a child she loves being at the center of this shifty scene, and yet like Justine she is hypervigilant—she can tell that something is off. "One of my first clear memories is having to deny the concrete truths of my life, of denying the clear pattern of them" (32). In particular, Dorothy shares with Justine a family that is weirdly self-enclosed, and she is likewise split from herself as a result. But Dorothy produces a different kind of split. Usually a "vision of my embattled father with my mother and me standing behind him" animates her. Like superhero partners she and her father "aimed for higher things; we had relinquished beauty and pleasure and turned our faces towards the harsh reality of the fight against cruelty and falsehood" (123).

At the same time, Dorothy begins to cultivate "beautiful and elaborate fantasies" about many things, including men and women whom she finds "unbearably beautiful" (117). She associates her drive for beauty with her mother's drive toward fictionalizing and femininity. Dorothy and her mother spend her youth drawing fantasy pictures together on construction paper in crayon. They tell each other "airy" stories about their visions, and then eat lavish desserts. At first, Dorothy draws countless Heavens "full of grinning winged children, candy bars, cake, ice cream, and toys" (81); then, on hearing her mother read aloud *Peter Pan*, Dorothy turns toward an addiction to Never-Never Land.

> Its very name made me feel a sadness like a big beautiful blanket I could wrap around myself. I tried to believe that Peter Pan might really come one night and fly me away; I was too old to believe this and I knew it, but I forced the bright polka-*dotted* canopy of this belief over my unhappy knowledge. (81) (italics mine)

At ten, Dorothy—nicknamed "Dotty," then—is already practiced at disavowing disquieting knowledge that she barely senses with an optimistic absorption in beauty. But the anomalous style of her attachment both to her unthought thought and its compensations resonates unpleasantly throughout her life. She lets slip to an already sexualized friend that Never-Never Land is her favorite fantasy world, and the friend immediately betrays the immature fantasy, making Dorothy the "queer" pariah at school. When strangers speak to her she becomes "struck dumb by trying too hard to discover the correct response" (115). This result is, in part, a relief, however: it confirms something inchoate about Dorothy's hyperorientation toward her family and the family's toward itself. The alien eyes of her peers force Dorothy to disfigure her family romance and family romance in general. This is played out as her physical withdrawal from the machinery of familial narcissism.

During Dorothy's early adolescence she gets quiet, fat, and disgusting, without knowing why. When I say "disgusting," I am not interpreting. Dorothy characterizes herself as "gross and unhealthy." When she is fifteen, her father abjectly enters her room to tell her that his frustration with the unjust world causes him to act out on her, and in the jumble of love and apology he utters he begins to molest and to rape her. This is no surprise to Dorothy, really: "underneath the fear and shame, underneath the excitement, it seemed that what was happening now between my father and me was only the physical expression of what always happened between us, even when he verbally reviled me. Tears came to my eyes; it seemed that his cruel words had clothed these loving caresses all along" (126).

This cruel love practice lasts for many years. At night, he grunts while she fragments in silence. During the day, he denounces her furiously—because she no longer obeys her mother. Dorothy looks down at her plate and eats. Subsequently, whenever she experiences anxiety, it is as though her organs explode through her body, in ways recognizable from the literature on incest but also, here, resonant as the bodily ground of what Justine calls Dorothy's soft and graceful corpulence. Dorothy says, "[M]ost of the time I felt as if my body had been turned inside out, that I was a walking deformity hung with visible blood-purple organs, lungs, heart, bladder, kidneys, spleen, the full ugliness of a human stripped of its skin" (161).

She comments that "these bodily memories are so unevenly submerged and revealed, so distorted . . . that they may as well be completely invented" (44). This is not to say that the post-traumatic subject is doomed to false or pseudomemory, but that the memory is mediated by fantasies and mis-recognitions so powerful and gratifying in their intensity that one must read them, and oneself, with distrust, even when the affect that binds one to memory feels necessary, an anchor. To create forms for managing the post-traumatic drives requires an acute visceral and intellectual sensorium that monitors at all times, judging and distinguishing, yet gathering up sensations generously. Monitoring is more important than the mastery of knowing. Much of the girls' creativity is sucked up by that patrolling activity, which enables self-deferral as well. But monitoring in itself assures no authenticity: it just keeps the subject close to the scene, the enigmatic representation.

In the language of case study rationality, both girls can be said to know negation as something productive, at once an expression of attachment and a cutting gesture that enables someone, usually the tormenter, to stop feeling overwhelmed. The older men teach the girls the value of the cut, and they spend their teens and twenties reproducing its cruelty wherever and whenever they feel the need to rise above the engulfing world of normal intimacy.[19] Yet the cruel cut is not merely dissociative, anti-intimate; it also binds the girls to optimistic habits of embodiment and attachment.[20] This is to say that the relation between impersonal formalism and the project of unique self-cultivation is all tied up in the novel. Self-protection and risk are indistinguishable here.

From a distance, the girls' nexus of self-abuse and pleasure produces formally antithetical sexualities. Justine loses and finds herself in S/M, while Dorothy practices a kind of distance learning, a mode of monitoring characterized by psychological sadism and sexual idealization.[21] Yet to the extent that these sexualities control the flow of risk and desire, they are formally identical. The girls share other pleasure styles as well, featuring the consumption of food and the production of intense intellection. Each, like sex, is a process of absorption and a way of being in the world, a way of bringing it in, entering it, and averting it. While optimistic, these habituated modes of being are also techniques of self-annihilation and negation, ways of using the episodic relief of particular exchanges in order not, for a minute, to be that ordinary failed person with that history. Even if one risks self-negation through such tendencies, not to be that person is an amazing thing. Strongly ambivalent, then, these three powerful modes of repetition, negation, and optimism are associated with the cultivation of the senses as well: food, thought, and sex are comforting as well as risky and raw-making modes of engagement and exchange.

So in one view these repetitions can be read as establishing a regime of self-continuity that amounts to the constellation called "who I am." At the same time the girls' capacity not to inhabit the case study version of their story ("Hey you!") that marks everything as a continuous symptom of the cultivated self suggests something else: an impulse to interfere with reproducing one's "personality." Their negativity can be read as a *departure from* rather than an *assumption of* a way of being "who they are." For the greater part of this essay I will turn toward this set of pleasures, which, I am arguing, interfere with negating rhythms of self-continuity. Responding to trauma's haunting plenitude not with ascesis but with a formalist abundance, the girls' tactic of counterabsorption marks their will to live otherwise ("Wait up!").

PLEASURE #1: FOOD (FOR THOUGHT)
Separately and together the girls "snack" constantly and "savagely" (15; 37; 81; 93; 241). Their mouths and their eyes consume, in order of appearance: potatoes, "a brown-bagged carton of milk," "rum-flavored marzipan candies, each wrapped in bright red tinfoil bearing a picture of a mysterious brown-haired lady in décolletage, bottled spring water" (12); sweet and sour pork (30); egg rolls (36); cheese curls, diet soda, chocolate cake, cookies, sandwiches, coffee, Gruyère brioche, Mystic Mint cookies (15);

dainty fried snacks (25); "tea . . . lumps of sugar and cream," "boiled dump-ling," (28); "white bags of candy" (44); "cream and eggs" (45); chili, pota-toes, beer, dry roasted peanuts (47); chili over spaghetti noodles, chocolate ice cream, ungnawable jawbreakers (48); cinnamon toast and hot chocolate (52); tuna sandwiches (55); mucusy eggs (56); gum (62); "old tea bags and carrot peels" (66); "blazing Popsicles" (66); Cream of Wheat (74); "apple cores, old potato chip bags" (75); "ice cream and . . . chicken pot pie . . . Almond Joys, Mallomars, Mellomints, and licorice ropes" (76); "cookies . . . gum" (78); eggs (80); "crackers and peanut butter . . . candy bars, cake, ice cream . . . cake and ice cream" (81); "orange and pink candy . . . Sloppy Joes . . . hot chocolate" (84); "cookies and tea" (86); cocoa (87); gum (91); ice cream (93); candy necklaces (94); eggs (98); "alcohol mixed with Coca-Cola" (105); "ice cream and vanilla wafers" (107); "Choco Chunk bars and French fries" (114); "meat . . . potatoes . . . iced tea" (118); sugar (119); "salad . . . scalloped potatoes . . . orange corn curls" (120); "potato chips and beer . . . bite-sized Heath Bars" (123); "pork chops and green beans . . . boxed lemon chiffon pie" (124); "carrots . . . potatoes" (128); "lime sherbet" (130); muffins (137); "gristle . . . milkshake" (141); "coffee with three spoons of sugar" (146); "a box of chocolates, some of which had ladies' faces painted on them" (154); "a chocolate . . . another chocolate" (155); ice cream sand-wiches (160); "a box of donuts and bag of potato chips" (161); "a bag of burgers, fries, and orange drink . . . French toast" (168); "two chocolate donuts wrapped in cellophane" (174); "mushroom fried rice with green peas and lurid red spare ribs" (175); "lumpy potatoes" (177); "cookies and coffee" (179); "salads . . . water" (185); "coffee . . . pizza . . . diet root beer" (193); "take-out salad" (195; 233); "cheese sandwich, potato chips, and candy . . . milkshake and double fries" (205); "lemon meringue pie" (206); "malteds and potato chips, jelly beans and roast beef sandwiches dripping gravy" (211); French toast (214); "can of soup . . . bread" (215); "wonderfully gooey apple pie" (221); "champagne with our omelettes" (225); "hot coffee and a bag of sugars, stirrers, and petroleum milk substitutes" (229); "muffins . . . bag of cookies" (232); "a bag of cashews, a bag of marzipan, and an apple" (234); cookies (238); grilled cheese sandwich (241); misshapen bran muffin (242); "a bag of potato chips and a bag of candy" (244); "a plate of jewel-like sushi and shiny purple seaweed . . . sake" (248); cookies (258); "pastries and puddings" (260); cakes (261); chocolate cake (264); "bags of potato chips and cookies" (272); martinis (281); "little mints and chewy candies" (290); and chamomile tea (309).

Forget the fat and calories: to live for one's snack is to live by the rhythm of one's own impulse for pleasure, as in creating "a paradise of trips to the grocery and take-out dinners" (76). "In this time of anorexic cuties" being a foodie is a way of both being and not being in the world, giving the girls leverage to engage in exchange and to withdraw from sharing anything with just anyone (95). Eating is *their* time. It's their *time*. When either woman travels, she marks time by eating. When she waits, she eats. When she thinks, she eats. She eats before and after sex. In response to the overwhelming feeling of "sickening boundlessness" or endless absorbing interiority, food shapes a space of time for her, an episode of alterity to herself that is nonetheless self-confirming (160). It provides and defeats structure. It creates consciousness (in its guise as pleasure memory) and its opposite (inarticulateness), too.[22] That is to say the girls' relation to eating is a scene, not a symptom: among other things, the practice of eating provides a way to negotiate one's incoherence while not organizing a personality to compensate for it.

Dorothy never feels full when she's on her own. Then, she can eat any spread infinitely. Only when she is absorbed in unoriginal acts—proofreading the law's text on Wall Street each night or transcribing the debates that take place in Granite's inner circle—does she feel something like satiety. To be unoriginal is to gain a reprieve from desire's self-articulating pressure: accordingly, the more intense the desire, the emptier the body feels. To empty out one's emptiness through work is something like negating the negation, at least for a minute, because work is absorbing, like eating. But Dorothy also shows that one cannot help but be original or to desire.

> It was in Ohio that I developed what my mother came to call my "unattractive habits." First, I stopped brushing my teeth, except on rare occasions. All at once, I hated putting the paste-laden brush into my nice warm mouth and scraping the intriguing texture of food from my teeth, annihilating the rich stew of flavors, the culinary history of my day, and replacing it with the vacuous mint-flavored aftertaste, the empty cavern of impersonal ivory. . . . In addition, I began giving in to gross and unhealthy cravings: candy bars, ice cream, cookies, sugar in wet spoonfuls from the bowl, Hershey's syrup drunk in gulps from the can, Reddi Wip [sic] shot down my throat, icing in huge fingerfulls from other people's pieces of cake. (64)

Dorothy shifts between the name-brand particularity of her attachment and the formless inner world of taste that she also creates. Her body is a kitchen in which the things of exchange become *thingness*, sensory knowledge, and material for a countertemporality ("the culinary history of my day") that enables her to "chop up and organize [her] life to lessen the impact of the outside world" (112). The violence of the chopping is accompanied by the pleasures of the result, which she appreciates, with all the pride of an author. "It was never enough," she notes (64). Frequently, she reads when she eats.

In the factory of Dorothy's abundant countersensorium, then, the personal is produced as a formally continuous but constantly mutating scene of gratifying repetition. The subtlety of her incremental attachment to tastes is strictly a form, and at the same time it *feels* like property, her inalienable hoard. But auto-pollution is not just a victory over something: in school and in her family Dorothy is a stray, a "deject," an outsider. It is not enough to say she embraces her negativity, because she doesn't.[23] The pain of unassimilability is unbearable while also remediated through the modes of self-care I have been describing. Eating cuts a swath in the anhedonia she experiences in the normal world by liberating her from the time and space of her sociability, where she is only inadequate. Devouring and its plangent aftereffects engender a lateral, endless present.

Collaborating with her body makes it a gift that keeps giving. But it gives only to her, meanwhile confirming its social negation with bodily grossness. That the two negatives of solipsism and hideousness do not make a positive here means that the rhythm of this process sets up an alternative way for self-interruption to make something of negation. Dorothy's misery and her social abjection seal her off from the shame of wanting to be normal after all. Yet her will-to-absorption in self-dissipation is a drive toward self-annihilation that seeks, at the same time, to be topped by its optimism for pleasure. She associates the annihilated version of herself with the subjected, abjected, and therefore impersonal one; her grandiosity produces something else, a creative force that thrives as long her enfleshment separates out into flavors, tastes, and smells.

Justine lives according to a similar scale of culinary plenitude, but its place in her sexual economy takes on a quite different shape, one involving cultivated objectification, rather than the subjective spreading we see in Dorothy's case. In one moment the world of Justine, "alone under the covers with her own smells, her fingers at her wet crotch, was now the world of the mall filled with fat, ugly people walking around eating and staring" (93). To have sexuality even in private is to be exposed to her own hypercritical gaze. An object of her own disgust exposed as *having had* appetites, Justine further degrades her desire because of its banality: after all, in the mall as in mas-turbation she seeks to stimulate desire while minimizing surprise.

Yet when Justine actually eats rather than fantasizes about it, the world seems manageable and pleasant: "When Justine left work she bought a bag of cookies and rode home on the subway eating them with queenly elation" (22). Justine's pleasure at public eating envelops her in a protective bubble; eating in public is better even than masturbating, because the outside is an anonymous space that enables episodic abandonment of what's been hurt in her. While Dorothy's saturation by the taste of her uniqueness constitutes a kind of homeopathic aggression at her stereotypically enfleshed iden-tity, Justine's mode of survival involves generating a pleasure in the world-situated gesture and its repetition rather than in any sensual or visual perfor-mance of counterauthenticity. When it works, each girl is relieved of herself in the act of taking in what she can bear to have of what she wants. The pro-cessual nature of Dorothy's sensual ingestion paradoxically enables her to shape the external body as a bad object while the sensual intellectual zone allows infinitely hoarded internal self-elaboration. In contrast, for Justine eating is a formalist strategy of impersonality, of time- and space-making, whether or not it appears "really" to be "her" creativity. They share a formal-ism of the invented gesture, organized for survival: what differs between them are the ways their compulsion to eat negotiates the economy of the personal and the impersonal.

It would be too grand to call any of these moments of food exchange "agency" in any transformative or transcendent sense. In *Two Girls, Fat and Thin* any individual's sustained emancipation from the hurt of history is un-imaginable. History is what hurts because that which repeats in conscious-ness, that which gives the pleasure at least of self-continuity, is what the subject deems her history. She is what she continues to have been. Trau-matically identified people in this sense can take a technical pleasure in their histories, insofar as their histories are what they have, their personal property. But to say this is not to say that the history that hurts is destiny, a gothic repetition. Optimistic compulsion in *Two Girls, Fat and Thin* produces a countertemporality that provides not narrative continuity but something more like the deep red areas on an infrared image. It involves attempts to experience moments of negative density.[24] Inhabiting such dense moments of sensuality stops time, makes time, and saturates the lived, imagined, and not-yet-imagined world. The impossible act the girls seek to repeat, for which food and eating serve as substitutes, merges will and repetition to produce something not uncomplicated or amnesiac, but something that as yet has no content, just inclination. What they achieve is not nothing; nor is it readable. Paying attention to what's absorbing marks a direction for the will to take. At one point Justine thinks, "The hell of it was, the fat woman was obviously very tough in some way" (195), then, "a man in an Armani suit . . . wildly waved a broken bottle and yelled 'I love you! I love you! I want to eat your shit and drink your piss!'" (196).

PLEASURE #2: (HISTORY IS WHAT) SMARTS

I have suggested that, for the girls, eating is a technique for pulling the world in and pushing it away according to their own terms and sense of pacing. It is neither an act of conscious intentional agency nor a manifestation of unconscious symptoms in any objective sense, although the narrative center of the novel, which tells the girls' stories one episode at a time, does use eating to establish the girls' way of participating in ordinary life. Yet along with making sense of their lives in the usual way, the novel shows another mode of organizing knowledge about persons. Technically it provides a sense that pleasure—a reiteration that makes a form, not necessarily something that feels good—also captures a way of being a *something* unbound to an identity that circulates or that can be tracked to personality. Christopher Bollas calls this the "unthought known," and argues that knowledge forms before it is experienced idiomatically, in terms of the subject's own patterning.[25] This suggests another way that traumatic repetition might generate knowledge beyond itself despite the manifestation of repetition as a kind of paralysis. The pedagogy of repetition involves a shift in the relation of content (the scene to which one returns) to form (the pacing and placement of one's attachment).

In *Caravaggio's Secrets*, Leo Bersani and Ulysse Dutoit describe the intricate relation between desire and form as the enigma of sexuality itself.[26] The enigmatic quality that allures derives from the sense that one's attachments are at best only symbolized in their objects, and that the objects are so charged by our regard for them that they remain enigmatic to us at the same time as they are never fully known. Bersani and Dutoit focus on the ways that sexual attachment is constituted by the risk of becoming open to the scene of unpredictable change that the misrecognition involved in erotic attachment brings. In their view, *jouissance* is a counter-traumatic shapelessness that shatters the ego, pleasing the subject's desire to be overwhelmed while marking a limit to what it can know. Nonetheless, attachment taps into a desire not-to-know as well, an aversion that has many simultaneous functions; preserving the object's enigmatic quality protects one from becoming bored with, alienated from, or overwhelmed by the object. At the same time the seriality of repetition protects the subject from experiencing the unbearable pull of her own ambivalence toward what she has attached to. In the world of *Two Girls, Fat and Thin*, this is why it is safer to open oneself up to reiterated forms than to persons or fetishes. The reliable rhythm of the girls' impulse to eat neutralizes the pressure of the pleasure motives it serves: eating is a way of admitting desire without having to "know" that its sensual enactment stands for anything but itself. It is an attachment to a process, not an object, with diverging implications for each of the girls. In both cases, though, having a masticating habit does not amount to an attempt to become null, numb, or stupid. *These girls are sharp cookies.* Here as everywhere in this novel, the visceral quality of attachment to a practice inevitably involves a kind of acute awareness as well.

The intellectual referent of the word "smart" derives from its root in physical pain. Smartness is what hurts, or to say that something smarts is to say that it hurts—it's sharp, it stings, and it's ruthless. It is as though to be smart is to pose a threat of impending acuteness (L. *acutus*—sharp). In this sense smartness is the opposite of eating, which foregrounds the pleasure of self-absorption, not its sting. In *Two Girls, Fat and Thin*, the fear of and attachment to that sting have multiple functions. As defense: hypervigilance enables pleasure in judging and explaining, including explaining away one's own contradictions; and it aims to ward off traumatic surprise. As libidinal drive: its constant activity works as well to find scenes for controlled acting out. For like eating, monitoring appears to control the shape and pacing of exchange. Hyperactively speaking, therefore, the counter-traumatic functions of smartness are almost indistinguishable from its traumatic effects. Mediated to people as a zone of personal perception and will, smartness can just as easily be seen as the site for grandiosity and dissimulation.

Both girls' hypervigilant minds munch the storied scenery of memory by reoccupying it optimistically with ideas. In itself, a new idea does not reeducate the mind, erasing or sublimating its knowledge. Rather, it interrupts the present and organizes the opportunity to identify with *pursuit*, with the raw energy of desire. As children they read with the voracious need to inhabit parallel worlds that operate, as Justine says, according to better rules. In this sense even the aesthetic is an instrument for providing a better idea than the one that governs actual living: all novels are utopian, by definition.

Definitism too appears to be an intellectual source for self-emancipatory optimism, but likewise, in the end, its content is irrelevant. For the girls, the pursuit of the ideal form is the pursuit of alterity. Risk, transformation, denegation, and beyond: a yet unenumerated possible destiny. Perhaps this is why Justine can only bear to get "ideas at the rate of about one a year" (18); it is still more risky to interfere with the reproduction of the life you know than to follow an instinct toward something unknown.

Intellection thus appears in the novel as content—philosophy and plot—on the one hand and as a hunger for a form of freedom on the other. The emancipatory form does not require a particular content but instead the capacity to be both surprised and confirmed by an attachment of which one knows little. For both girls the word for this unthought form is "beauty," in its spectacularly alien capacity to absorb a person, to take her out of her old way of being whether or not she finds a place elsewhere. The most thematic but not least dramatic instance of this double movement is in Dorothy's encounter with Anna Granite. Dorothy explains: "She showed me that human beings can live in strength and honor. And that sex is actually part of that strength and honor, not oppositional to it. And she was the first writer to do that, ever. To show that sex is not only loving but empowering and enlarging. Not only for men but for women. As you can imagine, this was a big revelation to me. And then the rest was just . . . the sheer beauty of her ideas" (27).

In this domain of Definitist thought, thinking and sex are modes of power that women and men wield with equal force. The couplet "thinking and sex" constitutes a utopianism whose violence and rage is embraced right up front as central to attachment and intimacy: Granite elicits a "muted snarl of urgency and need" from her followers (12).

Dorothy and Justine both see that Granite's followers are as likely to be nerds and strays as they are to be authoritarian masters. The rhetoric of greatness Granite speaks, for example, seems to be experienced by many of her followers as a kind of soft Nietzscheanism that rejects the emasculating proprieties of normative middle-class order. Dorothy's embrace of Definitism strikes a similar, but not identical, chord. She attaches to a vision of sexual emancipation that is far more iconoclastic and risky, embodying a will of intelligence beyond intention and rationality, a will afraid of nothing, neither death nor, what's scarier, living. What she calls the "beauty" of this possibility makes her weep with anger and gratitude. For Definitism is the first philosophy of living that accommodates the range of Dorothy's responses to the world—her softness (desire for intimacy) and her hardness (rage and intelligence). Only in this domain are they continuous attitudes and positive values rather than evidence of monstrous vulnerability that requires hiding. For Dorothy, to develop a self that can exist powerfully, not in compensation for abject objective powerlessness but in affirmation of her power, is to denegate the aspersions of her family, her father, and the taxonomizing cruelty of the normal world. Then again Dorothy is not actually transformed by Definitism. The beautiful idea turns out not to transform the girl's intuitions about navigating the world. When we meet Dorothy, she has regressed to her adolescent bubble of sadistic thought and culinary self-consolation. What, then, is the value of the ideational event?

That's the beauty of it. On an impulse, Dorothy decides to leave college to join the Definitist movement. "I could allow [Granite] to penetrate the tiny but vibrant internal Never-Never Land I'd lived in when there was no other place for me," she thinks, sensing that "the intimacy and understanding that I fantasized was such that it would rip my skin off" (167). To do that, though, she has to imagine that Granite will make that space beautiful, as she makes all others. "Beauty is part of what makes life livable" (133), Dorothy says, especially "strong, contemptuous beauty indifferent to anything but itself and its own growth" (132). Granite legitimates Dorothy's ruthlessness as a form not of monstrosity but beauty—in the abstract. Alas, when they meet, the girl struggles, feeling "my disappointment a dark wave under my need to worship" (169), for here was Granite "looking like a middle-aged house-wife in a Chanel dress. No, no, she didn't look like that. I don't want that recorded. . . . She had beautiful lids and eyes," a "beautiful black cape," a "beautiful tan" (28–29). "Then the light caught the necklace she wore, the deep blue hunks of precious stone that encircled her, and in a flash, I saw her haloed by the brilliant wattage of blue, the air about her ululating with an iridescent current of energy. . . . My fantasy mightily puffed out its sails" (170). As was the case in her fantasy of Peter Pan, Dorothy here cannot bear to be disappointed (again); her desire for the beautiful idea to saturate both the abstract and concrete zones of survival compels her to project beauty onto the smallest screen. The novel makes clear that Definitism requires such a commitment to misrecognizing impossibility as the beautiful: evaluating Bernard, another follower, Justine notes that "he arranged his perception into fantasies of beauty and strength, glory and striving, fantasies he nursed deep within himself. . . . Through this armor his deformed sensitivity strained to find the thundering abstracts of beauty and heroism that consoled it" (177). This is the compulsion to repeat optimism. Later, encountering Justine, Dorothy repeats this testing pattern. Paragraph by paragraph she judges her friend's physical, psychological, and intellectual adequacy to the beautiful idea and its transformative promise.

At the same time that she meets Granite, Dorothy renames herself. "Dotty Footie" becomes "Dorothy Never," a fantasy pseudonym borrowed from *Peter Pan*, a renaming that negates her family, marks her historical anonymity, and stakes out her attachment to a transformational harmony of desire and will through the idea. Granite asks Dorothy to tell the story of her life and then hires her to be a secretary and a scribe for the conversations held in the circle of philosophers that Granite convenes. Dorothy's job is not to comprehend the beautiful ideas that whirl around her, but to take them down as dictation—as sound, not as meaning.

> The experience was so charged, so heady that I lived those days in my head, my breath high and quivering on the pinnacle of my deserted body. . . . After the first hours had passed, my frayed perception forked into two—one navigating the landscape of words, phrases, and ideas, the other absorbing the sounds, inflections, and tonal habits of the voices. This secondary perception transmuted words and phrases into sounds that took on shapes of gentleness, aggression, hardness, softness, pride, and happiness, shapes that moved through the room, changing and reacting to one another, swelling and shrinking, nosing against the furniture, filling the apartment with their mobile, invisible, contradicting vibrancy, then fading away. (203, 209)

"Fortunately I went emotionally blank," Dorothy recalls (207), appreciating her post-traumatic capacity to dissociate in order not to interfere with the soundtrack she absorbs uncomprehendingly. This absorption marks another entry into the archive of beautiful forms she has amassed. And not surprisingly this time, as the sound fills her body she no longer needs its protective cover of fat, and she loses piles of weight. It is as though the sound substitutes for food, and as though the rhythmic pleasure of talk sublimates the solitary pleasure of eating. "All loneliness is a pinnacle," Granite pronounces (163). It is not loneliness as abandonment but as the impersonality of intellectual intimacy that frees Dorothy from the compensatory body she had developed as ballast against annihilation. Fat, the congealed form of history that hurts: as though it were indeed true that "the body remembers everything," the loss of fat reveals a new Dorothy. She begins to shop, to cultivate her now striking looks, and to fall in love with a musculature she hasn't seen since she was fifteen and struggling. She also begins to have sexual feeling.

Characteristically, smartness for Justine provides a scene of optimism and absorption much like Dorothy's, but for Justine smartness is far less personalized and embodied, less oriented toward savior-heroes in their magnificent iconicity. Instead, to identify with intellectual absorption is to develop an internal aesthetic that serves as an index for the feeling she can imagine having in a better life. That is, smartness is not utopian in the productive sense, but marks a yet unacknowledged affective tilting toward which she directs herself. Arguing for "the beauty of loneliness" and "the intrinsic value of beauty in writing," she does not make the connection explicit, and yet the isolation of writing constitutes for her a space of grandiosity without violence, a space of possibility (175, 235). "Stark" beauty is her chosen mode of public impersonality; through writing she passes as normal by withholding her perversity. No one can see and therefore touch her plenitude, and the hell of abandonment to herself is thereby safeguarded from further trauma.

Face to face, Dorothy experiences Justine as retiring and dutiful, marked by "methodical reserve," and otherwise "insubstantial" and tentatively alive (27–29, 12). But in her head, Justine is otherwise: gloriously judgmental like Dorothy, just less dramatic and vocal about it. She believes in her judgments, her pity, her contempt, her aversion, her ambivalence, and on the rare occasions when she has it, her approval. It is difficult to inhabit this grandiosity in public, though, and in this sense she and Dorothy are grotesque inversions of each other, each producing an impersonal body for the deterrence of others through strategies of hyperbole and litotes, hyper- and hyporepresentation. But the impersonality of the socialized flesh does not suggest that anyone's true personhood lies beneath, or is awaiting a safe space, or repair. Their bodily practices condition them for taking on the risk of *knowing* everything they can, without being anchored in a particular story that reduces subjectivity to the sum of biography. Embodied impersonality provides for the girls the time and space to judge freely, angrily, and bemusedly: to seek the experience of big feeling and the protection from exposure. Impersonalizing bodies facilitate escape from the very monitoring intelligence that the girls also cherish.

In this regard their overvaluation of the idea is akin to the pleasure of critical negation. The idea enables the girls to hold themselves, to embrace their own bodies at the pinnacle of their greatest humiliations. Their embodied cloaks of loneliness protect a cherished sense of bitter superiority and abjection. But, more cherished than the relation between contemptuous defensive knowledge and the libidinal stimulation of intellectual comfort are these forms of distance—of interference with the rhythm of the post-traumatic shuttle—that they have developed with an instinct toward surviving. The differences between them matter here, as content more than as form: Dorothy cultivates the idea as though it were an actual world *for her*, while Justine experiences in the alterity of thought a relief from the too intimate alterity of the world she lives in. For both girls, though, being mental provides almost a rhythmic relief from being reactive that protects what they know (without knowing it) about the possibility of a better or less bad relation to enfleshment, epistemology, fantasy, and intimacy.

It is with such strategies in mind, no doubt, that Adam Phillips titles his essay on intellectual subjectivity, "On Composure."[27] Phillips wants to understand why some people come to identify with their minds—not the mind as the true self but as an appendage that does things that can be trained and cultivated for the self's benefit: the image of a judge watching him/herself judge, for example, and taking pleasure as though the judging organ were elsewhere. Phillips argues that children with unstable caretaking environments will sometimes turn to the mind as the better mother. It holds you, it maps the world for you, and perhaps most important, it produces a space of composure between you and the world, so that you amount to more than a reactive impulse ("Hey, you!"). The space of time that composure produces enables you to set the scene of your entrance and makes the world come to you when you want it ("My close-up, Mr. DeMille") to some degree or another.

A number of consequences can be distilled from this structure. Phillips argues that the precociously mind-oriented child (read "intellectual") enters the world with "diffuse resentment," a certain self-confirming and sadistic thrill at the scene of optimism and disappointment.[28] Why is this, though? In part, disappointment can be channeled as though it were a judgment rather than a feeling, supporting the mytheme that the solitary and independent life of the brain precedes and is superior to the simple attachments of intimate proximity. On the other hand, no one experiences abandonment as a pleasure that simply feels good. Dorothy: "I clawed backward into the past and found no comfort in anything there unless 'comfort' could be had in the excruciating site of brute, ignorant love, cowed and trapped, exposed by the wildly panning camera of my memory" (162).

My argument so far has been that this recognition precisely brings the comfort or pleasure of recognition itself, but that this cannot be confused, say, with being known, or with happiness. Interrupting the ongoing logic of things, the mind enables alternative means and scenes of self-production without ever necessarily cultivating them. It is a camera that pans where it must but also where you will it—not that the will is smarter or more creative than the unconscious (far from it!). Cognition follows the affects. Usually, as Dorothy notes, there is "an awful thematic sameness under the deceptive novelty of the experience" (160). As composure approaches the posture of impersonality, it protects the subject's sensorial capacity to impoverish threatening objects while animating new ones and, more importantly, animates animation itself, spurring new processes of *paying attention*.[29] At least this is the counter-traumatic structure of mindfulness in *Two Girls, Fat and Thin*.

Psychoanalysis always raises anxieties for critics about its tendency to universalize individuality and normalize conventions of, say, individuation and autonomy as ideals of health that should be cultivated and always intelligible. Working between Winnicott and Lacan, Phillips articulates a different view, disidentifying health with the appearance of successful anything. Thinking about the form of the subject as related to his or her capacity to be composed, Phillips rethinks Freudian disease categories, pointing out that the pervert plays with his composure, the hysteric with composure's absence, and so on. In other words, the idea of composure tells us that the symptom lies. When the pervert gives form to perversion, this is his or her performance of composure, a private way of keeping the world at bay until he or she is ready. What looks like an absence of composure might well constitute its presence at the level of form, not representation. The subject who identifies with thought might be able to disavow her or his dependency and disappointment through the appearance of composure, and she or he can act as an autonomous author of the salient terms of accountability, judgment, and value with which she or he and the world shall be measured. Or, disappointed in the world's unhomeliness, the subject might experience the contingency of autonomy in a way that either impoverishes or overvalues the boundaries made by intellectual will. Composure then might feel desperate, like the drag of melancholy or the push of mania. Or, perhaps the subject absorbs unhomeliness as a just desert for being unlovable. Composure then might be experienced not as a condition of action but of dark affectlessness or simple neutrality. One cannot predict how and when—with intellection as the guardian of the bruised and disappointed self—someone will move toward any number of possible identifications. Composure is the formalist protector of fantasy, the subject's medium for misrecognizing what it takes to make some sense.

PLEASURE #3: SEX

Sex threatens composure, but offers a holding environment too. We have seen that, throughout the novel, all forms—all patterns or scenes of projection that can be misrecognized as objects-with-qualities—are managerial habits that orchestrate the subject's affective cadence while minimizing her or his risk of unwanted exposure or discomposure. A complex relation of fantasy to self-understanding ensues: what counts as discomposure might be a conventional style of instability rather than an instability that actually threatens the subject's core patterning—and therefore constitute a form of composure that takes on an antithetical style. One can never tell out of context, or maybe ever. Sex foregrounds the convolutions of this unthought known starkly. Even though I wish to remain myself, I may want also to experience the discomposure of intimate relationality, yet want only the discomposure I can imagine, plus a little of the right kind extra, and how can I bear the risk of experiencing the anything that might be beyond? How can I bear not seeking it? What's the relation between the contingency I'm used to, the kind I seek in relation, and the unbearable kind, since the pressures of proximity to the unbearable might be the motive for my attachment-seeking in the first place? These questions of the seeming and being of exposure and instability are central to the erotics of, the attachments and aversions to, the scene of sex in practice. Both confirming and interfering with patterns of self-intelligibility, sex's threat is objectively indistinguishable from its capacity to confirm. How do you know whether a change is the kind of change that involves a welcome loss of sovereignty? When is confirmation of a (conscious or unconscious) expectation the same thing as an assuring feeling of recognition and when is it merely formal, a "this is me"?

A sex event technically interferes with ordinary being, the kind that is usually not having sex, that spends time mostly not risking very much for the pleasure of a momentarily different body/mind relation. Tellingly, when the girls imbue ordinary acts of eating and thinking with qualities like "queenly elation," they are valuing the sense of mental uniqueness that they are able to project into the acts, which remain ordinary even as they open up to the extraordinary. It may look ordinary to eat a cookie or to be fat, but mentally an infinite domain of optimism opens up directed toward an enigmatic somewhere. In contrast, what the girls value most about sex is its unoriginality. The more mental work involved, the more dangerous it is.

For instance, orgasm seems to make you shatteringly different than your ego was a minute ago, but in another minute you are likely to be doing something utterly usual, like pissing, whispering, looking away, or walking into the kitchen and opening the refrigerator door. Is it not possible that the very unoriginality of the sexual experience, its banality, can also make it worth cherishing? This is not a rhetorical question but one that argues methodologically against the transparency of bodily response. Shattering is not always shattering, just as shame is only one way of coding sexual aversion; sentimentality, say, might be a much bigger threat to someone's defenses than any sexual event is, *pace* normative ideology.[30]

When people consent to inhabiting the potential for change that sexual events require, they are mainly consenting to enter a space whose potentially surprising consequences are kept to a minimum. The only requirement is that sexual subjects be able to manage any anxiety emerging from their failure—always possible—to be the *something* that they need or want to be. Such instability can have its comforts, nonetheless, if the subject can successfully control the degree of unwanted uniqueness engendered in the event. Bound optimistically to the impersonality of sex, she or he does not have to take personally *its* failure or *her* or *his* failure to do everything it is meant to do, in whatever context. So when Justine makes "what she hoped were attractive moaning noises" as a lover undresses her (149) and Dorothy describes "the mystery of masculine tenderness that enveloped me like the wings of a swan" (222), the girls perform rhetorically the comforting conventionality of sexual mimesis and the freeing impersonality of sexual sociability in general. There are phrases about sex that one can say; there are sounds that one can make; there are things one does and one doesn't do; there is what one can imagine. When one occupies the domain of those desires one is using fantasy norms to shape what feeling sexual is, in advance. Sex events might be expressive of one's true feelings or not, and they might be exciting, overwhelming, painful, or boring. One can never be sure, though, whether one will be confirmed or threatened either by the negativity or positivity that one attaches to the event. The struggle to master the implications of the impersonality of sex is central to the novel, at least, if not to living: for the girls in particular, I have suggested, this is a fundamentally empirical aesthetic question, a question of training the senses for building possible and beautiful worlds from within impossible ones.

Sex is the culminating counter-traumatic pleasure of *Two Girls, Fat and Thin*, then, because, when it's relational, its challenge to the girls' composure is the greatest, even greater than the adrenaline rush that comes from a good thought or piece of cake. Adrenaline is the addictive booty in this novel: its experience always involves tapping into one's creativity, even if the scene of stimulation repeats the most unpleasant or disappointing urges of need and desire. An idea, a possibility, takes over the girls. Suddenly as though they are all nerve endings, they turn and return toward mania, compelled to be compelled to repeat. "Justine was morbidly attracted to obsessions" (21); Dorothy attaches to scenarios with "wildest invention . . . growing more and more excited" (17). Romance narrative and violent sex are twins here the ways the girls, fat and thin, are also nominally twins. These genres of the viscera use heightened adrenaline (from longing and fear) to play out a threat to the subject's attachment to formalism itself.

All genres produce drama from their moments of potential failure. (What, the romance might not pan out, or its failure might not affirm the beauty of the elusive ideal? The hero might not survive, or the rule of law that his survival affirms might not be affirmed by his death?) Just as thinking and eating turn out to be ways of managing formally the risk of sociability, sex works dynamically in this novel. It wears its ordinary dress as the site in which the subject's structuring drama is repeated; it functions as a site of metacommentary about traumatic repetition; and it points to what it takes not to negate it but to break the stride of ordinary being's will to reproduce itself, its patterns.

I have described the girls' attachment to reading as a space for detaching from the normative world while cultivating a parallel sensorium from it. By the time they become readers both girls are hot for the dual historical functions of romance: as the site of grandiose alternative worlds and of recognizable intimate intensities. We cannot underestimate the gendered divisions that subject the girls to the thought that love plots, intellectual and sexual, will emancipate them from the deadening space of their own worlds. They read about suffering in Victorian literature, absorbed by its dramas of subordination. Further, like many middle-class American girls during the 1960s, they read Anne Frank's *Diary* and other Nazi and survivor tales from World War II, savoring and expanding these images of adolescent girl heroism.

This pedagogy of feminine suffering teaches many things. The girls learn to savor the story of bodily submission. They cultivate all sorts of scenes that repeat this submission and interfere with it too, by living the full range of their sensuality more fully as intellectuals than they do as social persons. As adolescents and adults, they read everything as romance, amalgamating the big passion of utopianism and the big passion of heterosexual lust. Even though one girl looks normal and the other grotesque from the perspective of white, middle-class suburban femininity, these forms of survival render the public body more impersonal to them than the mental body is. They end up in New York City, where the relief and pain of that impersonality is a fact of life. Thereby the power of the idea merges into sexuality.

One would think that Anna Granite's ideology of conscienceless power might not appeal to girls so femininely trained and so post-traumatic. But, and crucially, Anna Granite disseminates her ideology through romance novels. In effect, she turns all readers into adolescent girls. A utopia of the ruthless drives uses the genre of the ruthless drives: how to tell them apart? Which is the tenor and which the vehicle? Granite's novels, *The Bulwark*, *The Last Woman Alive*, and *The Gods Disdained*, are repeatedly characterized as trashy and preachy pornography. They are all about "the struggle of a few isolated, superior people to ward off the attacks of the mean-spirited majority as they created all the beautiful important things in the world while having incredible sex with each other" (163). This clearly ironic sentence is not ironic to Dorothy. Reading that the beautiful (fictional) Solitaire D'Anconti experiences trauma that forces "the hot anger of her pain into the icy steel of her intellect" makes Dorothy feel "possible," like a beautiful person whose social banishment is not fitting but the effect of a vicious and mendacious world (163–64). That Granite's plots feature women who submit and men who benefit from that submission is not supposed to be interesting. Indeed, Dorothy scorns Justine for suggesting as much, arguing that the power to submit without fear of loss is the pinnacle of anyone's individuality—if they can bear the beauty of it. We have seen that Dorothy cannot bear the ugliness of it when Granite turns out to be, after all, a bad practitioner of her theory. When turned down sexually by a younger man, Granite banishes him publicly from the cadre, wrecking the ideals for which Dorothy needs her idol to stand. Granite's belief in the ruthlessness of desire turns out to mean mainly her desire and not everyone's. To Dorothy, this threatens to make Granite's philosophy merely an individual's sexual alibi, not a way to retool the world for emancipated sexual personhood.

What would emancipated sexual personhood look like if she did encounter it? A cultivated individuality that merges inner ruthlessness with the beautiful form of desire in practice feels liberating to Dorothy in her intellectually organized affects. When she experiences it, however, the rhetorical archive for this fantasy is a romance novel, a vehicle central to the reproduction of feminine ideology in the first place. In *Two Girls, Fat and Thin*, the one relation involving sex that Dorothy seeks is with Knight Ludlow, "a wealthy New York financier" and colleague of Granite's. Engaged to someone else, Ludlow looks at Dorothy in a way so thrilling that her life changes overnight. She moves from her shabby apartment to a nice one, from shapeless clothes to shaped ones, and from exorbitant fat-eating to moderation. As they move toward becoming lovers, the language of her chapters takes up the song of romance: sparks fly and "streams of colored light" sway between them (218). "The ricocheting chatter in my mind became inaudible, the zipping comets of quasi thought slowed to melting putty. Rivulets of liquid gold, swollen with nodules of heat, spanned my limbs. A glimmering flower of blood and fire bloomed between my legs, its petals spanned my thighs" (222).

This ratcheted-up rhetorical blast crashes the moment Ludlow moves toward Dorothy's vagina. She turns to ice and then dissolves in tears. As she does this, her traumatic story leaks out, but this enhances their romance. Ludlow holds her, tells her his hard stories, and they sleep together for days until they make love happily. At this point the language of the soft and warm, flowering vagina reblossoms. Afterward they eat a big champagne breakfast, and he leaves to rejoin his fiancée. Dorothy is happy: she has been idealized. That's the end of sex for her. The memory stays perfect, before it fades.

Justine's history of painful sex takes on much the same trajectory as Dorothy's romantic one. "This memory [of sexual violence], with its ugly eroticism, was not in the least arousing; however she recognized something compelling in it, a compulsion akin to that of a starving lab animal which will keep pressing the button that once supplied it with food, even though the button now jolts its poor small body with increasing doses of electric shock" (235–36). The story of the starving lab animal suggests the bare relevance of content to what drives a being toward what negates it: the unbearable experience of being stuck in a way of being in life in the face of unlimited need is also the experience of competence at a certain form of living. The "poor small body" wants food, gets shocked, and is compelled to return to the place of pain by the possibility that shock will convert to food. Or, the small animal is compelled to return because returning is what it knows how to do. All the creature might know and know how to do is reduced to that one habit. The smarting beast is not using his smarts: knowledge is useless. It is compelled to create a form of living through repetitions that do not gratify it. But they do gratify it too, in the sense that this is a scene it recognizes. Recognizing oneself when one has survived shock provides a foundation for a mode of survival that is more than just a failure to die.

Heterosexual conventionality is, indeed, a painful maze for Justine—given her history, a perverse desire. Like loneliness, s/m performs for her the unnaturalness of normal intimacy by eroticizing form and boundary. It takes up the aspects of grandiose suffering she already associates with love and rescue plots. Her femininity is all tied up with training in the excellence of survival against the odds, the uninevitability of happiness, the pain of bodily pleasure. In this sense sexual trauma only slightly exacerbates ordinary sexuality. Thus on the one hand, it is not surprising that she turns toward a formalist mode of sex that foregrounds and replays the unfailing merger of violence and pleasure. On the other, and like Dorothy, when Justine meets Bryan, an artist and an advertising man who accosts her in a bar, the defensive impersonal version of Justine's social self develops a softer, more feminine persona than either the reader or she has seen. Bryan immediately gets Justine's persona as the gamine/terrorizer she has been. She responds to his percipience by recounting to him a sexually violent experience with a lover who "penetrated" and "opened" her up in a way that she could neither control nor wanted to control.[31] He takes her up on the promise of that story, frightening her with an image of "people being tied up and beaten, women getting fucked by dozens of guys" (201); they proceed to a whirl of soft romance and hard sex. Their relation feels normal, reciprocal—confusing. Bryan's surprising penetration discomposes the intellectual in Justine, shredding the "cloak" of loneliness that has protected her as well as emotionally repeating the surprise of intense childhood sexualization (173). It gives her pleasure to return to this complex tableau, although her narrator makes it clear that she still shifts positions constantly to get the responses from him she wants. But that Bryan knows how to be human in the context of heterosexual and s/m formalism opens Justine up to new and destabilizing practices.

What's stunning therefore is that each woman gets exactly what she wants out of consensual sex. She gets to be other than her default pattern. She gets to be impersonal by virtue of the imitative quality of the sex, its conventionality or formalism. At the same time she can identify with that impersonality and see it as an opening up of something that may or may not lead to something else. Finally, each girl gets to experience a simple feeling with another person. For Dorothy, this is a scene in which she can socially experience ownership of unimpeded "beautiful" femininity, while for Justine this is a scene in which vulnerability and defense recombine into a personality that can be recognized and desired. In other words, these enacted desires for simplicity, flow, and normalcy, in short, perversely allow into fantasy a certain conventional feminine rhetoric and sensorium, that from which they had been barred by their specific histories. Yet none of this is explicit or self-conscious: it is also as though small experiments with potential breaks from cruel optimism require the kind of unconsciousness and affective handoff we saw in this book's previous discussions of intuition and lateral agency.

The end of the novel suggests as much. Meeting Justine reclaims for Dorothy the desire for belonging that she once associated with Definitism. The energy released by these memories now attaches to Justine, not to the memories. This is why Dorothy sees their relation as "mind-boggling" (17): Justine becomes her newest object, her next opportunity to idealize and to become idealized by another human. Sex seems to interfere with idealization, but sex is only one route to love. As the novel closes, Bryan has just whipped Justine. At first, this is at her direction, but then it escalates beyond her consent (310). Meanwhile, Dorothy is acting violent and crazy in public, sputtering curses and wild accusations aloud on the New York City subway while reading Justine's article on Anna Granite in *Urban Vision*. Dorothy feels both accurately depicted and "raped" by the article. She marches up to Justine's apartment furiously and enters the room enraged. But seeing the scrawny, naked Justine tied to her bed all wounded, scarred, and fatigued, Dorothy takes up like a super hero, beating Bryan up and ejecting him from the room naked. Justine and Dorothy talk a little, but, exhausted by this show of violence and release, Justine falls asleep in Dorothy's arms. This is not a lesbian ending, exactly, since exhaustion is neither sex, love, nor object choice. It is not an orientation toward anything. On the other hand, this mutual fall into bed is not nothing. It's something else.

CODA: *Melodrama, after Trauma*

This is what we come to: the exhaustion of a repetition, and an impasse. What does it mean to turn an exhausted something into something other than itself, or anything? A lesson learned?

It may be that any commentary on their animated suspension at the close violates the spirit of the final scene, to the degree that the image of the two women hovers there as what it is. They need no longer to monitor. They no longer shuttle between the traumatic and the critical. It is our task to catch up to them, to find out what happened: wait up! Were we to take on the tactic that sustained them throughout their struggles, we would return to their desire for utopian beauty, for absorption in new attunements to the emancipating image or sound. We would have no choice but to be gratified that, finally, these two hypervigilant minds have come to rest in their bodies without being dead or crazy. It may be that the beauty of encountering these bodies in proximity requires the risk of acknowledging, even coveting, the possibility of a restful simplicity. How different is this scene, after all, from the end of *Pattern Recognition*, with its lovers drifting in bed? It's only simple in the moment, but not simple at all, given what has come before.

This beauty is born of a simple violence, too. Literally iconoclastic, it has beaten up on the heteroimago that has for so long provided the content for their girlish fantasy. Now the girls are literally beyond biography. Not only that, but the door has been closed on a boy. A newly sensible scene for attachment prevails. At least it amounts to a less bad world for anomalous women and sexuality, if not for sex. Perhaps it also sets forth a new lexicon for memory, and those lesbians and gay men Justine and Dorothy encounter suddenly become characters to whom they have paid too little attention (72, 116). We can extrapolate from this all sorts of practices of intimacy that do not refer to the birth or childhood family, property, or inheritance. Nor do they point to bourgeois subjectivity, the bodily and sensual cultivation of alternative worlds *inside* reflective individuals who can exchange stories about themselves without changing their actual lives. Gaitskill is so disciplined: we have no idea what kinds of subject will form from the closing event. We could, for example, read Dorothy as beneficent, capable of a love that needs no anchor in romantic inflation or murderous destruction. Or, we can read her as a monitoring top who now both rescues and fondles the adult, but diminutive, Justine Shade. Her father eerily haunts that potential version of the book's logic. So does another subject: the young Dorothy.

Earlier in the novel Dorothy reads *The Little Match Girl* the way she will later read of other suffering protagonists. She imagines rescuing the poor little girl, feeding her Cream of Wheat, and then sleeping with her, "her bony back pressed against my front, my arm wrapped around her waist" (74). At the end of the novel Justine *faces* Dorothy and falls asleep in her arms (312). Now Dorothy experiences "white flowers" blooming in her heart, and the erotic luminaries of Definitist romance who have "for so long" absorbed her libidinal energy suddenly dissolve. We know nothing about how Justine is feeling—the poor girl sleeps, impersonal as ever, but more relaxed.

In other words, the novel can be read as having a happy ending. Or, Dorothy's voice-over can be encountered as her loony and compulsive projection onto her attachment objects. For the end demonstrates again Dorothy's particular habit of idealizing something to achieve emancipation from herself while protecting her grandiosity. As in the discussion of apostrophe in "Cruel Optimism," here the voice-over that shapes the novel's final tableau might raise more questions than it resolves about whether intimacy and optimism are bearable if more than one person is awake, aware, and in the room.

Other questions about the narrative infrastructure might be productively raised along with the enigma of genre in Dorothy's rescue of Justine. This closing scene enables something political in the penumbra of narrative to be constructed in the readers' present. The novel is a historical novel, saturated by the politics of its moment, but the clarity of that perspective on the present remains in the shadows of the therapeutic idiom that dominates the narrative arc. Still, we can see in the double biography a thickly rendered historical scene to which this end is also a response. Collective infrastructures are collapsing all over the United States and the globe. I will focus on two: heterofamilial-economic and national-racial norms, fraying in the noise of collective life that suffuses the work.

The gendered division of labor is one formation mediating the political and the subjective. As far as careers go, what's available in the parental generation is masculine professional and feminine domestic misery, succeeded in the girls' lives by exciting and insecure occupational improvisation structured by the temporary relationship. *Two Girls* welcomes us to early neoliberalism, with its romance of the temporary, the flexible, and the entrepreneurial. But the end of the novel suspends that scene and wants the reader to pause for a bit, to look at what two women do together. It incites us to exemplify the "girls" into a case of something else beyond displays of sexual difference, beyond the title's corporeal types, and beyond anyone's voice. It incites us to impersonalize the girls newly. If we want, we can read in this scene a foundation for an actually feminist queer theory of a better good life—if, that is, we imagine Justine waking up rested, content, and ready to relate. This would involve following sexuality along all of the perverse paths it will travel—the traumatic, the conventionally romantic, the experimental, the meaningless, the funny, the hysterical. In the queer feminist utopian reading, one would pay less attention to visceral content and give more respect to the simple imperative for women to fight for women where the urgencies are. Because such an imperative can seem so trivial, private, self-referential, and minor in the "big picture" of things, feminists have paid a big cost for such simple visions, and their focus on women. Some have left feminism behind as white, heterosexual, and a bourgeois tic. Some would see that such attention to tenderness and affect sacrifices structural analysis and thereby reads as a victory for the neoliberal. Some might pay desperate attention to any evidence of alternative potentials for building new genres for collective life. The close of Two Girls, Fat and Thin provides a good case for any of these views.

The simplicity of the final tableau does put into relief the devastating failure of white, middle-class American subjectivity, whether feminist or not. Two Girls, Fat and Thin associates psychological interiority with the traumatic incapacity to disavow: trauma confounds the subject's censor, substituting its own wild aesthetic of distortion and repetition, and at the same time provides for the now impossible subject a counter-traumatic grandiosity that both harms and preserves her. This novel provides for us an easy way to recognize trauma: it happens through sex. But the girls know it takes more than this to contort a being. First, their families are traumatized and traumatic environments. I do not mean that all families are traumatic and traumatized, but these particular families are constructed as exemplary in their historical milieu for the ways they attached to a heteronormative good-life modality that was not good for anyone in it. The structuring "unthought known" of their lives is that the sexuality of the family, its amalgamated intimate and financial economy, its decision about how best to reproduce life in a perverse relation of fantasy to practice, is already a terrible context for the cultivation of anything. Sexual trauma shapes knowledge that the girls already have, rather than being the event that fully structures subsequent consciousness.[32]

I have told a psychological story here about the two girls' will to attach therefore first because this is how the novel explains the mental involution and bodily expression of the two girls, and I wanted to spin out a concept of impersonality that marks any ordinary subject and presents strategies for interfering with particular toxic intimacies so that a better present might be experienced affectively before there is a world structured for it. But as Carolyn Steedman argues, typically only some people—the middle classes—

get to have (complex) psychology, while others—on the economic bottom—are deemed as mere (simple) effects of social and material crises of survival.[33]

The complex interiority of Justine and Dorothy derives from their education in American conventionality. They are saturated by the mass cultural signs of the United States from the late 1960s through the 1980s. Like virtually every recent film about the 1960s, this novel locates the girls historically by depicting them listening to pop music, wearing pop style, eating pop food, and watching pop TV. On television they witness the civil rights actions of 1963, Martin Luther King, and metropolitan rioting. Their parents pronounce lots of historically predictable softly liberal opinions from their perch at a safe distance. The girls notice things but are not mobilized. Citizenship is for adults. In short, the two girls are not exemplary traumatic subjects, or children, or women, or any kind of exemplary Subject of History, whether of nations, capitalism, or sexuality. They are two middle-class white American girls, enclosed in nuclear families that live in communities so white that "the Jew" and "the Spic" are easy to spot from a distance. Economically more than comfortable, they have virtually no resources with which to escape the given world but themselves and books. It is entirely predictable that they would end up addressing the problem of living by diving inside their bodies and feelings. Partly, this is training, since, during adolescence, their parents send them to therapists. But even if this were not the case, the girls' isolation and involution are to be expected of children of the professional classes. Their interiority is the product, the cost, and the benefit of seeing themselves in the terms of bourgeois universalism, as autonomous individuals who demand some attention and independence, parental affirmation and private space. What if the girls had inhabited worlds in which the burden to make happiness was not indexed according to (masculine) power at work and (feminine) harmony at home and by the achievement of a family so complete it needs nothing else but itself? The girls would not be who they are (this is true whether you read them as psychological paradigms, as literary figures in a realist world dynamic, or both). In this sense, too, what is personal about them is also impersonal—not strategically but structurally, historically speaking.

So even if we could agree on a genre for the affective event of the girls' final moment of binding, their particular story can be only partly generalized, involving the exhaustion or discomposure of heterocultural trauma stories as the destiny for certain sectors of the white, professional, and metropolitan elite. When I say this I may sound moralistic and trumping. But I don't mean to sound that way just by naming the particular location out of which their drama comes. Only some people feel connected to the cultivation of selves, will, desire, and inflated poetic interiority. Dorothy's movement toward Definitism demonstrates this paradoxically, as it requires a new style of risky collective identification and de-privatization in order to promote the legitimacy of all individual will. The "Two Girls" twinning in the novel's title therefore suggests to me a third and final thought about the penumbra extending from its resonant end.

The novel's epigraph from Nabokov reads, "All one could do was to glimpse, amid the haze and chimeras, something real ahead." The closing image of Dorothy's and Justine's attachment might testify to something real. We can also read the conclusion as the new present from which we cannot predict, but only intuit, futures. History is what has hurt and it continues to make shadow lines, and we are always in the haze of the present, sensing new repetitions-to-be, some of which can be willed, others of which remain enigmatic. We are still unlearning the promise of realist representation to provide the detail-as-anchor, and still therefore are improvising how else we might know to pay attention.

We are also given a little help toward this reading. When Dorothy provides that image of their final bodily intimacy, she produces it as a soundtrack. "Her body against me was like a phrase of music" (313). The soundtrack is not accompanied by dialogue; it is as though we have returned to the melodramatic stage, where the smallest bodily gesture communicates so much about the ineloquence of our language. A musical phrase is powerful because it repeats: as we become attached to it, it helps us find a place before the plot tells what it means and where that place is. Melodrama is trauma's perfect vehicle in that regard, the unspeakable meeting the unsaid, the music bypassing the order of composure to make contact with the audience's affective intelligence. Melodrama is associated historically with the breakdown of political regimes (of class, of government, of family). These dissolutions release energies for social organization into the public that had been siphoned off into institutions. The transparency of melodramatic emotion responds directly to the enigma of a present no longer capable of being understood in terms of inheritance and its institutions—law, property, religion, family—whose oppressive histories have hurt but have also organized life consequentially. We can make a claim that the emphasis of melodrama shifts slightly in this contemporary genre. Melodrama consoles its audience with an aesthetic of transparent embodiment and emotional performance that produces continuity with the very past that is dissolving. But the aesthetics of the new ordinariness humbles the viewer with the enigmatic quality of institutions, affects, and bodies in the present. It is fundamentally a temporal mode, focusing on precarity but also on the urgent need to wrest the present both from the forms we know—the burden of inheritance, of personality, of normativity—and from the future-oriented ones to which the claims of the present are so often oppressively deferred.

So, the urgency not to take the present for granted as a rest stop between the enduring past and the momentous future provides another reason to conclude this essay with neither ringing optimism nor disappointment. To interfere with the work of trauma means to refuse its temporality, its insistence on saturating the present. Singly, the girls countertemporalize constantly through fantasy and habit in the ways I have described. Together, they break the time-stunting frame of girlhood by finally relaxing in each other's presence. No longer living within the mania of intellectual and erotic attachment and detachment, they drink a soothing cup of tea and unclench into consoling positions. To lean into the body of an intimate is a most personal thing. But what's personal about it is like the deep anonymity of sleepers finally disburdened of the weight of bearing themselves.

Our Professor Sedgwick, whose beautiful and acute thought has taught me how to read the meaningful stammering of repetition, has elsewhere instructed us not to think that feelings are merely constructed, and I doubt not that she is right that the body responds to stimulus as it will.[34] My angle on the question is slightly different. To me the evidence suggests a distinction between a structure of affect and what we call that affect when we encounter it. I may be or feel overwhelmed, I may be composed or feel composure; my panic might look like a stony silence, my composure might be a manic will to control, or not. What looks like a shamed response in one decade, may look angry in another one. One can experience the world not being there for one because of one's singularity or because one's singularity includes the kind of thing one appears to be to others. One might experience that as shame, but also many emotions at once. The subjects of structural subordination seem always to have tone-of-voice problems. All babies smile, but it might be gas. What really matters are the repetitions of relation, the buildup, the pressure over time that becomes a habit that seems intuitive. One assesses what affective events are according to one's education in attunement, in tracking repetition, form, and norm. And one might be wrong about everything. In contrast, an aesthetic that values the beauty of fantasy or of form can believe too much that the viscera are saying something undistorted when we encounter the scene of its investments. This is a paradox because the motive and aim of the aesthetic education are to train the viscera. The aspect I love most about a poetics of misrecognition is that it teaches us that our viscera have been taught and are teachable, if anything is. This view is also central to why I find impersonality—the state of the interruption of the personal, and the work of normativity to create conventions of the personal—such an optimistic concept for interfering with the march of individualities toward liberal freedoms and, additionally, the investment in emotional authenticity that structures bourgeois ideology and much critical theory of subjectivity.

I have tried to suggest, then, something quite different here. First, no model of subordination can rely on the view that affects are continuous with their appearance in an emotional vernacular if the critic wants to interfere with the reproduction of normative claims about the construction of attachment, intuition, and visceral capacities for relation. On this basis I have argued that pleasure does not always feel good, and that understanding the binding of subjects to both their negation and incoherence is key to rewiring the ways we think about what binds people to harmful conventions of personhood. Second, affects have content and form (the repetitions—of word, lyric, music, or sound). They are not species of preideological clarity, but quite the opposite: they are taught ("Hey, you!"), barely known ("Wait up!"), and often more sense than event. Two Girls, Fat and Thin articulates this haze of clarity and incoherence around emotions, as do the three zones of absorption the girls invent to interfere with the subordinations that feel inevitable. Third, the novel's conclusion tells us nothing conclusive about how not to be a case study subject, since all it represents is a fantasy that someday the self-consuming negotiation of ambivalence will stop and the subject can rest. Think of the relation of composition to composure. Learning to interrupt the present may have something to do with learning to make a political claim on the present, but that is not charted in the novel. The novel presents eating as creativity and self-annihilation; language as meaning and sound; the intellect as weapon and cushion. These clusters of image and pulsions of attachment might mean anything or be meaningless. The test is a broadly historical one, which unsettles what's personal and impersonal about being and having a history.

Post-Fordist Affect in *La Promesse* and *Rosetta*

I. *Nearly . . .*

In one sense, this chapter begins where the last one ended — in a scene where a contingent being tries, aversively and indirectly, to induce through an improvised relation with a semi-stranger an attachment that might become a solidarity that could produce more and better traction in the world; an attempt at a speculative intimate tethering more impulsive than strategic whose affective stakes are both unstated and profound. In *Two Girls, Fat and Thin*, this situation amounts to a suspension of violence that throws the historical present into relief as a thing to be overcome by a completely, and perhaps gratefully, enigmatic future. In the films *La Promesse* (1996) and *Rosetta*

4. Rosetta chants herself to sleep (Dardennes, *Rosetta*, 1999)

(1999), written and directed by Luc and Jean-Pierre Dardenne, the scene is of aspiring to a tractable *present*. Two nearly utopian moments in the films mark the core desperation, and historical specificity, of this desire.

In the first, we find Rosetta at the end of a very long day. She has made a friend, Riquet, and through that friendship found an off-the-books job at a waffle maker, escaped her alcoholic and sexually profligate mother, and, with Riquet, spent the evening imitating what it might be like sometime to have fun with a friend or in a couple. She is awkward at this thing called relaxing but she is game; she'll take the risk of submitting to someone else's pleasure economy in order to get that *thing* she wants, whose qualities she describes as she goes to sleep: "Your name is Rosetta. My name is Rosetta. You found a job. I found a job. You have a friend. I've got a friend. You have a normal life. I have a normal life. You won't fall through the cracks. I won't fall through the cracks. Good night. Good night."

Many reviews of *Rosetta* call this catechistic quasi-prayer the film's most heartbreaking moment: for Rosetta, all the world of possible desires has been pared down to a friend and a job, a state of attaining some bare minimum of social recognition. But this is an episode of intimacy, belonging, and sociability that, ultimately, Rosetta can have only with herself, in the private, hoarded space that's usually occupied by a cramping pain—a condition of attrition that the film suggests is a symbol and consequence of the intensity of aching life-making activity that she otherwise goes through every day merely to survive. Even the measured tone of Rosetta's repetitions expresses the wish to be able to use the French *rester*, which means not to rest exactly but to stay somewhere, over time, in a place to which one can return: *I rest here.*

When some Belgians saw *Rosetta* they understood this scene to exemplify a national crisis, and the government promptly sponsored and passed a law called the "Rosetta Plan" that forced businesses to hire the young Belgians who, like Rosetta, were desperately struggling to gain a foothold of any sort in the increasingly global economy.[1] Much contemporary theory defines citizenship as an amalgam of the legal and commercial activity of states and business and individual acts of participation and consumption, but Rosetta's speech about falling through the cracks and the effects of the cinematic event remind that citizenship, in its formal and informal senses of social belonging, is also an affective state where attachments that matter take shape.

Here, the affects of belonging are all tied up with what happens at the point of production. When the Dardennes describe *Rosetta* as a "war film," it is these aspects of the politics of everyday life and contemporary struggle to which they point.[2] Indeed, the film opens amid a tumbling chaos of camera and body movement as the diminutive girl is fired and physically fights two enormous men to keep from being ejected from another low-skill, low-paying, and repetitive job. She finally leaves that workplace to continue the circle she runs in every day, tracking a pattern from her home, to the town, to the bus, across a field, where she hides her precious "good shoes" — the ones that make her presentable to employers in the service economy — and into a trailer park where she lives, badly, with her mother.

Thus, by the time Rosetta makes her whispered, bedtime affirmation, we know the emotional costs of her contentment: the impersonal pulses of capitalist exchange have had devastating personal, including physical, effects and now, momentarily secure, she has optimism about the prospect of becoming what she pridefully calls "a good worker." This matters so desperately that she rejects state welfare, because she says that she wants to earn her value the way "normal" people do. Thus far she had taken in to her home cleaning and sewing work. But to be hired by a stranger who runs a workplace confirms her legitimate place in the world. Without membership in that army of laborers, she has had no room even for a little cramped fantasy about spaces of the good life or good times ahead; with a job, Rosetta's fantasy is not at a grandiose scale but evokes a scene of an entirely imaginable normalcy whose simplicity enables her to rest without anxiety and, for the first and only time in the film, to have a good night. It matters not that she is still unofficial, off the books in all the bureaucratic senses. Even in an extremely informal economy the goodness of the good life now *feels* possible to her and thus *feels* already like a confirming reality, calming her even before she lives it as an ongoing practice. The ongoing prospect of low-waged and uninteresting labor is for Rosetta nearly utopian; it makes possible imagining living the *proper* life that capitalism offers as a route to the *good* life. That the route is a rut matters not to Rosetta: when the world exists between the routinized rut and the ominous cracks, she chooses the rut, the impasse. What operates here are the affects of aspirational normativity, understanding the persistence of which in the project of life-building on the bottom of contemporary class society is the descriptive project of this chapter.

Likewise, in *La Promesse*, our protagonist, Igor, finds optimism for being in the world at the scene of hyperexploited, off-the-books, home-based labor and, as in *Rosetta*, the benefits of bad work are soul-making, not soul-killing. Like the sidekick in the horror movies from which his name comes, Igor works for a bad mastermind—his father, Roger, who runs a racket for illegal immigrant workers, providing for them false papers and substandard, shit-reeking housing in exchange for a never-ending series of exorbitant fees. When, inevitably, they become indebted to Roger, they are employed to work it off by building a big white house for him and his son. Meanwhile, Roger conscripts Igor to work on the white house as well. He also doctors the migrants' papers, collects their rent, and executes ordinary upkeep tasks. At the same time, Igor is apprenticed to an auto mechanic, who is not only teaching him a trade but also enabling him to build a go-cart in which to tool around with his buddies. But as the film begins, Roger insists that the son be available to do his bidding and gets Igor fired.[3] Roger forces this situation as, in his view, the child's labor obligations begin at home.

One day on the construction site Amidou, an illegal African immigrant who works to pay off his gambling debts, takes a hard fall. While the fall is not fatal, Amidou soon dies from it because Roger, afraid of being exposed as a smuggler, refuses to take him to the hospital. Roger and Igor bury the black Amidou in the foundation of the white house on which he died laboring, and lie to Amidou's wife, Assita, that her husband has fled town to avoid paying off his gambling debts.

But before Amidou dies he extracts from Igor the titular "promise" to take care of Assita and their newly born child. Igor is haunted by this promise, and his filial commitment is slowly displaced by his turn toward the obligation he incurred to his father's worker. Meanwhile, Assita is suspicious of Roger, who eventually contracts to sell her into prostitution to get her out of his hair.[4] At this point Igor steps in to hide her from Roger and save her from this fate: yet he does not tell her that Amidou is dead. Like Rosetta with

5.1–5.2. The hug and
the impasse (Dardennes,
La Promesse, 1996)

Riquet, Igor does not exactly know what he is doing when he enters a plot,
if not a life, with Assita. He works out of a headstrong, aggressive incoherence: he abandons an affect that he doesn't want to have, to risk having one
he can barely imagine.

For shelter, Igor takes Assita to the garage at which he formerly worked—
he's kept the keys to his previous home away from home. But Assita refuses
to play displaced house with Igor and it frustrates him, for he cannot bear
that Assita does not want to give him gratitude or any other sign of attachment. As they improvise their new relationship he is shocked to see that
she does not want reciprocity with him or trust him to have her interests at
heart. Indeed Assita puts a knife to his throat—for she can tell there's still
a secret somewhere. They bicker and scream, but ultimately he forces her to
shut up and submit to giving him what he wants: a hug.

What does the hug that he forces her to bear stand for? We know that
Igor has softly stalked Assita, peering in the pinhole in their family door,
seeing her in a white slip caring for her husband and child. The hug is enigmatic like Igor's face in those scenes, neither infantile nor sexual, or maybe
both, a muddy mess; and when Assita breaks from the clinch she just looks
at Igor, uncomprehending as he is, I think. Having experienced a moment of

relieving bodily simplicity, he leaves for a smoke and weeps in the dark. In the clinch he had conjured the unadorned affect of reciprocity or being-with that he has longed for, and without much realizing it, dedicates himself to securing the conditions of its repetition.

In these nearly peaceful episodic eruptions the productive instabilities of the contemporary capitalist economy engender new affective practices, in which children scavenge toward a sense of authentic social belonging by breaking from their parents' way of attaining the good life. At the same time, the will to attach that children manifest is not shared, really, by anyone, certainly not the people who make it possible. Happiness exists in the children's heads, in their commitment to bring life in line with the affect they want to continue experiencing, and above all in the triumph of their will to engender a silence in the enabling other that can seem like consent, thereby ensuring the continued affective experience of solidity and importance that might have been provided by parents and the family form.[5] I say "affect" rather than "emotion" here to emphasize that the children do not know fully what they're doing, flinging themselves at life in order to be in proximity to a feeling of something that is strangely both enigmatic and simplifying. Their objects of desire are really scenes they orchestrate in order to experience absorption, a sense of being held in a scene, of having reciprocity, and being unanxious somewhere. Yet their optimistic gestures also show how much aggression is involved in lining up life with fantasy, and the films track what it means to force hard bargains under duress to attain proximity to even the most vaguely, inarticulately defined pleasure.

These quiet moments in the middle of the films are also high points in these children's stories. They perform not the achieved materiality of a better life but the approximate feeling of belonging to a world that doesn't yet exist reliably. Both children are impulsive: they act urgently to calibrate life in an affective economy and then make emotional sense of it later. Yet this way of describing the cultivation of a world through recourse to impulse, gesture, and episodic improvisation does not take into account what we also see, that the creativity of the children keeps being rerouted to repeating some version of their parents' perverse approximations of the normative good life. It is as though the children, knowing nothing but that index of projected happiness, were compelled to repeat attachment to the very forms whose failure to secure the basic dignities of ordinary existence is central to the reproduction of the difficulty of their singular stories and lived struggle on the bottom of class society in the first place. This chapter is most broadly about the political and affective economies of normativity at the present time, the production as desire of a collective will to imagine oneself as a solitary agent who can and must live the good life promised by capitalist culture. It tells a story from the perspective of the economic bottom's thick space of contingency. It is about the fantasy of meritocracy, a fantasy of being deserving, and its relation to practices of intimacy, at home, at work, and in consumer worlds. It is a story about plenitude and scarcity—about so many bad jobs contingently available to so many contingent workers and never enough money, never enough love, and barely any rest, yet with ruthless fantasy abounding. It is a story about the calibrations of reciprocity and about how proximity to the fantasy life of normativity might be what remains to animate living on, for some on the contemporary economic bottom.

Finally, it is an account of normativity that sees normativity as something other than a synonym for privilege. Rather, in my view, to understand collective attachments to fundamentally stressful conventional lives, we need to think about normativity as aspirational and as an evolving and incoherent cluster of hegemonic promises about the present and future experience of social belonging that can be entered into in a number of ways, in affective transactions that take place alongside the more instrumental ones.

The all-too-present cause of the effects these films track is the volatile here and now of that porous domain of hyperexploitive entrepreneurial atomism that has been variously dubbed globalization, liberal sovereignty, late capitalism, post-Fordism, or neoliberalism. It is a scene of mass but not collective activity. It is a scene in which the lower you are on economic scales, and the less formal your relation to the economy, the more alone you are in the project of maintaining and reproducing life. Communities, when they exist, are at best fragile and contingent. The story from this perspective is about the historical present as a scene of constant bargaining with normalcy in the face of conditions that can barely support even the memory of the fantasy. How do fantasy-practice clusters such as those we've seen become the grounds for political and social conservatism? How can we understand the singular tragedies of Rosetta and Igor in light of the wave of uprisings in Paris (2006), Italy (2008), Greece (2010–2011), and the UK (2010–2011), where students marched to maintain the same state-secured labor and welfare protections enjoyed by their parents, who benefited from the postwar Western European promise of social democracy? What happens when the economic and social promise of a state becomes privatized like everything else, redistributed through emerging nonstate institutions and formal and informal economies?

In these films, what might have been political agency is diffused throughout the social, as the work of the reproduction of life absorbs most of the energy and creativity people have; and so much of it is absorbed by dramas of the tattered family, the lone institution of reciprocity remaining here for fantasy to attach itself to. But this does not mean that all world-building contexts are alike under stress: the Dardennes focus almost entirely on the destinies of white working-class and subproletarian citizens and migrants whose legal and social statuses are all shifting amid the forces inducing massive global migration. For everyone, regardless of their ethnic and racial origin, all sorts of normative emotions about how the fantasy and actuality of the good life might be tethered together stand in for affective urges for a better social world beyond what the conventional forms deliver. For the white citizens, the Belgian state still provides forms of visible relief in welfare and policing bureaucracies. But the state is not enough; it is a weakened environment mediated by individuals who may be benign or on the make but are always too late to prevent a crisis, and while its infrastructures can sustain the trains and provide the dole, they cannot maintain the world openly and robustly. At the same time the improvisations of labor make available alternative, non-kinship-organized spaces of positive reciprocity. Beyond that, the kids engage in their own lateral modes of world-building. Any of these scenes might generate new political or social genres of belonging, but at the moment of these films, they all amount to pleasures seized in the folds of productive contingency. There, there is no room to make a distinction among political, economic, and affective forms of existence, because the institutions of intimacy that constitute the everyday environments of the social are only viscerally distinct but actually, as we know, intricately and dynamically related to all sorts of institutional, economic, historical, and symbolic dynamics.

What follows includes an investigation of some psychoanalytic and materialist explanations of social attachment in the context of structural inequality, to see if we might find better ways of understanding how it is that forms associated with ordinary violence remain desirable—perhaps because of a kind of narcotic/utopian pleasure in their very familiarity. Using the Dardennes' films plus the work of Judith Butler and Lillian Rubin, I focus on some stories about the conscription of children to the worlds of their parents, the worlds of their parents' desires, and the gaps of disappointment and failure that the children see, because the articulation of children and neoliberalism is so crucial now in the academy, the middlebrow public, and the social policy and human rights communities, as an image of the contemporary ethical, political, and economic conundrums of structural subordination and social betrayal. This scene also enables us to consider the vertical attachments—say, of parents and children, bosses and workers— along with the horizontal, much less reliable ones, of friends, coworkers, and couples. The vertical and horizontal keep getting mixed up here, though: the daughter acts as the mother's mother, the father tells his son to call him Roger and gives him a ring to bind their fraternity. These confusions signify the immediate crisis out of which the children are trying to fight their way.

This is a way of describing the specificity of the experience of ordinariness—of, as Thomas Dumm writes, "ordinary life, the life-world, the everyday, the quotidian, the low, the common, the private, the personal"—in its visceral temporality today.[6] The ordinary, in La Promesse and Rosetta, is organized around the solicitation of children to the reproduction of what we should call not the good life but "the bad life"—that is, a life dedicated to moving toward the good life's normative/utopian zone but actually stuck in what we might call survival time, the time of struggling, drowning, holding onto the ledge, treading water—the time of *not-stopping*.

The Dardennes draw the Belgium of the 1990s as a colony of globalization with its legal citizens trying to maintain a grip on the waning shards of liberty, sovereignty, and economic hegemony:[7] it's a world of intensified economic and social volatility, a mainly deindustrialized, small business economy where impersonality and intimacy are enmeshed in a renewed regime of sweatshops and domestic labor.[8] This world is visually and physically crowded, both overwhelming and underwhelming in its assault, allowing little time to luxuriate in its sounds, tastes, and smells. As Achille Mbembe and Janet Roitman put it, about the African context, this "suggests that it is in everyday life that the crisis as a limitless experience and a field dramatizing particular forms of subjectivity is authored, receives its translations, is institutionalized, loses its exceptional character and in the end, [appears] as a 'normal,' ordinary and banal phenomenon."[9]

Mbembe and Roitman see crisis ordinariness as the condition for the production of revolutionary consciousness. But the Dardennes' scenario puts forth no hint of that, nor of the potentiality or revolutionary possibility that Michael Hardt and Antonio Negri attribute to the activity of immaterial

6. Igor plays with whiteness

labor in their analysis of the contemporary global mode of production.[10] In these films, the citizen's dissatisfaction leads to reinvestment in the normative promises of capital and intimacy under capital. The quality of that reinvestment is not political in any of the normative senses, though—it's a feeling of aspirational normalcy, the desire to feel normal, and to feel normalcy as a ground of dependable life, a life that does not have to keep being reinvented. That feeling does not require any particular forms of living to stimulate it; nor does it depend on the flourishing of the forms of living to which it attaches. Optimism attaches to their mere existence. The will to feel that feeling again becomes the first order object of desire. But this puts pressure on the infrastructure of the social world to be maintained despite its distributions of violence and negation.

A nearly comic, silent movie–style example from *La Promesse* plays out this activity beautifully, pointing additionally to what's singular about globalization's sensual flesh. It is Igor's job to white out the immigrant passports, making their bearers seem already legal. Yet when he arrives at Assita's papers and sees the contrast of her dark skin and her white teeth, Igor immediately moves to a mirror and whites out his own teeth, erasing working-class staining and emphasizing his racial whiteness as an homage to her smile and also to her blotted-out identity. It is also clear that he doesn't get it: his racial location, his privilege of citizenship, his dependency on her familial labor. Nothing happens from this moment of play, whose gestures are ordinary, forgettable, forgotten. In fact, in these films play itself is a momentary privilege crowded out constantly by risk, which is play with life-denting consequences. Both play and risk are shaped by the pressures of contemporary labor, with its demands for survival and incitement to fantasy without a scaffold, a net, or a retreat. Play allows a *sense* of normalcy, though, while risk tries to make some headway in the impasse: play is the performance of an interruption without risk. Yet it takes place as barely enjoyed comic relief from the risk that must be borne.

Thus, how to talk about the need to maintain binding to the normal in the context of crisis is a theoretical and political problem of more than consciousness. The Dardennes represent consciousness under present systemic economic, political, and intimate conditions as absorbed in regimes of bargaining with movement amid the slow train wreck that is always coming in the catastrophic time of capitalism, where if you're lucky you *get* to be exploited, and if you're lucky you can avoid one more day being the focus of a scene that hails and ejects you when it is your time to again become worthless. This is why exploitation is not what the children cast as the enemy. They want to be exploited, to enter the proletarian economy in the crummy service-sector jobs it is all too easy to disdain as the proof of someone's loserdom or tragedy. The risk would be opting out of the game. One does not *necessarily* require families or nations to secure this feeling; any reciprocal form will do—friendship, collegiality, a project, the state, a union, whatever has the capacity to deliver an affective, transpersonal sense of unconflictedness, belonging, and worth.

The history of sentimentality around children that sees them as the reason to have optimism—for if nothing else, their lives are not already ruined—thus takes on an ethical, political, and aesthetic purchase in these films. The audience is obligated to side with the child's will not to be defeated, even if the difference between defeat and all its others is the capacity to attach optimism for a less bad future to a blighted field of possibility. We are incited to have compassion for fruitless and even self-undermining—cruel—desires. In La Promesse, the promise of post-Fordist citizenship marks out agency not as that which changes the world but as that which bargains with it by developing affective bonds or "promise" within the regime of production that extends everywhere, as everyone is on the make. In Rosetta, belonging isn't an a priori but something that must be purchased by participation in the everyday economy. Community and civil society from this class perspective are not seen as resources for building anything, neither fantasy nor an ordinary life that can be trusted, rested in. Attachments are as brittle as the economic system that hails and then bails on its reserve army of workers.

It matters also that these films are not centrally organized around the consciousness and affects of migrants whose migration is animated by hope for a better good life, but around citizens who thought that the traditional forms of social reciprocity would provide scenes for life-building, not the attrition of being. For legal citizens (here, of Europe), the difference between having papers and not determines which economies you can participate in, and how. Yet the ease of attaining the paper identity that performs a simulacrum of secure social tethering smudges the legal/illegal distinction. In the economic lifeworld of these films, citizens without capital and migrants with fake papers are in proximate, interdependent boats structurally and affectively. All might as well be called survivalists, scavengers bargaining to maintain the paradox of entrepreneurial optimism against defeat by the capitalist destruction of life.[11]

In this fraying context, the children sometimes encounter private individuals who ameliorate the beatdown of overwhelming inequality, injustice, and just getting by in the folds of the modes of production—nice employers, for example. Sometimes they are even nice employers themselves: in *Rosetta*, the daughter who sews and markets the clothing they make compliments her mother on her creative sewing; in *La Promesse* Igor freely dispenses cigarettes and advice to the deracinated employees who work for him. Some government workers act compassionately, too, making it possible to imagine political institutions of a less bad life. Niceness here means manners, nothing more. But manners are not nothing, as we will see here and in the next chapter. They provide an infrastructure of sociality alongside of the other ones, one more potential opportunity for flourishing. Likewise, sometimes, there is leisure, especially where music and drink and unproductive randomness can be folded in, as in the father-son karaoke double date in *La Promesse* and the dinner-dancing moment in *Rosetta*. But when the camera pulls back, we see the ordinary experience of post-Fordist practice not just in the occasional moments of affect-lifting connection but in the constant movement of people and things through national boundaries, temporary homes, small and big business, and above all an informal economy of secrets, stashes, bargaining, and bribes that link women to small men, and small men to bigger ones.

Once anywhere in the chain, they can imagine their place in the big picture. For instance, when Rosetta screams at and beats up her mother, she is refusing the bargains her mother makes to be able to maintain her fantasy of normalcy. The mother's state of falling apart has reduced them to living at a trailer park ironically named Grand Canyon, a space of American wonder and leisure, but when the mother plants flowers or tries to make a middle-class dinner there, Rosetta destroys them, because the simulacrum of normalcy is a perversion in their context. She wants the real thing, the promise, and a relation of care that produces the ballast of a normal life.[12] Together they sew and sell clothes trying to get enough money to live. But when Rosetta is out making the profits, the mother accepts food and booze from the owner of the trailer park in exchange for sex; she also performs fellatio in lieu of parting with the money her daughter gives her to buy water, so that later she can buy drink. Brutal, that informal economy. Rosetta tells her to go to a state-run drying-out facility and the mother says she doesn't want to sober up, to which Rosetta replies, bargainingly, that she'll buy a sewing machine for the mother if she goes and dries out. The mother responds to the offer by pushing Rosetta into a pond of muddy water, nearly drowning her. But Rosetta knows how to tread water—that's what she knows.

In La Promesse, too, there's lots of bargaining in the grey economy: it's a coerced relation in which good manipulative skills can feel like agency. Roger's workers want to become illegals, migrate to benefit from the grey economy, and do not complain much when they are forced to appear and disappear at will; and what money they do acquire, we note, is often gambled away. When Amidou loses at gambling and complains that he's been cheated, Igor says, "It's not my problem you always lose. You should just stop playing." But in the informal economy where you may or may not get paid for what you do, where you don't exist on the identification papers the state recognizes, where you are always paid under the table if at all, you're always playing for the possibility of achieving, through the repetition of fraud, the ballast of capital or simply presence that will provide the social density of citizenship at the scale of a legitimate linkage to the reciprocal social world. The question is not whether citizenship as a guarantee of social reciprocity is fantasmatic, but how, and in what fantasmatic registers, it operates as such.

Even the category children is as volatile as the categories of citizen and worker. I call these protagonists "children," but actually that's an open question whose openness is an index of how hard it is to describe anyone in the flux of improvised survival habits that constitute existence in the contemporary economy. It is appropriate to call Rosetta and Igor children in that their stories are organized by intimacy with a parent with whom they live. At the same time, though, they are adolescents on the verge of seeking out sexual attachments and experience while also being adults economically, in that their days are organized mainly around the material reproduction of their lives. This convoluted regime of survival and low expectation is what childhood means now, for an increasing number: precocious adulthood. Jody Heyman's Forgotten Families documents the astronomical global expansion of the number of families in which the parents and older children work long hours daily in order to maintain inadequate housing and malnourishment, optimistically hoping that the sacrifice of their health will add up to something else, something better for the younger children.[13] In the family struggling to survive on the bottom, the ordinary splintering effects of exploitation or state violence in its open-secret arbitrariness continue to shape proximate norms of imaginary belonging whose theoretical availability comes to occupy the bottom line *and* the utopian horizon in the scene of survival, failure, and disappointment with which globalization impresses. Such are the paradoxes of cruel optimism.

So even if, in these two films, the promise of familial love is the conveyance for the incitement to misrecognize the bad life as a good one, this is also a story about the conditions under which fantasy takes the most conservative shape on the bottom of so many class structures. The adults want to pass the promise of the promise on to their children.[14] That may be the children's only sure inheritance—fantasy as the only capital assuredly passable from one contingent space to another. And of course here, as everywhere, the gendered division of labor mediates the attritions of capital and the intimate spaces in which the labor of living is imagined beyond the urgencies of necessity. As Gayatri Spivak writes of another example, "This is not the old particularism/universalism debate. It is the emergence of the generalized value form, global commensurability in the field of gender. All the diversity of daily life escapes this, yet it is inescapable."[15] *Rosetta* and *La Promesse* are training differently gendered children to take up a position not within normative institutions of intimacy but within something proximate to them. The hypervigilance required to maintain this proximity is the main visceral scene of post-Fordist affect. The fantasy of intimacy that will make one *feel* normal (as opposed to making one able to secure the conditions of dependable reciprocal life) provides a false logic of commensurateness and continuity between everyday appearance and a whole set of abstract value-generating relations. The aesthetic of the potentially good enough love enables crisis to feel ordinary and less of a threat than the affective bounty that makes it worth risking being amid capitalist social life.

But in the Dardennes' *mise en scène*, normative intimacy has been worn down to the nub of the formal and the gestural. The emotions associated with intimacy, like tenderness, are most easily assumed as scavenging strategies that the children are compelled to develop to get by. Igor acts genuinely sweet to the old woman whose wallet he steals in the opening scene; Rosetta acts in loving and protective ways toward her mother, whom she also beats for manifesting nonnormative appetites. Roger appeals to Igor for loyalty, although he has also lied to him, beat him, and destroyed his opportunity to be a kid and to cultivate a different life (also involving building things: but go-carts that move, not houses that require property). Yet Roger can still say, "The house, this whole thing, it's all for you!" To which Igor can only say, "Shut up! Shut up!" because there is no story to counter Roger with, no proof that it wasn't love, or that love was a bad idea. Apparently, the register of love is what there is to work with, when you are managing belonging to worlds that have no obligation to you.

But this is why optimism for belonging in a scene of potential reciprocity amid tragic impediments is, in these films, not merely cruel, even in its repetitions. The endings of these films tie the audience in identificatory knots of vicarious reciprocity that extend in affective and formal ways beyond the actual episode. Rosetta approaches her final shots having just had to quit her hard-won job in order to take care of her degenerating mother. She is miserable and defeated by her daughterly love and her commitment to not living outside the loop of a reciprocity whose feeling feels legitimate to her.

At the end, we see her dragging a big canister of gas. It is unclear whether she is about to commit suicide by asphyxiation, or to make a go of things the way she always does, and it doesn't matter: her body collapses in exhaustion as Riquet arrives. Riquet—whom she has previously beaten up, left to drown, turned in as a thief, and had a strange, unsteady, asexual night with, a night that ends with her sleeping, not alone, but whispering intimately with herself.[16] Riquet—who is stalking her in revenge for taking his job. He is the only resource for potential reciprocity she has. As the film closes, Rosetta weeps, looking off-screen toward he who is only a proximate friend, in the hope of stimulating his compassionate impulse to rescue her. And the film cuts to darkness.

Likewise, the close of *La Promesse* involves a scene of wishful gallantry. In the train station, just as Assita is about to escape Belgium, Igor's father, Igor, and the whole shoddy mess, Igor confesses one part of his secret. Perversely fulfilling and breaking "the promise" after which the picture is named, he gambles that revealing Amidou's death will keep Assita there, and indeed it binds her and her child to him and to the local scene of danger, violence, and poverty for the indefinite future. In the final shot, they walk away from the camera, together and not together, and as they become smaller the film cuts sharply to black. Both of these works thus end engendering in the audience

7. Rosetta's pathetic appeal

a kind of normativity hangover, a residue of the optimism of their advocacy for achieving whatever it was for which the protagonists were scavenging. Because Rosetta and Igor are cut off from the normal, the spectators become holders of the promise.

In classic Hollywood cinema and much of queer theory, such expectant "families we choose" endings would make these films, generically, comedies, and the anxieties we feel on the way would be just the effects of the conventional obstacles genres put out there that threaten the genre's failure.[17] In Foucault's rendering, such scenes of communicative tears and confession would mark the children's ascension into sexuality, that is, into the place where desiring acts evince the youths' subjugation to the clarifying taxonomic machinery of familial and social discipline. In *La Promesse* and *Rosetta* it is where they become sexual, but such evocations of the two clarifying institutions of social intelligibility, genre and gender, would mishear the tonalities of these particular episodes. In these scenarios, sexuality is not only an accession to being intelligible, but also a performance of affective avarice, a demand for a feeling fix that would inject a *sense* of normality.

What does it mean to want a sense of something rather than something? In the emergent regime of privatization that provokes aggressive fantasies of affective social confirmation in proximity to the political often without being in its register, genre shifts can point to new ways of apprehending improvisations within the ordinary. In the Dardennes' films, the formal achievement of genre and gender suggests not success but survival, a survival reeking of something that partakes of the new generic hybrid, *situation tragedy*: the marriage between tragedy and situation comedy where people are fated to express their flaws episodically, over and over, without learning, changing, being relieved, becoming better, or dying.[18] In the situation comedy, personality is figured as a limited set of repetitions that will inevi-

8. The never-ending
ending of *La Promesse*

tably appear in new situations—but what makes them comic and not tragic
is that in this genre's imaginary, *the world has the kind of room for us that enables
us to endure.* In contrast, in the situation tragedy, one moves between having
a little and being ejected from the social, where life is lived on the outside
of value, in terrifying nonplaces where one is a squatter, trying to make an
event in which one will matter to something or someone, even as a familiar joke (in the situation tragedy, protagonists often try heart-wrenchingly
to live as though they are in a situation comedy).[19] In reinventing some version of the couple, the family, or the love link, at the end, Rosetta and Igor
are repeating a desire they have fancied and longed for throughout: a desire
simply and minimally to be in the game. Not controlling the conditions of
labor, they take up positions within sexuality that at least enable a feeling of
vague normalcy that can be derived on the fly, in a do-it-yourself (DIY) fashion. They do this in gestures that try to force a sense of obligation in someone, which will just have to stand in as the achievement of their desire for
acknowledgment and a way of life.

Thus, we see forming here submission to necessity in the guise of desire;
a passionate attachment to a world in which they have no controlling share;
and aggression, an insistence on being proximate to the thing. If these motives stand as the promise of the scene that will provide them that holding
feeling they want, the proof that it's worth investing in these forms is not
too demanding. There is a very low evidentiary bar. The key here is *proximity*;
ownership has been relinquished as the children's fantasy. The geopolitical space of fantasy is not a nation or a plot of land secured by a deed but
a neighborhood. And just as both films feature careers involving soldering
and sewing, techniques that bind parts to bigger wholes, they restage at
the close our protagonists' coercive appeal to a relative stranger for rescue
and reciprocity, and all the stranger has to do is to be near, to stick around.

That this is an appeal to a proximate normativity is signified by their spatial placement outside the home (in a terminal, on the ground) but never very far afield at all; they are all in proximity to the natal and fantasmatic home, in the end. And, affectively speaking, is Riquet not a man on whom the silent Rosetta must depend; and is Assita not a mother/sister/lover/friend forced by Igor, by his sweet downcast eyes and aphonia, to submit?

Normalcy's embrace can only flicker, therefore, in the Dardennes' rendering of the contemporary historical moment. Each time it looks as though a reciprocal relation has been forged, the temporal and monetary economy in which the experience of belonging can be enjoyed is interrupted by other needs, the needs of others that seem always to take priority. Nonetheless, in the context of material and parental deprivation, Rosetta and Igor crowd the cramped space of any potentially transitional moment to maintain, for one more minute, their optimism about having a thing, a life, a scene of practices of belonging and dignity that can be iterated, repeated, and depended on without much being looked forward to.

So, what does it mean that the endings of these films solicit audience desire one more time for the protagonists to receive, finally, the help they seek because it feels like their last chance to experience, through openness to another, a good change amid the violence and numbing everywhere present? Since "at all costs" is no metaphor from this perch on the bottom of the class structure, here fantasy and survival are indistinguishable effects of the affects' own informal economy. To be made to *desire* a normativity hangover trains the audience in cruel optimism.

Thus, there is more to the story of the affect the children display than the tragedy of particular individual attachments to the feeling of optimism that someday they might rest in a sense of belonging; at stake is measuring the distribution of the subjective accommodation to the political economy of dependable reciprocity. Belgium, an exemplary hub of immigrant labor from Africa, other French postcolonies, Korea, and the generic European countryside, was a scene of expanding informal economies and welfare state shrinkage in the 1990s; from this perspective *Rosetta* and *La Promesse* are fiercely, deliberately actuarial in their depiction of the emotional effects of globalization. So much creativity and effort go into attempts to rescue oneself and sometimes others from drowning in scenes of personal and impersonal violence; and if here appeasement of the family constitutes the absorbing work of ordinariness as it usually does for children, this situation is intensified because now, again, urban families on the bottom are also sites of production. In *Rosetta* the drama is activated locally by the daughter's resentful and loving desire to support her mother and herself, to have a job that will enable the mother to cease her pathetic gestures of optimism and disappointment—"All you do is fuck and drink!" Rosetta repeatedly says; in *La Promesse* the drama is activated by the father's desire to repeat himself in his son, and the son's ambivalence about reproducing the multitude of exploitations this vision of the patriarchal good life involves. The women run a sweatshop for themselves, making clothing; Rosetta looks for other jobs in every other public zone of exchange she enters, such as food shops and clothing stores. The men import illegals, make money off them, and get them in debt to be paid off by forced labor on the house that is the father's entailment to his son.

This gives the Belgian family that occupies the reserve army of labor a paradoxical social location, as evinced in the children themselves. It participates in the informal economy, often acting as part of an informal petit bourgeoisie, with an informal chamber of commerce composed of like-minded, grey-economy profiteers, and at the same time engenders new social locations, shapeless spaces defined by who moves through them and how, marked by practices and modes of being so evanescent that they're hard to describe, to speak in, and to confront. Relative to other films, everyday communication in *Rosetta* and *La Promesse* is as convoluted as identity is now, wandering in the economo-affective lag time of transition, negotiation, untruth, and anxiety. Its voiceover would sound something like "Be next to me, don't overwhelm me, don't say anything, don't interfere with my desire to imagine how it would feel to have my needs recognized by you, say something, give me something, let's try, be quiet."

What's striking in the temporal imaginary of both the citizen and the migrant workers, then, is the ways they look forward to getting ahead, to making it, *and* to a condition of stasis, of being able to *be somewhere* and to make a life, exercising existence as a fact, not a project.[20] In other words, in this version of transnational class fantasy, mobility is a dream and a nightmare. The end of mobility as a fantasy of endless upwardness, and the shift to the aspiration toward achieving an impasse and stop-loss, is a subtle redirection of the fantasy bribes transacted to effect the reproduction of life under the present economic conditions.[21] Given these conditions, if one is an informal or unofficial worker, there is little room for imagining revolution or indeed any future beyond the scavenging present, though it happens.[22] Given these pressures, it is easy to see how post-Fordist subjectivity can shrink the imaginary social field to a repetition of actions that might be either building a foundation for staying or staving off defeat.

The desire for a less-bad bad life involves finding resting places; the reproduction of normativity occurs when rest is imagined nostalgically—that is, in the places where rest is supposed to have happened, a fantasy masquerading as screen memory or paramnesia. One might read these repetitions as nostalgia for nostalgia, a kind of desperate regression toward the desire to soon experience an imaginary security one *knows* without having ever had, and fair enough; but normativity where there is no foundation for the expectation of it beyond a lasting fantasy can also be read as a form of bargaining with what is overwhelming about the present, a bargaining against the fall between the cracks, the living death of repetition that's just one step above the fall into death by drowning or by hitting the concrete at full speed. It's a mode of living-on with the dread of an eternal present that gets drowned out by the noise of promised normativity's soothing bustle. This is an empirical question as well as a theoretical one, but one of the empirical questions is about the transmission, content, form, and force of fantasy. For in order for normative conservatism to take hold in fantasy, or in order for fantasy to join ideology, somewhere in there the children learn to fantasize that the bad life that threatens impossibility or death *could* be the good life that must materialize from all this labor. The intensity of the need to *feel* normal is created by economic conditions of nonreciprocity that are mimetically reproduced in households that try to maintain the affective forms of middle-class exchange while having an entirely different context of anxiety and economy to manage. What is it in the relation of fantasy to the everyday that enjambs the children in shaky fidelity to a practice of intimacy whose manifestation in their own lives could easily have produced their rejection of it?

11. *Psychoanalysis, Ethics, and the Infantile*

So far I have suggested that neoliberal economic and social conditions of reproducing everyday life shape the affective horizon of normativity in the Dardennes' films in a way that illuminates some more general questions about why the bad life is not repudiated by those whom it has failed. Mothers make dinner, fathers build houses and businesses, people are mostly reliable until things get stressed out and inconvenient, and a certain familiar tenderness is transacted transgenerationally. All of these gestures are not themselves objects of desire but a tightly proximate cluster of place-holders for what everyone seems to want, a space of a collective relief from the ongoing present in which living on is an activity of treading water and stopping loss amid unreliable dependencies. The parental gestures would work, would lubricate thriving, if only they could drown out or distract the scavenging hypervigilance toward survival and acknowledgment that constitutes the subjective practice of the children. But the dramatic action of the films emerges because the children come to cast parental gestures of life-building, reciprocity, and acknowledgment in the light of suspicion, as zombie forms through which normativity reproduces itself as an unlivable animating desire. Realism about love forces affect to become materialist. But this does not mean that the children detach from the fantasy forms they associate with parental love, however badly practiced. How to explain why the children protect their attachments to such fantasy, the lived version of which is at best anxious and at worse tragic?

From a certain political perspective, a feminist one, it has long been argued that love is a bargaining tool for convincing others to join in making a life that also provides a loophole through which people can view themselves nonetheless as fundamentally noninstrumental—selfless, sacrificial, magnanimous—in their intimacies.[23] The code phrase for this loophole is the distinction between the public and the private. This structure is what Jürgen Habermas points to as well when he distinguishes the modern bourgeois as someone who shifts between his identity as a calculating man of the market and his identity as an *homme* who locates his true self in the performance of intimacy in the theater of domestic space.[24] The displaced relation within the capitalist subject between his instrumental persona and his loving persona enables him to disidentify with what's aggressive in his pursuit of desire and interest in all spaces, and to see himself as fundamentally ethical because he means to have solidarity with some humans he knows. This perspective would suggest that the children in the Dardennes' films are caught in the contradictory knot of their parents' econo-affective practices, which similarly cast intimate well-intentioned activity as importantly life-affirming and only situationally aggressive, coercive, or disappointing.

Judith Butler's formidable work on "grievable life" produces a quite different account of attachments to "the bad life." From *The Psychic Life of Power* through *Precarious Life*, Butler also develops an account of social inequality that grows from the intricate and contradictory bindings of power within the family. But she pursues a *developmental* model of political subjectivity that sees infantile dependency as the seed of a kind of sadistic normativity in adults that can be interrupted by an ethical commitment to compassionate emotion. In recognizing the previously ungrieved "grievable life" or lives, the Butlerian progressive subject dismantles her pathological sense of defensive sovereignty or sovereign indifference on behalf of a healthy nonsovereign identification with those populations that need to be included in communities of compassion in order to gain access to the machineries of justice.

Since many people, including Belgian policymakers, responded to the Dardennes' films as though already trained in making ungrieved lives subjects of their transformative compassion, it would seem that these films would enact the emotion-work that Butler proposes. Yet, as we will see, in translating the psychoanalytic to the ethical by way of normativity, Butler writes the unconscious out of the story, producing subjects as ethical intentionalists who can make cognitive decisions to short-circuit foundational affective attachments in order to gain a better good life. One might note the political problems with this circuit of displacement: as I and others have argued, projects of compassionate recognition have enabled a habit of political obfuscation of the differences between emotional and material (legal, economic, and institutional) kinds of social reciprocity.[25] Self-transforming compassionate recognition and its cognate forms of solidarity *are* necessary for making political movements thrive contentiously against all sorts of privilege, but they have also provided a means for making minor structural adjustments seem like major events, because the theater of compassion is emotionally intense. Recognition all too often becomes an experiential end in itself, an emotional event that protects what is unconscious, impersonal, and unrelated to anyone's intentions about maintaining political privilege.

However, my focus here is not on Butler's argument about empathic capacities as central to justice, but on the developmental aspect of the account, which argues that the experience of sovereignty is a reaction formation against infantile dependency. Claiming that "[t]o desire the conditions of one's own subordination is . . . required to persist as oneself [such that we] embrace the very form of power—regulation, prohibition, suppression—that threatens one with dissolution in an effort, precisely, to persist in one's own existence," she enmeshes all sorts of unlike phenomena, conflating dependence with subordination, psychic self-dispossession with political injustice, and personal with political subjectivity.[26] This enmeshment is not an accident or unconscious in Butler's work—it is an explicit project of explanation about how "this condition of my formation" is expressed in "the sphere of politics."[27] More important for our purposes, the work equates infantile dependency with normative attachments and normative attachments with attachments to power and privilege. Is the infantile structure of dependency sublimated into love really the origin of all patience with injustice? Let me briefly open up some problems that such enmeshing generates for a concept of political subjectivity generally and of post-Fordist affect from the perspective of the economic bottom in particular. Here is the most developed version of the argument:

> The task is doubtless to think through this primary impressionability and vulnerability with a theory of power and recognition. To do this would no doubt be one way a politically informed psychoanalytic feminism could proceed. The "I" who cannot come into being without a "you" is also fundamentally dependent on a set of norms of recognition that originated neither with the "I" nor with the "you." What is prematurely, or belatedly, called the "I" is, at the outset, enthralled, even if it is to a violence, an abandonment, a mechanism; doubtless it seems better at that point to be enthralled with what is impoverished or abusive than not to be enthralled at all and so to lose the condition of one's being and becoming. . . . So the question of primary support for primary vulnerability is an ethical one for the infant and for the child. But there are broader ethical consequences from this situation, ones that pertain not only to the adult world but to the sphere of politics and its implicit ethical dimension.[28]

Butler and I are not clinicians: what matters here are arguments about how to understand passionate or irrational attachments to normative authority and normative worlds. To Butler, answering this means characterizing desires for autonomy as adult symptoms of a wounded narcissism of the dependent child. She insists that when adults imagine autonomy or sovereignty as synonymous with freedom, they are manifesting a humiliated reaction formation to having been duped, as an infant, into idealizing a love that was always self-dispossessing and never not disappointing.[29] As a result, Butler argues, the adult repudiates interdependency and becomes deeply authoritarian. She deems ethno-racisms, homophobia, and misogyny to be expressions of this compensation.[30] Nonetheless, she suggests that there is enough ambivalence in the subject's love of subjection that opportunities exist to choose not to reproduce attachments to subordination; the way to do this is to make ethical interventions into unconscious attachments, to produce a new vulnerability that will undo the humiliation of the original one.

As I argue in the next section, it is not at all clear that infantile dependency provides a bad education in the phenomenology of justice. But for the moment let's accept the claim that children organize their optimism for living through attachments they never consented to making, that they make do with what's around that might respond adequately to their needs. They may even come to be in love with the promise of the promise that there will be a moment of reciprocal *something* between themselves and the world, if they're good, that is, *if they become a good subject of the promise*, and they may mistake love for subjection to the will of others who have promised to care for/love them. W. R. D. Fairbairn provides a different angle on this, arguing that the child becomes attached not to subordinated dependency but to the scene of the opportunity to imagine the optimistic overcoming of what's disempowering about this dependency.[31] Likewise, Christopher Bollas has adapted Donald Winnicott to argue for thinking of the object of desire not as an object but as a transformational environment.[32] As I suggested in "Slow Death," an environment is a scene to which you can return that is characterized by a recognizable atmosphere. It is loose and porous, a space that you can enter in a number of ways and change within, without violating the fundamental attachment. Scenes like this magnetize a noncoherent cluster of desires for reciprocity, acknowledgment, or recognition that can converge into a mirage of solidity—it's a vitalist, pointillist notion of the object of desire. From this theoretical perspective on what love does to reproduce normativity, infantile dependency would not really be an experience of attaching to domination but a scene where the subject negotiates an overdetermined set of promises and potentials for recognition and even thriving. It might be more like an environment where the subject is trained to cathect with optimism, a relational affect whose practices and objects are themselves normatively mediated.

What we are talking about here is the hardest problem: understanding the difficulty of unlearning attachments to regimes of injustice. Justice itself is a technology of deferral or patience that keeps people engrossed politically, when they are, in the ongoing drama of optimism and disappointment.[33] Yet Butler's theoretical stance about power in relation to the law, normative authority, normative values, and structural privilege underdescribes the number of internally contradictory promises (of acknowledgment, amelioration, protection, retribution, balancing, delegation, discipline, and enabling to thrive) that its activity represents. It also neglects what *Rosetta* and *La Promesse* show intricately, that recognition and reciprocity can take many forms, some of which mime equality as collaboration, some of which produce contexts of trust in interdependency, some of which are coerced or tactical, and all of which are deeply ambiguous, compromised, and unstable.

Indeed, one analysis of the crisis scripted by the Dardennes would focus on the increasingly impossible task of recognizing what counts as reciprocity at any scale of sociality. In the scene of economic, national, and transnational life that has provided this essay's case, love is only slightly less contingent than work. During the last twenty years of state shrinkage and temp culture both at work and in the institutions of intimacy, the work of (re)production has been shaped by the increasing demand for flexibility and the increasing expectation that in love as at work, one might well be only a temporary employee, without affective or material benefits reliably in the present or the future. At moments like this the fantasy of an unconflicted, normative lifeworld can provide the affective pre-experience of a potential site of rest, even if one has known it only as at best a mirage of solidity and stability. This is why whatever account of attachment to normative fantasy we make needs a more complicated notion of object choice and of what it means to desire to have a cluster of affects and feelings in lieu of having a world.

Comfort in proximity to a vague object or scene that promises to deliver some ballast in sociality is not the same as enjoying supremacist pleasure, just as, psychoanalytically speaking, misrecognition is not the same as being mistaken. The hegemonic is, after all, not merely domination dressed more becomingly—it is a metastructure of consent. To see hegemony as domination and subordination is to disavow how much of dependable life relies on the sheerly optimistic formalism of attachment. As citizens of the promise of hegemonic sociability we have consented to consent to a story about the potentialities of the good life around which people execute all sorts of collateral agreements. This is why the people who enforce the reality-effect of this commitment to imminent generality are not just "the hegemons" like CEOs, heteros, Anglos, and U.S. Americans. Commitments to a society of the General Will are enforced by people who have varying access to power, both economic and intimate. From this point of view, instead of embracing ethics as a kind of emotional orthopedics of the political, we might also attend to the convolutions of attachment that involve a desire to stay proximate, no matter what, to the potential openings marked out by fantasies of the good life, self-continuity, or unconflictedness.

III. *Worlds of Pain*

I've been suggesting that Butler's attempt to explain the subject's love of subordination reads normativity too narrowly as an authoritarian desire. In trying to understand how bargaining gets confused with reciprocity and how participation in the economy gets confused with social belonging, this epistemology sees ambivalence as coming after object choice, which is fundamentally abject. What would happen if we saw subjectivization as happening historically, as training in affective sense perception and intuition? Since the 1960s, Lillian Rubin has completed a series of ethnographies of working-class families in the United States in the hope of understanding the ties that bind them to the scenes of deprivation in which they'd become literate as members of the social. Rubin's take on working-class attachment connects it to the cramped temporality of the everyday, twenty-five years before speedup had spread from the two-income, working-class household to the professional-managerial class itself.[34] "But with so little time for normal family life, there's little room for anyone or anything outside. Friendships founder, and adult social activities are put on hold as parents try to do in two days a week what usually takes seven—that is, to establish a sense of family life for themselves and their children. For those whose days off don't match, the problems of sustaining both the couple relationship and family life are magnified enormously."[35]

Meanwhile, the children watch the parents' worlds shrink inwardly to the scale of getting through the day—and the stress is so palpable that the kids learn to try to take up as little space as possible. They grow up feeling guilty about taking up space, seeing their parents as doing their best, but being powerless as well:

> However imperfectly articulated or understood, children in such families sense the adults' frustration and helplessness. Their own hurt notwithstanding, assigning blame to parents makes little sense to these children. Their anger either is turned inward and directed against self . . . . or projected outward and directed against other, less threatening objects. . . . For all children, life often feels fearful and uncontrollable. When a child's experience suggests that the adults on whom he must depend for sur-

vival have little control as well, his fears of being unprotected and over-whelmed are so great that he must either deny and repress his experience or succumb to his terror.[36]

Thus, the working-class child is directed away from critique or complaint. "Children in all families frequently are 'lonely or scared,' or both," she writes. "But the child in the working class family understands that often there's nothing his parents can do about it. They're stuck just as he is — stuck with a life over which they have relatively little control."[37] Rubin here does not describe children's consent to their or to anyone's subordination; nor does she describe love of familial compensations for social powerlessness in the mode of exaggerated patriarchalism and maternality. Instead, the children appear to her to be depressive realists, not idealizing, for the most part, their parents' struggles or modes of survival while at the same time feeling protective of them for the ordinariness of their social humiliation.[38] Another way to say this is that even before the children's lives can be let in as trans-formatively grievable, the parents' lives must be taken seriously as some-thing other than already wasted. It is the function of the children to do that.

How such fantasy becomes the inheritance of an impossible life is most beautifully described by Loïc Wacquant in his ethnography of Chicago's South Side. His informant, Kenny, is a man on the make: he scavenges to live, he builds some skills and lets them lapse, but never gives up his dreams. His dreams, though, are vague: to be a vet, to have a life, to be a star boxer, to make a family. Wacquant says that Kenny has little sense of how these ends might be achieved — the enabling fantasy lives in a disavowed discon-nect from the pressures of getting through the day: "Under such conditions of relentless and all-pervading social and economic insecurity, where exis-tence becomes reduced to the craft of day-to-day survival and where one must continually do one's best with whatever is at hand, that is, precious little, the present becomes so uncertain that it devours the future and pro-hibits thinking about it except as fantasy. . . . [I]n its own way, [it is] a *labor of social mourning* that does not say its name."[39]

Homosexuality, the love that dare not speak its name, echoes within this phrasing of the labor of social mourning: both phrases are about what must remain veiled in order that a scene of social belonging may still be endured. Such euphemisms protect the vulnerable subjects and the social order that ejects them from appropriateness. In Kenny's case, social mourning amid poverty must remain unstated directly, on behalf of not feeling defeated. To

Wacquant, Kenny manifests mourning without feeling it in an explicit way, but we would likely call it cruel optimism, a projection of sustaining but unworkable fantasy.[40]

Thus, perhaps this combination of disappointment and protectiveness can be misread as a hardwired love of subordination, but I think not. *Rosetta* and *La Promesse* show in countless ways the children's desire to protect their parents from experiencing, within the family, a repetition of the humiliation they know all too well outside of it. At the same time, these children are forced, by the parents' lack of fight, to fight the parents on behalf of a dignity and sense of possibility that they maintain only as a fantasy they pass down to their kids. This is clearly the case in Rosetta's constant refusal of her mother's homemaking gestures—making salmon, planting plants outside their caravan—because those things are effects of charity and sexual exchange, and "we are not beggars" and "you are not a whore." Likewise Igor never says no to his father, even after they kill Amidou, but instead falls silent, and though he rescues Assita from his father and she wants to go to the police, Igor says, "My father's wrong, but I'm no snitch." In the end, it is Assita who must physically overpower Roger, because Igor wants to protect him from facing the reality that the network of illegal patriarchalism has now been exposed not as making do or building a life but as the petty reproduction of exploitation's instrumentality at the level of the informal everyday. Igor begins to see it, but his body freezes, much as Rosetta's body is being eaten alive by an ulcer that cramps her up, but neither of them can reject the drowning parental body that is also pulling them down, perhaps for fear of becoming identical to the police, the state, the bosses, and inspectors who would see only practices and care little for the motives of love.

Given the films' geopolitical and historical specificity, what can we take away from thinking through these readings of the ways some children reproduce the forms of the bad life insofar as they are rooted in the family? We have seen that the child, the subordinated subject, learns early that relations of reciprocity are likely to be betrayed when the only way to survive the world is to resort to informal economies and the bribes and bargains of biopower, with its discourses of untruth. The films show the youths struggling to tell their truths without harming anyone. But to do so is impossible, because in their worlds love is constituted through acts of lying to protect the feelings of intimates, while at the same time, and behind the veil of lies, the ruthlessness for survival that anyone on the bottom of class society must mobilize ends up shaking up the intimate sphere as much as anything else. The subjects of survival require cultivating techniques of scavenging, syncretism, and mistrust. There is barely time to reflect on belonging, and no time not to react to threat; the tiny folds of moral peace and optimism these two films allow their protagonists cannot be sustained by personal will, after all, but by control over resources they do not have.

I close, therefore, not with a solution to the problem of aspirational normativity as expressed in the conventionalities of subaltern feeling, because, I am arguing, the subordinated sensorium of the worker, whose acts of rage and ruthlessness are mixed with forms of care, is an effect of the relation between capitalism's refusal of futurity in an overwhelmingly productive present and the normative promise of intimacy, which enables us to imagine that having a friend, or making a date, or looking longingly at someone who might, after all, show compassion for our struggles, is really where living takes place.

SIX **AFTER THE GOOD LIFE, AN IMPASSE**

Time Out, Human Resources, and the Precarious Present

1. *Always Now: Situation, Gesture, Impasse*

This chapter extends to the bourgeois family our attention to the relation between the reproduction of life and the attenuation of life in lived scenes of contemporary capitalist activity. Laurent Cantet's assessments of French labor in the late 1990s—*Ressources humaines* (1999) and *L'emploi du temps* (2001)—have been extolled as aesthetic reenactments of the impact of neoliberalism on the everyday life of formerly protected classes.[1] Documenting the shifting up of economic precarity into what Giorgio Agamben has called the new "planetary petty bourgeoisie" (PPB) comprised of unionized populations, entrepreneurs, small property owners, and the professional managerial class, the films detail major and minute recalibrations of relations among the state, the market, and how people live.[2] Their precarity is therefore significantly more than economic: it is structural in many senses and permeates the affective environment too. The films witness the blow to traditional props for optimism about life-building that had sustained the aspirationally upwardly mobile, and pay attention to how different kinds of people catch up to their new situation.

What does it mean even to propose that a spreading precarity provides the dominant *structure* and *experience* of the present moment, cutting across class and localities?[3] There is broad agreement on the emergence of this situation, but descriptions of the affected populations veer wildly from workers in regimes of immaterial labor and the historical working class to the global managerial class; neobohemians who go to university, live off part-time or temporary jobs, and sometimes the dole while making art; and, well, everyone whose bodies and lives are saturated by capitalist forces and rhythms.[4] In what sense, then, is it accurate to call this phenomenon a new global *class*—one that has indeed been termed the *precariat*?[5] This emergent taxonomy raises questions about to what degree precarity is an economic and political condition suffered by a population or by the subjects of capitalism generally; or a way of life; or an affective atmosphere; or an existential truth about contingencies of living, namely, that there are no guarantees that the life one intends can or will be built.[6]

At root, precarity is a condition of dependency—as a legal term, *precarious* describes the situation wherein your tenancy on your land is in someone else's hands.[7] Yet capitalist activity always induces destabilizing scenes of productive destruction—of resources and of lives being made and unmade according to the dictates and whims of the market. But, as David Harvey and many others argue, neoliberal economic practices mobilize this instability in unprecedented ways. The profit interests of the owners of neoliberal capital are served by the shrinkage of the social welfare state, the privatization of what had once been publicly held utilities and institutions, the increase in state, banking, and corporate pension insecurity, and the ever more "flexible" practices of contractual reciprocity between owners and workers, which ostensibly keeps business nimble and more capable of responding to market demand. Add to this the global transformation of unions from a force driving forward security and upward mobility to administrative entities managing workers' decreasing legitimacy for claims-making on profit and security, and you get a broad picture of the neoliberal feedback loop, with its efficiency at distributing and shaping the experience of insecurity throughout the class structure and across the globe.

Many analysts claim that the managerial classes of the industrialized West, in particular, have recently been forced to enter a new historical phase. Pundits have noted that the latest banking crisis in the United States was unusually "democratic" in its shattering of the expectations, rules, and norms of reciprocity that govern life across diverse locales and statuses.[8] Richard Sennett and Michael Hardt and Antonio Negri would have predicted this; they shape their otherwise dissimilar analyses of contemporary capitalist subjectivity by noting the increasing corrosion of *security* as a condition of life for workers across different concentrations of economic and political privilege.[9] But they also claim that, at the turn of the twenty-first century, security became less of an aspiration for the classes who had less access to it, and indeed that this labile labor environment produced a sense of freedom and potential for many members of the PPB. They report that some members saw labor as a system that could be gamed on behalf of forging a more satisfying life, others opted out of a live-to-work ideology altogether, and still others focused on developing their craft, not their lifestyles.

How this affective shift toward valuing lateral freedoms and creative ambitions over strict upward mobility will fare in the current economic crisis, amid expanding claims on the state and the frantic grasping to stay in labor as such, remains to be seen. A concrete example of this synergy between neoliberal interests and the shift in worker desires was evident in the "Precarious" movement itself: in its film and its polemic, for example, the group *Precarias de la Deriva* ("The Precarious Adrift") narrates both the frustration and free-feeling pleasure of the educated, underemployed classes of Europe as they move around cities, make deals and build networks, and insist on their centrality and not marginality to the social. In the rhetoric of a crisis of care, they demand a new metric of reciprocity for a new social ecology, wanting the state to guarantee basic conditions of flourishing—food, clothing, shelter, jobs—without anyone having to give up the flexible, wandering way of living they have carved out.[10] This view places what used to be antagonistic classes in apparent solidarity: both the managers and the multitude sense in this shift the radical potential for the destruction of work as we know it, while expecting the state to maintain its provision of economic security and infrastructural solidity.

In contrast, while agreeing that precarity has saturated the consciousness and economic life of subjects transnationally and across populations,

Jacques Rancière, in *Hatred of Democracy*, and Adam Phillips, in *Equals*, claim that the majority in the formerly protected classes increasingly "hate" the instabilities, incongruities, antagonisms, ambiguities, and messes that constitute their life in contemporary capitalist mass society. They argue that the PPB wants to hoard for itself not radical flexibility but the privilege of only moderately creative living and working amid relatively predictable security, while demanding from everyone else deference, docility, self-management, and predictability.[11] In their view, which is also Agamben's, the managers of capital and its service class are finding the threat of real vulnerability a crisis condition within the ordinary; their response to it has been fundamentally antidemocratic, producing at best gestural solidarities with other precarious populations.

Add to this Phillips's claim about the synergies of radical democracy and psychoanalysis. Phillips argues that the historic mission of psychoanalysis—to build skills for the subject's capacity to live and flourish under conditions of ongoing disorientation and insecurity—should find solidarity with the radical democratic embrace of the chaos, antagonisms, and interests of the least privileged that would characterize any true democracy. His strong claim is that the central sensual experience of equality and democracy is not knowing where one is. But people come to fear and hate these processes because they exert a constant pressure for negotiating social location. Cruel optimism or not, they feel attached to the soft hierarchies of inequality to provide a sense of *their place in the world*. The internal tensions between capitalism and democracy seem resolved as long as a little voting, a little privacy, and unimpeded consumer privilege prevail to prop up the sense that the good-life fantasy is available to everyone. Ideally, then, one would achieve both mental health and a commitment to equality if one embraced precarity as the condition of being and belonging.

Cantet's films resonate with these broad descriptions of affective placeness amid the situation of structural adjustment in contemporary Europe and the United States. They do not assume a globalized comparative perspective on class or on the good-life fantasy—they're not analytics or polemics—and so can only partly help to answer the question of what it means to enter insecurity from a variety of class locations. Yet even the most local perspective in these films is an outcome of globalization and neoliberal restructuring: none of these dramas would occur without shifts in state tax, labor, and welfare policy that promote the disempowerment of unions, a corporate culture that suppresses wages, benefits, and worker's rights, and the concomitant expansion of production systems scattered across spaces in Europe, Korea, and elsewhere. Focusing on dramatic reconfigurations of economic and affectional relations of "responsibility" among bosses, contract workers, and satellite intimates, Cantet's films stage how close the relatively privileged now are to living the affective life of those who have never been economically and institutionally secure. The hanging last line of *Human Resources*—*where is your place?*—could be spoken by anyone to anyone else in the films, is unanswerable, and is the least rhetorical question imaginable at this moment in time. Perhaps, in the impasse of the transitional present, where situations unfold in ongoing crisis, what were rhetorical questions become genuine ones.

This strange cohesion of neoliberal interest, psychoanalytic theory, and radical theoretical commitments to contingent conditions for the reinvigoration of social life suggests, in short, two things about contemporary precarity. One is that the precariat must be a fundamentally affective class, since the economic and political processes that put people there continue to structure inequalities according to locale, gender, race, histories of class and political privilege, available state resources, and skills.[12] The other is that, in the affective imaginary of this class, adaptation to a *sense* of precarity dramatizes the situation of the present. Throughout this book I have been calling the historical present a *situation* deliberately, to develop it as a concept for tracking transactions within the elongated *durée* of the present moment. As we know from situation comedy, a situation is a genre of living that one knows one's in but that one has to find out about, a circumstance embedded in life but not in one's control. A situation is a disturbance, a sense genre of animated suspension—not suspended animation. It has a punctum, like a photograph; it forces one to take notice, to become *interested* in potential changes to ordinariness. When a situation unfolds, people try to maintain themselves in it until they figure out how to adjust.

What makes the present historical moment a situation is not just that finally the wealthy are experiencing the material and sensual fragilities and unpredictability that have long been distributed to the poor and socially marginal. It is that adaptation to the adaptive imperative is producing a whole new precarious public sphere, defined by debates about how to rework insecurity in the ongoing present, and defined as well by an emerging aesthetic.[13] These shifts have provoked strange continuities in neoliberal and radical analyses of causality and futurity—for example, of how things got to be this way and whether better futures are even imaginable.[14]

Whereas in the Dardennes' work (see chapter 5, "Nearly Normal") play-risk and life-risk provide alternative folds of potentiality within the contingencies of contemporary capitalist precarity as seen from "below," for Cantet's more privileged population the increases in vulnerability and in risk seem to produce more confusion than optimism about what kinds of adjustment to prefer. For what defines this pressing situation is the problem of living in the ongoing now of it. The enduring present that is at once overpresent and enigmatic requires finding one's footing in new manners of being in it. The haunting question is how much of one's creativity and hypervigilant energy the situation will absorb before it destroys its subjects or finds a way to appear as merely a steady hum of livable crisis ordinariness.

Nonetheless, the situation is not, finally, proof that economic and political fragility everywhere has engendered a new globalized or mass-homogeneous class. That remains to be seen. It is that there has been a mass dissolution of a disavowal. The promise of the good life no longer masks the living precarity of this historical present. This is evidenced in the emergence of a new mask, a precarious visage that now graces myriad accounts of how people are living the end of both social and market democracy in Europe and the United States: a recession grimace has appeared, somewhere between a frown, a smile, and a tightened lip. As more people from more social locations are seen watching their dreams become foreclosed on in material and fantasmatic ways, the grimace produces another layer of face to create a space of delay while the subject and world adjust to how profoundly fantasmatic the good-life dreams were, after all.[15]

Cantet's films enact an aesthetic style of living and of mediation that tracks this disturbance. In the films, shifting relations among economic and political conditions of contingency refract in singular, simultaneous, and yet collective bodily performances of instability—the instability of the ongoing present as the ground for living. It is an aesthetic shaped by the fraying of norms, that is, of genres of reliable being. Fraying implies something slow, delicate, processual, something happening on its own time. Aesthetically, we observe this politico-affective condition mainly in messy situations, episodes, incidents, and gestures, and not often in the genre of the dramatic event.

A proprioceptive history, an archive of exemplary bodily adjustments, provides access to the affective reeducation that transpires in response to the stress fractures now appearing in the normative fantasy and its related economies. In "Precarity: A Savage Journey to the Heart of Embodied Capitalism," Vassilis Tsianos and Dimitris Papadopoulos list a whole series of nervous-system symptoms to attend to—although this analysis locates precarity only in the subjects of immaterial labor.[16] These include:

(a) vulnerability: the steadily experience of flexibility without any form of protection [sic]; (b) hyperactivity: the imperative to accommodate constant availability; (c) simultaneity: the ability to handle at the same [time] the different tempi and velocities of multiple activities; (d) recombination: the crossings between various networks, social spaces, and available resources; (e) post-sexuality: the other as dildo; (f) fluid intimacies: the bodily production of indeterminate gender relations; (g) restlessness: being exposed to and trying to cope with the overabundance of communication, cooperation and interactivity; (h) unsettledness: the continuous experience of mobility across different spaces and time lines; (i) affective exhaustion: emotional exploitation, or, emotion as an important element for the control of employability and multiple dependencies; (j) cunning: able to be deceitful, persistent, opportunistic, a trickster.

Precarious bodies, in other words, are not merely demonstrating a shift in the social contract, but in ordinary affective states. This instability requires, if not psychoanalytic training in contingency management, embarking on an intensified and stressed out learning curve about how to maintain footing, bearings, a way of being, and new modes of composure amid unraveling institutions and social relations of reciprocity.

Queer phenomenology, as a scene for putting into circulation a bodily orientation, provides another intellectual context for the rise of proprioception as a metric for apprehending the historical present. To turn toward cinematic bodies transacting in space is not to re-argue that cinema reenacts and transforms some universally haptic sense of the world that is registered as bodily flesh. Queer phenomenology—see especially work by Camilla Griggers, Laura Marks, Gail Weiss, Elspeth Probyn, and Sara Ahmed—has demanded a political analysis of the ongoing activity of bodily orientation and the modes of circulation through which subjects enter into contemporary worldliness, identity, and belonging. Aesthetic mediation here produces exemplary translations between singular and general patterns of orientation, self-projection, attachment, and a psychic, affectional, neural *sense* of proximity. In contrast to Tsianos and Papadopoulos's work, queer phenomenology is involved not mainly with gathering up evidence of symptoms of affective damage, but with following the tracks of longing and belonging to create new openings for how to live, and to offer the wild living or outside belonging that already takes place as opportunities for others to re-imagine the practice of making and building lives. In this work social attachments are evidenced in practice, including the practices of the senses that are always working in the now and are active and responsive without being expressive, necessarily, of ideologies, or truths, or anything.[17]

Interested in how people live through historical moments of loss, this chapter looks even more locally toward how bodies figure *glitches* in the conditions of the reproduction of life in the historical present. A glitch is an interruption amid a transition. I want to show how transactions of the body of the aestheticized or mediated subject absorb, register, reenact, refigure, and make possible a political understanding of shifts and hiccups in the relations among structural forces that alter a class's *sense* of things, its sensing of things.[18] It involves encountering what it feels like to be in the middle of a shift and to use reconfigurations of manner amid the persistence of the body in the world to embody not the continuities of institutionalized history but something incoherent or uncongealed in the ongoing activity of the social.[19] It is to see what is happening to systems of self-intelligibility through watching subjects getting, losing, and keeping their bearing within a thick present. It is to understand action that does not express internal states but measures a situation. Henri Lefebvre would call this a *rhythmanalysis*, but it is not the bodily rhythm forced by the architecture of the everyday and the modes of dressage that enable living in it that I focus on here. This chapter is a rhythmanalysis of a disturbance in the situation of the present and the adaptations improvised around it.[20]

Such a relation of embodied perturbation to adaptation is what Agamben points to when he claims that "By the end of the nineteenth century, the bourgeoisie had definitely lost its gestures."[21] Film, he argues, registers this "generalized catastrophe" by gathering up the lost gestures as a measure of what it means to be archaic.[22] As a genre, the gesture is not identical to the Brechtian concept of *gestus*, a mode of aesthetic communication that releases to the public occluded, illegitimate knowledge about the mode of production and its manifestation in typical people's individual and collective lives.[23] Instead, to Agamben, the gesture is a medial act, neither ends-nor means-oriented, a sign of being in the world, in the middle of the world, a sign of sociality. To elaborate, this version of the gesture is not a message; it is more formal than that—the performance of a shift that could turn into a disturbance, or what Deleuze would call a "problem-event."[24] The gesture does not mark time, if time is a movement forward, but makes time, holding the present open to attention and unpredicted exchange. The grimace is such a gesture. So is a deadpan nonresponse. A situation can grow around it or not, because it makes the smallest opening, a movement-created space. The gesture is thus only a potential event, the initiation of something present that could accrue density, whether dramatic or not. The movement could make a situation, and then the gesture would start to look different in it. In this view the present is not always a sense of something fleeting or a metaphysical experience of loss; nor is it mainly a dumping ground of anachronistic historical forces. When the disturbance of the gesture is lived as adjustment, remediation, or adaptation, the present is a stretch of time that is being sensed and shaped—an impasse.

It might seem amiss to call a live situation where actors do things an impasse, since the world remains largely organized by dedramatized clusters of causes, consequences, and microtransformations. I offer impasse both as a formal term for encountering the duration of the present, and a specific term for tracking the circulation of precariousness through diverse locales and bodies. The concept of the present as impasse opens up different ways that the interruption of norms of the reproduction of life can be adapted to, felt out, and lived. The impasse is a space of time lived without a narrative genre. Adaptation to it usually involves a gesture or undramatic action that points to and revises an unresolved situation. One takes a *pass* to avoid something or to get somewhere: it's a formal figure of transit. But the impasse is a *cul-de-sac*—indeed, the word *impasse* was invented to replace *cul-de-sac*, with its untoward implications in French. In a cul-de-sac one keeps moving, but one moves paradoxically, in the *same space*. An impasse is a holding station that doesn't hold securely but opens out into anxiety, that dogpaddling around a space whose contours remain obscure. An impasse is decompositional—in the unbound temporality of the stretch of time, it marks a delay that demands activity.[25] The activity can produce impacts and events, but one does not know where they are leading. That delay enables us to develop gestures of composure, of mannerly transaction, of being-with in the world as well as of rejection, refusal, detachment, psychosis, and all kinds of radical negation.

Yet not all stretches of life and time in the present are suspended in the same way. As the chapter proceeds, I'll focus on two kinds of impasse while gesturing toward and performing a third. First, there is the impasse after the dramatic event of a forced loss, such as after a broken heart, a sudden death, or a social catastrophe, when one no longer knows what to do or how to live and yet, while unknowing, must adjust. Second, there is what happens when one finds oneself adrift amid normative intimate or material terms of reciprocity without an event to have given the situation a name and procedures for managing it—coasting through life, as it were, until one discovers a loss of traction. Third, there are situations where managing the presence of a problem/event that dissolves the old sureties and forces improvisation and reflection on life-without-guarantees is a pleasure and a plus, not a loss. Agnes Varda's *The Gleaners and I* (2000) provides a problematic, exuberant example of happy life-without-guarantees in the impasse, as do the lateral pleasures of aesthetic interpretation itself.[26] (Note that these three versions of postoptimistic response echo the case material of chapter 1, "Cruel Optimism.")

Whatever else it is, and however one enters it, the historical present—as an impasse, a thick moment of ongoingness, a situation that can absorb many genres without having one itself—is a middle without boundaries, edges, a shape. It is experienced in transitions and transactions. It is the name for the space where the urgencies of livelihood are worked out all over again, without assurances of futurity, but nevertheless proceeding via durable norms of adaptation. People are destroyed in it, or discouraged but maintaining, or happily managing things, or playful and enthralled. Add to this the fading of security and upward mobility as national capitalist alibis for exploitation in the present. If the precariat is an affective class, then for the formerly psychically and economically protected members of the precariat there has been at least one enduring and collectively binding loss—of the gestures that maintained the disavowals and contradictions that sustained so many social democratic good-life fantasies. This is where the details of the dissolution, and how they are exemplified, and the fantasies that continue to bind people to fantasy, matter politically to the history of the present.[27]

II. *"It's normal to be a bit nervous"*: Ressources humaines

Jean-Claude Barbier's extremely useful "A Comparative Analysis of 'Employment Precariousness' in Europe"[28] claims that the word *précarité* originally referred only to lives mired in poverty, and only became attached to employment in the 1980s, when neoliberal restructuring in the guise of flexible labor was becoming a byword in national and transnational corporate politics.[29] Flexibility was sold as a freedom both for corporations responding to an increasingly dynamic or unstable economy and for people who saw being tied down to jobs as a hindrance both to pleasure and to upward mobility. Many have written about the consequences of this shift for the loosening and convolution of the traditional national-liberal terms of social obligation. Barbier argues that in the French case "precarity" underdescribes the variety of labor contracts that operate in the nation, but nonetheless the concept has become elastic, describing an affective atmosphere penetrating all classes. Finally, in parallel with this continuous extension of *précarité* to *précarité de l'emploi* and then to *précarité du travail*, a fourth extension of the scope of phenomena to which the notion referred led to the introduction of *précarisation*, that is, the process of society as a whole becoming more precarious and basically destabilized.

What has been called the French cinematic "New Realism" of the 1990s and after—a global style that amounts to a *Cinema of Precarity*—documents this shift in precarity from limited structure to pervasive life environment.[30] Returning to the hinge between the melodramatic realism associated with Hollywood cinema of the 1930s and 1940s and postwar Italian neorealism, the Cinema of Precarity melds melodrama and politics into a more reticent aesthetic to track the attrition of what had been sustaining national, social, economic, and political bonds and the abandonment of a variety of populations to being cast as waste.

Precarious cinema destabilizes the neat postwar shift from a bourgeois private idiom into a national public idiom in that the story it tells about what is exemplary in the privatization of public life and the fragility of all of the institutions and spaces for the reproduction of life—intimate, public, private, national, economic, transnational, environmental—emphasizes the present as a transitional zone where normative forms of reciprocity are wearing out, both in the world and aesthetically—barring the reproduction of inherited fantasies of what it means to want to add up to something—that story of the good life. The ongoing crisis of institutions, economies, and fantasy in the ordinary destabilizes exemplarity itself at these moments, and the films record the loneliness of collective singularity, the impacts of affective fraying, and the tiny optimism of recuperative gestures in the middle of it all, for those who can manage them. The Cinema of Precarity therefore attends to the proprioceptive—to bodies moving in space performing affectively laden gestures—to investigate new potential conditions of solidarity emerging from subjects not with similar historical identities or social locations but with similar adjustment styles to the pressures of the emergent new ordinariness.

Cantet's *Human Resources* is most explicit about this transition into the beyond of convention, and equates the aesthetic problem with the problem of living, of livelihood. It tells a simple, exemplary microhistory of the expansion of precarity in the story of what happens between two people, in one family, one factory, and one community, at a recent historic moment in France. And yet the very simplicity of this story—which sees in the details of the reproduction of life the end of a mode of production and of life—mobilizes multiple, terrible ironies. Cantet plants his scenario firmly in the irony I outlined at the start of this essay, where radical imaginaries for the reconfiguration of work and neoliberal interests in greater profit extraction through more "flexible" relations of obligation and responsibility to workers and business locales assumed a terrible synergy. In particular, the film is set as a thought experiment prior to the instantiation of the French socialist program to shorten the workweek to thirty-five hours (the 1998 film was predicting the state of things in 2000, when the policy legislating the so-called "trente-cinq" was enacted). This moment was marked as historic, as a collective event, because it involved state action to reshape the everyday lives of working citizens.

By subsidizing a more equal distribution and expansion of job opportunity (for so many were unemployed while so many others were working overtime), the socialists also made concessions to neoliberal corporate claims that labor must become more flexible and available to respond quickly to the rise and fall of market demand. Thus the thirty-five-hour week is actually a misnomer and instead points to an average to be calculated over a year: workers might be asked to increase or decrease their hours at any time. It is also worth noting that in France the salient distinction is between jobs *with status*—that is, legally protected jobs—and jobs without status—that is, precarious, temporary, and episodic jobs. Established workers had thought that they had jobs for life, steady, predictable time-extensive ruts created by showing up and doing enough rather than showing up and being anxious about constantly re-earning their jobs. The thirty-five-hour workweek has brought with it an increase of contract labor, a decrease in the power of unions, and a crisis in the terms of the national social contract, insofar as that contract is evidenced in economic policy.[31] Cantet's film predicted all of this.

If the collaboration of socialist and corporate interests was inauspicious in itself, the outcome of this mutual adaptation has also had world-distorting consequences. The second irony involves the perverse rhetorical synergies that emerge from the marriage of the language of market risk to that of class struggle: in *Human Resources*, the language of precarity and of the threatening "situation" is used not only by workers, whose lives and livelihoods are threatened by pressures on industry to increase both production and profits, but by the managers themselves. The first line that Rouet, the factory boss, says in *Human Resources* translates as, "Do not terrify him with our precarious situation." At a moment of fierce contestation between the interests of workers and capital, it is now possible to bracket or to claim as archaic long-standing debates about what it means for individuals, the masses, and the state to live democracy by asserting that everyone now lives capitalism in proximity to risk, threat, and ongoing anxiety at the situation that something autonomous called "life" seems to present equally, everywhere. Competing precarities can morph in an instant to sound like grounds for solidarity.

So in some sense, the new realism or melodramatic impasse of *Human Resources* is right on the surface and the precarious public sphere is just a development in capitalist/democratic crisis management of long-embedded historical contradictions. It is, after all, a tale in which states manage capital not on behalf of citizens but on behalf of profit to be enjoyed elsewhere, by a few, while maintaining the traditional manners of a liberal polis run by the presumption of good intentions on all sides and a theoretically equal distribution of vulnerability. What makes this situation historically specific, however, is *how* these struggles are played out in a shift between older and newer idioms of sociality, not only in wars of words but according to the metric of manners.

When the unions fight management in this film, for example, Mme. Arnoux, a furiously direct, classically belligerent union representative, is called crazy and irrational not only by the plant managers but by her fellow syndicalists. She pounds the table and calls the bosses vulgar liars, to which her male colleagues respond by saying, "what she is saying in her own way . . . ," rephrasing her claims in the tones of management, the language of reason, trust, coolness, and dispassion. Later, when she turns out to be right, she gloats that what they called crazy bad manners was really the last barrier to an appeasement that had already taken place, as though the union men's commitment to manners was greater than it was to facing what was incommensurable about the interests of the owners of capital and those of the workers.

Pressures to adapt all down the line increase, though, and the discourse fellowship gets increasingly brittle. As the film goes on, it focuses more and more on minor moments, not so much of lives colliding but of bodies demurring, averting, hesitating, double-talking, rushing into proximity but then recoiling. We watch the exhaustion of one mode of life, the spreading out of the edges of its loss into an endless ongoingness, and then a blockage of any imaginary for what else could happen next, apart from a slower chipping away at the good life that had been achieved. What's revelatory and painful about Cantet's version of this, additionally, is his sensitivity to national-capitalist restructuring as a catastrophe for democracy, starting in the most intimate spaces. What begins as relations of comfortable banter can only aspire, at the end, to a numbness made of a mix of defeat, anxiety, and stupefaction: a mixed space of delayed reaction that can allow the fantasy and memory of intimate feeling to persist along with the truth of the end of economic optimism. Upward mobility tips over into the impasse, into phrases like "it is what it is."

Two moments condense this shift revealingly. The filmic action begins and ends on a train, but what's in transit is what's at home. Franck returns to Normandy from Paris to take up a management position in the factory his father has worked in for over three decades. This return has "enormous symbolic" importance to Franck: as a child he went to summer camp run by the factory, attended their Christmas spectaculars, and it is clear that he's intimate with the parental social life that has extended from the father's work life. But although Franck has lived within walking distance of the factory his entire life, it is only on his very first day of wearing the tailored suit that marks his class difference from his uniformed father that he first sees his father's machine, and the labor his father does on it. "I wanted to show him my machine," the father says to his foreman. There's a lyric rhythm to the father's relation to his phrases, which are responded to rhythmically shot by shot: "You put down the part. The welder's at the back. A bolt drops into place by itself. You put the part on top. With practice, you do 700 an hour." Here, as at home in the family woodshop, the son looks on quietly at his father's competence, his face a little masked. But one foreman sees the scene of performing and watching differently: "It's not a zoo here. Even for your son. . . . You should know it's no circus here!" Another foreman interrupts the scene by berating the father for his slowed-down output.

Franck's illiteracy in his father's machine is likely a deliberate outcome of familial decisions probably made before the son was sentient. Franck em-

9. Franck brings the New Normal (Cantet, *Human Resources*, 1999)

bodies the postwar social democratic contract to grant the working classes access to *embourgeoisement*. His father owns a home and makes furniture in his well-machined woodshop; his mother tends house, makes meals, says the right things, polices manners, and keeps the family flowing. His sister, Sylvie, works in the father's factory and has married Olivier, a paternal look-alike, who also works there. They have two children, and their own, larger, home. But Franck, the "baby," is special. He embodies the familial invest-ment in upward mobility. Sent away to Paris and to business school, he has been educated prior to that *not to know* much about his family's work lives. He is cultural, social, economic capital that's been squirreled away, fussed over, not yet invested: it is appropriate, therefore, that he is named after money. In contrast, his parents have no names in the film's credits: "*le père*" and "*la mère*" are there as human resources for Franck.[32] They have invested their labor in him behind the scenes, as it were, and kept what the mother calls their "sacrifice" to themselves. In investing money, time, ignorance, and pride in their son this way, they reproduce the hierarchy of class defer-ence whose very legitimation splinters during the film. You see this in the very first family scene, where the father veers between awe of "my son" (a phrase he repeats throughout with pride) and soft paternalism. You see it too in the scenes where the parents apologize to him for making noise while he's working in the family living room.

At first the father is so proud of the son that he can barely approach him: as the son is an abstraction, a screen for fantasy investments, when he re-turns home his body perturbs and requires an adjustment, a shift that takes place at the level of manners. "You're not saying hello?" says the mother to the father, who hovers on the periphery of the intimate family crowd on the train station platform. Then, later, the father, more comfortable on the couch next to his son, erupts with advice about how the son, now unpre-

10. Franck and his father debate expectations at work

pared, can survive in the real world. The scene is shot in the romantic light of standard, soft Hollywood domestic comedy: ambient noise, the camera acting like an amused guest following the bantering conversation. This is the kind of forgettable conversation that happens in ordinary information and wisdom transmission across generations. But the final cut pins the tail on the plot to come.

> Le père: Tomorrow don't act smart with the boss. Find out what he wants first. . . . I mean it. He's not one of your professors. Work's not like school. You have to be serious.
> Franck: I'm only a trainee.
> Le père: It's no reason to stroll in unprepared.
> Franck: I won't stroll in unprepared. . . . I wasn't nervous. Now I am. Happy?
> Le père: It's normal to be a bit nervous.
> Franck: I don't know. . . . Maybe.

The bottom line here is that labor is not a casual space, and that to be a good worker is to be an anxious one. On the next day, the film takes a dive into the new normal. The atmospherics are of excitement, pride, awkwardness, and bodies jostling while inventing new habits of being and relating in space. By the end of the day, we see how out of synch the father is with the new capital, which Franck represents. But Franck is also in over his head. Well-mannered, he absorbs all kinds of sniping ambivalence in the management offices and on the production floor. He seems to absorb this hazing as the price of upward mobility; but, having learned nothing at home or in business school about the labor struggles of the twentieth century, he does not take the hazing as political commentary. Protected by his father's archaic deferentialism and the experience of unions as a cultural, rather than political, force, he retains the liberal fantasy that management and unions are on the same side and slips easily into the new model of universal precarity. Saying that he hopes that the new world of flexible labor will help bosses and workers economically and "will further implicate employees in company affairs," he expresses a desire to make the workers' forced adaptation feel like rational critical democracy and not the insult to their capacity to reproduce life that it is. He does not notice when the boss says, "We'll win it together!" that the referent of "we" excludes the workers. And when he offers a plan to circumvent the union by canvassing workers about the *trente-cinq* directly, he thinks he enacts classic public sphere ethics: the business ought to represent what the people want, and the unions are a self-interest group that hampers individual sovereignty and self-determination. He has no clue that he's providing an alibi for decisions about downsizing that have already been made: he's not yet suspicious of the class to which he's been educated.

Later, when Franck realizes that he's been used by the factory managers to justify downsizing, including the downsizing of his father, he becomes angry, reveals management secrets, works for the union, and helps to organize a strike. But the father is mortified by the son's political transformation. The end of the old normal produces tears "like a woman's," the mother says; and soon the son cries too, not like a woman but a lost child. The tear is a tear, a rip, a glitch. What do they do next, after the good life, after patronage, after loving paternalism, and without clarity about what makes sacrifice and risk worth it?

Franck's response is to rub his father's face in his own despair. Attacking him for refusing to stop work and join the strike, he strikes out at his father on the factory floor, in front of his entire community. Representing and contesting the new phase of capital, the son makes his father face the new normal.[33]

> Franck: You'll never stop. You're pathetic. I'm ashamed of you! Understand? I've been ashamed since I was small. Ashamed to be the son of a worker. Now I'm ashamed of being ashamed!
>
> Arnoux: No reason for shame.
>
> Franck: Tell him! He taught me! . . . Ashamed of his class. I have good news. You're not fired, you're retiring. Not because you worked hard for 30 years. It's a favor from the boss. He did it for me. Because he likes me. We talk as equals. That makes me sick. That!

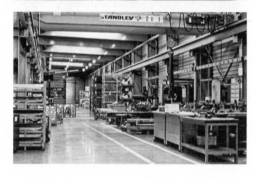

11.1–11.3. Franck and his father confront the new normal

Do you understand it makes me sick? [Sister tries to stop him] I know I'm unfair! I should thank him. I should thank him and mom for your sacrifices. You did it. Your son's on the bosses' side. I'll never be a worker. I'll have an interesting job. I'll earn money. I'll have responsibilities and power. The power to talk to you like this. The power to fire you like this. But you gave me your shame. I'll have it inside me all my life.

Embedding affective transmission in the historical, this scene of searing pedagogy links the power to talk and to act to visceral atmospheres of shame dissociated from explicit social performance but present everywhere in the intimate atmospheres of the reproduction of life. Shame is the trace of dis-avowed class anxiety, the darker side of aspiration's optimism. Franck tells his father that it is now Franck who has the power to be dissociated, to act as a beneficent patriarch of sorts, pretending, if he wanted to, that kindness has nothing to do with the shaming deference culture of the factory and the family. This inverts their historical relation, as the son's job had been to be good and deserving of his parents' investment in him, so that their class self-disidentification would not become expressed in his failure to aspire and achieve.

Out of shame, these subjects of capital have protected each other from frank talks about what *exactly* has been sacrificed in managing the domes-tic/industrial labor nexus that has constituted lifemaking. Out of love, these subjects of capital protect the fantasies of intimates by suppressing the costs of adjustment to labor's physical and affective demands. Out of love and shame, the subjects of class shame have all been being good, acting optimistic, building lives, and hoping that the affective bargains passed as obligation and care among them will not have been in error. Everyone's ap-propriateness had turned shame's threat into pride.

This scene of shock in the factory should not shock the father, in a way: just the previous year twenty-two workers were let go "in the shadow" of the company's threat to go out of business if adequate rates of profit were not protected. But here the father's early casual, intimate, teasing banter, bodily comfort, and paternalist transmission of expertise become exposed pub-licly as archaic, associated with the paternalist capitalist social relations that accompanied the gains made by socialist and social democratic workers' movements in the twentieth century. The old normal came with a body that absorbed the slings and arrows of working-class discipline into a kind of solidity and quiet grace. This solidity made the father a valued colleague who did not talk much, but gave helpful advice when he did—not only to Franck but to Alain, the father's French-African neighbor in the production line, who tells Franck about how the father taught him to work the machines. Now, Alain says, "You know, sometimes, without meaning to, I still look his way. . . . to see if he's satisfied. Seeing him cope helps me cope." Alain, not Franck, is the heir of the father's pride in his class attachments. At one level, coping here is a manner of being working-class, a rhythm of being. It says nothing about how anyone lines up affectively or emotionally behind their practices: purely formal, its performance of self-discontinuity produces continuity itself. But as the camera tracks the situation of the present in *Human Resources* and, later, in *Time Out*, this structure of labor-related affective splitting comes to pervade contemporary experience.

In the old normal the paternal face was the same as the body: it said a little, it absorbed a lot, it was a barrier sponge that enabled living on to be something to look forward to. What's new is that the father is being forced to be *seen seeing* his own desire to work under the radar as political, and to be *seen seeing* the political as saturating all of his most intimate fantasies, gestures, and ordinary casualness. This doubling dissolves his fantasmatic legitimations for doing the work that, as Alain says, "no one wants to do." His way of standing apart, sitting aside, writing a check, and whispering so as not to be a bother becomes identical to appeasing the bosses when they ask the workers to give back more hard-fought rights. When they speak of all this at home, he blusters and throws his family out. But in the intimate space of work he can no longer access his defenses.

The father's flesh registers his assimilation to the public news that there is no such thing as being under the radar by way of a disturbance in his facial composure. The father's quivering lip moves not toward speech but threatens to become out of control, to decompose. The quivering lower lip denotes someone overwhelmed by a wordless response without a way of saving face. He is stuck in the impasse of the present without routines left to prop up even a lip, let alone a person. Deleuze's and Guattari's much-commented-on concept of faciality posits the face as a porous relay between the chaos of subjectivization and the clarities of signification, an always failing barrier between the subject's composure and the affective instability that exists in a domain quite different from the body's proprioceptive dynamics. But here the class politics of bodily performance advises a different way of reading

12. Franck, imploded

that de-ontologizes the face and embeds its stunned expressivity in a historical zone of circulation, affect management, and self-projection.

Cantet cuts from the father's quivering lip to the empty factory because there is no outside to this situation. The scene of facial drama reminds us that disbelief can be a political emotion, but not in the usual sense, since it is not oriented toward opinion. It is, rather, the scene of stopping while being full of unacted-on sensation related to refusing a consensual real: an emotional space-time for adjustment, adjudication. Ordinarily, uncommitted emotions like this are deemed apolitical, even blockages to the political: and to the degree that negative political affects accompany nonparticipation in voting or political culture, one can see why this convention of reading detachment in dispassionateness persists. But disbelief stands here as a variety of political depression. And we know what the other telltale signs of that are: dramatic and undramatic versions of hopelessness, helplessness, dread, anxiety, stress, worry, lack of interest, and so on. What's the difference between the father's emotional neutralization in the old normal and his disbelief in the new? Neutralization was a vehicle for upward mobility and class aspiration; disbelief is a suspended affective transaction that enables life to move on insecurely in the impasse's enigmatic space.

Looking at the history of class-analytic cinema, moments of bodily stuckness like these are not unprecedented: the spectacle of stunned ineloquence as dreams of deferred gratification are remanded to permanent deferral is a central trope of the aesthetics of struggle. What makes this film's scenario an emanation of the present moment is its performance of the becoming-archaic of the dreamscapes and gratifications of capitalist modernity, and of the fantasies that enabled everyday life to be lived in small doses of leisure that promise to become longer scenes of aged enjoyment. By the last scene of the film the father has adapted, and saved parts of his dream: at a union picnic amid the strike, he plays with his grandchildren with a gentle exuberance that suggests that there's nothing now but the present and whatever sweetness he can squeeze into it, and he seems at peace with that.

Meanwhile, Franck seems to have inherited his father's disbelief. His young face has completely imploded and lost expression; he sits on the margins, still and plotless. Without an imaginable future or a home, on his way back to Paris without a plan, and emptied out of confidence and impulsive gestures, all he *has* is impassivity. It is as though all of the varieties of precarity have crept in to still his very marrow, and so he has to stop his body from transacting with anything. In the cinema of precarity, the shift in the portrayal of immobility from a normative, conventional, habituated solidity to a living paralysis, playful repetition, or animated still-life has become a convention of representing the impasse as a relief from the devastating pain of this unfinished class transition.

III. *Why Should You Be Spared?*: L'Emploi du temps

Cantet's attention to class-related varieties of impassivity as coping strategies and responses to neoliberal restructuring takes on a new set of connotations in his return to the situation in L'Emploi du temps. L'Emploi du temps also features a series of scenes that mark the development of proprioceptive skills that communicate changes in their case study subjects' transference with the situation of the historical present. Unlike Ressources humaines, though, no event marks the onset of the new normal, and indeed what's striking here is that no manner of being mannered is disturbed in the film's narration of the fraying of a life. Instead, we begin and end in the middle of a story, a story about drifting.

L'Emploi du temps tells the story of Vincent, a consultant who has been released from his labor contract sometime in the French 1990s. Vincent does not tell his family that he has been released from his contract, though, and his opacity to his parents, wife, and children is repeated in the physical atmosphere of the film when it opens, which also means that the film transmits the historical present as a situation, a moment held in abeyance. Vincent sleeps in a car, near a railroad, in the passenger seat, the windscreen foggy with his breath. It is a beautiful abstraction that suggests something enigmatic in the real from which it protects our gaze. Then a bus arrives and children spill out, passing before a space in the glass that is not yet misted

13.1–13.2. Vincent opens at an impasse (Cantet, *Time Out*, 2000)

up, and one imagines that imminent to this moment is a disaster—an instance of sexual perversion, a child kidnapping, a bad divorce, a suicide—an event, in other words, where a gesture could well become an act that destroys the ordinary thoughtlessness of the present and sends us into grey economies, underworlds or otherworlds that no one wants to live in, at least for long.

But this is not what happens in *L'Emploi du temps*, whose English translation, *Time Out*, inverts the vernacular sense of the phrase in French, which is *time-schedule*, or just *schedule*. Still, the English translation gets it right too, if time is defined by capitalist productivity. It is midday, and the man is not working. He is in a car, but it is not moving. When his cell phone rings, and the man talks to an intimate about being between meetings, we learn that the man is double-timing his life. He is not in meetings, as far as we can tell, and he is also taking a time-out from truth-telling to the interlocutor, who thinks that their intimate rhythms are being supported by schedules, the rhythms of encounter that produce value in the managerial class.[34]

In piling on multiple kinds of time-out, the film reveals instantly that Vincent is living a secret life. A secret life is that genre of being that takes place in myriad folds of the social, protected from specific gazes that would expose to normative judgment something awry in someone's tendencies.[35] In the first scene, we cannot tell what Vincent's affect is; the emotion he expresses is ordinary loving familial reliability, and he seems really to feel it when he says it. He smiles at the phone, after all. But we know that something is false, that a life about which we can only overhear is precarious, and that its inhabitants are clueless, because Vincent holds a secret.

This sense of professional shame, of the shield and poison of both normativity and the secret life, would likely have been in the mind of anyone who saw this film in France. It adapts a real case, that of the French citizen Jean-Claude Romand. Romand was a doctor who did not pass his boards, but dissimulated having done so for eighteen years. In 1993, sensing that his secret of failure and dissembling was about to emerge, he killed his family in a rampage and tried to kill himself too, also unsuccessfully.[36] Time Out also echoes uncannily in a U.S. case from 2004, the case of Mark Hacking, who murdered his wife, Lori, to avoid being exposed as a failed medical student.[37]

Yet the event that we dread when the film opens in a beautiful abstraction that is interrupted by realism is not what the film offers to us, at first or ever. The film sets us up constantly to want and to expect events and, as was the case in the Dardennes' films, this amounts to the public's affective education in confronting not knowing what it means to have a life and in staying proximate to the enigma and confusion of the situation as it plays out. We realize later that the image of children wandering around may emanate something the man identifies with or wants to be near, a wandering, purposeless fogginess, that privilege of childhood confirmed by the beautiful, almost subdermal quietness of Jocelyn Pook's soundtrack. But nothing returns us to this atmosphere of rest: the rest is disturbance. The aesthetics of disturbance are not in the idiom of the event's melodrama but in an idiom that does not exist yet, an idiom of life tipped over in the impasse.

Later, Vincent glosses this opening scene in another way. He is in a car on a narrow, icy road at the edge of a mountain at night—he could be killed and no one who knows him in his other life would know that or why he is there. In the car he is with Jean-Michel, another middle-aged white European man clearly honed for the professional managerial classes and who like Vincent has taken a wrong turn somewhere and who now simulates businessman-style legitimacy in the transnational grey economy. By this point Vincent is living among many lies, many multiple lives, and trying not to drown in any of them, which means avoiding the fate of the father in *Human Resources*, that of losing face in front of others who would then deny him his defenses, his enabling disavowals—his capacity to maintain cruel optimism.

Vincent has told his family that he works for the United Nations offices in Geneva, brokering the neoliberal hunger for new development opportunities in Africa. He tells his friends from college that he is brokering extraordinarily-high-interest-rate bank accounts in the Russian grey economy, and they invest in him based on their historic trust. He supports his family with the monies he's embezzled. In other words, globalization makes politically and economically imaginable what the cell phone lubricates in his intimacy: the outline of a postnormative life lived as a multiplication of normativities that seem to have arisen organically from relationships and networks rather than oppressive or disciplinary institutions. I say they seem organic because we know that the dedication of the state to fomenting neoliberal practices of interrupted accountability and fading meritocracy is a central context for the rise of a consultancy class that contracts to have episodic dealings as opposed to having institutionally shaped long-term relationships.

Jean-Michel had met Vincent after overhearing him in a hotel lobby pitching the Russian bank accounts to his friends. Later he says that Vincent was a bad method actor, disinvested in the story about beating the system that he was telling. But his friends, who already trust him, do not attend too closely to the details, and, for awhile, Vincent prospers. When Jean-Michel confronts Vincent, we think a blackmail plot will ensue, but he has the honor of thieves, it turns out, as he too lives an antinomian life regulated by surreptitious contracts and flexible norms. For a living, Jean-Michel sells fake designer watches; his warehouse is a room in the hotel whose lobby now serves as an office for an indefinite population of managers released from management who are still trying to do the thing they know how to—strike a deal, stay in the game.

Further, Jean-Michel serves the same class of aspirational consumers that Vincent is now tapping, people who like a good deal and do not want to pay very close attention to the details. It turns out that Vincent is Jean-Michel ten years ago. He used to be a member of the global diplomatic class, those civil servants whose job it is to manage the here and now of the political behind the scenes, under the radar. But Jean-Michel was a crook, got exposed, and lost his family, and his "name." The underground economy that circulates at

14.1–14.2. Vincent tells the truth on the edge of the cliff

night is the only one left in which he can simulate sovereignty. Both capitalist and middleman, he runs immigrant sweatshops, stores the goods himself, transports the goods stealthily across borders, and takes the profit. He occupies all places in the neoliberal economy—except the manufacturing, which he outsources to the migrant. What he wants from Vincent is a partner. For one can simulate managerial legitimacy, but one can never be one's own colleague, and it is lonely in the secret life.

Jean-Michel is therefore the only person to whom Vincent tells the truth about his life. On the night of their first surreptitious transfer of fake goods together, the car is dark and intimate, and the road to the border on the side of the mountain twists and winds dangerously. Vincent drives; Jean-Michel notes that he seems focused, almost at peace. Vincent's response is a dramatic monologue, delivered mostly in profile and shadow; the camera keeps glancing over at the icy cliff he drives on slowly, and shoots through the windscreen the car's own blind spots. The ordinary event of men driving at night merges the audience with the hermetic scene in which the men live out their pleasure and attachment to the risk of being in the unknowable and unknown. The most ordinary tracking shot also becomes, in this scene of exemplary historical consciousness, a performer of the hypervigilance necessary in the impasse.

> In the dark, the men talk.
>
> Vincent: I love to drive. When I first started working, driving was my favorite part. Alone in the car, thinking about nothing, smoking and listening to music. I could go on for hours. I think the only thing I really liked about my job was the driving. That ended up working against me. It felt so good in my car, I had difficulty leaving it. Sometimes I'd drive 200m for an appointment. Without thinking I'd miss the turnoff. I'd just keep driving.
>
> My boss started to get annoyed. But things could have been worse. They felt that I no longer had the company spirit. No one tried to keep me. Negotiating my departure was easy.

The mutual recognition of lost company spirit allows Vincent to drift away not just from being reliable but also from being intentional: in the present moment of neoliberal contingency, he discovers himself drifting and drifting off. What did it mean to have the company spirit, and then to lose it? Is this the same feeling as that exemplified in *The Man in the Grey Flannel Suit* (1955), namely, of hating the false self demanded by corporate-style upward mobility? Is company spirit even an affect or an emotion, or is collegiality a performance of "citizenship" that is entirely practice-based and normative, a mere ideologeme? Or is it deeper than that, a mode of mannerliness close to gallantry that both is instrumental and lubricates the kind of durable, life-affirming sociality that Arlie Hochschild points to as a distinguishing ambivalent demand of the contemporary workplace on worker subjectivity?[38] Eva Illouz's *Cold Intimacies: The Making of Emotional Capitalism* tells another bit of this story.[39] In her chapter "The Rise of *Homo Sentimentalis*," she tracks the early-twentieth-century implantation of psychological discourse in the evaluation of work. Scientific studies of women workers became models for evaluating workers generally, and suddenly emotion talk saturated determinations about the value of managers and employees who were not only obliged to be good at tasks but to participate in making work a place where people both were good and felt good. Thus the twentieth century witnessed the expansion of corporate demands that workers line up emotionally with workplace norms along with producing value adequately: responsibility and reciprocity came to require the performance of emotional compliance.[40] This is what distinguishes *Time Out* from *The Man in the Grey Flannel Suit*. In the latter, one had to be a team player, but the affective work was accomplished at home; it's the difference between a culture of consultants and a culture of executives.

We have already seen that method acting is a crucial part of being a successful entrepreneur and consultant. To be a good subject of neoliberal labor, one has to emit desire and identification with the affective ties of collegiality to make networks of shared obligation seem more grounded and permanent than the corporation will support structurally. A subplot of *Time Out* instantiates this imperative explicitly, in all of its ambiguities. At one point the family goes shopping on the money Vincent has stolen. There, they run into Jeffrey, an old colleague of Vincent's, who's been leaving heated phone messages, to which Vincent has not responded. But caught in the same public leisure space, Vincent has no choice but to act the part of friend, at least around his wife, Muriel. We learn a lot about the emotional demands and performance norms of the consultancy class in this scene. The men have worked together for ten years. Like an old lover, Jeffrey complains, "Is this a joke? Weren't we really close? We ate lunch together daily for ten years. All those late evenings. . . . Isn't that something?" Yet at first when the men meet they introduce their wives and their children to each other. The closeness was the closeness of colleagues, not of friends who share the whole range of life. This does not mean that their bond was fake or shallow, though. It meant something to Jeffrey: "Vincent, you were fired. Then you completely disappear. My concern is normal." Vincent: "I don't find it normal. We only worked together. . . . That means nothing now."

So, on the face of it Vincent was never taken in by the ideology of managerial affect. He complied physically with warm collegiality but never complied affectively with the atmospheric imperative. But his relation to labor-related affectivity is quite different when he talks of work with his wife. Throughout the film he relates his sense of precarity as a loss of "enthusiasm."[41] This is the only idiom in which he speaks to Muriel about the life he has cultivated away from her:

Vincent: Things aren't going the way I had hoped. I knew it would take time to adapt. I didn't think it would be this hard.

Muriel: You only started a few weeks ago. Doesn't it take time to get on the right track? Don't you think so?

Vincent: I get along well with my colleagues. That's not an issue. They're

15.1–15.2. Affective
truths, empirical lies

easy to talk to. Good atmosphere. But still perverse. That makes
lying easy. Tell myself everything's fine. That's a lie. I'm afraid
I'll disappoint.

Muriel: Afraid of what?

Vincent: Afraid I'll disappoint. Afraid I won't make the grade.

Muriel: You've had these worries before, but you always pull through.

Vincent: I can't handle anything right now. I'm just going along. Sometimes I don't even know what I'm supposed to do. What's expected of me. So I start to panic. A simple phone call becomes
overwhelming. I go from meeting to meeting. No time to sum
things up or take a step back. I can't think anymore. My mind is
blank. I look around me, at the people I work with. I see totally
unknown faces. Like moments of absence. . . . Sorry. I'm just
tired.

They smoke together, they speak in hushed tones, act tenderly, keep the
lights low. Vincent puts his head on her shoulder; she holds his head. This is
how intimates *act*, but what does it mean? At every moment of tenderness,
each time Vincent seems to let his guard down the camera betrays no irony,

soliciting the audience to advocate for his enthusiasm, itself a keyword in manager-speak—even as we know that he is duping his wife. It is as though the emotions are real even if the story is false. At the same time the emotions are placeholders for an affective confusion that only finds its genre in the film, and not manifestly in the lives depicted there.

At the same time, Muriel reveals a lot about what she fears learning even as she seems to long for Vincent to be candid. Throughout the film, Muriel cannot bear to witness the threat of giving up that Vincent always portends. Whenever the story he tells starts to crack, she rushes to fill it up with assurance: this is how you always are, this feeling is appropriate, there is no disturbance, your unhappiness is both endemic and temporary, episodic and predictable. She needs him to be on the same page she is on: maintaining intimacy requires bracketing out dissonance, fear, surprise, failure, and most of all, incoherence. Manners become the way they drown out the interference with their durable contract to act and feel tender about performing love.

So when she finally visits Vincent in Geneva and he does not take her to the apartment that he claims to own there, Muriel is disappointed. But in the abandoned, unheated farmhouse he squats in, she tries very sweetly to adjust and stay in synch with him. They have what seems like good sex, and after, she evaluates each of his body parts—his thighs have gotten smaller, his penis is fine, but his "tits are starting to fall." When he laughingly protests her "hard" judgment of him she says, "Mine are falling too. Why should you be spared?" She is observing him, searching him, exposing him to her verdict, but he prefers this exposure to what might come from her questions about his work life, and in the end of the scene he uses his sexual body to force her searching questions to become rhetorical ones.

Thus we keep seeing Vincent come home and leave home: home is at the base of the cul-de-sac. But the people who live with him there in cul-de-sac normativity have little clue that he is false and has drifted off. His impassivity reads like good manners. If he had the money, he could sustain that rhythm infinitely: the mild theatricality of intimate spaces is sustained by gestures and tones of caring that he is good at and that, we see elsewhere, he admires and finds satisfying and effective. Cynically, one might say that he loves tenderness because it's on the surface and demands little. Being tender with an intimate is to him like being a colleague: the gesture stands in for authentic emotional depth, but does not demand it.

Still, as Vincent and Muriel leave the farmhouse, she disappears momen-

16. Vincent, imploded

tarily into the snow and Vincent panics. Like any lover, he needs her to be where he needs her to be, to be reliable and solid, not lateral or secreted. His anchors in the normal turn out to be important and keep him from becoming destructive or psychotic; he bars the event that would splinter everything. Instead he acts mannerly with his children, Oedipal with his parents, softly masculine with his wife—doing whatever it takes to protect the privilege of drifting without entirely drifting off, or going off the cliff.

At the end of the film, it appears that Vincent has been caught out by his wife and family, and it seems as though his father has bailed him out, including finding him another job opportunity. Vincent has no choice but to return to the normative emotional performance of the PPB, and the open secret of zombie managerial enthusiasm permeates the room where he is interviewed: pale, wan, sadly smiling, pretending that he wants to be the head of a team of salespeople who receive no benefits, no contract, only the right to be associated with the shell of an institution. He is the least independent independent contractor imaginable: it does not matter what actual job he's doing, as the form of being in labor is what counts and not the value of the thing produced. His incapacity to lose everything, to go genuinely off the grid toward the horizon of his negativity, is not surprising, for there is nothing else for him in the impasse, no anarchist energy, no dramatic refusal, no gun and no gasoline for the road. In place of being happy, he gets one more chance at making faces in the social. The terms of reciprocity are fundamentally normative and gestural, and the time-outs he has taken recede like some twisted pastoral. In the impasse of the present he is no longer driving in spirals but in circles, in team meetings and modes of conviviality that fake optimism in the hope that eventually it will have to be worth it.

In this sense *Time Out* revises deferred gratification for the precarious era. It no longer involves suffering in the present for future enjoyment, but simulated, improvised, scavenged enjoyment in a present beyond which there is nothing. Upward mobility has been replaced by what we have been calling lateral or sideways mobility. The only membrane Cantet can find between absolute, psychotic-making, off-the-grid loss and imaginable life is the optimism of manners, composure, a formalism of being that requires the minima of affective attention or emotional performance and that allows subjects to keep things to themselves and represents the neoliberal privatization of all resources in an idiom of private emotion, in which the body is a container for the subject's affects while his face aspires to remain all surface.

Yet Muriel's question haunts: *Why should you be spared?* Explicitly, Muriel refers to aging and death, and to the slow decline into becoming sexually undesirable. She also refers to being seen and known, to being obligated and responsible. The story of bourgeois inauthenticity and secret lives is not limited to neoliberal time and space, though. Like "Where is your place" from *Human Resources*, "Why should you be spared?" expresses the precarious universal of the neoliberal moment. It is a rhetorical question in transition, open to many potential political and existential idioms, but having reached none of them yet; it is a measure of the low bar of belonging and reciprocity in times of crisis ordinariness. Living amid the breaking up of modernity's secure institutions of intimacy and reciprocity—the state, the corporation, the family, liberal publics—Cantet's protagonists live the impasse of the present between a quivering lip and a death mask, and without an imaginary for the terms and the register in which new claims on social resources of reciprocity could be made.

But should those claims be in the idiom of a new affective class, the precariat? Neoliberal interests are well served by the displacement of so many historical forms of social reciprocity onto emotional registers, especially when they dramatize experiences of freedom to come that have no social world for them yet. In this register of political optimism, what does it threaten to protest precarity to our heart's content? This is no rhetorical question. It goes to the heart of the tension between the affective sense of solidarity that might come through a collective detachment from the normative world and the divergent imaginaries of the better good life that its subjects would wish to bring into being, in compensation for their profound, collective, material, and fantasmatic loss.

1. *Affect, Noise, Silence, Protest: Ambient Citizenship*

Intensely political seasons spawn reveries of a different immediacy. People imagine alternative environments where authenticity trumps ideology, truths cannot be concealed, and communication feels intimate, face-to-face. In these times, even politicians imagine occupying a post–public sphere public where they might just somehow make an unmediated transmission to the body politic. "Somehow you just got to go over the heads of the filter and speak directly to the people," then-President George W. Bush commented in October 2003, echoing a long tradition of sentimental political fantasies and soon followed by condemnations of the "filter" by the Republican National Committee and the presidential campaign of John McCain and Sarah Palin.[1] What is "the filter" that demands circumnavigation? Bush seems to be inverting the meaning of his own, mixed, metaphor. A filter, after all, separates out noise from communication and, in so doing, makes communication possible. Jacques Attali and Michel Serres have both argued that there is no communication without noise, as noise interferes from within any utterance, threatening its tractability.[2] The performance of distortion that constitutes communication therefore demands discernment, or filtering. However steadfast one's commitment to truth, there is no avoiding the noise.

Yet Bush's wish to skirt the filter points to something profound in the desire for the political. He wants to transmit not the *message* but the *noise*. He wants the public to feel the funk, the live intensities and desires that make messages affectively immediate, seductive, and binding.[3] In his head a public's binding to the political is best achieved neither by policy nor ideology but *the affect of feeling political together*, an effect of having communicated true feeling without the distancing mediation of speech.[4] The transmission of noise performs political attachment as a sustaining intimate relation, without which great dramas of betrayal are felt and staged. In *The Ethical Soundscape*, Charles Hirschkind talks about the role of "maieutic listening" in constructing the intimate political publics of Egypt.[5] There, the feeling tones of the affective soundscape produce attachments to and investments in a sense of political and social mutuality that is performed in moments of collective audition. This process involves taking on *listening together* as itself an object/scene of desire. The attainment of that attunement produces a sense of shared worldness, apart from whatever aim or claim the listening public might later bring to a particular political world because of what they have heard.

From Hirschkind's perspective the social circulation of *noise*, of affective binding, converts the world to a space of moral action that seems juxtapolitical — proximate to, without being compromised by, the instrumentalities of power that govern social life.[6] Speaking above the filter would confirm to Bush's whole listening audience that they already share an affective environment; mobilizing "the ethical and therapeutic virtues of the ear"[7] would accomplish the visceral transmission of his assurance not only that he has made a better good life possible for Americans and humans around the globe, but that, affectively speaking, there is already a better sensorial world right here, right now, more intimate and secure and just as real as the world made by the media's anxiogenic sensationalist analysis. This vision locates the desire for the political in an alternative commons in the present that the senses confirm and circulate as though without mediation.

What exactly is the problem with "the filter"? The contemporary filtered or mediated political sphere in the United States transmits news 24/7 from a new ordinary created by crisis, in which life seems reduced to discussions about tactics for survival and who is to blame. The filter tells you that the public has entered a historical situation whose contours it does not know. It impresses itself upon mass consciousness as an epochal crisis, unfolding like a disaster film made up of human-interest stories and stories about institutions that have lost their way.[8] It is a moment on the verge of a post-normative phase, in which fantasmatic clarities about the conditions for enduring collectivity, historical continuity, and infrastructural stability have melted away, along with predictable relations between event and effect.

Living amidst war and environmental disaster, people are shown constantly being surprised at what does and does not seem to have a transformative impact. Living amid economic crisis, people are shown constantly being surprised at the amount, location, and enormity of moral and affective irregulation that come from fading rules of accountability and recognition. What will govern the terms and relations of reliable reciprocity among governments, intimates, workers, owners, churches, citizens, political parties, or strangers? What forms of life will secure the sense of affective democracy that people have been educated to expect from their publics? Nobody knows. The news about the recent past and the pressures of the near future demand constant emergency cleanup and hyperspeculation about what it means to live in the ongoing present among piles of cases where things didn't work out or seem to make sense, at least not yet. There are vigils; there is witnessing, testimony, and yelling. But there is not yet a consensual rubric that would shape these matters into an event. The affective structure of the situation is therefore anxious and the political emotions attached to it veer wildly from recognition of the enigma that is clearly there to explanations that *make sense*, the kind of satisfying sense that enables enduring.

Uncertainty is the material that Bush wished to bracket. His desire for a politics of ambient noise, prepropositional transmission, and intuitive reciprocity sought to displace the filtered story of instability and contradiction from the center of sociality. He also wishfully banished self-reflexive, cultivated opinion and judgment from their central public-sphere function. In short, as Jacques Rancière would put it, Bush's wishful feeling was to separate the political from politics as such.[9] In so doing he would cast the on-going activity of social antagonism to the realm of the epiphenomenal, in contrast to which the affective feedback loop of the political would make stronger the true soul-to-soul continuity between politicians and their public. Foucault used to call "sexuality" that noisy affectivity that Bush wanted to transmit from mouth to ear, heart to heart, gut to gut.[10] From his perspective, at least, the political is best lodged in the appetites.

These are not politically tendentious observations. Perhaps when Bush uttered his desire for affective communication to be the medium of the political, he was trying cynically to distract the public gaze from some of his particular actions. But the wish to inhabit a vaguely warm sense of already-established, autonomic, and atmospheric solidarity with the body politic is hardly his special desire. Indeed, in his preference for the noise of immediacy, he has many bedfellows in the body politic with whom he shares little else politically, namely, the ones who prefer political meetings in town halls, caucuses, demonstrations, and other intimate assemblies to the pleasure of disembodied migratory identification that constitutes mass publics. He also joins his antagonists in the nondominant classes who have long produced intimate publics to provide the feeling of immediacy and solidarity by establishing in the public sphere an affective register of belonging to inhabit when there are few adequate normative institutions to fall back on, rest in, or return to.

Public spheres are always affect worlds, worlds to which people are bound, when they are, by affective projections of a constantly negotiated common interestedness. But an intimate public is more specific. In an intimate public one senses that matters of survival are at stake and that collective mediation through narration and audition might provide some routes out of the impasse and the struggle of the present, or at least some sense that there would be recognition were the participants in the room together.[11] An intimate public promises the sense of being held in its penumbra. You do not need to audition for membership in it. Minimally, you need just to perform audition, to listen and to be interested in the scene's visceral impact.[12] You might have been drawn to it because of a curiosity about something minor, unassociated with catastrophe, like knitting or collecting something, or having a certain kind of sexuality, only after which it became a community of support, offering tones of suffering, humor, and cheerleading. Perhaps an illness led to seeking out a community of survival tacticians. In either case, any person can contribute to an intimate public a personal story about not being defeated by what is overwhelming. More likely, though, participants take things in and sometimes circulate what they hear, captioning them with opinion or wonder. But they do not have to do anything to belong. They can be passive and lurk, deciding when to appear and disappear, and consider the freedom to come and go the exercise of sovereign freedom.

Indeed, in liberal societies, freedom includes freedom from the obligation to pay attention to much, whether personal or political—no-one is obliged to be conscious or socially active in their modes and scenes of belonging. For many this means that political attention is usually something delegated and politics is something overheard, encountered indirectly and unsystematically, through a kind of communication more akin to gossip than to cultivated rationality.[13] But there is nothing fundamentally passive or superficial in overhearing the political. What hits a person encountering the dissemination of news about power has nothing to do with how thorough or cultivated their knowledge is or how they integrate the impact into living. Amidst all of the chaos, crisis, and injustice in front of us, the desire for alternative filters that produce the sense—if not the scene—of a more livable and intimate sociality is another name for the desire for the political.

This is why an intimate attachment to the political can amount to a relation of cruel optimism. I have argued throughout this book that an optimistic attachment is cruel when the object/scene of desire is itself an obstacle to fulfilling the very wants that bring people to it: but its life-organizing status can trump interfering with the damage it provokes. It may be a relation of cruel optimism, when, despite an awareness that the normative political sphere appears as a shrunken, broken, or distant place of activity among elites, members of the body politic return periodically to its recommitment ceremonies and scenes. Voting is one thing; collective caring, listening, and scanning the airwaves, are others. All of these modes of orientation and having a feeling about it confirm our attachment to the system and thereby confirm the system and the legitimacy of the affects that make one feel bound to it, even if the manifest content of the binding has the negative force of cynicism or the dark attenuation of political depression.

How and why does this attachment persist? Is it out of habit? Is it in hopes of the potentiality embedded in the political as such? Or, from a stance of critical engagement, an investment in the possibility of its repair? The exhausting repetition of the politically depressed position that seeks repair of what may be constitutively broken can eventually split the activity of optimism from expectation and demand.[14] Maintaining this split enables one to sustain one's attachment to the political as such and to one's sense of membership in the idea of the polity, which is a virtual—but sensual, not abstract—space of the commons. And so, detaching from it could induce many potential losses along with new freedoms.

Grant Farred calls fidelity to the political without expectation of recognition, representation, or return a profoundly ethical act.[15] His exemplary case derives from voting patterns of African Americans in the 2004 presidential election, but the anxiety about the costs of this ethical commitment has only increased with the election of Barack Obama as the President of the emotional infrastructure of the United States as well as of its governing and administrative ones.[16] What is the relation between the "Yes We Can!" optimism for the political and how politics actually works? What is the effect of Obama's optimization of political optimism against the political depression of the historically disappointed, especially given any President's limited sovereignty as a transformative agent in ordinary life? How can we track the divergences between politically orchestrated emotions and their affective environments? Traditionally, political solidarity is a more of a structure than a feeling—an identification with other people who are similarly committed to a project that does not require affective continuity or warm personal feeling to sustain itself. But maintaining solidarity requires skills for adjudicating incommensurate visions of the better good life. The atrophy of these skills is at risk when politics is reduced to the demand for affective attunement, insofar as the sense of belonging is threatened by the inconvenience of antagonistic aims. Add to this the possibility that "the political" as we know it in mass democracy *requires* such a splitting of attachment and expectation. Splitting off political optimism from the way things are can sustain many kinds of the cruelest optimism.

This chapter looks at some instances of contemporary art that are situated in the desire for the political to be routed through the affective eavesdropping that shapes the *sense* of immediacy among mass mediated intimate publics in the historical present. Located in traditions of silent protest, this art aims broadly to remobilize and redirect the normative noise that binds the affective public of the political to normative politics as such. Without having speech as a cushion, affect shapes the event. Participants in contemporary political life witness this aesthetic all the time, in genres of portable and improvised performative memorializing from dramatic self-immolation to the silent vigil. In Deleuze's and Guattari's sense, it is minor work of political depression that both demonstrates a widespread sense of futility about slowing the mounting crisis of ordinary life in the present, and still, makes a world from political affect in which practices of politics might be invented that do not yet exist.

This aesthetic of reticent immediacy derives from a long transnational tradition not only of radical art but also of popular religious and secular nonviolence, especially around trauma and mourning, most famously exemplified, perhaps, by the silent visual performances of Argentina's *Las Madres de la Playa de Mayo* (Mothers of the Plaza de Mayo). In the United States, silent protest originated with the "voiceless speech" tactic of suffrage and the performative silence of antilynching protests. Its big years were 1916 and 1917. On many occasions, thousands of women risked a paradoxical arrest for "disturbing the peace" by standing mute and still in public with banners and placards that made their suffrage arguments for them. A multiauthored pro-suffrage novel, *The Sturdy Oak*, first published in *The Pictorial Review* (1917), dramatizes these protests and the insane responses they induced in publics who could not bear the affective and ethical claim transmitted on the feminist frequency.[17] The novel echoes contemporary newspaper reports of the responses the transgression caused: mainly, people ignored the voiceless speech or manifested resentment at feeling compelled to stop; sometimes, they were curious and took in the arguments; sometimes, the pause and the quiet, slow reading interrupted something profound in their political orientation.

In the very same year, ten thousand African Americans marched against lynching in silent protest in New York City, an act of discipline so astonishing that the spectating crowds, too, organized to contribute absolute silence. In both cases the silence was broken by the police, who, one imagines, could not bear confronting such fully organized political will. Such acts of aggressive passivity always seek to expose the corruption of, or toxic noise within, political speech, as well as to measure the perverse relation between ideals of the political and the practice of politics. However, the gesture of performative withdrawal always goes farther than that too, inducing, as if electronically, new sensual routes for political potentiality from the place where conscience meets knowledge.

What does it say about the contemporary historical moment that so much art-activism mobilizes not classic public sphere communication but noise, the activity of visceral immediacy that communication rationalizes, brackets, idealizes, and disrespects? Why is it so hard to detach from the life-destructive forms of the normative political world, without that detachment providing tacit permission for that world to reproduce itself as such? This chapter rethinks publicness by looking at some cases in which the body politic in the politically depressive position tries to break the double-bind of cruel optimism, *not* reentering the normative public sphere while seeking a way, nonetheless, to maintain its desire for the political.

The body of work this chapter remobilizes suggests that the new crisis ordinary is engendering peculiar forms of something like "ambient citizenship"—politics as a scene in which the drama of the distribution of affect/noise meets up with scenarios of *movement*. In the perspective it opens up on the way the political suffuses the ordinary, ambient citizenship is a complicated thing, a mode of belonging, really, that circulates through and around the political in formal and informal ways, with an affective, emotional, economic, and juridical force that is at once clarifying and diffuse. As sound, ambience provides atmospheres and spaces in which movement happens through persons: listeners dissolve into an ongoing present whose ongoingness is neither necessarily comfortable nor uncomfortable, avant-garde nor Muzak, but, most formally, a space of abeyance. As an atmosphere induced by sonic diffusion it is a habitation without edges, a soft impasse. As movement, as ambit, it is akin to ambition (whose original sense was to go around soliciting for votes), but even then it's a gathering modality.

At the same time the noise of the political measures the materiality of status and power, in a number of ways. There is, of course, the noise of the reproduction of life, which charts relations of ownership and control in the everyday. Ambient citizenship is also the place where the question emerges of whose noise matters, whose immediacy-pressures rule the tendency of the situation—who controls the zoning. But this is not only about distinguishing who matters, and how. The moral valuation of noise affects the status of melodrama in the political as such. Melodramatic political performance sometimes claims to perform the scale and measure of just legitimacy and sometimes claims that an Other suffers from aural bloat that is out of control. (Think about whose anger is deemed honorable and whose is deemed a threat; whose sentimentality is a sign of moral virtue and whose a sign of weakness that needs to get regulated.) This adjudication of the noise is especially what happens in a democracy when groups speak as minor, refusing to delegate attention to "representative" authority: some noise is sanctioned and invited to dilate, while some noise calls out the police. Mass politics is melodramatic, and noise politics is at the heart of the popular:

ambient citizenship registers the normative distinctions in terms of who has the formal and informal right to take up soundspace.

Ambient art in the recessive mode is a counter-style appropriate to the impasse of the present that appears degenerating and excitable, without being, exactly, open. Building on the analysis of lateral agency in chapter 3, "Slow Death," this chapter forces into view more of its immanent meanings: roundabout movement, aural diffusion, a collectively prehensible atmospherics, and an orientation toward the world with no predictable rhythm. Radically identified art so disposed tracks the affective ups and downs of the overwhelmed body politic, moving across exuberance and quietness and poking at the relation between the political desire on which it insists and the comforts and clarities it is willing to risk losing in order to instantiate a representation of that desire. It points to ways that the sovereign sensorium does not have to be reproduced in kind, scale, or intensity.

All politically performative acts of vocal negation are pedagogical, singular moments inflated to embody something generally awry in the social. But what kinds of things might it reveal about politics and the political to be driven to negate one's own political voice? Silent protest can be a tactic for withering the reigning terms of fidelity to publicness. Refusing publicness itself can also be the same thing as starving the ideal of a general public, or detaching from a desire for the political as such. Alternatively, it can be the opposite, the reassertion of a commitment to civil society, but aimed at a different generality than imagined by the reigning terms. Silence, too, can protect antinomies. It can preserve a political relation—relying on what goes without saying and therefore making a cynical, defeated, or aspirational bargain with normativity. When is public withdrawal a gesture seeking to sustain attachment and attain repair, and what does that have to do with trying to incite conscience in others, forcing them to experience affectively the political condition of being out of control in the middle of managing the world?

Performative silence is therefore not simply political speech that might as well be spoken. It is also really silence, by which I mean noise: that circulating, transpersonal, permeating, viscerally connective affective atmosphere that feels as though it has escaped "the filter" to indicate, for good or for ill, a sensorium for a potential social world now lived as collective affect, or a revitalized political one. My claim will be that contemporary instances of this aesthetic pattern partly point to modes of mainstream political power so corrupted as to defy optimism about political speech as such. They provide actively recessive commentary on the overdetermined conditions of the current transition, where basic presumptions about reciprocity are up in the air, clouding up the conditions of social intimacy. Questions of injustice meet crises of infrastructural health and belonging that striate emotional, political, economic, natural, and built environments. Noise interferes, makes interference. Interference made loud within political communication makes time for adjustment and counter-thought. The question to which the artists return repeatedly, in different ways, is how to turn the noise of attachment to the political into interference with the parts of it that have made politics as such seem to so many like a ridiculously bad object choice.

This chapter looks at representative instances of avant-garde art situated in the United States but intelligible in the Euro-American tradition, broadly seen.[18] It tracks modernist and postmodernist-style counterdramatics or shock dramatics associated with the tradition that arcs from surrealist antibourgeois art through Warholian flat transgressions. It ends with a look at the anarchist/DIY (do-it-yourself) aesthetic of the ordinary that, at least, points to a politics and aesthetics that is genuinely dedramatized and embedded in the new ordinariness, which is organized by a postspectacular articulation of banality, catastrophe, and structural crisis.[19] What the cases share is a focus on the sonic aspects of ambient citizenship. The first, Cynthia Madansky's The PSA Project, is a powerfully executed instance of conventionally modernist propaganda-style avant-garde work against the war in Iraq. The second involves security camera art, focusing on the Surveillance Camera Players' play on the secrecy strategies of contemporary Western-liberal surveillance.[20] The third case takes up the "sonic activism" of the collaborative Ultra-red, and especially its project "Organizing the Silence." Emerging from the intersection of postmodern and identity politics, this queer-related work uses "silence" to mean speech that has had no political "voice" or impact; it converts this silence not into polemic but into registers of reflective political feeling. The chapter's final cases are examples of social commentary to one side of a manifestly political idiom. Juxtapolitical, they wander the zone of the body politic without referring or recommitting to the project of civil society. These works, by Slater Bradley and Liza Johnson, use ambient sound to stand in for a speechlessness resulting from a failure within the political: politics itself is a lost object, a foregone conclusion, concluded. These works open up different ways to detach from the cruel optimism of a civil society politics, if not from the desire for the political as such. The question is whether and how that loss might make an opening.

11. Sounding out the War

Politically engaged video art has long utilized soundtrack noise as an interpretive mirror of political violence. Cynthia Madansky's exemplary The PSA Project (2004–present) is a series of fifteen public service announcements against the Iraq war, each organized under a different keyword, for example, Occupation, Color, Anthem, Skin.[21] This series of terms seeks to recode the national viscera: to take the color palette of terrorism (Red, Orange, Yellow, Blue, Green, in descending order of threat intensity), and to shift it back to the National Symbolic: "Red is not terror; white is not security; blue is not homeland." The PSA Project turns to conventional avant-garde strategies to reroute the audience's visceral national associations. To dilute the saturating power of state-sanctioned propaganda, it reprocesses and defamiliarizes realist film and video footage. To reframe the contours of the historical present, it mobilizes montage, merging popular memories of Vietnam, 1968, civil rights, and postwar commodity optimism with contemporary political footage from U.S. military action. Interlaced are shots of domestic things, to perform visually the complicity of those who think that their ordinary domestic privacy is neither political nor part of the war machine.

In these ways and others, the series frames and distorts conventional icons that have been transmitted as monumentalized memory for the nation: like Forrest Gump and other chronicles of the post-Vietnam era, it revises popular memory to offer a more ambient, diffuse, lived register of political immediacy. But here, as the iconicity of planes and bombs and flags and bodies and ordinary commodities is both intensified and distorted, The PSA Project reproduces the stentorian tone of the struggle over national signs that has long been central to the reproduction of patriotism.

Moving quickly among processed images of the war already associated with the military-global ordinary, Madansky's historical present is itself a relic of war, an often slow-motion reenactment of its shattering resonance in events as big as death and as gestural as a whoop or a glance. The series documents the profoundly intimate and collective consequences of not being able to take the ordinary for granted. The video reproduces this insecurity about ordinary spectatorial comportment: as the eye and ear are hailed unevenly and unpredictably, listening and watching becomes awk-

17.1–17.3. The PSA Project #1: Color Theory (Madansky, 2005)

18.1–18.5. Madansky, PSA: Icons of the U.S. ordinary

19.1 and 19.2. Civilian and soldier
break through the silence

ward. Forced to cruise, to coast, and to be open to receiving impacts whose generic expectations cannot be prepared for in advance, the audience is nonetheless not being prepared to be open to everything. The eye is made to separate from the present as a space of continuity or narrative cohesion and to feel not assured about much. But its mission remains to witness the flaws in the national symbolic as it saturates the everyday; to feel the impact of imperial violence; and, tacitly, to convert the outrage to the senses into collective critique.

Meanwhile, the ear is forbidden to accrete meaning and is made to dissipate and float between boredom and interest. In addition to achieving sensorial dishabituation by washing out, scratching, darkening, and distorting the visual field, *The PSA Project* suffuses the aesthetic space with an alternating stream of mainly synthesized theramin-related sound plus thickly hissing static. The model is generally that of silent film, defined not at all by silence but by barriers to the representation of speech.

Only once does the video work with human voices, and they are shocking to hear: the murder of an Iraqi citizen and the pleasure in military competence expressed by a soldier in the area. The highly mediated performance of vocal immediacy *feels* like the real thing is happening in the real time an objective judge encounters: the audience audits the war as though unedited, and as it sees what a relatively unmoving camera sees in the generic movements of tanks, it hears the whooping exuberance of soldiers as they shoot and kill the enemy.

One could tell a story about the long history that produces this moment of banality and shock. But to relate historical narrative is not The PSA Project's main aim: it stuns its audience into the historical present as a sense experience of anachronism, as the "here we go again" sinking feeling of patriotism turned toxic in a way that needs to be exposed and opened to repair. Scavenging is the method of such a moment, and the centrality of tattering to all of the scapes scraped up by The PSA Project bears that out—landscapes, soundscapes, and imagescapes fray. Nevertheless, Madansky never lets things get too out of control, negative, or far from meaning: each surreally distended chapter is bookended by hyperbolic counterhegemonic captions and slogans such as the ones in the figures above.

Why refer to this audience as the body politic as such, since its demographic must have been presumed both to be much smaller and also to be cosmopolitan?[22] Creations of the mass media, public service announcements are direct communications to a general public: using the tools of immediacy that merge advertising with propaganda, they require the notion of a general public whose well-being requires that some action be performed.[23] Indeed, the genre of Madansky's series argues for an ethical as well as a material obligation for the public to identify with itself as generally as possible in order to engender a dynamic of political responsibility. It is entirely conventional within its genre, even if the message is counternormative. But The PSA Project's construction and its aesthetics presume quite a different spectatorial scene as well, a smaller, nondominant insider space of like-minded antagonists to the war, neocolonialism, conservative patriotic subjectivity, and the Bush administration itself. The didacticism, literalism, sarcasm, and ironies of the piece presume an already tight binding of collective, but not mass-general, solidarity.

In other words, the narrative avant-gardism and polytonal dissonance of The PSA Project confirm the audience's cultural and emotional capital. As such, the political avant-garde serves its audience the way a movie about trauma on the Lifetime channel provides for its own: its aim is not to make its consumers more vulnerable, as they are already in some sense socially marginal, but to provide a scene for being together in the political. In performing a massive collective sensual disidentification, the progressive sensorium implied here functions as an ethical placeholder for a potential political world. It implies also that the positive substance of the alternative political life with which the audience can identify can go without saying, as it is in an apparently known zone of progressive consensus bound by a different static than the general noise of the U.S. body politic. Not challenging its audience politically, but only aesthetically, The PSA Project preaches to the choir.

Preaching to the choir is always undervalued. But, as a world-confirming strategy of address that performs solidarity and asserts righteousness, it is absolutely necessary to do. When an intimate public is secreted in its own noise, it rehearses affectively what the world will feel like when its vision gains mass traction. At the same time, though, the strength of any political movement depends on persevering in the face of the inevitable kinds of internal dissent that will put at odds people also bonded through critique. But perhaps reinforcing intimate binding is the main function of avant-garde counternormative political work. The relation of these strategies to its secondary aim—to magnetize the political desires of a larger public—raises different and more troubling questions. To offer solidarity through an uncanny and lightly discomfiting aesthetics that keeps its own commitments and program implicit is to conflate solidarity with aesthetic sophistication—that is, with a privileged class location.

I am not posing questions about the value of avant-garde modernism as such, but addressing the question of how political art, shaped by the urgency to induce consciousness and convergence, engages the desire for the political across planes of self-idealization and paranoia.[24] Take, in contrast, the surrealist-inspired performance tactics of so much security camera or CCTV art. In its address to the power of state and capital, this scene of politico-aesthetic work is similarly antiauthoritarian. But its mode tends to be extroverted and expansive, providing a different perspective on how the remediation of a political subjectivity constituted by the aural and the ambient can interrupt normative strategies of affective orchestration.

CCTV art contrasts significantly with Madansky's approach to the in-your-faceness of its counter-public aesthetic that provides for its audience an affective experience of democracy-in-potential, an intimate public to come. The popular frequency on which CCTV art transmits converts and disrupts the popular frequency of the visual culture of contemporary policing itself. Taking on the power elite's rendition of the body politic as something inconvenient at best and criminal at worst—as though a threat to its own democratic existence—this genre focuses on the nonreciprocity of the gaze between the camera that makes publics and the publics that look back. It expands the stentorian and acidic tonalities of the avant-garde to take on the absurdities of neosituationist tragicomedy; often, it moves from pedagogies of sophistication to the energetics of carnival.

Now also a theatre for security cameras, commercial and public space was never unzoned and neutral but controlled and policed by a wide spectrum of interests on behalf of the collective security of persons, nations, and private property. But, since the installation in the late 1960s of CCTV (closed-circuit television) cameras throughout the United States and the United Kingdom, and especially since the bombings that rocked New York and London in 2001 and 2004, these kinds of supervisory practices have been made more aggressively public. During a general time of neoliberal disidentification with the state, this expansion was justified by reference to the state and capital's need for a more active and proactive chilling effect on crime and counterpolitics: this is to say that, during this period, crime and counterhegemonic politics came to seem as species of the same force of threat and disruption.

As Talal Asad has argued, the civilizational claims of liberal political modernity have enabled people to feel free in everyday life by placing the explicit performance of state violence in occulted zones, namely, specific neighborhoods and prisons on the spatial margins.[25] To the bourgeoisie and the classes organized by being "respectable," this practice made the police look less like an apparatus of force and more like border collies nudging everyday atmospheres into order.[26] But disciplinary surveillance and its apparatus are no longer located in that offstage, and having good manners does not any longer guarantee even the privileged races, genders, and classes a status under the radar. Shared between the police and private capital patrolling its own property, the ordering function of the explicit camera in performance smudges the terms of their and the public's accountability and responsibility.[27] Surveillance art counterperformance responds to this new explicit proliferation, which merges the idiom of disciplinary security with the protective language of care, by advancing a series of strategic misrecognitions of these dynamic but enigmatic social relations, particularly by misrecognizing the camera as an affectional agent with human or animal emotions.

Much critical theoretical and radical work has been done on the banalization of the "society of control" through the technological proliferation of "video sniffing"[28] and other information trackers organized by owners of property, including the state.[29] In theory, the subject of democracy is a being without qualities, included in the space of politics because of some formal compliance with a rule (of blood, of birth). But the anonymity of the informatic citizen has a different status: what's being recorded is not their citizenship status, but evidence of their potential intentions, of *who they might become*. In this sense, every moment of everyday life is now an audition for citizenship, with every potential "passer-by a culprit."[30] In the security state, no one knows when the citizen's audition for citizenship is happening, through what channels, and according to what standards. Security camera art against the open secret materializes this aspect of the scene as well, characterizing practical liberty in the contemporary world as the permission the security apparatus gives the citizen to enjoy minor wandering.

Here the focus is on the camera's specifically affective and emotional qualities in relation to the distortion of sound, and their implication in the political dynamics of embodied contemporary citizenship. Acting as exemplary members of the public whose bodies are exposed to provide evidence for classification and control, the actors refuse to maintain the fiction that the cameras are relatively passive parts of the built environment—recorders, eavesdroppers. In this idiom, it is not just that ambient citizens of the contemporary public look back: they act back, take over the frame, and they perform this by a disruption in speech. The Surveillance Camera Players of New York City provide this chapter's exemplary case.

The Surveillance Camera Players are a comic project with a DIY aesthetic, inspired by underground or guerilla activity but also by traditions of carnival that resurfaced in situationism: their exuberance is catching, as they've been imitated all over the world. Their book, *We Are Watching You*, provides rich documentation of their tactical, ephemeral, spectatorial events. The book is also full of failed performances to minuscule audiences and a series of lame, badly organized, and ineffectual collaborative efforts to taunt and transgress the operative norms of securitization. The police who embody the security state seem to find the actors harmless and funny, too. So, even though SCP's self-exemplifying enactment of the body politic's refusal to be docile risks more violent suppression than solicited by the kinds of high-art performances that take place in museums, galleries, and other areas zoned for alternative experience, the riskier risks did not pay off in soliciting responses or undoing the composure of power. Yet the group persisted, documenting the efforts and the failures and disseminating tactics for future failures.

20.1–20.7. *We Are Watching You*
(Surveillance Camera Players, 2001)

When the SCP puts on plays in front of the cameras, it uses the method of the voiceless speech, here in the genre of silent film intertitles. Its method is to flirt with, seduce, and take over the security camera's gaze. The actors are having fun and performing affective solidarity by giving the camera too much of what it wants. By producing blockages so that the camera cannot see beyond the people filling up its lens, SCP usurps the camera's capacity to choose the objects of its focus and allows the nonactors in the vicinity the opportunity genuinely to wander and maintain some semblance of anonymity.

Additionally, hiding actors' bodies behind cardboard outlines of general subjects on the way to being socially productive (working and shopping, for example), SCP does the security analysts' work for them, interpreting bodies at the outset as types available for classification according to actual and potential threat. The collective therefore forces the scene of citizenship back into the overdetermined time of security: its disciplinary performance, its paranoid structure (the enigma of other people is the enemy), and its utopianism (policing will convert insecurity into security). By publicly embodying ambient citizenship, while silently refusing to reproduce the open secret of securitization, the Surveillance Camera Players change the terms and rhythms of reciprocity that constitute the scene of politics as it is lived.

Its aim is not, mainly, to dissolve the public's political and sensual imaginary, though. As in The PSA Project, the SCP's strategy of détournement turns the question of threat levels back on their makers. It also manifests the normative rules of ambient citizenship, by foregrounding how everyday wandering is actually highly orchestrated by the law and affectively embedded norms. The usual presumption of individual sovereignty is here revealed as the activity of generic subjects performing the work of general belonging to contemporary market democracy.

This aesthetic project reconstructs the body politic as an intentional actor who addresses the state as an interlocutor, not a structure, and whose pleasure is not in an unconscious or random freedom but in the production of interference, noise in the system. I suggested earlier that most politics is overheard: the paradox of the political deployment of silent comedy is not just in the way it reveals that, under the current regime of public security, overhearing goes both ways. Performing interference in public risks making explicit a whole lot of open secrets about the ordinary conditions of liberty-in-crisis in the United States.

One of security culture's open secrets is, as I have said, that there never were free sovereign subjects of politics or the market, but rather monitored subjects who are permitted to pass by and get on with things if their comportment does not go awry. (The intensity of monitoring is more explicit in areas where targeted populations are deemed normatively incompetent to enact profitable forms of docility and reciprocity, but the distinction between normative and carceral control is mainly one of emphasis.) A second open secret addresses the presumption that the ambient body politic of mass democracy enjoys a right to anonymity in the everyday.[31] The Surveillance Camera Players' counteraesthetic refutes the expansion of random and deliberate identification by refusing the anonymity of the camera—of the technology's capacity to seem neutral, to be open-secreted, and to hold secrets about the ways it turns bodies into information just in case on behalf of potential scenarios.[32] When the Players play out the logic of pervasive security by upending the usual hierarchies of information and citizen performance, they open up how very affectively attuned the war on terror has always been. I have argued that the "war on terror" is a war on an emotion and a war on and through the senses.[33] I mean this not generally, in a paranoid way—the senses mediate all knowledge and ideology, after all, and what we call "political persuasion" must entail shaping political affections. But the Surveillance Camera Players' tactics remind us that the deliberate state invasion of visceral intuition transpires not only through zoning, propaganda, and profiling technologies but through torture itself, which no longer looks exceptional, but like a *genre* of working on the political affects.

To take the most dramatic examples, it has been well documented that prisoners held by the United States at Guantánamo and Abu Ghraib were sonically tortured, broken down in the solitary confinement of their cells through random shifts between utter silence and unbearable and unrelieved noise and harsh music.[34] Both sonic strategies completely produce politics through the affects and break down the subject into a heap of destroyed capacities for reciprocity with the world. The politics of pure noise destroys defenses against being overwhelmed: one cannot close all of the senses down without becoming closed down oneself. Stuart Grassian's work on solitary confinement's psychopathological effects tracks the processes by which sensual destruction becomes psychological.[35] They include an intensified disruption of the prisoner's affective capacity to perceive undistorted relations of event to effect; unwonted ideation and the disruption of impulse control; affective flooding as a manifestation of psychic disorganization; and paranoia expressed as the magnification of the smallest gesture into the biggest threat.

scp's mode of art activism mimics the secrecy of the state by reenacting its self-preservative silence and at the same time performs as slapstick the irrelevance of the body politic to the conditions of its endurance. It echoes the echo chamber that tortures citizens who have no control over their bodies and the information to which the state asserts a right of control. It demands performatively that the public understand security culture as a concentrated project of saturating the senses and establishing a new sense of the ordinary as that which cannot be taken for granted without a thick film of data archived by the state that verifies continuities and anomalies in the ongoingness of life.

scp's antic slapstick also measures the real loss to collective life that occurs when the state and capital are allowed to banalize terrorism by associating it with the scene of anything noticeable in the ordinary. The success of that association makes it possible to allow a politics of the unreadable gesture or coded phrase to turn all ordinary activity into suspicion about the pervasive likelihood of anyone becoming-terrorist. Comedy here is a refusal to allow the security state's saturation of the ordinary to go without saying.[36]

Indeed, a politics of cartoonish simplicity diminishes the state, making it seem just a camera, as it were. This is an old tactic for diminishing affectively what it is much harder to diminish effectively. But the simple joyousness of scp's comic disruptions also interrupts the association of politics with pain, discipline, shame, oppression, disappointment, and the self-inflating atmosphere of profound courage that often accompanies assertions of political depression. It tries to reopen the possibility of the political as it is lived to becoming a space of genuine flourishing.

Thus the most powerful pedagogy in this case relates to the cheerleading that comedy can contribute in order to motivate the body politic to perform modes of intimate, physical, live reciprocity in the ordinary spaces of life itself. Security camera aesthetics always involve a proprioceptive pedagogy, an incitement toward a revitalized, awkward, ungainly counterdressage for the occupant of contemporary political space, who is not always a citizen. Auditioning for future citizenship is awkward, and mostly the performance fails. But comedy, Bergson writes, is the encrustation of the machinic on living, breathing humanity.[37] To become machinic like the camera, to embody the anomalies within anonymity, to embody the citizen as a generic and not a universal cartoon, is to produce the body politic not as an abstraction but as an embodied being whose ambition is that its ambience be part of a society of accountability, not of ownership, a space of belonging whose terms are negotiated in the sensual time of democracy rather in what's being redacted, rendered, and enclosed.[38] In the meantime, traditions of silent film iconicity and slapstick absurdity tap into and try to shift the shape of knowledge and life in the historical present.

III. Silence on the Record

We have been following how the contemporary security state produces, in reaction, avant-garde melodrama and tragicomedy in the satirical mode. Both piercing modes are mimetic of the open secret that an affective politics keeps the political subjects of mass democracies attached to the desire for the political. In the next case—the work of the sound activist group Ultra-red—the politico-aesthetic strategy of rerouting the ambient noise of the sentimental state into a record of the state's failures and the inhabitants' hopes is, in a sense, a simpler project. As I suggested at the outset, Ultra-red's project, *Organizing the Silence*, conceives of "silence" in the conventional idiom of identity politics: silence as the name for speech that has had no transformative impact. Ultra-red always works on behalf of the poor, the dispossessed—the politically inconvenient. The collective figures "silence" not as at all silent, therefore, but a description of what happens to potentially transformative political claims-making that affronts the presumption that democracy exists merely when the sense of its existence can be felt.

For Ultra-red, organizing the silence and organizing the noise of the political are, then, the same thing. The collective is inspired by Adorno's claim that modern normative senses are atrophied.[39] What is the opposite of an atrophied sense? They turn to John Cage, here, to think about the senses that are "failing to thrive" as echo chambers. They imagine an alternative sensorium filled with the sounds of what is undefeated in the body although not flourishing in the world.[40] Ultra-red then makes a world for an aesthetic dynamic that disrupts over- and understimulation, demanding not the convoluted identifications and disidentifications of *The PSA Project*, nor the comic play of the countersurveillance actors: here, genuineness reigns. Ultra-red's ethnographic seriousness converts political and social alienation into material that taps into the idiom of a popular sentimentality, yet that would displace the empty form of intimacy captured in conventional political speech.

Organize

the silence.

AIDS where is your rage . . . I am confused . . . I heard something very disturbing on the news . . . I'm frustrated grieved disappointed overwhelmed saddened by the silence that still exists in our communities . . . And still to this day I'm baffled by that . . . When I listened to the silence I heard behind it an anger . . . Tired of being stigmatized . . . AIDS where is your rage . . .

21.1–21.2. Ultra Red records "the silence"

Using sophisticated real-time recording, mixing, and amplifying equipment, Ultra-red enters a community and interviews activists, organizers, or participants who work with and from a subjugated or silenced population: people with AIDS, prisoners, *sans-papiers*, the poor. (They title a recent project: "Fifteen Sounds from the War on the Poor.") They then invite a selection of these interviewees to come to a performance. This performance takes place either inside, in a gallery space, or outside, in an urban one. There, they invite attendees to put their statement on what the collective calls "the record." No one, to my knowledge, ever asks what "the record" is: it goes without saying that going on the record involves speaking and being recorded for any potential public that might encounter the archive. Ultra-red records any statement that its subjects want to put on the record in the new historical present that the performance engenders. The collective engineers on-site a sound loop that aspires to become the collectively dense archive of a new historical sensorium. What statement would you put on the historical record if you got one shot at it?

But Ultra-red's method is more selective than reproducing testimony about whatever situation it was that brought this loosely affiliated group together. Members of Ultra-red came to notice that, along with telling their stories about injustice, their interviewees talked a lot about their feelings: both inequality and political work made them exhausted, depressed, frustrated, exuberant, and so on. So Ultra-red embarked on a project of sifting out political feeling statements from the statements generally.[41] As the interviewees spoke their speech into the record a technician would remix it and play back the voices in a new feedback loop made up of sentences reflecting on political feeling, until the room was thick with the hangover of everyone's feelings and the noise of a newly collective atmosphere. Ultra-red then engineered videos re-performing the feeling statements and worked with sound-artists like Matmos to create dance mixes on CD.

The *mise en scène* of the performance site and the video is somewhere between funereal, corporate, and avant-garde minimalist—quite an achievement. Long white tables represent both the unwritten record and coffins; the performers saying phrases about how it feels to be politically irrelevant to the culture's self-idealizing version of the reproduction of life and the orchestration of death are well dressed, well behaved, and distant in a cool enough way that the whole scene could be hip or simply abstract. It moves not from mouth to ear, as in the structure of Foucauldian sexuality, but from ear to all the other senses, including the flesh. Reinvesting the mundane *dres-*

sage of the body politic with the legitimation of the historical record, Ultra-red manages to straddle, on the one hand, the enormity of the change that would have to happen for these activists to matter politically and, on the other, soundtracks so minimalist that spectators can hear their own breathing while they watch.

The repeated and accreting verbalization of Ultra-red's archive engenders an intensifying atmospherics that enables the drama of subordination and its ordinariness to articulate with the pleasurable merging of speech and noise. This filter does not delaminate meaning from noise, but makes the noise viscerally meaningful, or at least that is its aim; in other words, it becomes slowly apparent that to cast the political as a feedback loop is another way to understand the ambiance of the classic public sphere. Ultra-red takes over this process as a project, though, not just to make new opinion directed toward the state or civil society, as it exists, but as new noise for a body politic, new visceral political sounds. These statements are then synthesized, remixed, and distributed to other communities and venues. The "record" Ultra-red makes is not therefore a dead, filed archive that exists to establish and legitimate norms, but a circulating thing that engenders rhythm. This strategy does not turn mourning into militancy but, again, phrases politics as a kind of dressage, a habit of being in the present.

As a reading of the political in the historical present, "Organizing the Silence" provides an index not just to a description of the problem but to political art as the scene for an invention of a new mannerliness, a new rhythm for being in the social, a new proprioception, quite apart from whatever is collective about the "consciousness" that gets engendered by the particular utterances that circulate. This links its avant-gardism to the sentimental register of the popular pedagogy of pleasure around AIDS that Tavia Nyong'o reports on in "I've Got You Under My Skin."[42] Additionally, it shares with popular reeducation projects the seduction of the body politic's body toward reattaching to the political by a route that does not have to pass through the institutional frustrations of mainstream politics or ideological policing of self-consistency. The sense of freedom-in-attachment that becoming the referent of "the record" can make releases the body politic from merely echoing in its own head. Then, the feedback loop of the social is no longer abandoned to the kind of meaninglessness that is otherwise endemic to the sonic politics of solitary confinement that haunts the popular drive for the noise of political immediacy.

One response to political abandonment is to revolt, to fight the power in genres of direct action. The subjects of precarity that this book tracks have chosen primarily not to fight, but to get caught up in a circuit of adjustment and gestural transformation in order to stay in proximity to some aspirations that had gotten attached to the normative good life. Literally, by changing the sensorial experience of immediate things in the world, this chapter's cases have interfered with that pattern of treading water in the impasse. To overhear the political, and to speak back from a position of not being addressed as the majority to be represented in it, is to seek to interfere with the feedback loop whose continuity is at the core of whatever normativity has found traction. Interference with the feedback loop of a genre is one version of ideological iconoclasm. It affirms a model of a civil society that is civil, but in a new manner.

This work is radical in a traditional sense, taking up the position of the interfering intellectual, the counterconceptual aesthetic activist reorganizing the senses along with common sense. What follows is exemplary of a growing body of work with a different aim. It is similarly avant-garde in its aesthetic refusal of Aristotelian narrative satisfaction, character identification, and other conventionally naturalized genres of ambient citizenship. It abjures inflated political conventions of representation, speaking, listening, imitating, lurking, and projective identification. This work speaks most strongly to the possibility of breaking the patterns of cruel optimism of normative liberal civil society models in its turning away from those models. I say turning away rather than refusal, because these works are not in a melodramatic modality. They are aversive to the in-your-face modes of on-the-street protest. They manifest a politically depressed position, but without seeking repair in an idiom recognizable in the dominant terms.[43]

Instead, this art strays beneath the radar where things go without saying not because they are censored or normative, but because, as the body politic wanders around stunned in the crisis ordinary, it is not clear what to say. If the state's cameras are *silent* in the security camera art, these alternative lenses are *quiet*, attentive to the noise of the social and giving it form without returning it to political shape. This impasse is not too comfortable, though: there's queasiness in the air. Normative idioms of power and distinction are almost entirely outside of the frame, and yet hover everywhere. Stunningly quiet witnessing work by Slater Bradley and Liza Johnson provides the exemplary cases for this segment. Given the implicit context from which the works emerge, they document failures of democracy and social security in the United States. At the same time, they point toward the waning of the melodramatic hegemony that both inflates the noise of the political to constitute evidence of authentic immediacy within the body politic and casts the events that conventionally constitute the collective present in an inflated dynamic of trauma and recovery. The artists address postcatastrophic life not only as what happens after great pain. They gaze at the extended duration of an ordinariness in which what has fallen apart is being measured, reoccupied, and joined with that which is not yet destroyed or which, even better, is stronger. They connect to allusive things, too, tapping into the register of fantasies that have not yet found narrative circulation. For both artists, it is as though the aesthetic eye were looking around for political reciprocity but will not take just *anything* that returns the gaze.

In addition to working in genres like rock video and minidrama, Slater Bradley makes video art that records or reenacts stretches of time with an undramatic flatness that challenges the intense atmospherics of transgressive deflation that have shaped so much of the mainstream avant-garde tradition of twentieth-century political art—say, from the Surrealists to the Critical Art Ensemble. Bradley champions the DIY aesthetic of the simple conceptualizing experiment that shuttles between the present-at-hand and the ready-to-hand of Heideggerian phenomenology.[44]

Focusing on historical events that the U.S. body politic (and the global entertainment culture that consumes its mediatized dramas) experienced both collectively and in the singular autonomic zones of experience, Bradley's deflationary aesthetic stretches out the space between cause and effect, and stimulus and response. He thereby splits off loop from feedback, throwing the spectator into a space that does not exist yet as genre. Seeing and hearing the potentiality that constitutes the event in the outflow of its initial happening, Bradley deems the spectatorial angle as important only insofar as it can be induced into a space of not-yet-being-situated. At the same time, because his work is in proximity to the dramatics of events, a space of potential political agency circulates in the atmosphere. The video is virtually a gesture of world-unmaking that is not the same as the catastrophic loss of experience in conventional trauma-time.

Two videos in particular bear out these propositions: JFK, Jr. (1999) and *The Land of Artistic Expression* (2002). The first involves a two-and-a-half-minute

22.1–22.8. *JFK, Jr.* (Slater Bradley, 2000)

film that shows a woman of indeterminate age—she could be anywhere from fifteen to twenty-five—placing a commemorative rose on the pile of other flowers commemorating the life and death of John Fitzgerald Kennedy Jr., Carolyn Bessette Kennedy, and Lauren Bessette in 1999. The camera stands in line behind, but not directly behind, that woman at the memorial. People are jostling but quiet too: strangers in line to signify something. The camera zooms in glancingly at her freckled arms, her neck, her back, resting a bit on her large hoop earrings; it looks over her shoulder, reads her card, and then reads other testimonial placards over her shoulder, as she reads them. Yet it does not take on anything like her "perspective," if we think of the not-quite parallel positioning of the camera's gaze as a proprioceptive expression of the woman's, or anyone's, internal state. From this action we do learn a bit about her. The card reads:

To John, Carolyn, and L ___:
Even though I never met yous I want you to no [sic] you will always be happy and remembered by me. Love, Patricia (Astoria, Queens)

Patricia's identity is in the details: her name, neighborhood, and something about a sensibility in proximity to the political but not at all in its idiom. As I have argued previously about this event, to the members of the body politic who cared about it, the death of JFK Jr. was the death of an exemplary member of the body politic.[45] Kennedy represented proximity both to representative political sovereignty in its inflated mode and ordinary citizen sovereignty in its distance from control over life and death. "Patricia" writes, therefore, to the family intimately, and yet as a stranger. She attempts sovereign affective performativity very sweetly: her act of sympathy asserts his repair through her mourning—"you will always be happy and remembered."

In other words, Patricia writes to the exemplary Kennedy as though any member of a democracy has the right to call herself exemplary, denying the hierarchies and divisions that structure politics—especially the oligarchic politics that the Kennedys represent. In this she measures the difference that we have been tracking for this entire chapter, between *politics* as a scene of antagonism and *the political* as that which magnetizes a desire for intimacy, sociality, affective solidarity, and happiness. As chapter 2, "Cruel Optimism," argues, a lyrical address to the dead—apostrophe—works best when they are absent and you are affectively and mentally in sovereign control over the ways that they are "in" you. The condition of Patricia's expressive freedom is the absence of her interlocutors, whose death disables the potential anxiety of status shame and enables the assertion of a defiant right to the kinds of commentary, judgment, and sympathy that constitute fan culture as such. We also have no idea how "Patricia" would reflect on her act if asked about it.

While all of this unravels onscreen, the screen itself is going through changes. The shot shifts size from a partly matted image to a columnar shot of the girl squeezed between wider mattes that push her into the middle third of the frame, crowding her the way a body might be crowded while waiting in the line to the memorial pile of cards and flowers. The lens focuses on her stiff body movements and brackets out the larger space she moves in; at the same time it shifts between a flowing image and a stuttering, erratic, robotic one; and meanwhile it cuts from ambient sound to no sound and back again. Because this is a film loop, the flow of the installation does not go from full to depleted, but circles back to the jerky rhythms that resist predictable counterpoint. The citizen and the sounds of citizenship are not in synch. The technical interruptions may reenact glitches in the flow of life, but they do not seem to imitate death or to call for the spectator's melodramatic performance of whatever mourning she might have gone through in response to these deaths. They point to the insecurity of knowing how to embody live liberal democracy. At times the camera seems to stalk the girl, or to expose the girl to ridicule, implicitly accusing her of bathos and condescending to her infelicitous writing. But, as the camera doesn't caption, that judgment would be the spectator's noise, his/her antidemocratic leanings made audible. Then, it seems that Patricia might be aware of all of the vulnerability that occurs when the body politic shows up in public. As she places a wrapped rose on the pile she looks over her shoulder diagonally—not at the camera—as if seeking out some clue about how to act.

The camera "eavesdrops" on the card she writes, but, covered with her thumb, it is only partly legible. Likewise, a poster that she reads, titled "Who's a Hero?" features cut-off lines, with words obscured by the flowers drooping over them.[46] The lyric fracture does nothing, though, to make the expressed affect feel incomplete. The film is not seeking her or anyone out to discover spontaneous overflows of emotion. The excesses of public mourning are conventional. But, this does not mean that they are shallowly felt. Going through the motions without performing the emotions in public, its subject may or may not have felt the impact of the melodramatic mode even within herself.

23. *The Land of Artistic Expression*
(Slate Bradley, 2001)

Bradley's video *The Land of Artistic Expression* takes this pursuit of and respect for the opacity of emotional performance in the context of collectively processed trauma to a more extreme place than even the previous case. Bradley shot this video on 9/11/2001.[47] Having seen the news on television, he went up to his roof and turned on his camera. A matte on the top of the screen says HOME VIDEO as though this footage were taken from the television itself—because, as the security camera example highlighted, one can no longer see any footage outside of its potentiality as *evidence*.

The camera, completely quiet apart from whatever the microphone picks up, inadvertently gathers up another, human, spectator. On a roof across the street someone emerges to stand there and look at Manhattan. The smoke rising from where the Twin Towers were is far away enough for the soundscape of the scene to be random, dispersed, virtually silent. The neighbor on the roof is completely alone, and entirely quiet. He is recording the event, but not with a machine. Bradley's camera is even more alone in this scene of non-relation, watching without inciting or, more significantly, inviting.

There is no "community" here, if community signifies an active, interdependent network that delivers reciprocal recognition and affective synchronization. There is at best only an inoperative community, a community in affective proximity, political potentiality.[48] Yet, what the camera shows has none of the affect associated with the desire to belong or to cultivate any utopianism of the ongoing present; nor is there any of the optimism that autonomous or singular beings could generate in an affectively continuous zone. This film loop projects trauma as ordinary life: flat screen, flat affect, it is a melodramatic hole not quite full of not-quite-boredom. It is an aesthetic of an animated gaze almost completely still, without evidence even of a move to acknowledge, or empathize. Yet, the tacit context of 9/11 enforces that it is not quite dissociated from politics or the political, either. The aesthetic of animated suspension, in the time and space of cinematic prehension, performs the impasse of the present.

Liza Johnson's *South of Ten* also makes out the historical present as a space of survival that is entirely dedramatized, but more deliberate human activity shapes the cinematic space than was evident in Bradley's aesthetic worlding. This is a post-Katrina film, but it neither takes place in New Orleans nor tracks the multiple disasters that the name "Katrina" now implies. The "Ten" of the title is U.S. Interstate 10: "south of ten" is the Gulf Coast of Mississippi, an area that was hit hard by the hurricane. However, Mississippi was itself bypassed by the press-shaped noise of the national imaginary, whose dramatic sense of exemplarity preferred to mourn and imagine rescue for New Orleans, an already fully sentimentalized zone of cultural production and racialized exoticism. There is always hope that sentimental treasuring will protect one's valued objects, but the materially crumbling political and physical infrastructure of Mississippi measured some limitation to what feeling could do. To track devastation in the places only spottily invested with sentiment and long riven by an unidealizably sordid class and racist history might be not to encounter evidence that one had already been interested, virtuous, and well-intentioned.

South of Ten looks not toward the past, however—that's in the air. Even while documenting the racial and class hierarchies of life available to view south of Interstate 10, it shows the owners of property and the workers, too, figuring out the ongoing present. The film is silent except for the ambient noise of ongoing life. People are *tending*: tending things, tending to things, having tendencies to go in this, then that direction. The wealthy tend to be alone, surveying the overwhelming scene, moving inefficiently. The poor and more disenfranchised tend to have projects: of being outside together, relaxing, or scavenging, working, and recovering. The wealthy tend to be white, and solitary: more poor whites and poor people of color are scattered all over the space. Nevertheless, the conditions for solidarity persist. It seems that all of the talking has already happened, and *everyone* is in survival time. This, and not the optimism of political being as such, is what it means to live collectively, within a kind of loose solidarity, in the crisis-shaped ordinary of *South of Ten*.

In contrast to the earlier examples, then, where silence manifests a drama of blocked citizenship through which artists and activists refilter explicitly political sensual immediacy, this film's perspective is *quiet*. The soundtrack opens the filmic shot to the ongoing activity of making life up *again*; the

24.1–24.3. *South of Ten* (Liza Johnson, 2006)

aesthetic attention to absorption, to standing back to capture the historical mood of the present in suspension within the unfolding situation, is the piece's exemplary achievement.

South of Ten is only ten minutes long. The camera sits and watches, pans gently across a variety of blighted fields. The color is the color of an ordinary, saturated, sunny day: Johnson does not emphasize the heavy atmospherics of the affective or actual weather. Nonetheless, there is an atmosphere. One can tell that some places are *close*, close to airless, as when a seeming family moves through a too small space to find a booth where they can sit without resting, exhausted, not talking.[49] Most spaces are too big, though, requiring the camera to pan to find what is there of life: workers coordinate their bodies and then take a rest, sit somewhere looking and smoking; scavengers wander around a space, but the aim is not random at all. Adults do the thing they can do in the destroyed place of the ongoing present to begin the gesture-by-gesture work of cleaning up and figuring out how to make it all add up again to a life. There is no need for talk; ambient sound measures the elastic proximity of people in a collective moment who move physically closer and farther away from each other but are isolated, too, in a sense, like castaways on the same island taken up with getting on with things, leaving dramatic expressive subjectivity for later, or never.

At the same time, South of Ten does tap into the age-old marriage of liberal realism and white sentimentality: the atmosphere connotes suffering, witnessing, and innocence.[50] Along with documenting the racial and class hierarchies of life for adults, the film repeatedly stages the post-catastrophic scenario from the perspective of a sweet group of kids of color. This glancing referentiality solicits old-timey U.S. melodramatic identification with the innocent, the imminent, the incompetent, and the not-yet-responsible and, so, not-yet-failed. However, the Katrina crisis produces new pressures on managerial realism, new pressures on composure and comportment, new pressures on genre, tone, and mode. The filmic atmosphere neither demands nor foregrounds the performance of drama—suffering, empathic, or otherwise. People seem more caught up in speculation and fatigue than they do in affective inflation or unraveling. The film watches without adding intensities. This means that the waning of the melodramatic mode is accompanied by a new conventional unraveling of the relation of image to affect as well.

South of Ten casts postcatastrophic existence not as wounded or healed life but in process: the time of gathering, wandering, and scavenging the im-

25.1–25.2. *South of Ten* (Liza Johnson, 2006)

passe. The kids are neither manifestly virtuous nor wise. Mainly they are playing: riding bikes, circulating. They play and collect what's on the ground because that is their usual mode of passing time. But this age-appropriateness produces a tacit contrast between the traditionally sentimental subjects and their elders. Scavenging is a game for kids; for the adults it is life itself now, amidst crisis. Crisis turns out not to be fast, but stretched and slow: the adults work, take breaks, sit down, stare out. This is what life south of Interstate 10 has been reduced to.

In these latter films, the body in recovery from disaster is in the vicinity of mainstream politics, but has other things to do than to work out the historical present in its idiom, pragmatically or fantasmatically. Emotion might intersect politics, but that is just one nodal point among many, and not the most important. The disaster-shaped present interferes with the ordinary tragic attrition of life by tending toward moments of comedy and play, work and wandering, and focus and distraction, and not by taking up a position in the intimate zones of political immediacy that orient the body politic to the belief that world-building at a historic scale requires the drama of inflated sovereignty, or politics.

v. Cruel Optimism and the Desire for the Political

These last films might appear to some as quietist, as politically depressive aversions to the political sans gestures of repair of the political. They are indeed performances of departure from the circuit of reseduction and despair that so often absorbs genuine energy for social change. They are perhaps doing some of the delicate work of detaching from the cruel optimism of a political fetish. But as there is no social movement in aesthetic sight, is this refusal to go through the motions and emotions of fidelity to politics a sign of ethical failure? The depressive position, in Klein and Sedgwick, is taken up by a subject who acknowledges the broken circuit of reciprocity between herself and her world but who, refusing to see that cleavage as an end as such, takes it as an opportunity to repair both herself and the world. But, as Anna Potamianou argues in *Hope*, such an arc and rhythm can also amount to attempts to sustain optimism for irreparable objects. The compulsion to repeat a toxic optimism can suture someone or a world to a cramped and unimaginative space of committed replication, *just in case* it will be different. Political realism can be tyrannical; it can become a foundation for change. Political fantasy can be ridiculous and self-defeating; it can ground and sustain an aspirational thinking beyond pragmatics that insists on a new materialism.

Facing the fact that no *form* of being in the political or politics — including withdrawing from them — will solve the problem of shaping the impasse of the historical present, what alternatives remain for remaking the fantasmatic/material infrastructure of collective life? Is the best one can hope for *realistically* a stubborn collective refusal to give out, wear out, or admit defeat? In that case, optimism might not be cruel at all, but the bare minimum evidence of not having given up on social change as such.

Indeed, throughout this book, this is what we have seen: many varieties of turning away from politics and the political, a becoming-private that ranges from a desperate self-hoarding (in *Rosetta*, *Two Girls*) to embodiments of the neoliberal subject aspiration that equates entrepreneurial activity with sovereign, democratic personhood (in *Human Resources*, *Time Out*). By looking at the play between political intensities and performative aesthetic distortions of ambient citizenship, this chapter has pursued attempts to multiply idioms for the habitation of the desire for the political — for belonging — in domains proximate to contemporary politics. Yet this archive might look minor because it is not situated in the gestures of heroic action we associate with the political; because it turns rather toward deflation, distraction, and aleatory wavering in unusual arcs of attentiveness; and because some of these cases do not counter hegemonic ideologies with philosophies of refusal. In so doing, though, it resonates with the strategies of the global anticapitalist movements whose counternoise has surfaced in this book whenever it looked like the impasse created from the waning of economic and fantasmatic infrastructures of the good life was only a coming apart of the social at all of its seams.

David Graeber and J.K. Gibson-Graham have written brilliantly of the potentiality for reinventing the bodily practice of politics and therefore the production of political subjects projecting out to each other affective assurance and solidarity. In their work, anarchism (Graeber) and neocommunitarianism (Gibson-Graham) neither involve chaos nor the kinds of recognition and closeness we usually understand "community" to signify.[51] They advance a kind of philosophical pragmatism that involves becoming a political subject whose solidarities and commitments are neither to ends nor to imagining the pragmatics of a consensual community, but to embodied processes of making solidarity itself. This orientation toward relating politics and the political would be something like the skeptical, perfectionist position of Cavellian ethics, and something like Agamben's "means without end," where the pure mediality of being in the present of the political and the sensual is what matters and not any ends or preconditions.

In this view one's individual or a collective attachment to the political would ideally be an attachment to the process of maintaining attachment. In psychoanalytic terms, the anarchist political depressive would enact repair by performing a commitment to repairing *politics* without needing clarity or consensus on either of the two traditionally legitimating motives for political action: an ends-oriented consensually held good-life fantasy or confirmation of the transformative effectiveness of one's actions. One "does politics" to be in the political with others, in a becoming-democratic that involves sentience, focus, and a comic sense of the pleasure of coming together once again. Achieving and succeeding are not the measures for assessing whether the desire for the political was ridiculous: a kind of affective consonance is, amidst the noise of ongoing antagonism and debate.

This sense of democracy as an untethering from assurance about social location would be something like Rancière's view in *Disagreement* and *Hatred of Democracy* that being in the middle of the bedlam of world-making embodies the visceral experience of democracy as such. It goes also to

Gibson-Graham's aesthetics of the local, which recognizes "particularity and contingency, honor[s] difference and otherness, and cultivate[s]" the improvisations of "local capacity" and community in the absence of traditional relations of obligation and trust between citizens and their local and more distant governments, and between workers and employers who always claim some reality for the working life of meritocracy.[52] This locates politics in a commitment to the present activity of the senses. It sees the work of citizenship as a dense sensual activity of performative belonging to the now in which potentiality is affirmed.

Lateral politics is therefore, in its own way, mimetic of the historical sensorium that this book has shown to be gathering up the chaos of the present moment. I believe that the return of DIY practices such as these emerges from the hope that changing the white noise of politics into something alive right now can magnetize people to induce images of the good life amidst the exhausting pragmatics of the ordinary's "new normal." To call the new embrace of populist potentiality in the stretched-out historical present a symptom of the intensified transition from the liberal to the post-neoliberal world in which many nationals find themselves is not to belittle it, though. It is to observe that Europe and the United States (not identically, not at the same time) have been forced to adjust emotionally to the process of living with the political depression produced by brutal relations of ownership, control, security, and their fantastmatic justifications in liberal political economies.

I have argued throughout this book that the neoliberal present is a space of transition, not only between modes of production and modes of life, but between different animating, sustaining fantasies. This shift generates intensities so present that they impose historical consciousness on its subjects as a moment without edges, and recent pasts and near futures blend into a stretched-out time that people move around in to collect evidence and find a nonsovereign footing. For the time being, the atmospheres and encounters of the new ordinary orchestrate political time by reinventing sovereignty in the interval between crisis and response: while political demonstrations remain exceptional, posting something, clicking on a hyperlink, or sending an email continue the old model of citizenship as an event of circulating opinion, now folded into the ongoing demand to respond to the next new intensified pressure, just like the last one, and the next.

Now, as in the past, these actions emerge in an atmosphere of belatedness and outrage at not mattering. The model of anarchist/DIY performativity aims to revitalize political action, though, not first by mapping out the better good life but by valuing political action as the action of not being worn out by politics. The carnival and chaos that produce the intimate sociality of political depression where action is delegated to representatives and fantasy are drowned out, in these worlds, by the noise of a new politics that sees those messes as ordinary, vitalizing, interesting, absorbing, personal, playful, and curious. At the same time, the hope that new norms, forms, intuitions, and habits might be invented to reinvent publicness has brought activist theorists and artists back to the question of what kind of form a gesture is, what kind of imminent expressivity it holds, and what kind of affective pedagogy might be effected by it. This is what Sedgwick would call *weak theory*. I believe that its return is in the hope that changing the white noise of politics into something focused but polymorphous can magnetize people to a project of inducing images of the good life that emerge from the sense of loose solidarity in the political that now occupies the ordinary amidst the exhausting pragmatics of the everyday.

But how different is this fantasy of politically affective immediacy from the presidential fantasy that opened this chapter? It is also possible that this shift to a more sustainable optimism through absorption in the present process may merely recast the neoliberal orchestration of political emotion's intimate viscera, producing distractions that inflate the relative importance of the *sense* of belonging in relation to dealing with the hard questions of distributing resources, risk, and vulnerability in the polis. It is a sign of how desperately overwhelming the infrastructural pressures are now—from environmental to economic disparities and depletion—that localism and xenophobias are resurfacing in the political at the same time as more inclusive forms of popular imaginary emerge.

I do not promote the alternative of lateral politics unambivalently, therefore, but situate my optimism for its optimism in the noise of the transitional moment, in the way it slows down our gaze at performatively democratic activity by linking it to a context where solidarity comes from the scavenging for survival that absorbs increasingly more people's lives, rather than from an anxiety about reasserting the potentiality within the political as it has long been known and exerted pressure on fantasy. The urgency is to reinvent, from the scene of survival, new idioms of the political, and of belonging itself, which requires debating what the baselines of survival should be in the near future, which is, now, the future we are making.

Cruel Optimism claims that a new ordinary has emerged in the displacement of the political from a state-citizen relation to a something else that is always being encountered and invented among people inventing life together, when they can. To recast the ordinary this way is to hazard the value of conventional, archaic political emotions and their objects/scenes. But this is what it means to take the measure of the impasse of the present: to see what is halting, stuttering, and aching about being in the middle of detaching from a waning fantasy of the good life; and to produce some better ways of mediating the sense of a historical moment that is affectively felt but undefined in the social world that is supposed to provide some comforts of belonging, so that it would be possible to imagine a potentialized present that does not reproduce all of the conventional collateral damage.

Pace Žižek, the energy that generates this sustaining commitment to the work of undoing a world while making one *requires* fantasy to motor programs of action, to distort the present on behalf of what the present can become. It requires a surrealistic affectsphere to counter the one that already exists, enabling a confrontation with the fact that any action of making a claim on the present involves bruising processes of detachment from anchors in the world, along with optimistic projections of a world that is worth our attachment to it. All of the affective paradoxes of the political in relation to mass demands for social change uttered from the impasse of the present extend from this, cruel optimism's double bind: even with an image of a better good life available to sustain your optimism, it is awkward and it is threatening to detach from what is already not working.

26. Riva Lehrer, *If Body: Riva and Zora in Middle Age*, 2007. Collection of Michael and Michelle Minns.

NOTE ON THE COVER IMAGE

If Body: Riva and Zora in Middle Age

The painting here and also on the paperback edition's cover is Riva Lehrer's *If Body: Riva and Zora in Middle Age*. In the painting, Zora, the dog, blind in one eye and barred by the cone she wears from touching where it's tender, looks into the air and seems happy. Why? She looks happy because she's still and her face tilts up and because her tail seems intimately to brush Riva on the floor in the background. Riva, her face half covered, is probably weeping. But Riva is not in an absolute heap, destroyed by discomposure. She is using her hand to hold her face half-together and to touch what Zora cannot also touch. At the same time, she hides what Zora cannot also hide, so that the dog has a face for two, it seems: aimed, perhaps, toward the light. Part of the story lies in the title's opening phrase: *If Body*. There is no verb, no action, only a tendency that's subjunctive, propositional. There is an IF but no THEN: and so, if one follows the IF, what does one find, then? If body, pain. If body, misery. If body, attrition, vulnerability, wearing out. If body, bound to life. If body, fabric, hair, prosthesis, and surfaces that are grounds and backgrounds too. If body, other bodies: unseen and in proximity, abstract and touchable. If body, imitation—Riva covers her face as though she can be blind like Zora, but the difference between being and likeness is played out a hundredfold, and she is not blind, only tender, trying to stay in synch. If body, there's Riva and Zora, hanging there and hanging in there, in the middle.

If body, there's always a space in the middle, even when there is touching. Riva is riven in the middle—spina bifida. But this is not the middle to which the title refers—that's age, the middle age—which, in dog and human years, amounts to an actuarial guess about an arc of existing. In what sense does this tableau of the two vulnerable bodies cover *Cruel Optimism*? Zora and Riva seem at peace with each other's bodily being, and seem to have given each other what they came for: companionship, reciprocity, care, protection. Bodies make each other a little more possible: but they can't do everything. My sight can't give you your sight, my performative blindness may not even be empathy, and my mix of ability and impairment doesn't impinge much on yours. What we do have together, in the middle of this thing, is a brush with solidarity, and that's real. Zora and Riva are a team, a brace of utopian realists; they see things jointly, partially. A fantasy from the middle of disrepair doesn't add up to repair. It adds up to a confidence that proceeds without denying fragility. Within the ordinary that means having adventures and being in the impasse together, waiting for the other shoe to drop, and also, allowing for some healing and resting, waiting for it not to drop. If body, then everything can follow.

So this scene would seem not to represent a relation of cruel optimism, because no projection or misrecognition is depicted, because so many kinds of reciprocity are on offer, and because there is an "and" that appears to work for both of these beings in the stretch of time that is the ongoing present of the presence of the two. But even in those circumstances mortality and vulnerability hover as the velvet uncanny of the situation. Even when you get what you want, you can't have what you want. Even the best relation, the one that deserves the optimism you attach to it, can turn out cruelly when conditions beyond your or any dog's control suddenly cleave your confidence about the scenes of increasing austerity beyond the one here that stretches out infinitely into aesthetic time. The if-bodies should be so lucky to be able to imitate the painting; if only they could follow indefinitely the dog's tilt toward life. The painting is an aspirational concept. Disability, vulnerability, queerness, femininity, companion species solidarity—there is so much experimental suturing to be tried and so much confidence to be maintained, but because there is so much there is optimism that sitting in the situation will allow more of a flourishing. Sitting is sitting, and preparation for moving, and the painting is a gesture.

It's a political problem, of course, the body. *If Body* is a performance of optimism that lives not just with existential contingency but also with what goes without painting, the structural cruelty of risk, exposure, and affording things like the cone around Zora's neck: medicine and whatever else it takes to maintain a holding environment for love. As a work, a cover, a cover song, a tribute, a displacement, and a restyling, *If Body* hovers in the long moment after the two-as-two have sat for the portrait of their undefeated mutual attachment to living on in phase beyond the frame.

Introduction

Thanks much to Anahid Nersessian and Tom Mitchell for reading the original draft of this introduction with such acuteness and alacrity; and to Roger Rouse for his last-minute engagement.

1 There is a vast literature on the relation of the emergence of neoliberal economic and state practices in relation to social and cultural formations and forms of subjectivity. Highlights include David Harvey, *A Brief History of Neoliberalism*; Wendy Brown's *Edgework*; Aihwa Ong's *Neoliberalism as Exception*; Bob Jessop's *The Future of the Capitalist State*; and many pieces by Silvia Federici, including "Precarious Labor" and "The Reproduction of Labour Power in the Global Economy."

2 I use the language of "precarity" here in concert with the global political movement of the "precarious" that has emerged during this same period of the good-
life fantasy's *frayage*. Seeking to forge transcategorical alliances (trans- local,
national, class, legal, sexual, etc.) against the fading of social democratic institutions and toward the invention of new communities of care and political belonging, this movement is the politically mobilized response to the more general
scenario of impasse and adjustment that I am tracing here. (See chapters 5–7 for
a more thorough engagement with precarity and precariousness.) I should note
that this version of "precarity" resonates only obliquely with the ethical notion
of "precariousness" advanced by Judith Butler in *Precarious Life* and elsewhere.
Butler's usage is vernacular—meaning "vulnerable"—and does not refer to the
meme's political mobilization in Europe, South America, and the United States.
But of course to the extent that we both see in political injustice the amplification
of vulnerability that feels like vulnerability, our engagements with the formation
of political subjectivity and what it might become are in significant solidarity.

3 Thanks to Katie Stewart for this crisp reformulation of the original sentence.

4 This phrase was offered to this project by Srinivas Aravamudan.

5 Berlant, "Unfeeling Kerry," introduced the concept of the historical present in
dramatic transition as in the genre of the "impasse," and "Starved" made a claim
for its potentially positive valences in sexual episodes of improvisation and sovereign unraveling.

6 Badiou, *Manifesto for Philosophy*, 52–56.

7 Massumi: "A technical object continues to evolve, but within the bounds of its
definition. It changes but not noticeably enough to merit a new official name. If
it does jump the bounds of its nominal identity, it is because an event has tran-
spired. Something new has arrived in the world. In a very particular context, a new
singularity has irrupted, making the context a genitive 'situation' again. 'More'
has come. A new life: more to reality." Massumi, "Too-Blue: Colour-Patch for an
Expanded Empiricism," 183.

8 See Deleuze, *The Logic of Sense*, 19. Also informing this discussion of the Deleuzean
event are: Massumi, *A User's Guide to Capitalism and Schizophrenia*, 68–69; Patton,
"The World Seen from Within."

9 It has become a convention to take cheap shots at Fredric Jameson's assessment
of postmodern affective aversions to historical process in *Postmodernism*. Chapter 2, "Intuitionists," makes a substantial argument about the waning of affect.
This section otherwise rephrases material from Berlant, "Thinking about Feeling
Historical."

10 Agamben, *Means without End*.

11 Raymond Williams, *Marxism and Literature*, 115–35.

12 Jameson, *Signatures of the Visible*, 29.

13 Lefebvre, *Rhythmanalysis*, 38–45.

14 Cavell, "The Uncanniness of the Ordinary" and "The Wittgensteinian Event"; Das, *Life and Words*.

15 Taylor, *The Archive and the Repertoire*. See also Vogler, "The Moral of the Story," for an extended brief against character-based realism.

16 I first elaborated this argument in "The Subject of True Feeling," and then extended it in *The Female Complaint*. See also Karyn Ball's elaboration in "Traumatic Concepts."

17 Marcuse, "Aggressiveness in Advanced Industrial Society," 256.

18 Support for this view of affect as a metapsychological cluster of activities related to the senses and emotions without originating in any particular place can be found in André Green, *The Fabric of Affect in the Psychoanalytic Discourse*. Green worries about the conflation of metapsychology with phenomenology, however, whereas here I am claiming that the overdetermination of affectual forces demands a genuinely transdisciplinary capacity for awareness, evidence, and explanation, one that tracks the convergence and dispersal of affective logics with serious rigor and fidelity to focalizing principles but without worry about reproducing the disciplines that are merely professional.

19 Muñoz, *Cruising Utopia*, 1.

20 Hage, *Against Paranoid Nationalism*, 9.

21 See Deleuze and Guattari, "Percept, Affect, and Concept," 163–99.

22 Massumi, "The Future Birth of the Affective Fact," and *Parables for the Virtual*, 35–36.

23 Žižek, *Organs without Bodies*.

24 Brennan, *The Transmission of Affect*.

25 Raymond Williams, *Marxism and Literature*, 132, and *The Long Revolution*, 63.

26 For a compelling performance of this dynamic of incomplete yet comprehensive subjective and structural determination see Franco "Bifo" Berardi, *Precarious Rhapsody*.

27 For Jameson's classic essays on history's expression and censorship in form, see *Ideologies of Theory*, vol. 1.

ONE *Cruel Optimism*

1 Emmanuel Ghent's contribution to this sentence is the word "surrender," which, he has argued, has an importantly different valence than the word "submission" with great consequences to the ways this essay calibrates the difference between being absorbed in something and being dominated by it. Daniel Stern's phrase "the present moment" introduces here a conceptualization of "the present" as a duration that is not just always lost and fleeting but is that which people slow down by projecting or moving it into space. Ghent, "Masochism, Submission, Surrender"; and Stern, *The Present Moment in Psychotherapy and Everyday Life*.

2 For examples of case studies in cruel optimism, see Frank, *What's the Matter with Kansas?*, and Michael Warner, *The Trouble with Normal*.

3 Barbara Johnson, "Apostrophe, Animation, and Abortion."

4 One senses that Johnson conjures, in this scene, the absent presence of the Lacanian *objet petit a*; but in many ways Johnson's work on rhetorical intersubjectivity is closer to Mikkel Borch-Jacobsen's construction of projection in mimetic attachment in *The Freudian Subject*.

5 Barbara Johnson, "Muteness Envy."

6 For further elaboration of enduring in transference with the object, see Benjamin, "'What Angel Would Hear Me?'" In accounting for the analysand's insistence on being found or recognized somewhere, by someone, this wonderful essay also over-aligns the formal optimism of attachment as such and the *affects* of self-preserving desire.

7 Barbara Johnson, "Metaphor, Metonym, Voice in *Their Eyes Were Watching God*" and "Thresholds of Difference."

8 Barbara Johnson, "Bringing Out D.A. Miller."

9 See Bersani and Phillips, *Intimacies*, and Tim Dean, *Unlimited Intimacy*.

10 Freud, "Mourning and Melancholia," 244. Thanks to Tom Stillinger for introducing this to me decades ago.

11 The phrase "political depression" emerges from discussions in a working group on Public Feelings: special appreciation goes to Ann Cvetkovich, Katie Stewart, Debbie Gould, Rebecca Zorach, and Mary Patten.

12 Sedgwick, "Teaching/Depression." http://www.barnard.columbia.edu.

13 Berlant, *The Queen of America Goes to Washington City*, 222.

14 Ashbery, "Untitled." This poem has since been revised into "Ignorance of the Law Is No Excuse."

15 Ashbery, "Filigrane."

16 The neighbor has been slowly emerging as a figure for adjudicating the complexities of intimacy, recognition, and misrecognition in situations of unequal power. See, for example, Joan Copjec's analysis of the transferential relations among colonial/colonized neighbors in *Read My Desire*, 65–116; Žižek, "Love Thy Neighbor? No Thanks!"; and Amy Hempel's story, "Beach Town," in which, in order not to experience the atrophy of her own life, a narrator sits in her backyard listening to her neighbor's conversation with another woman about the neighbor's betrayal and abandonment by her husband.

17 Žižek, "Passion—Regular or Decaf?"

18 Marx, *Economic and Philosophical Manuscripts*, 162.

19 "Indeed what Reason may not go to School to the Wisdom of Bees, Ants, and Spiders? What wise hand teacheth them to do what Reason cannot teach us? Ruder heads stand amazed at those prodigious pieces of Nature, Whales, Elephants, Dromedaries and Camels; these, I confess, are the Colossus and majestick pieces

of her hand: but in these narrow Engines there is more curious Mathematicks; and the civility of these little Citizens more neatly sets forth Wisdom of their Maker," Browne, *Sir Thomas Browne: Selected Writings*, 15. Other famous bees, like Virgil's, might also obtain here.

20   Bradin Cormack suggested to me that, in breaking with heaven, Ashbery breaks with Milton as well: see the poem "On His Blindness," which closes with "They also serve who only stand and wait." Milton, "On His Blindness." Ashbery is breaking with Milton's account of standing: it is no longer God's watch but that of he who approaches. The waiting here too is now luscious and sensual, open and unhidden, having nothing to do with servitude. But in alignment with Milton, it's not sight that's privileged by Ashbery but the hearing that becomes more intensified when one is not, as it were, constantly searching and driving. As for Eliot, the famous lines from *Ash Wednesday* speak here: "Because I do not hope to turn again/Because I do not hope/Because I do not hope to turn/Desiring this man's gift and that man's scope/I no longer strive to strive towards such things/(Why should the aged eagle stretch its wings?)/Why should I mourn/The vanished power of the usual reign? Because I do not hope to know again . . ." One might also note the poem's proximity to Theodore Roethke's "I Knew a Woman": "How well her wishes went! She stroked my chin/She taught me Turn, and Counter-turn, and stand;/She taught me Touch, that undulant white skin:/I nibbled meekly from her proffered hand;/She was the sickle; I, poor I, the rake,/Coming behind her for her pretty sake/(But what prodigious mowing did we make.)" Roethke, "I Knew a Woman," 151. All of Ashbery's emendations tend toward a radical revision of what glorious impassivity might mean to someone not as an opposite to action, but as most apposite.

21   The whole phrase is worth reading: " 'Chloe liked Olivia . . .' Do not start. Do not blush. Let us admit in the privacy of our own society that these things sometimes happen. Sometimes women do like women." Woolf, *A Room of One's Own*.

22   To be seized by the event is to become a subject organized by fidelity to the unknowns released into the field of possibility by the event's truth processes. Alain Badiou links the truth potentials in the love encounter to less personal seizures of affect, including revolutionary activity. Badiou, *Ethics*, 41, 43, 118.

23   Habermas, *The Structural Transformation of the Public Sphere*, 30–50.

24   Cooter notes his brother's "Geoffrey Holder" laugh, which places this story in the mid-1970s, which is when Holder would have been famous for his role in *Live and Let Die* and also as the spokesman for 7UP, "the uncola."

25   Johnson, "Exchange Value," 28–29. Hereafter cited in the text.

26   From the OED: 'Chump change': *slang* (orig. in African American usage) a small or negligible sum of money; small change. 1967 'ICEBERG SLIM' *Pimp* xx. 285 Western whores were lazy and satisfied with making 'chump change.'

27   For more on the correlation between the worker's competence and physical unhealth, see chapter 3, "Slow Death (Obesity, Sovereignty, Lateral Agency)."

28 On the importance of Black People's Topographical Research Centers to nationalist political education projects within Black metropolitan communities across the United States during the 1970s, see Yusuf Nuruddin, "The Promises and Pitfalls of Reparations," on The National Coalition of Blacks for Reparations in America (NCOBRA) website: http://www.ncobra.org.

29 Ryman, *Was*, 168. Hereafter cited in the text.

30 Deleuze and Guattari, "What Is a Minor Literature?," 59–69.

TWO Intuitionists

1 "Affective realism" here points to genres of adjustment to the immediacy of happenings in the historical present, and has no ambition to provide a general or a historically particular theory of affective realism as an aesthetic mode with codifiable qualities. For impressive accounts of how that might be formulated, see Jernigan, "Affective Realism"; and Flatley, *Affective Mapping*. For the realist cookie, see Proust.

2 Bergson, *Matter and Memory*.

3 Here of course I am summarizing a century's worth of work on the relation of propertied to subjective privacy. A good short account of this psychic and material compartmentalization can be found in Eagleton, "Capitalism and Form." The concept of distributed *sensibilities* comes from Rancière, *The Politics of Aesthetics*. The problem of future-orientation as prison or opening within normativity is being fought out, tacitly, between Lee Edelman in *No Future* and José Muñoz in *Cruising Utopia*.

4 See, for example, the varied approaches to the domination and inventiveness of affect in relation to action in: Ahmed, *The Cultural Politics of Emotion*; Clough et al., *The Affective Turn*; Muñoz, *Between Psychoanalysis and Affect*; Probyn, *Blush*; Staiger, Cvetkovich, and Reynolds, eds., *Political Emotions*.

5 The previous paragraph takes material from Berlant, "Neither Monstrous nor Pastoral."

6 Gould, *Moving Politics*.

7 Sontag, "The Way We Live Now." Hereafter cited in the text.

8 Harootunian, "Remembering the Historical Present."

9 "Plane of immanence" is Gilles Deleuze's and Félix Guattari's term for the absorption, embeddedness, and consistency of life as it moves. See, among other things, *A Thousand Plateaus*.

10 The "whatever" point is Giorgio Agamben's conception of the "being-such, that it always matters," the formal, impersonal punctum that would be the ethical ground of anyone's membership in the social, their lovability. "Thus whatever singularity (the Loveable) is never the intelligence of some thing, this or that quality

or essence, but only the intelligence of an intelligibility." See *The Coming Community*, 2.

11 Lefebvre, *Rhythmanalysis*, 38–45.

12 "Pathogeography" is a concept invented by Mary Patten and Rebecca Zorach for Feel Tank Chicago to describe the emotional temperature of a space, refunctioning the Situationist term "psychogeography." See http://www.pathogeographies .net. I am interested here more in pathocartography, affective mapping.

13 One might say, then, that to eventilize an occurrence would be to force it from its status as object (use value) to thing (resistant, attractive enigma). For the extensive consequence of the object/thing distinction, see Bill Brown, "Thing Theory." For Foucault on eventilization and the historical present, see "What Is Enlightenment?" and throughout *The Archaeology of Knowledge*.

14 See Postone, "Lukàcs and the Dialectical Critique of Capitalism," 94–98, and *Time, Labor, and Social Domination*, esp. 186–25; and Harootunian, "Remembering the Historical Present." Žižek's career of denouncing the disavowals that enable the ordinary to endure began with *The Sublime Object of Ideology*.

15 Lukàcs, *The Historical Novel*, 32, 38, 48, 58–63, 195–96.

16 Raymond Williams, *Marxism and Literature*, 132, and *The Long Revolution*, 63.

17 Jameson, *Postmodernism*, 10–11.

18 See Berlant, *The Female Complaint*, 3–4 and throughout, for a more extensive discussion of genre as affectual contract.

19 See Rohy, "Ahistorical," 64–68. I'd also like to thank Benjamin Blattberg for sharing with me "The Style of the So-Called Inanimate: Commodity Style in *Sister Carrie* and *Pattern Recognition*," a paper that, like all *Pattern Recognition* criticism, thinks about pasts in the novel in relation to imminent futures but not as histories of the present; the paper also proposes interestingly that the novel plays out a difference between ahistoricism (which, as immanence, it sees as a good) and antihistoricism (which it sees as ideology) in ways that might fruitfully cross over into a conceptualization of its aesthetic and historical self-contemporaneity.

20 Jameson, *The Political Unconscious*, 6.

21 Ibid., 76.

22 Harootunian, "Remembering the Historical Present," 485.

23 See Kristin Ross's critique of the historical emptiness of everyday life theory (and its relation to colonialism) in *Fast Cars, Clean Bodies*.

24 Massumi, "Too-Blue," 177–83.

25 *The Intuitionist* hereafter cited in the text.

26 *Pattern Recognition* hereafter cited in the text.

27 Intuitionism seems not to refer to the philosophical project associated with L. E. J. Brower; Whitehead is more likely to be in conversation with Bergson.

28 This brief summary derives from Bob Altemeyer's *The Authoritarians*. To track the

development of "authoritarian personality" theory since Adorno et al., see Altemeyer's introduction.

29 Patricia Williams, *The Alchemy of Race and Rights*, 222.

30 Stewart, *Ordinary Affects*, 4.

31 Deleuze and Guattari, "Capitalism: A Very Special Delirium," 216.

32 See Berlant, "Thinking about Feeling Historical."

33 I entirely respect Caruth's work and claim, but think that the relation of trauma to styles of representation is far richer in terms of the implied temporal imaginary of the symptom than *Unclaimed Experience* argues. Caruth's later work attributes the creativity and aesthetic richness that might accompany post-traumatic life to the life drive, and thus preserves the autonomy of trauma from the ordinary, a view against which I am arguing.

34 For a related analysis of the tradition of traumatic temporality, see Clough et al., *The Affective Turn*, 1–33.

35 Caruth, *Unclaimed Experience*, 1–9.

36 Ruth Leys points to two styles of traumatic symptom, the mimetic and antimimetic, arguing that trauma's shattering of boundaries as such produces a constant shift between seeing the subject of trauma as shattered into symptom (mimetic) or produced as dissociative being (antimimetic). My analysis is clearly on the antimimetic side of things, but as the focus of this book is on dramas of adjustment and processual subjectivity during times of historical transition, trauma's focus on the logic of exception underdescribes the range of response styles that emerge in these extended situations. See Leys, *Trauma: A Genealogy*.

37 Phillips, "Freud and the Uses of Forgetting."

38 See the historical details surrounding the emergence and suppression of "the falling man" of 9/11 in Junod, "The Falling Man." See also DeLillo, *Falling Man*; and the documentary *9/11: The Falling Man*, dir. Henry Singer (2005).

39 François, *Open Secrets*.

40 Fred Moten, *In the Break*, especially 63–122.

41 Spivak, "Forum: The Legacy of Jacques Derrida." The term "telepoesis" is from Derrida, *The Politics of Friendship*, 32 (translation modified). See also Spivak's use of the concept in "Harlem," 116.

THREE *Slow Death*

Many thanks to Dipesh Chakrabarty, Geoff Eley, Dana Luciano, Nasser Hussain, Roger Rouse, Adam Thurschwell, and Martha Umphrey for their meticulous engagements, as well as to audiences at Amherst, Johns Hopkins, the University of Wisconsin, the University of Chicago, APA, ASA, and Cleveland State. Special nostalgic thanks to Virginia Chang, my original collaborator in the Obesity and Poverty conference (2002).

1 See Harvey, "The Body as an Accumulation Strategy." To call Harvey polemical is not to devalue his profound contributions to understanding the productive destructiveness of capital: in his work, a polemic is a call for precision, not a way of drowning it out.

2 Mbembe, "Necropolitics," 12. See Agamben, *Homo Sacer*, *Remnants of Auschwitz*, and *State of Exception*.

3 See Sarat and Hussain, "On Lawful Lawlessness," 1307; see also Hussain, *The Jurisprudence of Emergency*.

4 For a related critique of the metaphysicalization of the sovereignty concept, see Balke, "Derrida and Foucault on Sovereignty." In "The Life and Times of Sovereignty," Daniel Morris helped me to elaborate and clarify what it might mean to temporalize this concept.

5 See Bataille, *Literature and Evil*, 173; and *The Unfinished System of Nonknowledge*.

6 Foucault, "17 March 1976," 238–63.

7 Ibid., 243–44. Ultimately Foucault's model of the endemic and of biopower is far more focused on power distributed through delegated state practices than is this chapter.

8 See, for example, the place of sovereignty in the conceptualization of sociality and publicness throughout Michael Warner's *Publics and Counterpublics*. In "Derrida and Foucault on Sovereignty," Balke argues that late Derrida also presumes the metaphysical and foundational equivalence of self-mastery, autonomy, and sovereignty in the operation of the Western polis and its individuals.

9 See Laclau, "Universalism, Particularism, and the Question of Identity," 107, and Gilroy, *Against Race*, 220, 230. See also Armstrong, *The Radical Aesthetic*, 236. The antinomian activity of the contemporary U.S. state shows how powerful an as-if or fantasmatic assumption of sovereignty can be in the hands of those otherwise bound by an obligation to legal proceduralism.

10 The future anteriority of the subject is central to the problematics of death-in-life in Barthes, *Camera Lucida* and *A Lover's Discourse*, and Cornell, *The Imaginary Domain*. See also, as a problem, this mode of the will-have-been as confronted by Lee Edelman, *No Future*.

11 Available in World Health Organization documents as early as 1998, and registering typical anxiety about the joke-and-threat status of obesity in public-sphere Western rhetoric about it, *globesity* is now in wide circulation in medical and commercial venues: see, for example, Anderson, "Buzzwords *du Jour*"; Eberwine, "Globesity"; Blackman, "The Enormity of Obesity"; and multiple articles in *Journal of the American Medical Association* and other medical journals. For a recent academic deployment, see Kulick and Meneley, "Introduction."

12 "Anti-will" is Patricia Williams's brilliant phrase for the mass personality or collective identity deemed so instinctive and appetitive that it is defined by its compulsions. Williams, *The Alchemy of Race and Rights*, 219.

13 For the actuarially based establishing arguments, see National Center for Health Statistics (a subdivision of Centers for Disease Control and Prevention), "Prevalence of Overweight and Obesity Among Adults: United States, 1999–2002"; the CDC general obesity homepage at http://www.cdc.gov; International Obesity Task Force, http://www.obesite.chaire.ulaval.ca; the several World Health Organization Obesity reports at http://www.who.int/en; and Mokdad et al., "The Spread of the Obesity Epidemic in the United States, 1991–1998." For debunking arguments, see Oliver, *Fat Politics*, and Campos, *The Obesity Myth*, and the prescient Richard Klein, *Eat Fat*. For geopolitically relativizing arguments, see Gremillion, "The Cultural Politics of Body Size."

14 See Dumm, *A Politics of the Ordinary*, 10–49.

15 For a great habitation of the Lyotardian "temporalization of space and spatialization of time," see Quick, "Time and the Event."

16 Brennan, *The Transmission of Affect*.

17 The "event" has been accumulating much critical attention via Jean-François Lyotard, Gilles Deleuze, Jean-Luc Nancy, Alain Badiou, and the post-Freudians, all of whom focus on the event as an experience of radical contingency. I concur with this sense to the extent that the event always points to an impactive experience, but, with the exception of Freud's *après-coup* and Deleuze's perturbation, event theorizers use extreme and melodramatic anti-foundational languages of nothingness, shattering, cleavage, and so on to describe impact, disregarding what about the event is at the same time ordinary, forgettable, charming, boring, inconsequential, or subtle. See the Preface for an expanded argument about ordinariness and the event. I am thinking with Jameson's work on genre here, to initiate a way of describing events that allows calibrations of their resonance to articulate different registers of impact (including the vagaries of the vague, the null, and the whatever) and the conventionality of even memorable affective experiences. See Jameson, *The Political Unconscious*. For kindred views, see Collins, "The Great Effects of Small Things"; and Stewart, *Ordinary Affects*. See also the ruminations on the ongoingness of the historical event in Sewell, *Logics of History*.

18 A related view on how to think about the temporality of environments in late capitalism, focused on the environment in its natural sense along with its epistemological one, can be found in Barbara Adam's wonderful *Timescapes of Modernity*.

19 In the nineteenth century it might have been called morbidity, that is, death as a way of life, but in this instantiation, in slow death, the focus is on the articulation of the structural and the experiential. Not defining a group of individuals merely afflicted with the same ailment, slow death describes populations *marked out for wearing out*. Thanks to Dana Luciano for discussions about this.

20 For more on the anti-intellectual utility of an actuarial imaginary in the orchestration of public politically related emotion, see Berlant, "The Epistemology of State Emotion."

21 Such a description as this, pointing to disavowed ways of living that thrive within the "same" temporal regime or horizon of history, resonates with Agamben's use of "zone of indifference" or undifferentiation [*zone di indifferenza*] to describe the thriving antinomianism within political life under contemporary regimes of national/global law (Agamben, *State of Exception*, 23). At the same time that a discourse and practice of obligation to the law endures to resanctify the sacred rights of human subjects, a variety of zones in which the law is suspended also emerges, negating conventions of rights protection in order to protect the *idea* of protection. This is not just a phenomenon of state practices but also of popular support for the suspension of legal protections on behalf of legal freedom. The problem in Agamben's important description of this multiplication of distinctions into a zone of incoherence is that a structuralism perdures in the idea of bare life as that which is included as the excluded. Agamben overterritorializes what is fundamentally a temporal, symbolizing, and expanding penumbra suffusing and confusing the law. The concept of indistinction should be much stronger, enabling discussion of the foundational disavowals within democratic practice of parceling out freedom and unfreedom, legitimacy and all its formal and informal others. This argument about the activity of displacement is akin to Talal Asad's argument about the institutions of hypocrisy that protect cruel and unusual punishment within liberal legal regimes. Asad shows powerfully how out of sight is *not* out of mind. See Asad, "On Torture, or Cruel, Inhuman, and Degrading Treatment."

22 Elizabeth Kolbert's "XXXL: Why Are We So Fat?" provides the best brief history of the rollout of this crisis to date. Flegal et al. provides the most up-to-date obesity statistics, with 32–35 percent of Americans *obese* through 2008, but with the rate of increase in obesity status having flatlined around 2003–2004.

23 See U.S. Congress, "Personal Responsibility in Food Consumption Act of 2005." Introduced and passed in the House in March 2004, the Senate version of the hamburger bill passed on October 19, 2005. For a legal/cultural reading of this event, see Lithwick, "My Big Fattening Greek Salad."

24 The Center for Science in the Public Interest maintains a frequently revised data page concerning normative and legal trends in enforcing nutritional pedagogy: http://www.cspinet.org. As for norm tracking, early in this process the French fry took a beating that had nothing to do with the right-wing vitriol against the old Europe that manifested after 9/11. In 2005 an article appeared in the *New York Times* stating aghast that the French fry is now the most frequently and voluminously eaten vegetable by all children in the United States over fifteen months old; this was soon succeeded by a controversial claim that childhood consumption of French fries leads to increased incidence of adult breast cancer; and soon succeeded by the virtual omnipresence of Michael Pollan as the voice of conscience and manageable health, with his slogan: "Eat food. Not too much. Mostly plants." See Tarkan, "Bananas? Maybe. Peas and Kale? Dream On"; Melanie Warner, "Cali-

fornia Wants to Serve a Health Warning with That Order"; and Rabin, "Study or No, Fries Are Still Bad News." See also the response from business, Investors .com, "California's Low-Fact Diet"; Pollan, "Unhappy Meals"; De Noon, "Michelle Obama's Plan to End Childhood Obesity Epidemic."

25 The Obama administration's "Let's Move" initiative covers the gamut from gardening and exercise to actual recipes for cooking and activism. See http://www .letsmove.gov. As with previous administrations, the focus is on changing consumption habits through consensual corporate and institutional "partnerships." http://www.cdc.gov.

26 Oliver, Campos, and Klein fight the "cold facts" of the obesity epidemic with their own cold facts, many of which are taken from "fat activists" who proffer their own antinormative analyses of what should constitute definitions of health and sickness. Speaking a debunking language in the register of scandal to drown out the register of crisis, they do not write with a nuanced understanding of their participation in the discursive and always processual construction of disease historically. See Oliver, *Fat Politics*; Campos, *Obesity Myth*; and Klein, *Eat Fat*.

27 See World Health Organization, "Controlling the Global Obesity Epidemic"; MSNBC, "'Globesity' Gains Ground as Leading Killer"; Dickson and Schofield, "Globalization and Globesity"; and Eberwine, "Globesity."

28 Besides the cornucopia of evidence in the widely reprinted blog Nanny State Liberation Front, http://nannystateliberationfront.net, a decade-long, well-argued, and documented polemic by Jacob Sullum tracks the solidification of the nanny state socialism meme in relation to obesity, from "Public Health vs. The Nanny State?" (2000), "The Link between Fat Ad Budgets and Fat Children" (2004), "An Epidemic of Meddling" (2007), to "Fat Load: A Slimmer America Won't Save Taxpayers Money" (2009). See also note 45.

29 Medical sociology and cultural epidemiology are developing groundbreaking approaches relating social capital to other forms of inequality in relation to health, but the field is yet young in terms of thinking about the relation of formal to informal health ideologies and infrastructures. For summary examples, see Song, Son, and Lin, "Social Capital and Health," and Muntaner's more critical commentaries, "Commentary" and, with Lynch and Smith, "Social Capital, Disorganized Communities, and the Third Way."

30 Davidson, "Unequal Burden," http://www.kaisernetwork.org.

31 For wonderful analyses of addiction's disruption of the agency/intentionality phantasm, see Brodie and Redfield, eds., *High Anxieties*.

32 CNN, "Fat Americans Getting Even Fatter." See Sturm, "Increases in Clinically Severe Obesity in the United States, 1986–2000." The United Kingdom is comparably described: see Economic and Social Research Council, "Diet and Obesity in the UK." This increase is also being tracked among adolescents: see Miech et al.,

"Trends in the Association of Poverty with Overweight among US Adolescents, 1971–2004."

33 See Gardner and Halweil, "Underfed and Overfed." The pandemic nature of unhealthy overweight is registered in countless places. See research summaries in Kimm and Obarzanek, "Childhood Obesity"; Popkin, "Using Research on the Obesity Pandemic as a Guide to a Unified Vision of Nutrition"; and Walker, "The Obesity Pandemic." While increasing homogeneity of food distribution in global urban and suburban contexts has made unhealthy weights a global medical concern, at the same time the norms of what constitutes evidence of bodily thriving remain resolutely local. See Angier, "Who Is Fat?"

34 A substantial literature exists on the translocal impact of U.S. food policy and neoliberal market practices (often called reforms) on global food production. A good general introduction to the field is Lang and Heasman, *Food Wars*. But for a sense of the texture of the debates, it is most instructive to track the series of reports on food production, politics, policies, and consequences at the World Trade Organization and World Social Forum Meetings at alternet.org and open democracy.org.

35 Each time I gave the talk on which this chapter is based, sensible people have argued back that obesity and overweight are forms of resistance to the hegemony of the productive/bourgeois body as well as to white class-aspirational beauty culture. My counterargument is that while many forms of ordinary behavior can be phrased in terms of blockage, defense, or aggression, people are more vague and incoherent than that characterization would suggest. There is, in any case, a difference between eating and being fat, and both kinds of activity can be noncommunicative gestures, or ways of detaching from or merely interrupting a moment. Tracking this activity of the shifting subject requires quite a different imaginary in reference to what it means to do something than the transformative fantasy that saturates the concept of resistance and protest. The case is an obstacle to our appetite for drama. So, maybe, and sometimes—but mainly not.

36 For a valuable European history of state and medical moralization around bodies as manifest in food, see Turner, "The Government of the Body."

37 See Hicks, "America on the Move."

38 See Surgeon General, "The Surgeon General's Call to Action to Prevent and Decrease Overweight and Obesity"; for later emendations of Satcher's plan, see USA Today, "Surgeon General: 'Obesity Rivals Tobacco as Health Ill,'" and the current page at the CDC, http://www.cdc.gov. There is a vast clinical literature responding to this cluster of empirical claims; see, for example, Manson et al., "The Escalating Pandemics of Obesity and Sedentary Lifestyle."

39 Schlosser, *Fast Food Nation*, 242–43.

40 The literature on pangenerational disability from obesity and obesity-related

illnesses is often focused on diabetes and hypertension. See, for example, the front-page *New York Times* series on diabetes: Urbina, Kleinfield, and Santora, "Bad Blood," and Scollan-Koliopoulos, "Consideration for Legacies about Diabetes and Self-Care for the Family with a Multigenerational Occurrence of Type 2 Diabetes."

41 In Harvey, "The Body as Accumulation Strategy," 103–4.

42 The National Depression Screening Day website is http://www.mentalhealth screening.org. See also Jacobson, "The Epidemic of Obesity"; Shomon, "National Depression Screening Day Offers Public an Open Invitation to Learn about Treatment Options, Expectations"; and Simon et al., "Depression and Work Productivity."

43 See, for example, the argument against setting "moral panic" versus the obesity epidemic in the blog *Inquisition 21st Century*, http://www.inquisition21.com, and the 100+ articles on the libertarian Cato Institute website, at www.catoinstitute .org, with titles such as "Obesity and 'Public Health'?," "Fat Scare Leads to Government Girth," "What You Eat is Your Business," and "Big Reasons for Fat Skepticism." Rush Limbaugh even blamed the obesity epidemic on "the left," the welfare state, and the United Nations; see Media Matters, "Limbaugh Blamed the Left for Obesity Crisis."

44 There have been two "Declaration of the World Food Summit" instantiations, in 1996 and 2002. The archive of the transnational collaboration, mostly among financially stressed nations but including the United States, is located on the United Nations website at http://www.un.org. The U.S. government's speeches focus on bank financing of entrepreneurial initiatives. The 2002 Declaration explicitly acknowledges that no progress is being made in the eradication of world poverty despite all of the money, planning, and good intentions directed toward that end at these meetings.

45 All statistics on obesity are debated, especially those about children. The Centers for Disease Control and Prevention page on obesity and overweight puts the national percentages at 68 percent in 2010, but slides willy-nilly between obesity and overweight statistics. http://www.cdc.gov. For debates about the empirical base of the situation, see the special issue on the obesity epidemic of *The Journal of Clinical Endocrinology and Metabolism* 89, no. 6 (June 2004), featuring many articles focusing on the debate about how to diagnose and treat children. See especially Slyper, "The Pediatric Obesity Epidemic." These debates in the medical literature produce popular literature such as Pick, "Slim Chance"; and Brown, "Well-Intentioned Food Police May Create Havoc with Children's Diets." The current CDC statistics viz. childhood are at http://www.cdc.gov.

46 Brownell and Battle Horgen, *Food Fight*, 15; see also 23–24.

47 There is a vast literature on constrained physical environments and the obesity increase; a good place to begin is the Obesity and the Built Environment website

of the National Institute of Environmental Health Sciences: http://www.niehs.nih
.gov.

48 Nestle and Jacobson, "Halting the Obesity Epidemic."

49 See U.S. Department of Health and Human Services, "Overweight and Obesity."
    Daniel Zu's "Musings on the Fat City" lays out the problem of thinking about
    health-related movement within the urban ordinary really imaginatively.

50 Critser, Fat Land, 7.

51 See ibid.

52 See Wise, "Collateral Damage."

53 See Critser, Fat Land; Nestle, "Hunger in the United States"; and U.S. Conference
    of Mayors, "A Status Report on Hunger and Homelessness in America's Cities
    2001." For counter-arguments as to whether food insecurity is increasing—a de-
    bate about methods of measurement—see Nord et al. "Household Food Secu-
    rity in the United States, 2000." The important thing here is just to note that,
    in the contemporary United States, mass unhealth due to significantly excess
    weight and mass hunger are not antithetical states or historical contradictions
    but propped strangely and perversely onto each other.

54 See Tilghman, "Obesity and Diabetes in African American Women." See also
    Freedman et al., "Racial and Ethnic Differences in Secular Trends for Childhood
    BMI, Weight, and Height."

55 See Chang, "The Social Stratification of Obesity."

56 See Adams et al., "Overweight, Obesity, and Mortality in a Large Prospective Co-
    hort of Persons 50 to 71 Years Old."

57 For a variety of comparisons among women's eating and mobility patterns, see
    Sobal and Stunkard, "Socioeconomic Status and Obesity," and Lovejoy, "Dis-
    turbances in the Social Body." See also Chang, "U.S. Obesity, Weight Gain, and
    Socioeconomic Status"; Chang and Lauderdale, "Income Disparities in Body
    Mass Index and Obesity in the United States, 1971–2002"; and Chang and Chris-
    takis, "Income Inequality and Weight Status in US Metropolitan Areas." Chang's
    work alone demonstrates the lability of contemporary accounts of the class and
    racial indicators of overweight and obesity. In "U.S. Obesity, Weight Gain, and
    Socioeconomic Status," she argues that poverty-related obesity presents a variety
    of significant health care challenges in the United States, while claiming that
    the rate of increase in obesity currently varies significantly across class lines and
    locale, and that middle-class nonwhites are increasing their degree of overweight
    faster than are the poor. In "Income Inequality," though, she and her co-author
    note that varying degrees of economic inequality in different metropolitan areas
    do not much affect individuals' risk of obesity, except for white women, who con-
    tinue to use weight status as a means of class mobility. The implication of the
    latter article is that income inequality in the United States does not *create* weight-

related ill-health; but the implication of "Income Disparities" is that there is, nonetheless, *a high correlation* between individual income and unhealthy weight, because the poor are indeed more likely to be significantly overweight than everyone else. This tension between causality and correlation is what creates much of the polemical and methodological debate over whether weight-related unhealthiness in the United States presents an epidemic, a problem, or even an interesting phenomenon.

58 For a useful summary of the current literature, see Brown, "Everyday Life for Black American Adults." While the specter of shorter life has been tracked in the medical and popular press for a while, the clearest current epidemiological representation of this phenomenon is Olshansky et al., "A Potential Decline in Life Expectancy in the United States in the 21st Century." The popular debate continues. Just after the publication of Stein, "Obesity May Stall Trend of Increasing Longevity," a counterargument was staged in Gibbs, "Obesity, An Overblown Epidemic?"

59 See Logwood, "Food for Our Souls," 98.

60 For the general problem of disciplinary moralizing at vulnerable populations, see Gilliom, *Overseers of the Poor*; on the specifically medical side, see Fitzpatrick, *The Tyranny of Health.*

61 For surveys of size and eating motivation in the historical and anthropological disciplines, see Gremillion, "The Cultural Politics of Body Size," and Mintz and DuBois, "The Anthropology of Food and Eating." The seeming impossibility of not seeing behaviors as symptoms, as condensations and displacement, of "larger" social forces is striking. The symptom as case becomes a map of a historical field. It is always an expression of a social relation. For ethnographic or observational material that suggests otherwise, showing ingestion as an activity of self-abeyance, see Shipler, *The Working Poor*, and DeParle, *American Dream*. See also note 38.

62 See Valverde, *Diseases of the Will.*

63 In using eating in excess of minimal caloric requirements for the reproduction of life as a way to think about lateral agency and some contexts of its materialization, I am refuting the kinds of misconstrual that characterize the subjects of appetites (i.e. people) as always fully present to their motives, desires, feelings, and experiences, or as even desiring to be. For a brilliant performance of this error, which goes through all the actuarial and historical material one could want while insisting on a hypercognitive historical actor presently obsessed with eating and fat, see Klein, *Eat Fat*. For a beautifully written but even more self-contradictory performance of this perspective, see especially Probyn, "Eating Sex." Adapting Deleuze's and Guattari's articulation of the sexual and the alimentary, Probyn argues paradoxically that eating is a performative part of the becoming-x central to the ongoing undoing of the subject in assemblages of processual sensual ac-

tivity *and* that the appetitive is nonetheless exemplary as a grounding site of self-discovery, self-confirmation, identity, and ethics.

64 The "slow food" movement emerging in Europe in the 1990s responds to many of the environmental factors this chapter details; along with its critique of neoliberal agricultural policies, it translates the impulsive improvisation around recalibrating the pacing of the day into a collective program for deliberative being in the world in a way opposed to the immediatist productive one of anxious capital. For a terrific analysis of the phenomenon, see Leitch, "Slow Food and the Politics of Pork Fat."

65 See Rubin, *Worlds of Pain*, and Heymann, *Forgotten Families*.

66 One could use such a model of agency to talk about the self-disenfranchisement of U.S. voters—the slow death of the body politic—much as one can talk about modes of negative agency in domains more immune from the presumption of sovereignty. See chapter 7, "On the Desire for the Political."

67 Thanks to Kris Cohen for the Baudrillard citation. I hadn't known about this history of the phrase "slow death" before writing this piece. While the vision of the exhaustion of the capitalist subject expressed by the melodramatic Situationist model of Baudrillard and, also, Bataille does share some parts of this analysis of contemporary obstacles to bodily flourishing, it does not get at the overdetermined gestural invention of other bodily temporalities, nor the complexities of optimism, that I am laying out here. Baudrillard, *Symbolic Exchange and Death*, 38–42. Lotringer's "Remember Foucault" provides a great, rich history of their use of the concept.

68 See, for example, Davis, *Late Victorian Holocausts*.

69 See, for example, Notes from Nowhere, *We Are Everywhere*; Sitrin, *Horizontalism*; Shukaitis et al., *Constituent Imagination*; Holmes, *Unleashing the Collective Phantoms*. See also chapters 5–7 for more anticapitalist activist bibliography.

FOUR *Two Girls, Fat and Thin*

1 Sedgwick, *Fat Art, Thin Art*, 160. This essay was written originally for a *festschrift* dedicated to Eve Kosofsky Sedgwick.

2 By "phrase" I refer both to Marx's "The Eighteenth Brumaire of Napoleon Bonaparte" and Lyotard's *The Differend*, where the concept of the phrase resonates musically—a form generated through repetition that comes to seem like the origin and limit of meaning, rather than a scene of it. The *differend* is what goes beyond the phrase; it is what, in Marx, the bourgeoisie cannot afford to avow and which, therefore, is everywhere enacted in the tawdry pleasure and violence of ordinary discipline and taboo.

3 See the keyword "Phantasy" in Laplanche and Pontalis, *The Language of Psycho-Analysis*.

4 On this question, see Bersani, *The Freudian Body*; de Lauretis, *The Practice of Love*; Laplanche and Pontalis, "Fantasy and the Origins of Sexuality"; Rose, *States of Fantasy*; Žižek, "Remapping Ideology" and *Enjoy Your Symptom!*, 1–28, 165–93.

5 See Sedgwick, "The Beast in the Closet: James and the Writing of Homosexual Panic" and "Queer Performativity: Henry James's *The Art of the Novel*."

6 See Adorno, "Television as Ideology."

7 Sedgwick, "Paranoid Reading and Reparative Reading."

8 Christopher Bollas puts forth the phrase "unthought known" for those knowledges one has inarticulately or has left unarticulated, and which one expresses in practices of being rather than in language. See *The Shadow of the Object*.

9 I learned to recognize the overvaluation of this mode of self-reflective, self-elaborating personhood as a major effect of the liberal project, dating from John Stuart Mill, from Elaine Hadley, *Living Liberalism*. See also Lloyd and Taylor, *Culture and the State*.

10 See Eley, *A Crooked Line*.

11 See Sedgwick, *Tendencies*; *Fat Art, Thin Art*; and *A Dialogue on Love*.

12 In the end, of course, it's a dialectic between the Althusserian "Hey, you!" and "Wait up!" but these locutions are not antitheses either, because they each mark the subject's lag (*nachträglichkeit*) with respect to the meanings and desires that organize her.

13 On repetition and convention as antidotes to the formlessness of subjects, see Bollas, *The Shadow of the Object*, and Sedgwick, *Epistemology of the Closet*. See also Bersani, *The Freudian Body*.

14 Jameson, *The Political Unconscious*.

15 Sedgwick, "The Use of Being Fat," in *Fat Art, Thin Art*, 15.

16 Berlant, *The Queen of America Goes to Washington City*, 92.

17 Gaitskill, *Because They Wanted To*; *Two Girls, Fat and Thin*; and *Bad Behavior*. Other relevant stories include "Suntan"; with Peter Trachtenberg, "Walt and Beth: A Love Story"; "Veronica" (now a full-length novel); and "Folksong." All subsequent references to *Two Girls* will be cited in the body of the essay.

18 Thanks to Howard Helsinger for the *Pale Fire* reminder. The literary history whose repetition saturates this novel requires a story of its own.

19 On "normal intimacy," see Berlant, "Introduction," in *Intimacy*. On normative case study intimacy, see Vogler, "Sex and Talk," in the same volume. Vogler's procedures for tracking the contradictions between the ideology of more intimacy and the seemingly actual need for less of it are central to the essay's conceptualization of impersonality. We are working with quite a different model than the more subjectivized psychoanalytic model of "impersonal narcissism" on offer in Bersani's and Phillips's *Intimacies*.

20 Freud's essay on "Femininity" argues that female masochism emerges from the lack of sanction for women's justified anger in and at the world. Much contempo-

rary feminist theory follows through this line, although not Deleuze's "Coldness and Cruelty," which mainly forgets to remember women.

21 I refer to Freud's description of the child's desire to master the relation of control to loss of control in the *fort/da* game. The child's "loss" and "recovery" of the top is read generally as the bargaining any subject does to retain a notion that her or his intelligibility or continuity in the world is a function of her or his will. However, the capacity of the ego to respond to contingency via a principle of form should not imply that the subject "really" is contingent and only masterful in a compensatory way. Each position, repeated countless times, is its own pleasure, and the playing child is also increasing his capacity to be in the room with myriad potentialities.

22 In *Kafka: Toward a Minor Literature*, Deleuze and Guattari comment that cultural minoritization—a relation of displacement within a hegemonic frame, a non-position of internal exteriority to ideal collective norms—is reenacted in the displacement of speech and writing by eating. Eating performs a displacement that is already a social fact: it stuffs the mouth that cannot anyway be heard, except as a distortion.

23 In Julia Kristeva's version of abjection the abjected subject becomes a thing—a stray, a deject. One cannot, in my reading of this text, embrace one's abjection, because that would imply a capacity to disavow one's expulsion from personhood. That's the difference between a notion of subordination as *subjectifying* (I am an x kind of person) and desubjectifying (I am not a person, I have no form, I am a negative). I have suggested throughout this essay that these positions are inassimilable but proximate, articulated in the relation of a psychologically-oriented subjectivity and an impersonal one, at least in *Two Girls, Fat and Thin*, and perhaps beyond. See Kristeva, *Powers of Horror*.

24 See Stewart, *A Space on the Side of the Road*.

25 See Bollas, *The Shadow of the Object*, 4.

26 Bersani and Dutoit, *Caravaggio's Secrets*.

27 Phillips, "On Composure."

28 Ibid., 44.

29 Phillips, "First Hates," 24.

30 Here I allude to an argument I make elsewhere against the presumption of shame as the primary sexual affect (recognizable by queers). While I agree with Sedgwick that subjects' responses may well be hardwired, it does not much matter to me, as I maintain the importance both of reading the gap between affect and the emotional vernaculars that stage its scene and also of the need to find analytic ways to attend to the subject's affective surplus. The multiple tethers of the subject to the world (and of the world's affect of the subject), expressed in relational activity and the work of intuition, are rarely registered in psychoanalytic and affect theory, which still tend to see the subject as having one or two clear and dominant

channels of experience and which therefore often fail the analytic situation of describing the overdetermining work of ideology, atmosphere, the unconscious, distraction, ambivalence, attention—in short, the many ways the subject takes up a position in any episode and in the world. See Sedgwick and Frank, "Shame in the Cybernetic Fold"; Warner, *The Trouble with Normal*; Berlant, "Thinking about Feeling Historical" and "Starved."

31 This story, of the man who introduces a female protagonist to self-estranging but exciting sexual violence, is a staple of Gaitskill's *oeuvre*. See, for example, "A Romantic Weekend," "An Affair, Edited," "Something Nice," and "Secretary," in *Bad Behavior*, and "The Blanket" and "The Dentist," in *Because They Wanted To*.

32 Traditionally the Freudian *après-coup* is structured by a primary trauma that finds form in a later repetition (such as a childhood molestation that generates symptoms later on in life, after what looks like an irrational phobic symptom appears). Often, and in this novel, I am suggesting, the inverse relation applies.

33 Carolyn Steedman, *Landscape for a Good Woman*. Sometimes this distribution happens because critics make it so, but it is also the case that the mode of explanation of therapy culture takes on distinct class articulations.

34 Sedgwick and Frank, "Shame in the Cybernetic Fold," and Sedgwick, "A Poem Is Being Written," in *Tendencies*.

FIVE *Nearly Utopian, Nearly Normal*

Thanks to Melanie Hawthorne, Roger Rouse, and myriad audiences for their engaged and clarifying responses. This essay was first written to express my gratitude to and training by the work of Fredric Jameson.

1 "Belgium: Rosetta Plan launched to boost youth employment," *European Industrial Relations Observatory On-line*. A bill called the "Rosetta Plan" was initiated in Belgium shortly after the film appeared, to try to develop more jobs for youth chronically underemployed within the first six months of leaving school. Reviews suggest that the film was seen as barely fictive in its dramatization of generally contingent economic conditions as well as those among youth, but Rosetta was read as strongly exemplary of a generation of the willing, able, and economically unacknowledged.

2 Camhi, "Soldiers' Stories: A New Kind of War Film."

3 The utopian potentials of the impersonality of an apprentice relationship are followed through, complexly, in the Dardennes' next film, *Le Fils* (2002).

4 This essay focuses on labor, kinship, and the children as the scene of the *event* in the Dardennes' films; but that *La Promesse* specifically articulates the global traffic in manual labor and sex must not go unnoticed, as the kinds of ambivalence raised by the global market for subproletarian migrant labor do not usually apply

to the outrage around sexual traffic, which seems more often to provoke more moral clarity against indentured servitude, bodily exploitation, and actual or virtual slavery. See, for example, the magazine *Migration*, produced by the Geneva-based nongovernmental organization, The International Organization for Migration. *Migration* covers many crises of survival, including defining migration as trauma, but its moments of greatest clarity are in the essays on the sexual trafficking of children and young women (including an announcement of a new organization by the entertainer Ricky Martin called "People for Children," which arose from his experience of meeting former sex slaves in India). See http://www.iom .int.

5 Kehr, "Their Method Is to Push Toward Moments of Truth." Kehr interviews the Dardenne brothers in this article, suggesting that "Though the Dardennes' films are scrupulously naturalistic, they all belong to the suspense genre, though it is a suspense of character, not of plot. It is not so much a question of what will happen next, as of how the characters arrive, or fail to arrive, at a decision to act." The "suspense of character" is played out, in their films, intergenerationally: the suspense is how the children will act, not the adults, who are bullied about by chaotic appetites.

6 Dumm, *A Politics of the Ordinary*, 1.

7 Catherine Labio argues that the structural and subjective effects on contemporary Belgium of the changes wrought by the European Union and neoliberal economics are quite different than those felt in France or Germany. She attributes this shift to historical factors such as Belgium's long colonial history in Africa but relatively short national history as a federalized state. It is only in the last few decades that a project of building a national metaculture has commenced; at the same time class breaches between the rich and poor are becoming more accentuated there as everywhere. See "Editor's Preface: The Federalization of Memory"; and Murphy, "Landscapes for Whom?"

8 See "Uncertainties of the Informal Economy: A Belgian Perspective," *European Industrial Relations Observatory On-line*. See also, for a fantastic synthesis of the transnational problematic of economic precariousness and "precarity" among youth across Europe, Mitropoulos, "Pre-cari-us?" It is also worth saying here that the Dardenne output of the 2000s, *L'Enfant* and *Le Fils*, draws the same "economo-affective" picture as that of the 1990s.

9 Mbembe and Roitman, "Figures of the Subject in Times of Crisis," 155.

10 Hardt and Negri, *Empire*, 290–94. See also Dyer-Witheford, "Empire, Immaterial Labor, the New Combinations, and the Global Worker."

11 On the capitalist destruction of life in the project of making value, see Harvey, *Spaces of Hope*.

12 Rosetta's rejection of her mother's faux gentility taps into a long tradition of talk-

ing about working-class "decency" or "respectability." The locus classicus of academic discussion of this phenomenon is Peter Bailey, "'Will the Real Bill Banks Please Stand Up?" For recent analyses of and contributions to this literature see Charlesworth, *A Phenomenology of Working-Class Experience*; Kiter Edwards, "We're Decent People"; Siegel, "The Failure of Condescension"; and Steedman, *Landscape for a Good Woman*.

13 Heymann, *Forgotten Families*.

14 This desire to pass on a desire for a better good life that looks like the present unhampered by individual failures or defeats, and unsupported by the economic, social, and political positions of a historical moment, is documented by all of the major class analyses of familial reproduction from Carol Stack's *All Our Kin* to David Shipler's *The Working Poor*. See also n. 34 and n. 39.

15 Spivak, "Other Things Are Never Equal: A Speech."

16 Bert Cardullo considers this final moment a redemptive one in which a Christian relation of mercy is articulated. See "Rosetta Stone: A Consideration of the Dardenne Brothers' *Rosetta*."

17 "Families we choose" is Kath Weston's term for improvised institutions of queer intimacy, in *Families We Choose*.

18 Now in somewhat spreading usage to describe genres of aesthetic embarrassment like the BBC's *The Office* or *Blackadder*, the genre phrase "situation tragedy" describes episodes of personality caught up in a form of despair not existential or heroic but shaped within the stresses of ordinary life under capitalism. (Not "everyday life" in the classic sense, where subjects are busy making do, but ordinary life, where projects of affect management provide registers for experiencing the structural contingencies of survival.) "Situation tragedy" emerged in the anti-Thatcherite critique of the "This Vicious Cabaret" insert in Alan Moore's and David Lloyd's *V for Vendetta*. The genre links the effects of draconian economic to erotophobic politics on a stunned body politic that now lives in catastrophic time, an experience of a paralyzed but aware spectatorship of its own demise as a public; because nothing is ever worked through, and the public is stuck in repeated viewings of its own annihilation, it is *situation* tragedy and not, say, melodrama. Moore's and Lloyd's not unfamiliar countercultural imaginary enmeshes cuttingly ironic Weimar-style kitsch-decadence with a love of pop culture, both of which are seen to house the exuberance, longing for intimate and social reciprocity, and anarchic *joie de vivre* that, they argue, can never be entirely defeated by creeping or accelerated fascism or constitutional crisis. The immediate context for the phrase is "At last the 1998 show!/The situation tragedy!/Grand opera slick with soap!/Cliff-hangers with no hope!/The water-colour in the flooded gallery . . ." In the "grand opera slick with soap" that is the BBC's *The Office*, when David Brent is finally ejected from his fantasmatic place as the funniest good boss imaginable, he spends all of his time in cars, in waiting rooms, and on benches, trying to

make something happen. When he haunts his old "haunt" compulsively, he becomes the figure of embarrassment, the person who cannot "not" be exposed in his thwarted desires and therefore the figure for *everyone's* potential ejection into the social death of no work and no love, the nearness of which it becomes harder and harder to protect oneself from knowing.

19 Using the periodizing language of supermodernity to mark the ascent of neoliberalism, Marc Augé argues that the emerging centrality of the "nonplace" (malls, terminals, hospitals) as a zone of episodic experience exemplary of the displacements that contemporary Europeans manage complicates everyday life theory's conception of the dynamic relation of ordinary space to the production of subjective life. He focuses especially on the need to consider the impact of life lived among social spaces that interrupt grounding logics of value and norms of intelligibility and self-identity. My claim is on the affective side of things, that supermodernity/neoliberalism produces the situation tragedy as a way of expressing the costs of what's ordinary now, the potential within any grounding space to become a nonplace for anyone whose inconvenience to the reproduction of value becomes suddenly, once again, apparent. Augé, *Non-Places.*

20 "This 'life world' is not only the field where individuals' existence unfolds in practice; it is where they exercise existence—that is, live their lives out and confront the very forms of their death." Mbembe, *On the Postcolony*, 15. We might also address, here, the alternative temporalities to a counter–human rights conception of living on, as in Alain Badiou's *Ethics*, 14–15, where the person's capacity to take up subjectivity requires a conception of the Good beyond that reality which is presented to him as the ground of experience; or Giorgio Agamben's flattened temporality of the Aristotelian lifeworld, where the prevarications and temporizations of the law/*bios* in the zone of indistinction that constitutes official understandings of belonging in the social is contrasted to *zoe*, the fact of living that connects live matter and that doesn't require historicizing to justify a world organized around sustaining its existence. This view extends to that put forth as a radicalized rights consciousness in Patricia Williams's visionary *The Alchemy of Race and Rights*, 165. What's important here is to enumerate, in any case, what it means, historically and politically, to "exercise existence." Agamben returns to this in his advocacy of *zoe* over *bios* in all the work including and after *Means without End.*

21 "Fantasy bribe" is Fredric Jameson's term for what capitalism, and commodity genres particularly, hold out as a kind of affective profit for its participants. See his "Reification and Utopia in Mass Culture," 144.

22 Recent worker revolts in Paris and Dubai, for example, forced concessions by exposing and exploiting the economy's dependence on docile workers. But for many, strikes threaten the already too tight margin of survival for the marginal worker, and the more common response to exploitation is to grit it out just in case a life can be built in the process of it being worn out by poverty, as docu-

mented in Shipler's *The Working Poor* and Heymann's *Forgotten Families*. See Fattah, "In Dubai, an Outcry from Asians for Workplace Rights"; Sciolino, Crampton, and de la Baume, "Not '68, but French Youths Hear Similar Cry to Rise Up"; and Smith, "Four Ways to Fire a Frenchman."

23 For the history of this argument, see Coontz, *Marriage, A History*.

24 Habermas, *The Structural Transformation of the Public Sphere*, esp. 47–56.

25 Berlant, "The Subject of True Feeling: Pain, Privacy, and Politics"; Povinelli, *The Cunning of Recognition*; and Markell, *Bound by Recognition*. Much of this work emerged from discussions of the Late Liberalism project of the University of Chicago. None of the above claims that affective recognition has *never* been part of the significant political, economic, and social empowerment of minoritized or negated communities — it *always* is. But more often, the intensities of affective performance are not matched in scale by transformations in the law, the distribution of wealth, the administrations of institutions, or the normative collective practices of communities.

26 Butler, *The Psychic Life of Power*, 9.

27 Butler, *Precarious Life*, 27.

28 Ibid., 45–46.

29 Ibid., 26–27.

30 Ibid., 37–41.

31 Fairbairn, *Psychoanalytic Studies of the Personality*, esp. 59–151.

32 Bollas, "The Transformational Object."

33 On "technologies of patience," see Berlant, *The Queen of America*, 222.

34 Rubin, *Worlds of Pain*, and Carol Stack, *All Our Kin*, provide the classic analyses of this phenomenon; the ensuing bibliography is extensive. For a great literature review, which focuses on parental pain rather than childhood experiences of class, see Gorman, "Reconsidering *Worlds of Pain*." With variations on styles of survival their findings about defensive affective binding as a condition for the reproduction of normative fantasy are supported entirely by ethnographies of working-class children and youth from each of the following decades. High points of different kinds include Bourdieu, et al., *The Weight of the World*; Hochschild, *The Managed Heart*; DeParle, *American Dream*; and Heymann, *Forgotten Families*.

35 Rubin, *Worlds of Pain*, xxv.

36 Ibid., 27–29.

37 Ibid., 27.

38 Steedman performs a like congeries of ambivalence, silence, and secrecy entailed in her experience of the transactions of parental love in her working-class household in *Landscape for a Good Woman*.

39 Wacquant, "Inside 'The Zone,'" 156. For cognate readings of a cleavage in the relation of lived life on the bottom of class society and aspirational normativity with a particular focus on youth, see Connolly and Healy, "Symbolic Violence and

the Neighborhood"; Kiter Edwards, "We're Decent People"; Lareau, *Unequal Child-hoods*; and MacTavish and Salamon, "Pathways of Youth Development in a Rural Trailer Park."

40 This paragraph reworks material in Berlant, "Compassion (and Withholding)," 8.

SIX *After the Good Life, an Impasse*

The epigraph is from "Statement Due," 365.

1 The precarity bibliography is enormous; what follows is an exemplary and resource-rich collection of this discussion as it has developed. See Berardi, "Pre-carious Rhapsody" and "The Insurgence of the European Precariat"; Neilson and Rossiter, "From Precarity to Precariousness and Back Again"; Grimm and Ronne-berger, "Interview with Sergio Bologna"; The Invisible Committee, *The Coming In-surrection*; "Multitudes, Creative Organisation and the Precarious Condition of New Media Labour," a special issue of *Fibreculture* 5 (2005): http://journal.fibreculture .org; *Mute Magazine* special issue "Precarious Reader" (2005), at http://www .metamute.org; the blogs "Understanding Precarity" at http://precariousunder standing.blogsome.com; *Upping the Anti: A Journal of Theory and Action* at http:// uppingtheanti.org; and *European Left* at http://www.european-left.org; the jour-nal *Multitudes*, at http://multitudes.samizdat.net/; and the Preclab, at http://www .preclab.net.

2 Agamben, *The Coming Community*, 64–66.

3 For a longer argument about the relation of structure to experience in thinking about affect, see Berlant, "Thinking About Feeling Historical."

4 On the contemporary, "neo-bohemian" economy of lateral improvisation, see Lloyd, *Neo-Bohemia*; see also Sennett, *The Corrosion of Character*, and Ross, *Nice Work if You Can Get It.*

5 Loïc Wacquant attributes "precariat" to *Droits Devants*, a French activist group linked with the global *sans-papiers* movement. See Wacquant, "Territorial Stigma-tization in the Age of Advanced Marginality," and *Droits Devants*. See also Neilson and Rossiter, "Precarity as a Political Concept."

6 I learned about the need to create analytical infrastructures for representing the overdetermined and open dynamics of the historical present ("without guaran-tees") from Stuart Hall: see throughout his *Stuart Hall: Critical Dialogues in Cultural Studies.*

7 Precarious, *adj.* [< classical Latin precarius given as a favour, depending on the favour of another, (of property) held by tenancy at will, uncertain, doubtful, sup-pliant (< prec-, prex prayer, entreaty (see PRECES n.) + -{amac}rius -ARY suf-fix1) + -OUS suffix. Compare French précaire (of a right, tenancy, etc.) held or enjoyed by the favour of and at the pleasure of another person (1336 in an iso-

lated attestation in Middle French as precoire, subsequently from 1585), exposed to risk, insecure, unstable (1618). With sense 1 compare earlier PRECARY adj. With senses 3 and 4 compare PRECATORIOUS adj. and earlier PRECATORY adj.] 1. Esp. of a right, tenancy, etc.: held or enjoyed by the favour of and at the pleasure of another person; vulnerable to the will or decision of others. Also fig. Now rare or merged in other senses, exc. in technical use with reference to tenancies. *Oxford English Dictionary Online*, s.v. "Precarious."

8   Krueger, "Does the Financial Crisis Threaten Your Job?"

9   Hardt and Negri, *Multitude*, 133–37, 216–19, and Sennett, *The Corrosion of Character*.

10   See, for example, Precarias a la Deriva, "Bodies, Lies, and Video Tape: Between the Logic of Security and the Logic of Care."

11   Rancière, *Hatred of Democracy*, *The Politics of Aesthetics*, and *Disagreement*; and Phillips, *Equals*.

12   On the need to continue traversing structural and cultural definitions of class, see especially Eley and Nield, *The Future of Class in History*, 139–201.

13   See Ross, *Nice Work If You Can Get It*.

14   Is belatedness the existential temporality of contemporary life? Anti-precarity activists challenge norms of capitalist time by demanding a better *present*. How is that possible? Emergency is another genre of the present. As the state demands mass austerity to pay for capitalists' excesses, these movements counter-demand a more democratic relation among work, play, intimacy, and security.

15   For a frequently updated archive of the grimace, see the "Times Topics" section called "Foreclosures," at http://topics.nytimes.com.

16   Tsianos and Papadopoulos, "Precarity."

17   Ahmed, *Queer Phenomenology*; Griggers, *Becoming-Woman*; Marks, *Touch*; Probyn, *Blush*; Weiss, *Body Images*.

18   Stewart, *Ordinary Affects*.

19   Agamben's model of *manner* sees it as exemplary singularity, whereas I am looking at a class of adjustments that I think are exemplary generalities, responses to a collectively felt glitch in the ongoingness of life. See *The Coming Community*, 27–29.

20   Lefebvre, *Rhythmanalysis*.

21   Agamben, "Notes on Gesture," 49–58.

22   Ibid., 51–53.

23   Brecht, "A Short Organum for the Theatre."

24   See Patton, "The World Seen From Within."

25   This paragraph reworks material in Berlant, "Starved."

26   In *The Gleaners and I*, Alain, a lonely man, walks hours to the city every day, averse to normative production schedules and domestic life but perfectly happy to have a conversation and to teach French to migrants; Jean Laplanche, a psychoanalyst and married man, lives on a vineyard while, presumably, theorizing the enigmatic signifier that passes between us as the currency for optimism/attachment. Then

there is Varda herself: perfectly happy to distribute her cool attention on whatever is around, circulating her voiceover whether or not another speaking being
is there, and all the while seeking waste that is not fully wasted, from potatoes
to mirrors. Life lives after all in *The Gleaners and I*: there are always more things to
attach to, including garbage, a cat, and, for Varda, her own specular face. She induces a spectatorial mirroring rhythm so that she is never alone, but is always
being spoken to by the being in things. Like Bordowitz, her impasse is created by
conversation, travel, encounter, and the spreading out of a seeking insistence: her
style of *élan vital*.

Her curiosity and sensually absorptive collecting is not a plot or an inscription
of life in a narrative: it spreads out, it is there, and it is lovely. But here the other
shoe drops. The shape of the whole film cannot help but point to what's unequal
across economies of contemporary existence: life made from what one has inherited, from what one has earned, from what the state has made available, and
from what gets left behind daily when the markets close up and discard the un-
sellable. Even here, in what looks like a democratic distribution of the capacity
for enjoyment in the impasse, there is a story about the difference between scavenging and gleaning that is also a story about affect in a historical present that
is shaped by the unequal distribution of "free time" managed by the fading welfare state. The scavenger-gleaner is about to go under. The scavenger-gleaner, the
peasant looking for potatoes in the fields that have been culled and left behind, is
starving. The potatoes are flourishing more than the peasant. The peasant aspires
not to become-potato, but to become better at being than the potato, to enjoy
surplus rather than being surplus. Scavenger-gleaners are everywhere homeless,
in danger of embodying the *inutile*. The gleaner that Varda embodies enjoys the
artist's mien, the life of the modernist flaneuse, the being whose mode of living
is unthreatened as long as it moves, even if death looms on the horizon as the
sad end of sentience as such. But for most gleaner-scavengers, displacement and
homelessness are not metaphors for a curious mind.

27 Ehrenreich, *Nickel and Dimed* and *Bait and Switch*; Cottle, *Hardest Times*.

28 Barbier, "A Comparative Analysis of 'Employment Precariousness' in Europe."

29 Jenkins, *Employment Relations in France*.

30 Other writer-directors of this heavily atmospheric witnessing mode of contemporary capitalist *fraying* include the Dardennes (see chapter 5), Hooman Bahrani,
Cristian Mungiu, Fatih Akin, Jiă Zhāngkē, Kelly Reichardt, Mike White, Courtney
Hunt, and Debra Granik, and sometimes, as in *71 Fragments of a Chronology of Chance*
(1994), Michael Haneke. In his recent "Neo-Neo Realism," A. O. Scott attempts to
define the mode of class witnessing in these filmmakers' films. See also Higbee,
"Elle est-où, ta place? The Social-Realist Melodramas of Laurent Cantet."

31 Barbier, "A Comparative Analysis," 6. There are debates about the *trente-cinq's* effec-
tivity, though. See Hayden, "France's Thirty-Five Hour Week."

32 At one point Mme. Arnaux calls the father Jean-Claude, but this is not registered in the credits as his name.

33 The "new normal" meme took fire during the George W. Bush administration but now tends to signify the need to adjust to diminished standards of growth and security in the financial and labor sectors as well as the need to confront spreading precarity in market, health, and environmental domains. See Carolyn Baum, "'New Normal' Tops 2009 List of Overused Phrases," http://www.bloomberg.com, and Paul Kedrosky's chart at "Infectious Greed," at http://paul.kedrosky.com.

34 On the genre of meetings and contemporary time, see Albert, *Parecon*.

35 I learned to think about the secret life from the dissertation of Emily Shelton. Shelton, "My Secret Life."

36 A website on the Romand incident is at http://jc.romand.free.fr.

37 On Mark and Lori Hacking, see TruTV, available at http://www.trutv.com/library/crime.

38 Hochschild, *The Managed Heart* and *The Commercialization of Intimate Life*.

39 Illouz, *Cold Intimacies*, especially 1–39. See also Ehrenreich and Sennett.

40 See Cottle, *Hardest Times*, and Hochschild, *The Managed Heart* and *The Commercialization of Intimate Life*. This emotional idiom also saturates the policy literature about unemployment, where the long-term unemployed are called discouraged workers and characterized simultaneously as an economic and an affective class.

41 Barbara Ehrenreich notes that the production of enthusiasm is a major performance requirement for the white-collar unemployed in the United States as well. Ehrenreich, *Bait and Switch*, 230–46.

SEVEN *On the Desire for the Political*

Thanks to the artists for their generosity in making the work available to me and to the book. Thanks also to Corey Creekmur, Haans Mott, Dont Rhine, Gregg Bordowitz, and Amelia Jones for transformative conversations; and to interlocutors at ASA, the Open University, McGill University, and Concordia University for thickening my archive and helping me to work this thing through.

1 Bumiller, "Trying to Bypass the Good-News Filter." See also President Bush's news conference with President Mwai Kibaki of Kenya at http://findarticles.com. The Republican National Committee deployment of "liberal media filter" can be confirmed at "GOP Seeks Donations to Get Bush Plans 'Past the Liberal Media.'" The McCain/Palin campaign also infused its attacks on the media with fantasies of bypassing bad filters and performing political immediacy: see, for example, Palin's statement during the vice presidential debate against Joseph Biden: "I like being able to answer these tough questions without the filter, even, of the main-

stream media kind of telling viewers what they've just heard. I'd rather be able to just speak to the American people like we just did." Transcript available on CNN.com. Palin has gone on to develop Facebook and Twitter platforms for daily voice-authenticity events. Early news reporting on the Obama administration refers frequently to the President's facility at sidestepping the "media filter" as well; "Organizing for America" constantly sends out "personalized" mass mailings from the President and his minions.

2   Serres, *The Parasite*; Attali, *Noise*.

3   The classic "liveness" bibliography includes: Auslander, *Liveness*; Doane, "Information, Crisis, Catastrophe"; Feuer, "The Concept of Live Television"; Halttunen, *Murder Most Foul*; Phelan, *Unmarked*; Dolan, "Performance, Utopia, and the 'Utopian Performative.'" See also Berlant, "Live Sex Acts," in *The Queen of America*.

4   See Berlant, "The Subject of True Feeling."

5   Hirschkind, *The Ethical Soundscape*, 22.

6   For more on the "juxtapolitical" nature of intimate publics, Berlant, *The Female Complaint*, 22.

7   Hirschkind, 9.

8   Stewart, *Ordinary Affects*.

9   On the distinction between politics (the police, the arts of power) and the political (the domain and activity of dissensus on behalf of the parties of no part) see Rancière, *Disagreement*, especially chapters 1 and 2. On the "new normal," see chapter 6, "After the Good Life." The incoherence or "schizophrenia" across survival gestures in the new normal has now been termed "the new abnormal," as journalists register the deep and confused relation of economic to affective disruption. See Leonard, "The New Abnormal."

10 Documenting the transmission of sexuality not as a genital activity but as a transition from mouth to ear—seeing sexuality as a discourse expressed with the mediation of professional expertise in mind—is the general project of Foucault, *The History of Sexuality*. The specific metaphorization of sexuality as that which moves from mouth to ear is contained in "The Confession of the Flesh," 218.

11 See Berlant, *The Female Complaint*.

12 Hearing has long been central to public sphere theory without it much being a topic or problem—see Michael Warner's examples of overhearing as the source of interpellation into publicness in *Publics and Counterpublics*, for example.

13 It might be worth noting that overhearing the political has been central to all accounts of the public sphere after Althusser—Michael Warner's examples in "Public and Private," in *Publics and Counterpublics*, are exemplary here, resituating Althusser's illustrations of interpellation in "Ideology and Ideological State Apparatuses"—although the focus has always seemed to be on evaluating the sovereign agency expressed in speech events that organize the world according to con-

ventional political genres. For a great exercise in thinking through this kind of thought, see Weinberger, "What I Heard about Iraq in 2005."

14　I learned to think about this model of reparation from Melanie Klein, but most powerfully through Eve Sedgwick. See Klein and Rivière, *Love, Hate, and Reparation* and Sedgwick, *Touching Feeling*.

15　Farred, "A Fidelity to Politics."

16　I owe the phrase "emotional infrastructure" to a conversation with Ruthie Gilmore; I elaborate on it at http://supervalentthought.wordpress.com.

17　Jordan, *The Sturdy Oak*. A full history of the genre of the voiceless speech has not yet been written. Contemporary references include: Anthony, Gage, and Harper, *History of Woman Suffrage*, vol. 6, 285, 386, 533; National American Woman Suffrage Association et al., *The Handbook of the National American Woman Suffrage Association*, 35, 43, 118; Oldfield, *International Woman Suffrage*, vol. 1, 68; Constable, "Women's Voiceless Speech": Blatch and Lutz, *Challenging Years*, 191–92. More recent historical references and discussions include: Baker, *Votes for Women*, 167; DuBois, *Harriot Stanton Blatch and the Winning of Woman Suffrage*, 153; Cohen, "The Impersonal Public Sphere"; and Southard, "Militancy, Power, and Identity."

　　The antilynching parade of silence has been documented widely both recently and at its contemporary moment. The *New York Times* article on this parade was published July 29, 1917. Many documents are available at the online exhibit, Harlem, 1900–1940, accessed at http://www.si.umich.edu. There were copycat silent protests throughout the country. For the short version of the main event with a decent primary and secondary bibliography, see Wintz and Finkelman, *Encyclopedia of the Harlem Renaissance*, vol. 2, 751–752. See also Zangrando, *The NAACP Crusade Against Lynching, 1909–1950*, 37–38; Ellis, *Race, War, and Surveillance*, 129; and Jackson, "Re-Living Memories."

18　For some background on this particular characterization of avant-garde traditions, see Rees, *A History of Experimental Film and Video*.

19　For an introduction to the DIY aesthetic, see Lupton, "Why DIY?"

20　For brief histories of CCTV, see Roberts, "All-Seeing Eye"; Abbas, "CCTV"; the article "Closed-Circuit Television" at http://www.absoluteastronomy.com; and Norris, McCahill, and Wood, "The Growth of CCTV." See also Norris, Moran, and Armstrong, *Surveillance, Closed Circuit Television, and Social Control*. For excellent archives of security camera art, see "The Video Art History Archive," at http://www.arthistoryarchive.com; and the website "We make money not art," at http://www.we-make-money-not-art.com. Work by particular artists not discussed explicitly that nonetheless contributes to the generalizations I make about this medium includes: Heath Bunting, *Irational*, at http://www.irational.org; Sophie Calle, *Two Works* [with Fabio Balducci, *Unfinished* (video that absorbs *Cash Machine*) and *Cash Machine* (installation)] at http://www.eai.org; *The (in)security camera*, an installation created in 2003 by Benjamin Chang, Silvia Ruzanka, and Dmitry Strakovsky at http://silviaruzanka.com/; David Claerbout, "Still, Moving," at http://touchingharmstheart.com; Darko Fritz, *Self-Surveillance*, at http://darkofritz.net; Jill Magid, *Evidence Locker*, at http://jillmagid.net; Norman, *The Contemporary Picturesque*; Shannon Plumb, *Shannon Plumb: Behind the Curtain*, at http://www.aldrichart.org. I would also point people to Harry Shearer's silent video-feed pieces called "silent debates" from the 2008 presidential campaign, at http://www.mydamnchannel.com.

21 Madansky's website is well-stocked with documentation: http://www.madansky.com.

22 *The PSA Project* has been shown in galleries and festivals around the world and was also screened on the Sundance Channel, an arts cable network broadcasting from the United States.

23 A fascinating history remains to be written of the public service announcement as a performative genre that injects immediacy into the relation of the state and related systems to the body politic. Developed in the United States during the Second World War (1941) to create an appetite for sacrifice on behalf of the war effort, their very purpose is to produce consciousness of the present as an ongoing historical moment whose shape will have been an effect of the actions of myriad individual sovereigns. For a primary document, see Pimlott, "Public Service Advertising." See also Fleegler, " 'Forget All Differences until the Forces of Freedom Are Triumphant.' "

24 See Berlant, "Opulism." See also Mazzarella, "The Myth of the Multitude."

25 Asad, "On Torture, or Cruel, Inhuman, and Degrading Treatment."

26 On comportment, respectability, and class difference, see Skeggs, "Ambivalent Femininities" and *Class, Self, Culture*.

27 Schneider, *The Explicit Body in Performance*.

28 Motevalli, " 'Video Sniffers' Subverting Surveillance for Art."

29 Deleuze, "Societies of Control" and "Postscript on the Societies of Control."

30 Graham, " 'Every Passer-by a Culprit?' "

31 I am grateful to have learned to think about anonymity during exam preparation with Eduardo de Almeida.

32 On the scenario as genre of heuristic realism, see Taylor, *The Archive and the Repertoire*, especially 53–78. The CCTV camera might not be anonymous insofar as sometimes its owner is known; but it is always anonymous insofar as (a) it looks as if its eye were uninterested, neutral, and generic; (b) the people turning the film into information are unknown; and (c) it becomes such an ordinary part of the infrastructure of publicity that the radar goes under the radar, as it were.

33 For more on the war on terror as a war on an emotion, see Berlant, "The Epistemology of State Emotion."

34 The literature on the sonic abuse of prisoners at Abu Ghraib and Guantánamo Bay is widespread. For a compendium, see the indispensable Kusick, "Music as Torture/Music as Weapon," and Shatz, "Short Cuts."

35 Grassian, "Psychopathological Effects of Solitary Confinement."

36 I learned to think about comedy as a membrane for dissociating from the political without detaching from it from Abbas, "Chen Danqing: Painting After Tiananmen"; and Yurchak, "The Cynical Reason of Late Socialism." The whole career of Slavoj Žižek is also testament to this strategy of remaining proximate. See also Anna Tsing's explicitly half-joking "Inside the Economy of Appearances."

37 Bergson, *Laughter.*

38 Rancière, *Hatred of Democracy.*

39 Ultra-red's manifesto can be found at http://www.ultrared.org.

40 See Ultra-red, "Deadrooms: From the Death of Ambient Music to Listening Material," at http://www.ultrared.org.

41 Some of Ultra-red's sampling can be found at http://www.myspace.com/publicrec.

42 Nyong'o, "I've Got You Under My Skin."

43 I refer here to the "differend," the phrase that measures power by way of incommensurate idioms of complaint, appeal, and justice in Jean-François Lyotard's *The Differend.*

44 For an introduction to the Heideggerian concepts (which come from *Being and Time*), see Inwood, *A Heidegger Dictionary.*

45 Berlant, "Uncle Sam Needs a Wife: Citizenship and Denegation," *The Female Complaint,* especially 161–67.

46 Blank underscore marks here signify obscured words on the memorial sign.

> Who's a Hero?
> Did he ever tell you he's a hero?
> He's the one who had the common touch.
> He liked all the people and a life of common stuff.
> Did he ever tell you he's a hero?
> For the gifts he gave to _____ children.
> Who would not have had the _____
> To Soar Like An Eagle or Debut in the _____
> Did he ever tell you he's a _____
> Now he'll never get that _____

47 Slater Bradley described the process of making *The Land of Artistic Expression* at a panel, "The Spectacle of Death: The Role of Disaster and Tragedy in Shaping Community," on Tuesday, March 21, 2004, at the Museum of Contemporary Art, Chicago.

48 A concept of the community that has not passed through the sieve of normativity but takes shape in a relation of simultaneity, singularity, and the solidarity of the

potentiality of being arises in multiple spaces of political theory now associated with autonomous politics and neo-anarchism. See the next section of this essay, and Nancy, *The Inoperative Community*; and Agamben, *The Coming Community*.

49 Johnson tells me that this scene takes place in a FEMA (Federal Emergency Management Agency) trailer, but no kinds of context for the scene are manifest in the work: they either require local knowledge or require the spectator to confront the affective, scenic exemplarity of what's on screen.

50 See Berlant, "The Subject of True Feeling," and *The Female Complaint*, especially "Poor Eliza."

51 See Graeber, *Fragments of an Anarchist Anthropology* and *Possibilities*; and Gibson-Graham, *A Postcapitalist Politics*. I focus on Graeber and Graham as exemplars, but the new anarchism is exemplified most widely by the autonomia movement associated in the United States with Antonio Negri but in Italy with a broader set of activities. See, for example, Virno, *A Grammar of the Multitude*, and Berardi, *Precarious Rhapsody*. I do not believe this is identical to the apparatus of chaotic democracy denounced as "post-politics" in Slavoj Žižek's rejoinders to Deleuze and Jacques Rancière. The general question of whether the reinvention of the political requires a withdrawal from it, insofar as it is associated with a polis-structuring state, the conflation of the state with the police, and the neutralization of political demand, remains a contentious debate in political theory. See Žižek, *Violence*, and Rancière, *Disagreement*.

52 Gibson-Graham, "An Ethics of the Local," 51.

Abbas, Ackbar. "Chen Danqing: Painting After Tiananmen." *Public Culture* 8, no. 3 (1996): 409–40.

Abbas, Niran. "CCTV: City Watch." In *London from Punk to Blair*. Edited by Joe Kerr, Andrew Gibson, and Mike Seaborne. London: Reaktion Books, 2003.

Adam, Barbara. *Timescapes of Modernity: The Environment and Invisible Hazards*. New York and London: Routledge, 1998.

Adams, Kenneth F., Arthur Schatzkin, Tamara B. Harris, Victor Kipnis, Traci Mouw, Rachel Ballard-Barbash, Albert Hollenbeck, and Michael F. Leitzmann. "Overweight, Obesity, and Mortality in a Large Prospective Cohort of Persons 50 to 71 Years Old." *New England Journal of Medicine* 355, no. 8 (2006): 763–78.

Adorno, Theodor. "Commitment." Translated by Francis McDonagh. *New Left Review* I (1974): 87–88.

———. "Television as Ideology." In *Critical Models: Interventions and Catchwords.* Translated by Henry W. Pickford. New York: Columbia University Press, 1998.

Agamben, Giorgio. *The Coming Community.* Translated by Michael Hardt. Minneapolis: University of Minnesota Press, 1993.

———. *Homo Sacer: Sovereign Power and Bare Life.* Translated by Daniel Heller-Roazen. Stanford, Calif.: Stanford University Press, 1995.

———. *Means without End: Notes on Politics.* Translated by Vincenzo Binetti and Cesare Casarino. Minneapolis: University of Minnesota Press, 2000.

———. "Notes on Gesture." In *Means Without End: Notes on Politics.* Translated by Vincenzo Binetti and Cesare Casarino. Minneapolis: University of Minnesota Press, 2000.

———. *Remnants of Auschwitz: The Witness and the Archive.* Translated by Daniel Heller-Roazen. New York: Zone Books, 1999.

———. *State of Exception.* Translated by Kevin Attell. Chicago: University of Chicago Press, 2005.

Ahmed, Sara. *The Cultural Politics of Emotion.* Edinburgh: Edinburgh University Press, 2004.

———. *Promise of Happiness.* Durham, N.C.: Duke University Press, 2010.

———. *Queer Phenomenology: Orientations, Objects, Others.* Durham, N.C.: Duke University Press, 2006.

Albert, Michael. *Parecon: Life after Capitalism.* London: Verso, 2003.

Altemeyer, Robert. *The Authoritarians.* 2007. http://home.cc.umanitoba.ca/~altemey.

Althusser, Louis. "Ideology and Ideological State Apparatuses." In *Lenin and Philosophy.* Translated by Ben Brewster. New York: Monthly Review Press, 1971.

Anderson, George. "Buzzwords du Jour: Prosumers, Metrosexuals, Globesity." *Retail Wire,* September 26, 2003. http://retailwire.com.

Angier, Natalie. "Who Is Fat? It Depends on Culture." *New York Times,* November 7, 2000: F1.

Armstrong, Isobel. *The Radical Aesthetic.* Oxford: Oxford University Press, 2000.

Asad, Talal. "On Torture, or Cruel, Inhuman, and Degrading Treatment." In *Social Suffering.* Edited by Arthur Kleinman, Veena Das, and Margaret Lock. Berkeley: University of California Press, 1997.

Ashbery, John. "Filigrane." *The New Yorker,* November 7, 2005: 89.

———. "Ignorance of the Law is No Excuse." *New York Review of Books* 51, no. 5 (March 25, 2004). http://www.nybooks.com.

———. "Untitled." *The New Yorker,* November 7, 2005: 88.

Associated Press. "GOP Seeks Donations to Get Bush Plans Past the Liberal Media." *Editor & Publisher,* January 26, 2005.

Attali, Jacques. *Noise: The Political Economy of Music*. Translated by Brian Massumi. Minneapolis: University of Minnesota Press, 1985.

Augé, Marc. *Non-Places: Introduction to an Anthropology of Supermodernity*. Translated by John Howe. London: Verso, 1995.

Auslander, Philip. *Liveness: Performance in a Mediatized Culture*. New York: Routledge, 1999.

Badiou, Alain. *Ethics: An Essay on the Understanding of Evil*. Translated by Peter Hallward. Introduction by Slavoj Žižek. London and New York: Verso, 2001.

———. *Manifesto for Philosophy*. Translated by Norman Madarasz. Albany: State University of New York Press, 1999.

Bailey, Peter. "'Will the Real Bill Banks Please Stand Up?': Towards a Role Analysis of Mid-Victorian Working-Class Respectability." *Journal of Social History* 12, no. 3 (1979): 336–53.

Baker, Jean H., ed. *Votes for Women: The Struggle for Suffrage Revisited*. New York: Oxford University Press, 2002.

Balke, Friedrich. "Derrida and Foucault on Sovereignty." *German Law Journal* 6, no. 1 (January 2005). http://www.germanlawjournal.com.

Ball, Karyn. "Traumatic Concepts: Latency and Crisis in Deleuze's Evolutionary Theory of Cinema." In *Traumatizing Theory: The Cultural Politics of Affect in and Beyond Psychoanalysis*. Edited by Karyn Ball. New York: Other Press, 2007.

Barbier, Jean-Claude. "A Comparative Analysis of 'Employment Precariousness' in Europe." Paper presented at the Economic and Social Research Council's seminar "Learning from Employment and Welfare Policies in Europe," Paris, March 15, 2004. http://www.cee-recherche.fr.

Barthes, Roland. *Camera Lucida: Reflections on Photography*. Translated by Richard Howard. New York: Hill and Wang, 1981.

———. *A Lover's Discourse: Fragments*. Translated by Richard Howard. New York: Hill and Wang, 1978.

Bataille, Georges. *Literature and Evil*. Translated by Alastair Hamilton. London: Calder and Boyars, 1973.

———. *The Unfinished System of Nonknowledge*. Edited and introduction by Stuart Kendall. Translated by Michelle Kendall and Stuart Kendall. Minneapolis: University of Minnesota Press, 2001.

Baudrillard, Jean. "From the System to the Destiny of Objects." In *The Ecstasy of Communication*. Edited by Sylvère Lotringer. Translated by Bernard Schütze and Caroline Schütze. New York: Semiotext(e), 1987.

———. *In the Shadow of the Silent Majorities . . . Or the End of the Social and Other Essays*. Translated by Paul Foss, Paul Patton, and John Johnston. New York: Semiotext(e), 1983.

———. *Symbolic Exchange and Death*. Translated by Iain Hamilton Grant. Introduction by Mike Gane. London: Sage, 1993.

Baum, Carolyn. "'New Normal' Tops 2009 List of Overused Phrases." *Bloomberg*, December 22, 2009. http://www.bloomberg.com.

Benjamin, Jessica. "'What Angel Would Hear Me?': The Erotics of Transference." *Psychoanalytic Inquiry* 14 (1994): 535–57.

Berardi, Franco "Bifo." "The Insurgence of the European Precariat." 2006. http://www.generation-online.org.

———. *Precarious Rhapsody: Semiocapitalism and the Pathologies of the Post-Alpha Generation.* Edited by Erik Empson and Stevphen Shukaitis. Translated by Arianna Bove, Erik Empson, Michael Goddard, Giusppina Mecchia, Antonella Schintu, and Steve Wright. Brooklyn, N.Y.: Minor Compositions, 2009.

Bergson, Henri. *Laughter: An Essay on the Meaning of the Comic.* Translated by Fred Rothwell. New York: MacMillan, 1914.

———. 1912. *Matter and Memory.* Translated by Nancy Margaret Paul and W. Scott Palmer. New York: Zone Books, 1991.

Berlant, Lauren. *The Anatomy of National Fantasy: Hawthorne, Utopia, and Everyday Life.* Chicago: University of Chicago Press, 1991.

———. "Compassion (and Withholding)." In *Compassion: The Culture and Politics of an Emotion.* Edited by Lauren Berlant. New York: Routledge, 2004.

———. "The Epistemology of State Emotion." In *Dissent in Dangerous Times.* Edited by Austin Sarat. Ann Arbor: University of Michigan Press, 2005.

———. *The Female Complaint: The Unfinished Business of Sentimentality in American Culture.* Durham, N.C.: Duke University Press, 2008.

———. "Introduction." In *Intimacy.* Edited by Lauren Berlant. Chicago: University of Chicago Press, 2000.

———. "Neither Monstrous nor Pastoral, but Scary and Sweet: Some Thoughts on Sex and Emotional Performance in Intimacies and What Do Gay Men Want?" *Women & Performance: A Journal of Feminist Theory* 19, no. 2 (July 2009): 261–73.

———. "Opulism." *SAQ* 110, no. 1 (winter 2011), 235–42.

———. *The Queen of America Goes to Washington City: Essays on Sex and Citizenship.* Durham, N.C.: Duke University Press, 1997.

———. "Starved." *SAQ* 106, no. 3 (2007): 433–44.

———. "The Subject of True Feeling: Pain, Privacy, and Politics." In *Left Legalism/Left Critique.* Edited by Janet Halley and Wendy Brown. Durham, N.C.: Duke University Press, 2002.

———. "Thinking about Feeling Historical." *Emotion, Space, and Society* 1 (2008): 4–9.

———. "Two Girls, Fat and Thin." In *Regarding Sedgwick.* Edited by Stephen M. Barber and David L. Clark. New York and London: Routledge, 2002.

———. "Unfeeling Kerry." *Theory and Event* 8, no. 2 (2005).

Berlant, Lauren, and Michael Warner. "Sex in Public." *Critical Inquiry* 24, no. 2 (winter 1998): 547–67.

Bersani, Leo. *The Freudian Body: Psychoanalysis and Art*. New York: Columbia University Press, 1990.

———. "Is the Rectum a Grave?" *October* 43 (winter 1987): 197–222.

Bersani, Leo, and Ulysse Dutoit, eds. *Caravaggio's Secrets*. Cambridge, Mass.: MIT Press, 1998.

Bersani, Leo, and Adam Phillips. *Intimacies*. Chicago: University of Chicago Press, 2008.

Blackman, Stuart. "The Enormity of Obesity." *The Scientist* 18, no. 10 (May 24, 2004): 10.

Blatch, Harriot Stanton, and Alma Lutz. *Challenging Years: The Memoirs of Harriot Stanton Blatch*. New York: G. P. Putnam's Sons, 1940.

Blattberg, Benjamin. "The Style of the So-Called Inanimate: Commodity Style in *Sister Carrie* and *Pattern Recognition*." Unpublished paper, 2007.

Bnet.com. "The President's News Conference with President Mwai Kibaki of Kenya." October 6, 2003.

Bollas, Christopher. *The Shadow of the Object: Psychoanalysis of the Unthought Known*. New York: Columbia University Press, 1987.

———. "The Transformational Object." In *The Shadow of the Object: Psychoanalysis of the Unthought Known*. New York: Columbia University Press, 1987.

Borch-Jacobsen, Mikkel. *The Freudian Subject*. Translated by Catherine Potter. Introduction by François Roustang. Stanford, Calif.: Stanford University Press, 1988.

Bourdieu, Pierre, Alain Accardo, Priscilla Parkhurst Ferguson, and Susan Emanuel. *The Weight of the World: Social Suffering in Contemporary Societies*. Stanford, Calif.: Stanford University Press, 1999.

Brecht, Bertolt. 1949. "A Short Organum for the Theatre." In *Brecht on Theatre: The Development of an Aesthetic*. Edited and translated by John Willett. London: Methuen, 1964.

Brennan, Teresa. *The Transmission of Affect*. Ithaca, N.Y.: Cornell University Press, 2004.

Brodie, Janet Farrell, and Mark Redfield, eds. *High Anxieties: Cultural Studies in Addiction*. Berkeley: University of California Press, 2002.

Brown, Bill. "Thing Theory." *Critical Inquiry* 28, no. 1 (autumn 2001): 1–22.

Brown, Debra J. "Everyday Life for Black American Adults: Stress, Emotions, and Blood Pressure." *Western Journal of Nursing Research* 26, no. 5 (2004): 499–514.

Brown, Harriet. "Well-Intentioned Food Police May Create Havoc with Children's Diets." *New York Times*, May 30, 2006.

Brown, Wendy. *Edgework: Critical Essays on Knowledge and Politics*. Princeton: Princeton University Press, 2005.

Browne, Sir Thomas. *Sir Thomas Browne: Selected Writings*. Edited by Claire Preston. New York: Routledge, 2003.

Brownell, Kelly, and Katherine Battle Horgen. *Food Fight: The Inside Story of the Food Industry, America's Obesity Crisis and What We Can Do about It*. Chicago: University of Chicago Press, 2004.

Bumiller, Elisabeth. "Trying to Bypass the Good-News Filter." *New York Times*, October 20, 2003.

Butler, Judith. *Bodies that Matter: On the Discursive Limits of "Sex."* New York: Routledge, 1993.

———. *Gender Trouble: Feminism and the Subversion of Identity.* New York: Routledge, 1990.

———. *Precarious Life: The Powers of Mourning and Violence.* London: Verso, 2004.

———. *The Psychic Life of Power: Theories in Subjection.* Stanford, Calif.: Stanford University Press, 1977.

Camhi, Leslie. "Soldiers' Stories: A New Kind of War Film; Work as a Matter of Life and Death." *Village Voice*, November 3–9, 1999.

Campos, Paul. *The Obesity Myth: Why America's Obsession with Weight is Hazardous to Your Health.* New York: Penguin, 2004.

Cardullo, Bert. "Rosetta Stone: A Consideration of the Dardenne Brothers' *Rosetta.*" *Journal of Religion and Film* 6, no. 1 (April 2002).

Caruth, Cathy. *Unclaimed Experience: Trauma, Narrative, and History.* Baltimore: Johns Hopkins University Press, 1996.

Cavell, Stanley. "The Uncanniness of the Ordinary." In *In Quest of the Ordinary: Lines of Skepticism and Romanticism.* Chicago: University of Chicago Press, 1994.

———. "The Wittgensteinian Event." In *Philosophy the Day after Tomorrow.* Cambridge, Mass.: Harvard University Press, 2006.

Center for Science in the Public Interest. "Menu Labeling," http://www.cspinet.org/menulabeling.

Centers for Disease Control and Prevention. "Childhood Overweight and Obesity" homepage. http://www.cdc.gov/obesity/childhood.

———. "Obesity" homepage.

Chang, Virginia W. "The Social Stratification of Obesity: Bodily Assets and the Stylization of Health." PhD diss. University of Chicago, 2003. AAT 3077046.

———. "U.S. Obesity, Weight Gain, and Socioeconomic Status." *CHERP Policy Brief* 3, no. 1 (fall 2005).

Chang, Virginia, and Nicholas A. Christakis. "Income Inequality and Weight Status in U.S. Metropolitan Areas." *Social Science & Medicine* 61, no. 1 (July 2005): 83–96.

Chang, Virginia, and Diane Lauderdale. "Income Disparities in Body Mass Index and Obesity in the United States, 1971–2002." *Archives of Internal Medicine* 165, no. 18 (October 10, 2005): 2122–28.

Charlesworth, Simon J. *A Phenomenology of Working-Class Experience.* Cambridge: Cambridge University Press, 2000.

Cixous, Hélène. "The Laugh of the Medusa." Translated by Keith Cohen and Paula Cohen. *Signs* 1, no. 4 (summer 1976): 875–93.

Clough, Patricia Ticineto, et al. *The Affective Turn: Theorizing the Social.* Durham, N.C.: Duke University Press, 2007.

CNN. "Fat Americans Getting Even Fatter: Extreme Obesity is Ballooning in U.S. Adults." October 14, 2003.

Cohen, Kris. "The Impersonal Public Sphere." Unpublished paper, 2005. http://www.studioincite.com.

Collins, Douglas. "The Great Effects of Small Things: Insignificance with Immanence in Critical Theory." *Anthropoetics* 8, no. 2 (fall 2002/winter 2003). http://www.anthropoetics.ucla.edu.

Connolly, Paul, and Julie Healy. "Symbolic Violence and the Neighborhood: The Educational Aspirations of 7–8 Year Old Working-Class Girls." *The British Journal of Sociology* 55, no. 4 (2004): 511–29.

Constable, Anna. "Women's Voiceless Speech." *New York Times*, January 5, 1913.

Coontz, Stephanie. *Marriage, a History: From Obedience to Intimacy, or How Love Conquered Marriage*. New York: Viking, 2005.

Copjec, Joan. *Read My Desire: Lacan against the Historicists*. Cambridge, Mass.: MIT Press, 1994.

Cornell, Drucilla. *The Imaginary Domain: Abortion, Pornography and Sexual Harassment*. New York: Routledge, 1995.

Cottle, Thomas J. *Hardest Times: The Trauma of Long Term Unemployment*. Westport, Conn.: Praeger, 2000.

Critser, Greg. *Fat Land: How Americans Became the Fattest People in the World*. London: Penguin, 2003.

Cusick, Suzanne G. "Music as Torture/Music as Weapon." TRANS *Revista Transcultural de Música* 10 (2006). http://redalyc.uaemex.mx.

Das, Veena. *Life and Words: Violence and the Descent into the Ordinary*. Berkeley: University of California Press, 2007.

Davidson, Patricia. "Unequal Burden." Paper given in Washington D.C. at the National Black Women's Health Project conference, April 11, 2003, www.kaisernetwork.org.

Davis, Mike. *Late Victorian Holocausts: El Niño Famines and the Making of the Third World*. New York: Verso, 2001.

Dean, Tim. *Unlimited Intimacy: Reflections on the Subculture of Barebacking*. Chicago: University of Chicago Press, 2009.

Debord, Guy. *The Society of the Spectacle*. Translated by Ken Knabb. London: Rebel Press, 1983.

de Lauretis, Teresa. *The Practice of Love: Lesbian Sexuality and Perverse Desire*. Bloomington: Indiana University Press, 1994.

———. "Statement Due." *Critical Inquiry* 30, no. 2 (winter 2004): 365–68.

Deleuze, Gilles. "Coldness and Cruelty." In *Masochism: Coldness and Cruelty, and Venus in Furs*. New York: Zone Books, 1991.

———. *The Logic of Sense*. Edited by Constantin V. Boundas. Translated by Mark Lester and Charles Stivale. New York: Columbia University Press, 1990.

————. "Postscript on the Societies of Control." *October* 59 (winter 1992): 3–7.

————. "Societies of Control." *L'autre journal*, no. 1 (May 1990).

Deleuze, Gilles, and Félix Guattari. "Capitalism: A Very Special Delirium." In *Hatred of Capitalism*. Edited by Chris Kraus and Sylvère Lotringer. New York: Semiotext(e), 2001.

————. *Kafka: Toward a Minor Literature*. Translated by Dana Polan. Minneapolis: University of Minnesota Press, 1986.

————. "Percept, Affect, and Concept." In *What Is Philosophy?* Translated by Hugh Tomlinson and Graham Burchell. New York: Columbia University Press, 1994.

————. *A Thousand Plateaus: Capitalism and Schizophrenia*. London and New York: Continuum, 1987.

————. "What is a Minor Literature?" In *Out There: Marginalization and Contemporary Cultures*. Translated by Dana Polan. Edited by Russell Ferguson et al. Cambridge, Mass.: MIT Press, 1990.

DeLillo, Don. *Falling Man: A Novel*. New York: Scribner, 2007.

De Noon, Daniel J. "Michelle Obama's Plan to End Childhood Obesity Epidemic: Goal; Cut Child Obesity From 20% to 5% by 2030." *WebMD Health News*, May 11, 2010.

DeParle, Jason. *American Dream: Three Women, Ten Kids, and a Nation's Drive to End Welfare*. New York: Viking, 2004.

Derrida, Jacques. *The Politics of Friendship*. Translated by George Collins. New York: Verso, 1997.

Dickson, Geoff, and Grant Schofield. "Globalization and Globesity: The Impact of the 2008 Beijing Olympics on China." *International Journal of Sports Management and Marketing* 1, no. 1/2 (2005): 169–79.

Doane, Mary Ann. "Information, Crisis, Catastrophe." In *Logics of Television: Essays in Cultural Criticism*. Edited by Patricia Mellencamp. Bloomington: Indiana University Press, 1990.

Dolan, Jill. "Performance, Utopia, and the 'Utopian Performative.'" *Theatre Journal* 53, no. 3 (2001): 455–79.

Dubey, Madhu. *Signs and Cities: Black Literary Postmodernism*. Chicago: University of Chicago Press, 2003.

DuBois, Ellen Carol. *Harriot Stanton Blatch and the Winning of Woman Suffrage*. New Haven: Yale University Press, 1997.

Dumm, Thomas L. *A Politics of the Ordinary*. New York: New York University Press, 1999.

Dyer-Witheford, Nick. "Empire, Immaterial Labor, the New Combinations, and the Global Worker." *Rethinking Marxism* 13, no. 3/4 (winter 2001): 70–80.

Eagleton, Terry. "Capitalism and Form." *New Left Review* 14 (March/April 2002): 119–31.

Eberwine, Donna. "Globesity: The Crisis of Growing Proportions." *Perspectives in Health Magazine* 7, no. 3 (2002): 6–11.

Economic and Social Research Council. "Diet and Obesity in the UK."

Edelman, Lee. *No Future: Queer Theory and the Death Drive.* Durham, N.C.: Duke University Press, 2005.

Edwards, Margie L. Kiter. "We're Decent People: Constructing and Managing Family Identity in Rural Working Class Communities." *Journal of Marriage and Family* 66, no. 2 (May 2004): 515–29.

Ehrenreich, Barbara. *Bait and Switch: The Futile Pursuit of the American Dream.* New York: Henry Holt and Co., 2005.

———. *Nickel and Dimed: On (Not) Getting By in America.* New York: Metropolitan Books, 2001.

Eley, Geoff. *A Crooked Line: From Cultural History to the History of Society.* Ann Arbor: University of Michigan Press, 2006.

Eley, Geoff, and Keith Nield. *The Future of Class in History: What's Left of the Social?* Ann Arbor: University of Michigan Press, 2007.

Ellis, Mark. *Race, War, and Surveillance: African Americans and the United States during World War I.* Bloomington: Indiana University Press, 2001.

European Industrial Relations Observatory. "Belgium: Rosetta Plan Launched to Boost Youth Employment." *European Industrial Relations Observatory On-line,* November 28, 1999.

———. "Uncertainties of the Informal Economy: A Belgian Perspective." *European Industrial Relations Observatory On-line,* August 28, 1998.

Fairbairn, W. R. D. 1952. *Psychoanalytic Studies of the Personality.* London: Routledge, 1990.

Farred, Grant. "A Fidelity to Politics: Shame and the African-American Vote in the 2004 Election." *Social Identities* 12, no. 2 (2006): 213–26.

Fattah, Hassan M. "In Dubai, an Outcry from Asians for Workplace Rights." *New York Times,* March 26, 2006.

Federici, Silvia. "Precarious Labor: A Feminist Viewpoint." http://inthemiddleofthe whirlwind.wordpress.com.

———. "The Reproduction of Labour-Power in the Global Economy: Marxist Theory and the Unfinished Feminist Revolution." http://caringlabor.wordpress.com.

Feuer, Jane. "The Concept of Live Television: Ontology as Ideology." In *Regarding Television: Critical Approaches; An Anthology.* Edited by E. Ann Kaplan. Los Angeles: American Film Institute, 1983.

Fitzpatrick, Michael. *The Tyranny of Health: Doctors and the Regulation of Lifestyle.* London: Routledge, 2001.

Flatley, Jonathan. *Affective Mapping: Melancholia and the Politics of Modernism.* Cambridge, Mass.: Harvard University Press, 2008.

Fleegler, Robert L. "'Forget All Differences until the Forces of Freedom Are Triumphant': The World War II-Era Quest for Ethnic and Religious Tolerance." *Journal of American Ethnic History* 27, no. 2 (winter 2008): 59–84.

Flegal, Katherine, Margaret D. Carroll, Cynthia L. Ogden, and Lester R. Curtin. "Prevalence and Trends in Obesity among U.S. Adults, 1999–2008." *Journal of the American Medical Association* 303, no. 2 (2010): 235–41.

Foucault, Michel. "17 March 1976." Translated by David Macey. In *Society Must Be Defended: Lectures at the College de France, 1975–76*. Edited by Mauro Bertani et al. New York: Picador, 2003.

———. 1969. *The Archaeology of Knowledge and the Discourse on Language*. Translated by A. M. Sheridan Smith. New York: Pantheon, 1994.

———. "The Confession of the Flesh." Translated by Colin Gordon. In *Power/Knowledge: Selected Interviews and Other Writings 1972–1977*. Edited by Colin Gordon. New York: Pantheon Books, 1980.

———. 1978. *The History of Sexuality, Vol. 1*. Translated by Robert Hurley. New York: Vintage Books, 1980.

———. "Questions of Method." In *The Foucault Effect: Studies in Governmentality*. Edited by Graham Burchell, Colin Gordon, and Peter Miller. Chicago: University of Chicago Press, 1991.

———. "What is Enlightenment?" Translated by Catherine Porter. In *The Foucault Reader*. Edited by Paul Rabinow. New York: Pantheon Books, 1984.

François, Anne-Lise. *Open Secrets: The Literature of Uncounted Experience*. Stanford, Calif.: Stanford University Press, 2008.

Frank, Thomas. *What's the Matter with Kansas? How Conservatives Won the Heart of America*. New York: Metropolitan, 2004.

Freedman, David S., et al. "Racial and Ethnic Differences in Secular Trends for Childhood BMI, Weight, and Height." *Obesity* 14 (February 2006): 301–308.

Freud, Sigmund. 1917 [1915]. "Mourning and Melancholia." In Vol. 14 of *The Standard Edition of the Complete Psychological Works of Sigmund Freud*. Translated and edited by James Strachey. London: Hogarth, 1957. Hereafter S.E.

———. 1933. "Femininity." Lecture 33, *New Introductory Lectures*. In S.E. 22.

Gaitskill, Mary. *Bad Behavior*. New York: Vintage, 1988.

———. *Because They Wanted To*. New York: Scribner, 1997.

———. "Folksong." *Nerve* (1999). http://www.nerve.com/content/folk-song-1999.

———. "Suntan." *Word*, July 12, 1999. http://deadword.com/site/habit/suntan/index.html.

———. *Two Girls, Fat and Thin*. New York: Vintage, 1991.

———. "Veronica." *POZ* (August 1998).

Gaitskill, Mary, and Peter Trachtenberg. "Walt and Beth: A Love Story." *Word*, July 7, 1999. Previously available at http://www.word.com. Print copy in possession of author.

Gardner, Gary, and Brian Halweil. "Underfed and Overfed: The Global Epidemic of Malnutrition." *Worldwatch* (March 2000), http://www.worldwatch.org.

Ghent, Emmanuel. "Masochism, Submission, Surrender: Masochism as a Perversion of Surrender." *Contemporary Psychoanalysis* 26, no.1 (1990): 108–36.

Gibbs, W. Wayt. "Obesity, An Overblown Epidemic?" *Scientific American*, May 23, 2005.

Gibson, William. *Pattern Recognition*. New York: Putnam, 2003.

Gibson-Graham, J. K. "An Ethics of the Local." *Rethinking Marxism* 15, no. 1 (2003): 49–74.

———. *A Postcapitalist Politics*. Minneapolis: University of Minnesota Press, 2006.

Gilliom, John. *Overseers of the Poor: Surveillance, Resistance, and the Limits of Privacy*. Chicago: University of Chicago Press, 2001.

Gilroy, Paul. *Against Race: Imagining Political Culture beyond the Color Line*. New York: Belknap Press, 2000.

Golding, Sue. "Curiosity." In *The Eight Technologies of Otherness*. Edited by Sue Goulding. New York and London: Routledge, 1997.

Gorman, Thomas J. "Reconsidering *Worlds of Pain*: Life in the Working Class(es)." *Sociological Review* 15, no. 4 (2000): 693–717.

Gould, Deborah B. *Moving Politics: Emotion and ACT UP's Fight against AIDS*. Chicago: University of Chicago Press, 2009.

Graeber, David. *Fragments of an Anarchist Anthropology*. Chicago: Prickly Paradigm Press, 2004.

———. *Possibilities: Essays on Hierarchy, Rebellion, and Desire*. Oakland, Calif.: AK Press, 2007.

Graham, Colin. "'Every Passer-by a Culprit?'" *Third Text* 19, no. 5 (September 2005): 567–80.

Grassian, Stuart. "Psychopathological Effects of Solitary Confinement." *American Journal of Psychiatry* 140 (November 11, 1983): 1450–54.

Green, André. 1973. *The Fabric of Affect in the Psychoanalytic Discourse*. Translated by Alan Sheridan. New York and London: Routledge, 1999.

Gremillion, Helen. "The Cultural Politics of Body Size." *Annual Review of Anthropology* 34 (October 2005): 13–32.

Griggers, Camilla. *Becoming-Woman*. Minneapolis: University of Minnesota Press, 1997.

Grimm, Sabine, and Klaus Ronneberger. "Interview with Sergio Bologna: An Invisible History of Work." *Springerin* 1 (2007).

Habermas, Jürgen. *The Structural Transformation of the Public Sphere: An Inquiry into a Category of Bourgeois Society*. Translated by Thomas Burger. Cambridge, Mass.: MIT Press, 1989.

Hadley, Elaine. *Living Liberalism: Practical Citizenship in Mid-Victorian Britain*. Chicago: University of Chicago Press, 2010.

Hage, Ghassan. *Against Paranoid Nationalism: Searching for Hope in a Shrinking Society*. Annandale, NSW, Australia: Pluto Press, 2003.

Halttunen, Karen. *Murder Most Foul: The Killer and the American Gothic Imagination*. Cambridge, Mass.: Harvard University Press, 2000.

Hardt, Michael, and Antonio Negri. *Empire*. Cambridge, Mass.: Harvard University Press, 2001.

————. *Multitude: War and Democracy in the Age of Empire.* Cambridge, Mass.: Harvard University Press, 2004.

Harootunian, Harry. *History's Disquiet: Modernity, Cultural Practice, and the Question of Everyday Life.* New York: Columbia University Press, 2000.

————. "Remembering the Historical Present." *Critical Inquiry* 33 (spring 2007): 471–94.

————. "Shadowing History: National Narratives and the Persistence of the Everyday." *Cultural Studies* 18, no. 2/3 (2004): 181–200.

Harvey, David. "The Body as an Accumulation Strategy." In *Spaces of Hope.* Berkeley: University of California Press, 2000.

————. *A Brief History of Neoliberalism.* New York: Oxford University Press, 2007.

————. *The Condition of Postmodernity: An Enquiry into the Origins of Cultural Change.* Cambridge, Mass.: Blackwell, 1989.

————. *Spaces of Hope.* Berkeley: University of California Press, 2000.

Hayden, Anders. "France's 35-Hour Week: Attack on Business? Win-Win Reform? Or Betrayal of Disadvantaged Workers?" *Politics and Society* 34, no. 4 (December 2006): 503–42.

Hempel, Amy. "Beach Town." In *The Collected Stories of Amy Hempel.* New York: Scribner, 2006.

Heymann, Jody. *Forgotten Families: Ending the Growing Crisis Confronting Children and Working Parents in the Global Economy.* New York: Oxford University Press, 2006.

Hicks, Bernard. "America on the Move: The National Health Campaign for 2003." *American Fitness* (January/February 2003).

Higbee, Will. "'Elle est-où, ta place?' The Social-Realist Melodramas of Laurent Cantet: *Ressources humaines* and *Emploi du temps.*" *French Cultural Studies* 15 (2004): 235–50.

Hirschkind, Charles. *The Ethical Soundscape: Cassette Sermons and Islamic Counterpublics.* New York: Columbia University Press, 2006.

Hochschild, Arlie. *The Commercialization of Intimate Life: Notes from Home and Work.* Berkeley: University of California Press, 2003.

————. *The Managed Heart: Commercialization of Human Feeling.* Berkeley: University of California Press, 1983.

Holmes, Brian. *Unleashing the Collective Phantoms: Essays in Reverse Imagineering.* New York: Autonomedia, 2008.

Hussain, Nasser. *The Jurisprudence of Emergency: Colonialism and the Rule of Law.* Ann Arbor: University of Michigan Press, 2003.

Illouz, Eva. *Cold Intimacies: The Making of Emotional Capitalism.* Cambridge, U.K.: Polity Press, 2007.

Investors.com. "California's Low-Fact Diet."

The Invisible Committee. *The Coming Insurrection.* New York: Semiotext(e), 2009.

Inwood, Michael. *A Heidegger Dictionary.* London: Wiley-Blackwell, 1999.

Jackson, Phyllis. "Re-Living Memories: Picturing Death." *Ijele: Art Journal of the African World* 5 (2002). http://www.africaresource.com.

Jacobson, Miriam. "The Epidemic of Obesity: The Costs to Employers and Practical Solutions." Paper given at the Washington Business Group on Health Summit on Obesity, Cardiovascular Disease and Diabetes, December 5, 2002.

Jameson, Fredric. *The Geopolitical Aesthetic: Cinema and Space in the World System*. Indianapolis: Indiana University Press, 1992.

———. *Ideologies of Theory: Essays, 1971–1986*. Vol. 1, *Situations of Theory*. Minneapolis: University of Minnesota Press, 1988.

———. *The Political Unconscious: Narrative as a Socially Symbolic Act*. Ithaca, N.Y.: Cornell University Press, 1983.

———. *Postmodernism, or, The Cultural Logic of Late Capitalism*. Durham, N.C.: Duke University Press, 1991.

———. "Reification and Utopia in Mass Culture." *Social Text* 1 (winter 1979): 130–48.

———. *Signatures of the Visible*. London: Routledge, 1992.

Jenkins, Alan. *Employment Relations in France: Evolution and Innovation*. New York: Kluwer Academic / Plenum Publishers, 2000.

Jernigan, Adam. "Affective Realism: Economies of Feeling in Postwar American Fiction." PhD diss. University of Chicago. Forthcoming.

Jessop, Bob. *The Future of the Capitalist State*. Malden, Mass.: Polity Press, 2002.

Johnson, Barbara. "Apostrophe, Animation, and Abortion." *Diacritics* 16, no. 1 (1986): 26–47.

———. "Bringing Out D. A. Miller." *Narrative* 10, no. 1 (2002): 3–8.

———. "Metaphor, Metonym, Voice in *Their Eyes Were Watching God*." In *A World of Difference*. Baltimore: Johns Hopkins University Press, 1987.

———. "Muteness Envy." In *The Feminist Difference: Literature, Psychoanalysis, Race and Gender*. Cambridge: Harvard University Press, 1998.

———. "Thresholds of Difference: Structures of Address in Zora Neale Hurston." In *A World of Difference*. Baltimore: Johns Hopkins University Press, 1987.

Johnson, Charles. 1986. "Exchange Value." In *The Sorcerer's Apprentice: Tales and Conjurations*. New York: Plume, 1994.

Jordan, Elizabeth, ed. 1916–1917. *The Sturdy Oak: A Composite Novel of American Politics*. Columbus: Ohio State University Press, 1998.

Junod, Tom. 2003. "The Falling Man." Reprinted in *Esquire*, September 11, 2008.

Kedrosky, Paul. "Infectious Greed." http://paul.kedrosky.com.

Kehr, Dave. "Their Method Is to Push Toward Moments of Truth." *New York Times*, January 5, 2003.

Kimm, Sue Y., and Eva Obarzanek. "Childhood Obesity: A New Pandemic of the New Millennium." *Pediatrics* 110, no. 5 (November 2002): 1003–7.

Kiter Edwards, Margie L. "We're Decent People: Constructing and Managing Family

Identity in Rural Working-Class Communities." *Journal of Marriage and Family* 66, no. 2 (May 2004): 515–29.

Klein, Melanie, and Joan Rivière. *Love, Hate and Reparation.* New York: W. W. Norton and Co., 1964.

Klein, Richard. *Eat Fat.* New York: Pantheon, 1996.

Kolbert, Elizabeth. "XXXL: Why Are We So Fat?" *The New Yorker,* July 20, 2009. http://www.newyorker.com.

Kristeva, Julia. *Powers of Horror: An Essay on Abjection.* New York: Columbia University Press, 1982.

Krueger, Alan B. "Does the Financial Crisis Threaten Your Job?" *New York Times,* September 29, 2008.

Kulick, Don, and Anne Meneley. "Introduction." In *Fat: The Anthropology of an Obsession.* New York: Tarcher/Penguin, 2005.

Labio, Catherine. "Editor's Preface: The Federalization of Memory." *Yale French Studies* 102 (fall 2002): 1–8.

Laclau, Ernesto. "Universalism, Particularism, and the Question of Identity." In *The Identity in Question.* Edited by John Rajchman. London and New York: Routledge, 1995.

Lang, Tim, and Michael Heasman. *Food Wars: The Global Battle for Mouths, Minds, and Markets.* London: Earthscan, 2004.

Laplanche, Jean, and J.B. Pontalis. "Fantasy and the Origins of Sexuality." In *Formations of Fantasy.* Edited by Victor Burgin, James Donald, and Cora Kaplan. London: Methuen, 1986.

———. *The Language of Psychoanalysis.* Translated by Donald Nicholson-Smith. New York: W. W. Norton and Co., 1967.

———. "Phantasy." In *The Language of Psycho-Analysis.* Translated by Donald Nicholson-Smith. New York: W. W. Norton and Co., 1967.

Lareau, Annette. *Unequal Childhoods: Class, Race, and Family Life.* Berkeley: University of California Press, 2003.

Lefebvre, Henri. *Rhythmanalysis: Space, Time and Everyday Life.* Translated by Stuart Elden and Gerald Moore. London: Continuum, 2004.

Leitch, Alison. "Slow Food and the Politics of Pork Fat: Italian Food and European Identity." *Ethnos* 68, no. 4 (December 2003): 437–62.

Leonard, Devin. "The New Abnormal." *Bloomberg Businessweek,* July 29, 2010.

"Let's Move" Initiative. http://www.letsmove.gov.

Leys, Ruth. *Trauma: A Genealogy.* Chicago: University of Chicago Press, 2000.

Lithwick, Dahlia. "My Big Fattening Greek Salad: Are French Fries the New Marlboros?" *Slate,* August 14, 2003.

Lloyd, David, and Paul Thomas. *Culture and the State.* London and New York: Routledge, 1998.

Lloyd, Richard D. *Neo-Bohemia: Art and Commerce in the Postindustrial City*. New York and London: Routledge, 2005.

Logwood, Dyann. "Food for Our Souls." In *Body Outlaws: Young Women Write About Body Image & Identity*. Edited by Ophira Edut. Seattle: Seal Press, 1998.

Lotringer, Sylvère. "Remember Foucault." *October* 126 (fall 2008): 3–22.

Lovejoy, Meg. "Disturbances in the Social Body: Differences in Body Image and Eating Problems Among African American and White Women." *Gender and Society* 15, no. 2 (April 2001): 239–61.

Lukàcs, Georg. 1962. *The Historical Novel*. Lincoln: University of Nebraska Press, 1983.

Lupton, Ellen. "Why DIY?" *Design Writing Research*, August 2009.

Lyotard, Jean-François. *The Differend: Phrases in Dispute*. Translated by Georges Van Den Abbeele. Minneapolis: University of Minnesota Press, 1988.

MacTavish, Katherine A., and Sonya Salamon. "Pathways of Youth Development in a Rural Trailer Park." *Family Relations* 55 (April 2006): 163–74.

Manson, JoAnn E., et al. "The Escalating Pandemics of Obesity and Sedentary Lifestyle: A Call to Action for Clinicians." *Archives of Internal Medicine* (February 9, 2004): 249–58.

Marcuse, Herbert. "Aggressiveness in Advanced Industrial Society." *Negations: Essays in Critical Theory*. Boston: Beacon Press, 1968.

Markell, Patchen. *Bound by Recognition*. Princeton: Princeton University Press, 2003.

Marks, Laura U. *Touch: Sensuous Theory and Multisensory Media*. Minneapolis: University of Minnesota Press, 2002.

Marx, Karl. *Economic and Philosophical Manuscripts*. Translated by Gregor Benton, 1974. http://www.sozialistische-klassiker.org.

———. "The Eighteenth Brumaire of Napoleon Bonaparte." In *The Marx-Engels Reader*. Edited by Robert C. Tucker. 2nd ed. New York: Norton, 1978.

Massumi, Brian. "The Future Birth of the Affective Fact." Paper presented in Montreal at the conference "Genealogies of Biopolitics," 2005.

———. *Parables for the Virtual: Movement, Affect, Sensation*. Durham, N.C.: Duke University Press, 2002.

———. "Too-Blue: Color-Patch for an Expanded Empiricism." *Cultural Studies* 14, no. 2 (April 2000): 253–302.

———. *A User's Guide to Capitalism and Schizophrenia: Deviations from Deleuze and Guattari*. Cambridge, Mass.: MIT, 1999.

Mazzarella, William. "The Myth of the Multitude, or, Who's Afraid of the Crowd?" *Critical Inquiry* 36, no. 4 (summer 2010): 697–727.

Mbembe, Achille. "Necropolitics." Translated by Libby Meintjes. *Public Culture* 15, no. 1 (winter 2003): 11–40.

———. *On the Postcolony*. Berkeley: University of California Press, 2001.

Mbembe, Achille, and Janet Roitman. "Figures of the Subject in Times of Crisis." In

The Geography of Identity. Edited by Patricia Yaeger. Ann Arbor: University of Michigan Press, 1996.

Media Matters. "Limbaugh Blamed the Left for Obesity Crisis." August 29, 2006.

Miech, Richard A., et al. "Trends in the Association of Poverty With Overweight among U.S. Adolescents, 1971–2004." *Journal of the American Medical Association* 295, no. 20 (May 24/31, 2006): 2385–93.

Milton, John. "On His Blindness." In *The Poetical Works of John Milton*, vol. 3. London: Bell and Daldy, 1866.

Mintz, Sidney W., and Christine M. Du Bois. "The Anthropology of Food and Eating." *Annual Review of Anthropology* 31 (October 2002): 99–119.

Mitropoulos, Angela. "Precari-us?" *Mute*, January 9, 2006.

Mokdad, Ali H., et al. "The Spread of the Obesity Epidemic in the United States, 1991–1998." *Journal of the American Medical Association* 282, no. 16 (October 27, 1999): 1519–22.

Moore, Alan, and David Lloyd. *V for Vendetta*. New York: DC Comics, 1982–1985.

Morley, David, and Kuan-Hsing Chen, eds. *Stuart Hall: Critical Dialogues in Cultural Studies*. London and New York: Routledge, 1996.

Morris, Daniel. "The Life and Times of Sovereignty." Unpublished paper, 2002.

Moten, Fred. *In the Break: The Aesthetics of the Black Radical Tradition*. Minneapolis: University of Minnesota Press, 2003.

Moten, Fred, and Stefano Harney. "Policy." Roundtable: Research Architecture. http://roundtable.kein.org.

Motevalli, Golnar. "'Video Sniffers' Subverting Surveillance for Art." *Reuters*, May 27, 2008.

MSNBC. "'Globesity' Gains Ground as Leading Killer: Weight Problems Spreading to Even Poorest Countries." May 10, 2005.

Muñoz, José Esteban. *Cruising Utopia: The Then and There of Queer Futurity*. New York: NYU Press, 2009.

———, ed. "Between Psychoanalysis and Affect: A Public Feelings Project." In *Women and Performance* 19, no. 2 (2009).

Muntaner, Charles. "Commentary: Social Capital, Social Class, and the Slow Progress of Psychosocial Epidemiology." *International Journal of Epidemiology* 33 (2004): 1–7.

Muntaner, Charles, John Lynch, and George Davey Smith. "Social Capital, Disorganized Communities, and the Third Way: Understanding the Retreat from Structural Inequalities in Epidemiology and Public Health." *International Journal of Health Services* 31, no. 2 (2001): 213–37.

———. "Social Capital and the Third Way in Public Health." *Critical Public Health* 10, no. 2 (June 2000): 107–24.

Murphy, Alexander B. "Landscapes for Whom? The Twentieth-Century Remaking of Brussels." *Yale French Studies* 102 (2002): 190–206.

Nancy, Jean-Luc. *The Inoperative Community*. Translated by Peter Conner et al. Edited by Peter Conner. Minneapolis: University of Minnesota Press, 1991.

Nanny State Liberation Front. http://nannystateliberationfront.net.

National American Woman Suffrage Association, Harriet Taylor Upton, Susan Walker Fitzgerald, Hannah J. Patterson, Nettie Rogers Shuler, Justina Leavitt Wilson, League of Women Voters (U.S.). Congress. *The Handbook of the National American Woman Suffrage Association*. 1912.

National Center for Health Statistics. "Prevalence of Overweight and Obesity Among Adults: United States, 1999–2002."

Neilson, Brett, and Ned Rossiter. "From Precarity to Precariousness and Back Again: Labour, Life and Unstable Networks." *Understanding Precarity*, July 31, 2006.

———. "Precarity as a Political Concept, or, Fordism as Exception." *Theory, Culture, and Society* 25 (2008): 51–72.

Nestle, Marion. "Hunger in the United States: Policy Implications." In *Food: A Reader*. Edited by Carole M. Counihan. New York and London: Routledge, 2002.

Nestle, Marion, and Michael F. Jacobson. "Halting the Obesity Epidemic: A Public Health Policy Approach." *Public Health Reports* 115 (January-February 2000): 12–24.

New York Times. "Negroes in Protest March in Fifth Avenue." *New York Times*, July 29, 1917.

Nietzsche, Friedrich. *On the Genealogy of Morals*. Edited by Walter Kaufmann. New York: Vintage, 1967.

Nord, Mark, et al. "Household Food Security in the United States, 2000." *Food Assistance and Nutrition Research Report*, no. 21. Washington, D.C.: USDA, Economic Research Service, 2002. http://www.ers.usda.gov.

Norman, Nils. *The Contemporary Picturesque*. London: Book Works, 2000.

Norris, Clive, Mike McCahill, and David Wood. "The Growth of CCTV: A Global Perspective on the International Diffusion of Video Surveillance in Publicly Accessible Space." *Surveillance and Society* 2, no. 2/3: 110–35.

Norris, Clive, Jade Moran, and Gary Armstrong. *Surveillance, Closed Circuit Television, and Social Control*. Aldershot, U.K.: Ashgate, 1998.

Notes from Nowhere. *We Are Everywhere: The Irresistible Rise of Global Anti-Capitalism*. London: Verso, 2003.

Nuruddin, Yusuf. "The Promises and Pitfalls of Reparations," http://www.ncobra.org.

Nyong'o, Tavia. "I've Got You Under My Skin: Queer Assemblages, Lyrical Nostalgia and the African Diaspora." *Performance Research* 12, no. 3 (2007): 42–54.

Oldfield, Sybil, ed. 1912–1913. *International Woman Suffrage: Jus Suffragii, 1913–1920*. Vol. 1. London: Routledge, 2003.

Oliver, J. Eric. *Fat Politics: The Real Story Behind America's Obesity Epidemic*. New York: Oxford University Press, 2006.

Olshansky, S. Jay, et al. "A Potential Decline in Life Expectancy in the United States in the 21st Century." *New England Journal of Medicine* 352, no. 11 (March 17, 2005): 1138–45.

Ong, Aihwa. *Neoliberalism as Exception: Mutations in Citizenship and Sovereignty.* Durham, N.C.: Duke University Press, 2006.

Palin, Sarah, and Joseph Biden. "Transcript of Palin, Biden Debate." October 2, 2008. http://www.cnn.com.

"Partnership for a Healthier America." http://www.ahealthieramerica.org.

Patton, Paul. "The World Seen from Within: Deleuze and the Philosophy of Events." *Theory and Event* 1, no. 1 (1997).

Phelan, Peggy. *Mourning Sex: Performing Public Memories.* New York: Routledge, 1997.

———. *Unmarked: The Politics of Performance.* New York: Routledge, 1993.

Phillips, Adam. *Equals.* New York: Basic Books, 2002.

———. "First Hates: Phobias in Theory." In *On Kissing, Tickling, and Being Bored: Psychoanalytic Essays on the Unexamined Life.* Cambridge, Mass.: Harvard University Press, 1993.

———. "Freud and the Uses of Forgetting." In *On Flirtation: Psychoanalytic Essays on the Uncommitted Life.* Cambridge, Mass.: Harvard University Press, 1994.

———. "On Composure." In *On Kissing, Tickling, and Being Bored: Psychoanalytic Essays on the Unexamined Life.* Cambridge, Mass.: Harvard University Press, 1993.

Pick, Grant. "Slim Chance." *Chicago Tribune Magazine*, April 25, 2004: 12–17, 26.

Pimlott, J. A. R. "Public Service Advertising: The Advertising Council." *Public Opinion Quarterly* 12, no. 2 (1948): 209–19.

Pollan, Michael. "Unhappy Meals." *New York Times*, January 28, 2007. http://www.nytimes.com.

Popkin, Barry M. "Using Research on the Obesity Pandemic as a Guide to a Unified Vision of Nutrition." *Public Health Nutrition* 8, no. 6 (September 2005): 724–29.

Postone, Moishe. "Lukàcs and the Dialectical Critique of Capitalism." In *New Dialectics and Political Economy.* Edited by Robert Albriton and John Simoulidis. London: Palgrave, 2003.

———. *Time, Labor, and Social Domination: A Reinterpretation of Marx's Critical Theory.* Cambridge and New York: Cambridge University Press, 1993.

Potamianou, Anna. *Hope: A Shield in the Economy of Borderline States.* London and New York: Routledge, 1997.

Povinelli, Elizabeth A. *The Cunning of Recognition: Indigenous Alterities and the Making of Australian Multiculturalism.* Durham, N.C.: Duke University Press, 2002.

Precarias a la Deriva. "Bodies, Lies, and Video Tape: Between the Logic of Security and the Logic of Care." *Diagonal* (February 2005). http://www.chtodelat.org.

Probyn, Elspeth. *Blush: Faces of Shame.* Minneapolis: University of Minnesota Press, 2005.

———. "Eating Sex." In *Carnal Longings: FoodSexIdentities.* London: Routledge, 2000.

Proust, Marcel. 1913. *Swann's Way*. Translated by Lydia Davis. New York: Viking Press, 2003.

Quick, Andrew. "Time and the Event." *Cultural Values* 2, no. 2/3 (April 1998): 223–42.

Rabin, Roni. "Study or No, Fries Are Still Bad News." *Newsday*, September 20, 2005.

Rancière, Jacques. *Disagreement: Politics and Philosophy*. Translated by Julie Rose. Minneapolis: University of Minnesota Press, 1998.

———. *Hatred of Democracy*. Translated by Steve Corcoran. London and New York: Verso, 2006.

———. *The Politics of Aesthetics: The Distribution of the Sensible*. Translated by Gabriel Rockhill. New York: Continuum, 2004.

Rees, A. L. *A History of Experimental Film and Video*. London: BFI, 1999.

Renov, Michael. "Video Confessions." In *Resolutions: Contemporary Video Practices*. Edited by Michael Renov and Erika Suderberg. Minneapolis: University of Minnesota Press, 1996.

Roberts, Nahshon. "All-Seeing Eye: The History of Video Surveillance." http://www.ez-surveillance.com/blog/.

Roethke, Theodore. "I Knew a Woman." In *Words for the Wind: The Collected Verse of Theodore Roethke*. Bloomington: Indiana University Press, 1961.

Rohy, Valerie. "Ahistorical." GLQ 12, no. 1 (2006): 61–83.

Rose, Jacqueline. *States of Fantasy*. New York: Oxford University Press, 1995.

Ross, Andrew. *Nice Work If You Can Get It: Life and Labor in Precarious Times*. New York: NYU Press, 2009.

Ross, Kristin. *Fast Cars, Clean Bodies: Decolonization and the Reordering of French Culture*. Cambridge, Mass.: MIT Press, 1995.

Rubin, Lillian B. *Worlds of Pain: Life in the Working Class Family*. New York: Basic Books, 1977.

Ryman, Geoff. *Was*. New York: Penguin, 1992.

Sarat, Austin, and Nasser Hussain. "On Lawful Lawlessness: George Ryan, Executive Clemency, and the Rhetoric of Sparing Life." *Stanford Law Review* 56 (April 2004): 1307–44.

Schlosser, Eric. *Fast Food Nation: The Dark Side of the All-American Meal*. New York: Houghton Mifflin, 2001.

Schneider, Rebecca. *The Explicit Body in Performance*. London and New York: Routledge, 1997.

Sciolino, Elaine, Thomas Crampton, and Maria de la Baume. "Not '68, but French Youths Hear Similar Cry to Rise Up." *New York Times*, March 17, 2006.

Scollan-Koliopoulos, Melissa. "Consideration for Legacies about Diabetes and Self-Care for the Family with a Multigenerational Occurrence of Type 2 Diabetes." *Nursing and Health Sciences* 6, no. 3 (September 2004): 223–227.

Scott, A. O. "Neo-Neo Realism." *The New York Times Magazine*, March 22, 2009.

Sedgwick, Eve Kosofsky. "The Beast in the Closet: James and the Writing of Homosexual Panic." In *Epistemology of the Closet*. Berkeley: University of California Press,
1990.

———. *A Dialogue on Love*. Boston: Beacon, 1999.

———. *Epistemology of the Closet*. Berkeley: University of California Press, 1990.

———. *Fat Art, Thin Art*. Durham, N.C.: Duke University Press, 1994.

———. "Paranoid Reading and Reparative Reading; Or, You're So Paranoid, You Probably Think This Introduction Is about You." In *Novel Gazing: Queer Readings in Fiction*.
Edited by Eve Kosofsky Sedgwick. Durham, N.C.: Duke University Press, 1997.

———. "Queer Performativity: Henry James's *The Art of the Novel*." GLQ 1, no. 1 (1993):
1–16.

———. "Teaching/Depression." *The Scholar and the Feminist Online* 4, no. 2 (2006).

———. *Tendencies*. Durham, N.C.: Duke University Press, 1993.

———. *Touching Feeling: Affect, Pedagogy, Performativity*. Durham, N.C.: Duke University Press, 2003.

Sedgwick, Eve Kosofsky, and Adam Frank. "Shame in the Cybernetic Fold." *Critical Inquiry* 21, no. 2 (winter 1995): 496–522.

Sennett, Richard. *The Corrosion of Character: The Personal Consequences of Work in the New Capitalism*. New York: Norton, 1998.

Serres, Michel. 1980. *The Parasite*. Translated by Lawrence R. Schehr. Minneapolis: University of Minnesota Press, 2007.

Sewell, William H. *The Logics of History: Social Theory and Social Transformation*. Chicago:
University of Chicago Press, 2005.

Shatz, Adam. "Short Cuts." *London Review of Books*, July 23, 2009.

Shelton, Emily. "My Secret Life: Photographs, Melancholy Realisms, and Modern Personhood." Ph.D. diss. University of Chicago, 2002.

Shipler, David. *The Working Poor: Invisible in America*. New York: Vintage, 2004.

Shomon, Mary. "National Depression Screening Day Offers Public an Open Invitation to Learn about Treatment Options, Expectations." About.com, October 2001.

Shukaitis, Stevphen, David Graeber, and Erika Biddle, eds. *Constituent Imagination: Mili-
tant Investigations, Collective Theorization*. Oakland, Calif.: AK Press, 2007.

Siegel, Daniel. "The Failure of Condescension." *Victorian Literature and Culture* 33, no. 2
(2005): 395–414.

Simon, Gregory E., et al. "Depression and Work Productivity: The Comparative Costs
of Treatment Versus Nontreatment." *Journal of Occupational and Environmental Medicine* 43, no. 1 (January 2001): 2–9.

Sitrin, Marina. *Horizontalism: Voices of Popular Power in Argentina*. Oakland, Calif.: AK
Press, 2006.

Skeggs, Beverley. "Ambivalent Femininities." In *Formations of Class and Gender: Becoming
Respectable*. London: Sage, 1997.

———. *Class, Self, Culture*. London: Routledge, 2004.

Slyper, Arnold H. "The Pediatric Obesity Epidemic: Causes and Controversies." *The Journal of Clinical Endocrinology and Metabolism* 89, no. 6 (June 2004): 2540–47.

Smith, Craig S. "Four Ways to Fire a Frenchman." *New York Times*, March 26, 2006.

Snediker, Michael D. *Queer Optimism: Lyric Personhood and Other Felicitous Persuasions*. Minneapolis: University of Minnesota Press, 2009.

Sobal, Jeffrey, and Albert J. Stunkard. "Socioeconomic Status and Obesity: A Review of the Literature." *Psychological Bulletin* 105, no. 2 (March 1989): 260–75.

Song, Lijun, Joonmo Son, and Nan Lin. "Social Capital and Health." In *The New Blackwell Companion to Medical Sociology*. Edited by William C. Cockerham. Chichester, U.K.: Wiley-Blackwell, 2001.

Sontag, Susan. 1986. "The Way We Live Now." In *The Way We Live Now*. Susan Sontag and Howard Hodgkin. London: Jonathan Cape, Ltd., 1991.

Southard, Belinda A. Stillion. "Militancy, Power, and Identity: The Silent Sentinels as Women Fighting for Political Voice." *Rhetoric and Public Affairs* 10, no. 3 (2007): 399–418.

Spivak, Gayatri Chakravorty. "Forum: The Legacy of Jacques Derrida." PMLA 120, no. 2 (March 2005): 492.

———. "Harlem." *Social Text* 22, no. 4 (2004): 113–39.

———. "Other Things Are Never Equal: A Speech." *Rethinking Marxism* 12, no. 4 (2000): 37–45.

———. "The Politics of Translation." In *Destabilizing Theory: Contemporary Feminist Debates*. Edited by Michèle Barrett and Anne Phillips. Stanford: Stanford University Press, 1992.

———. "Subaltern Studies: Deconstructing Historiography." In *In Other Worlds: Essays in Cultural Politics*. New York: Routledge, 1987.

Stack, Carol. *All Our Kin*. New York: Harper and Row, 1974.

Staiger, Janet, Ann Cvetkovich, and Ann Reynolds, eds. *Political Emotions*. New York and London: Routledge, 2010.

Stanton, Elizabeth Cady, Susan Brownell Anthony, Matilda Joslyn Gage, and Ida Husted Harper. *History of Woman Suffrage*, Vol. 6. New York: J. J. Little and Ives Co., 1922.

Steedman, Carolyn. *Landscape for a Good Woman: A Story of Two Lives*. New Brunswick, N.J.: Rutgers University Press, 1987.

Stein, Rob. "Obesity May Stall Trend of Increasing Longevity." *Washington Post*, March 17, 2005.

Stern, Daniel. *The Present Moment in Psychotherapy and Everyday Life*. New York: W. W. Norton, 2004.

Stewart, Kathleen. *Ordinary Affects*. Durham, N.C.: Duke University Press, 2007.

———. *A Space on the Side of the Road: Cultural Poetics in an "Other" America*. Princeton, N.J.: Princeton University Press, 1996.

Sturm, Roland. "Increases in Clinically Severe Obesity in the United States, 1986–2000." *Archives of Internal Medicine*, October 13, 2003: 2146–48.

Sullum, Jacob. "Are You Sure You Want Fries With That?: Mandatory Calorie Counts cross the Line between Informing and Nagging." *Reason*, August 20, 2008.

———. "An Epidemic of Meddling: The Totalitarian Implications of Public Health." *Reason*, May, 2007.

———. "Fat Load: A Slimmer America Won't Save Taxpayers Money." *Reason*, August 5, 2009.

———. "The Link between Fat Ad Budgets and Fat Children." *Reason*, June 11, 2004.

Sullum, Jacob, and Thomas J. DiLorenzo. "Public Health vs. The Nanny State?" *The Independent Institute*, October 26, 2000.

Surgeon General. "The Surgeon General's Call to Action to Prevent and Decrease Overweight and Obesity," http://www.surgeongeneral.gov.

Tarkan, Laurie. "Bananas? Maybe. Peas and Kale? Dream On." *New York Times*, June 21, 2005.

Taussig, Michael. *The Nervous System*. London and New York: Routledge, 1991.

Taylor, Diana. *The Archive and the Repertoire: Performing Cultural Memory in the Americas*. Durham, N.C.: Duke University Press, 2003.

Thrift, Nigel. *Non-Representational Theory: Space, Politics, Affect*. London: Routledge, 2007.

Tilghman, Joan. "Obesity and Diabetes in African American Women." *Journal of the Association of Black Nursing Faculty* 14 (May/June, 2003).

Tsianos, Vassilis, and Dimitris Papadopoulos. "Precarity: A Savage Journey to the Heart of Embodied Capitalism." *Transversal* (October 2006).

Tsing, Anna. "Inside the Economy of Appearances." *Public Culture* 12, no. 1 (2000): 115–44.

Turner, Bryan S. "The Government of the Body: Medical Regimens and the Rationalization of Diet." *The British Journal of Sociology* 33, no. 2 (June 1982): 254–69.

Urbina, Ian, N.R. Kleinfield, and Marc Santora. "Bad Blood." *New York Times*, January 9–12, 2006.

USA Today. "Surgeon General: Obesity Rivals Tobacco as Health Ill." December 13, 2001.

U.S. Conference of Mayors. "A Status Report on Hunger and Homelessness in America's Cities 2001: A 27-City Survey." December 2001.

U.S. Congress. House. "Personal Responsibility in Food Consumption Act of 2005." HR 554. 109th Cong., 1st. Sess. *Congressional Record* (October 19, 2005).

U.S. Department of Health and Human Services. "Overweight and Obesity: What You Can Do."

Valverde, Mariana. *Diseases of the Will: Alcohol and the Dilemmas of Freedom*. Cambridge: Cambridge University Press, 1998.

Virno, Paolo. *A Grammar of the Multitude: For an Analysis of Contemporary Forms of Life*.

Translated by Isabella Bertoletti, James Cascaito, and Andrea Casson. New York: Semiotext(e)/MIT Press, 2004.

Vogler, Candace. "The Moral of the Story." *Critical Inquiry* 34, no. 1 (autumn 2007): 5–35.

———. "Sex and Talk." In *Intimacy*. Edited by Lauren Berlant. Chicago: University of Chicago Press, 2000.

Wacquant, Loïc. "Inside 'The Zone': The Social Art of the Hustler in the American Ghetto." In *The Weight of the World: Social Suffering in Contemporary Society*. Edited by Pierre Bourdieu et al. Stanford, Calif.: Stanford University Press, 1993.

———. "Territorial Stigmatization in the Age of Advanced Marginality." *Thesis Eleven* 91 (2007): 66–77.

Walker, Alexander R. P. "The Obesity Pandemic: Is It beyond Control?" *Journal of the Royal Society for the Promotion of Health* 123 (September 2003): 150–51.

Warner, Melanie. "California Wants to Serve a Health Warning with That Order." *New York Times*, September 21, 2005: C1.

Warner, Michael. *Publics and Counterpublics*. New York: Zone Books, 2005.

———. *The Trouble with Normal: Sex, Politics, and the Ethics of a Queer Life*. New York: Free Press, 1999.

Weinberger, Eliot. "What I Heard about Iraq in 2005." *London Review of Books* 28, no. 1 (January 5, 2006).

Weiss, Gail. *Body Images: Embodiment as Intercorporeality*. London and New York: Routledge, 1998.

Weston, Kath. *Families We Choose: Lesbians, Gays, Kinship*. New York: Columbia University Press, 1997.

Whitehead, Colson. *The Intuitionist: A Novel*. New York, Doubleday, 1998.

Williams, Patricia. *The Alchemy of Race and Rights: Diary of a Law Professor*. Cambridge, Mass.: Harvard University Press, 1991.

———. *The Rooster's Egg*. Cambridge, Mass.: Harvard University Press, 1995.

Williams, Raymond. *The Long Revolution*. London: Penguin, 1965.

———. *Marxism and Literature*. Oxford: Oxford University Press, 1977.

Wintz, Cary D., and Paul Finkelman. *Encyclopedia of the Harlem Renaissance*. Vol. 2. New York: Taylor and Francis, 2002.

Wise, Tim. "Collateral Damage: Poor Whites and the Unintended Consequences of Racial Privilege." *Z Magazine*, October 5, 2003.

Woolf, Virginia. 1929. *A Room of One's Own*. New York: Harcourt, Brace, and Jovanovich, 1957.

World Health Organization. "Controlling the Global Obesity Epidemic," http://www.who.int/en.

———. *Obesity Reports*, http://www.who.int/en.

Young, Iris Marion. *Throwing Like a Girl and Other Essays in Feminist Philosophy and Social Theory*. Indianapolis: Indiana University Press, 1990.

Yurchak, Alexei. "The Cynical Reason of Late Socialism: Power, Pretense, and the Anek-dot." *Public Culture* 9, no. 2 (1997): 161–88.

Zangrando, Robert L. *The NAACP Crusade Against Lynching, 1909–1950.* Philadelphia: Temple University Press, 1980.

Žižek, Slavoj. *Enjoy Your Symptom! Jacques Lacan in Hollywood and Out.* New York: Routledge, 1992.

———. "Love Thy Neighbor? No Thanks!" In *The Psychoanalysis of Race.* Edited by Christopher Lane. New York: Columbia University Press, 1998.

———. "Neighbors and Other Monsters: A Plea for Ethical Violence." In *The Neighbor: Three Inquiries in Political Theology.* Chicago: University of Chicago Press, 2005.

———. *Organs without Bodies: Deleuze and Consequences.* London and New York: Routledge, 2004.

———. "Passion—Regular or Decaf?" In *These Times,* February 27, 2004.

———. "Remapping Ideology." In *The Sublime Object of Ideology.* London: Verso, 1989.

———. *The Sublime Object of Ideology.* London: Verso, 1989.

———. *Violence.* New York: Picador, 2008.

Zu, Daniel. "Musings on the Fat City: Are Obesity and Urban Forms Linked?" *Urban Geography* 24, no. 1 (2003): 75–84.

Page numbers in *italics* refer to illustrations; those followed by "n" indicate endnotes.

abjection, 136, 287n23

Achmat, Zackie, 55, 56

adaptation or adjustment. *See specific works and topics*

Adorno, Theodor, 13, 123, 245

advertising, 112, 237

affect: Jameson on, 65; Marxist cultural theory and, 63–69; as metaphysical category, 15–16; metapsychology and, 271n18; nervous system as autonomous, 14; present, affective perception of, 4; structure of, vs. what we call it, 158–59. *See also specific topics*

affective intelligence, 73, 77, 157

affective realism, 11, 52, 274n1

affect theory, 14, 53, 287n30

Against Paranoid Nationalism (Hage), 14

Agamben, Giorgio: "being-such, that it always matters," 274n10; on gestures, 7, 198; manner, model of, 294n19; "means without ends," 260; on planetary petty bourgeois, 191; on sovereignty, 96; on zoe and bios, 291n20; "zone of indifference," 279n21

ageing, in Cantet's Time Out, 222

agency, lateral, 114–17

Ahmed, Sara, 12–13

AIDS and HIV, 55–63, 103

Althusser, Louis, 52, 286n12, 297nn12–13

ambient citizenship, 230–31

ambient noise. See noise and silence

American dream, 29–32, 37–38

Americanists and historicism, 67

anarchism, 260, 301n48, 301n51

Anderson, Benedict, 65

anonymity: of the camera, 243, 299n32; cities as anonymous spaces, 68–69; in Gibson's Pattern Recognition, 86–87

Anti-Oedipus (Deleuze and Guattari), 67

anxiety: fatness and, 107–8; of formlessness, 125; good workers and, 206; impasse and, 199; presentism and, 4; trauma and, 80

apostrophe, 25–26, 252–53

"Apostrophe, Animation, and Abortion" (Johnson), 25–27

"Appetites/Sovereignty" (Pentecost), 118

après-coup or Nachträglichkeit, 80–81, 278n17, 286n12, 288n32

art, avant-garde. See political desire and the body politic in avant-garde art

Asad, Talal, 239, 279n21

Ashbery, John, 28–36, 273n20

Ash Wednesday (Eliot), 273n20

atmosphere: Deleuze's "perturbation," 6; historical novels and, 66; materialism of, 100

atrophied senses, 245

attachment: impersonality and, 125–26, 127–28; lag and, 125; optimism as manifested in, 13; political, 227–28; Sedgwick's deshaming of fantasmatic attachment, 122–23; sexual, 138–39; wearing out of the subject, 27–28. See also cruel optimism; objects of desire; specific topics and works

Attali, Jacques, 224

Augé, Marc, 8, 291n19

autonomia movement, 301n51

autonomous politics, 301n48

autonomy: in Ashbery's untitled poem, 30; Butler on, 183; sovereignty and, 96

avant-garde art. See political desire and the body politic in avant-garde art

Badiou, Alain, 5, 32, 127, 273n22, 291n20

bad life in the Dardennes' Rosetta and La Promesse, 169, 180–86

Balke, Friedrich, 277n8

Barbier, Jean-Claude, 200–201

bargaining in the Dardennes' Rosetta and La Promesse, 171–73, 180

Barthelme, Donald, 30

Bataille, Georges, 96, 97, 285n67

Battle Horgen, Katherine, 110

Baudrillard, Jean, 67, 119, 285n67

"Beach Town" (Hempel), 272n16

beauty in Gaitskill's Two Girls, Fat and Thin, 131, 140–43, 153

belatedness, 294n14

Belgium, 162–63, 168, 169, 178, 289n7

belonging in the Dardennes' Rosetta and La Promesse, 163, 168

Benjamin, Jessica, 272n6

Bergson, Henri, 52, 244

Bersani, Leo, 27, 138–39

Bessette, Lauren, 252

biopolitics and slow death, 101–2

biopower, 97, 105–6, 277n7

Blattberg, Benjamin, 275n19

bodies: in Cantet's *Time Out*, 220; class politics of bodily performance in Cantet's *Human Resources*, 209–12; embodied impersonality, 143; as political problem, 267; precarious, 196–98; queer phenomenology, 197–98; under regimes of production of value, 108. *See also* obesity

body politic. *See* political desire and the body politic in avant-garde art

Bollas, Christopher, 138, 184, 286n8

Borch-Jacobson, Mikkel, 272n4

Bordowitz, Gregg, 55–63, 56, 61

bourgeois: Habermas on, 181; planetary petty bourgeois (PPB), 191–94, 221

Bradley, Slater, 232

Brennan, Teresa, 15, 100

Brothers, Joyce, 107

Brower, L. E. J., 275n27

Browne, Thomas, 32, 272n19

Brownell, Kelly, 110

Bush, George W., 223–26

Butler, Judith, 181–85, 270n2

Cage, John, 245

Campos, Paul, 280n26

Cantet, Laurent: adaptation, the precariat, and the historical present in films of, 194–96; *L'emploi du temps (Time Out)*, 191–92, 212–22; *Ressources humaines (Human Resources)*, 191–92, 202–12

capitalism: capitalist time challenged by anti-precarity activists, 294n14; in the Dardennes' *Rosetta* and *La Promesse*, 166; emotional, 217–18, 296n40; health, rationalization of, 95–96; historical present and, 67–68; Johnson's "Exchange Value," 36–43; obesity and, 104–5; the ordinary disorganized by, 8–9; post-Fordism in the Dardennes' *Rosetta* and *La Promesse*, 171–80; precarity and, 192–93; sovereignty and, 42

Cardullo, Bert, 290n16

Caruth, Cathy, 80–81, 276n33

case study and Gaitskill's *Two Girls, Fat and Thin*, 129–33

catastrophe. *See* crisis or catastrophe

Cavell, Stanley, 9

Cayce, Edgar, 76

CCTV art, 238–45, 299n32

Chang, Virginia W., 283n57

children: Foucault on ascension into sexuality, 176; inheritance and, 174; optimism attached to, 171; as volatile category, 173–74. *See also* family

children and social attachment. *See Rosetta and La Promesse*

Cinema of Precarity, 201–2, 212. *See also* precarity

circulation: being in circulation, 42; of global commodities, 104; in Johnson's "Exchange Value," 42–43; noise, social circulation of, 224–26; queer phenomenology and, 197

cities and anonymity, 68–69, 87–88

citizenship: ambient, 230–31; Bradley's JFK, Jr. and glitches in, 253; in the Dardennes' *Rosetta* and *La Promesse*, 163, 170, 173, 179; security state and, 240

class: bodily performance, class politics of, 209–12; decency or respectability and, 289n12; in Johnson's "Exchange Value," 38; obesity and, 112–13, 116, 283n57; precariat, 192, 195, 222; psychology and, 155–56; Rubin on working-class attachment, 186–87. *See also* bourgeois; labor

Cold Intimacies (Illouz), 217

"Coldness and Cruelty" (Deleuze), 287n20

Cold War, 107–8

comedy, political, 240–45. *See also* situation comedy

community, inoperative, 254, 300n48

"A Comparative Analysis of 'Employment Precariousness' in Europe" (Barbier), 200–201

compassionate recognition, 182

composure, 144–46, 240

control, 96, 239–40, 287n21

conversation, 57–59

Copjec, Joan, 272n16

crisis or catastrophe: in Bordowitz's Habit, 63; as genre, 7; in Gibson's Pattern Recognition, 76–78, 92–93; Katrina and postcatastrophe, 255–58; news 24/7 and, 225; obesity and, 102; the ordinary as impasse shaped by, 8; slow death misrepresented as, 101–2; trauma vs. crisis ordinariness, 10, 81–82; in Whitehead's The Intuitionist, 73–76, 92–93. See also trauma

crisis time, 57, 59

critical theory and optimism, 121

Critser, Greg, 111–12

the cruel cut, 132

cruel optimism: definitions of, 1, 24–25; as deictic, 27–28; double bind of, 51; as lived imminence, 28; love and politics and, 266–67; magnetic attraction of, 48; political attachment and, 227–28; social mourning as, 187–88. See also specific works and topics

Cruising Utopia (Muñoz), 13

cultural minoritization, 287n22

cultural theory, on trauma, 80

curating, 87

Dardenne, Luc and Jean-Pierre. See Rosetta and La Promesse (Dardenne & Dardenne)

Dean, Tim, 27

death and dying, 58–59, 96. See also slow death

Definitism, in Gaitskill's Two Girls, Fat and Thin, 140–41

Deleuze, Gilles: on affect, 14; Anti-Oedipus (Deleuze and Guattari), 67; "Coldness and Cruelty," 287n20; on cultural minoritization, 287n22; faciality, 210; on percept, 127; on perturbation, 6, 278n17; "plane of immanence," 274n9; "problem-events," 198; "What is a Minor Literature?" (Deleuze and Guattari), 48

depression: detachment and the depressive position, 27; obesity and, 109–10; political, 259–61

Derrida, Jacques, 277n8

desire for the political. See political desire and the body politic in avant-garde art

desire in Whitehead's The Intuitionist, 75

detachment, 27, 34–36, 229–30, 263

developmental model of political subjectivity, 181–85

differend, 300n43

The Differend (Lyotard), 285n2

disease: AIDS and HIV, 55–63, 103; from obesity, 113–14; time and chronic illness, 62

DIY aesthetic, 240, 250, 261

doppelgangers in Gibson's Pattern Recognition, 84

downward mobility, obesity and, 112

dread, in Whitehead's The Intuitionist, 88

Dumm, Thomas, 169

Dutoit, Ulysse, 138–39

eating and food: displacement and, 287n22; in Gaitskill's Two Girls, Fat and Thin, 133–38; medicalization of, 102–3, 115; nutritional pedagogy and the French fry, 279n24; pleasure and self-interruption, 115–17; slow food movement, 115. See also obesity

Ehrenreich, Barbara, 296n41

Eliot, T. S., 273n20

emergency as genre, 294n14

emotional capitalism, 217–18, 296n40

L'emploi du temps (*Time Out*) (Cantet), 191–92, 194–96, 212–22

emptiness and food in Gaitskill's *Two Girls, Fat and Thin*, 135

endemics, 97

endurance, compromised, 48

enthusiasm, managerial, 218–20, 296n41

environment: event vs., 100–101; infantile dependency and, 184; obesity and, 114; object of desire as transformational environment, 184

episodic nature of events, 101

epistemology, affective, 64–65

eventilization, 64, 275n13

events: Badiou on being seized by, 32, 273n22; environment vs., 100–101; episodic nature of, 101; gestures as, 198–99; as manifestation of radical contingency, 278n17; sex events, 146–47; situations vs., 5

everyday life theory, 8, 68–69. *See also* the ordinary and the everyday

"Exchange Value" (Johnson), 36–43

exhaustion: in "Cruel Optimism," 42; in Gaitskill's *Two Girls, Fat and Thin*, 152; from the "new normal," 261; by politics, 262; "Slow Death," 116

faciality, 210

Fairbairn, W. R. D., 184

falling man figure, 85–86

family: in Cantet's *Human Resources*, 204–5; in the Dardennes' *Rosetta* and *La Promesse*, 173–74, 178–79; "families we choose," 176, 290n17; in Gaitskill's *Two Girls, Fat and Thin*, 129–31, 155

fan culture, 78

fantasy and the poetics of misrecognition, 122. *See also specific topics, such as good life or attachment*

Farred, Grant, 228

Fat Land (Critser), 111–12

fatness. *See* obesity

The Female Complaint (Berlant), 20, 66

"Femininity" (Freud), 286n20

feminist perspective on love, 181

feminist queer theory, 154–55

Le Fils (Dardenne & Dardenne), 288n3

filters, 223–26, 296n1

flaneurs and flaneuses, 8, 78, 295n26

flexibility in labor, 193, 200–202

food. *See* eating and food; obesity

food insecurity, 106–7, 113, 283n53

Forgotten Families (Heyman), 173–74

formlessness, anxiety of, 125

Foucault, Michel: on ascension into sexuality, 176; eventilization, 64; on sexuality, 226, 247, 297n10; on sovereignty, endemics, and biopower, 97, 277n7

François, Anne-Lise, 86

free indirect discourse, 26–27

freelancers in Gibson's *Pattern Recognition*, 76

Freud, Sigmund: on control, 287n21; "Femininity," 286n20; on libidinal position, 27; *Nachträglichkeit* or *après-coup*, 80–81, 278n17, 286n12, 288n32; on negation, 123

Gaitskill, Mary. *See Two Girls, Fat and Thin* (Gaitskill)

Garland, Judy, 46

gayness in Ashbery's untitled poem, 32, 34. *See also* queerness

gender: labor, gendered division of, 154–55, 174; in Whitehead's *The Intuitionist*, 71–75; women's intuition, 70

generalization as method, 12

genetics and obesity, 110

genre: adjustments to the present and, 20; affective contracts compromised by, 66; as defense, 45; drama produced from moments of potential failure, 148; historicism and, 67; new genres, 7; tempo-

genre (*continued*)

 ral and aesthetic, 5–6; waning of, 6–7.
 See also specific genres

gestures: Agamben on, 7, 198; as genre,
 198; loss of, 198

Ghent, Emmanuel, 271n1

Gibson, William, 69–70, 76–79, 82–87,
 153

Gibson-Graham, J. K., 260–61

Gilroy, Paul, 98

The Gleaners and I (Varda), 200, 294n26

glitches, 198, 253

good life: in the Dardennes' *Rosetta* and
 La Promesse, 163–64, 166, 180; obesity,
 morbidity, and, 114; and wearing out of
 the subject, 27–28

Gould, Deborah, 57

governmentality and death, 96

Graeber, David, 260

Grassian, Stuart, 243

Green, André, 16, 271n18

grey economy. *See* informal economy

grievable life, 181–82

Guattari, Felix: *Anti-Oedipus* (Deleuze and
 Guattari), 67; on cultural minoritization, 287n22; faciality, 210; "plane of
 immanence," 274n9; "What is a Minor
 Literature?" (Deleuze and Guattari), 48

Habermas, Jürgen, 33–34, 181

Habit (Bordowitz), 55–63

habit and habituation: in Bordowitz's
 Habit, 55–63; in Gibson's *Pattern Recognition*, 78; rehabituation, 12, 17, 53–57;
 ritual, 61–62; sex as, 146; trauma and, 81

Hacking, Mark, 214

Hadley, Elaine, 124

Hage, Ghasan, 14

haggling in Gibson's *Pattern Recognition*,
 86–87

Hall, Stuart, 293n6

happenings and trauma, 80

Hardt, Michael, 169–70, 193

Harootunian, Harry, 59, 64, 67–68

Harvey, David, 95, 108, 277n1

"healing" in Whitehead's *The Intuitionist*
 and Gibson's *Pattern Recognition*, 92

health: rationalization of, under capitalism, 95–96, 108; as side effect of normativity, 106; social capital and, 104,
 280n29. *See also* AIDS and HIV; obesity

hegemony as metastructure of consent,
 185

Hempel, Amy, 272n16

Heyman, Jody, 173–74

Hirschkind, Charles, 224

historical novels, 63–69, 154

historical present: overview, 51–55; affectivity of, relayed by aesthetic transmission, 66–67; affectsphere and event in
 Whitehead's *The Intuitionist* and Gibson's
 Pattern Recognition, 69–79; Bordowitz's
 Habit, 55–63; cultural Marxist view of
 historical novels and affect, 63–69; the
 Dardennes' *Rosetta* and *La Promesse* and,
 167; precarity and, 200; sense of anachronism in Madansky's *The PSA Project*,
 237; as situation, 195–96, 212; Sontag's
 "The Way We Live Now," 57–59; trauma
 and anonymity in Whitehead's *The Intuitionist* and Gibson's *Pattern Recognition*,
 79–93; trauma as genre for viewing,
 9–10

historicism: Americanists and, 67; historical novel and aesthetic expression,
 64–65; in Whitehead's *The Intuitionist*, 75

"history is what hurts" (Jameson), 121,
 126, 137, 157

hoarding in Johnson's "Exchange Value,"
 40–42

Hochschild, Arlie, 217

Holder, Geoffrey, 273n24

hope, 13–14

Hope: A Shield in the Economy of Borderline States (Potamianou), 13–14

Human Resources (Cantet), 191–92, 194–96, 202–12

hunger, 106–7, 113, 283n53

Hurricane Katrina and postcatastrophe, 255–58

hypervigilance: in Cantet's Time Out, 217; in the Dardennes' Rosetta and La Promesse, 181; in Gaitskill's Two Girls, Fat and Thin, 130, 139, 153; in Whitehead's The Intuitionist and Gibson's Pattern Recognition, 54, 78, 87

"I Bought a Little City" (Barthelme), 30

idea, overvaluation of, 143–44

ideology theory, 52, 53

If Body: Riva and Zora in Middle Age (Lehrer), 264, 265–67

"I Knew a Woman" (Roethke), 273n20

illness. See disease

Illouz, Eva, 217

impasse: in Ashbery's untitled poem, 33–36; in Cantet's Human Resources, 204–12; in Cantet's Time Out, 217, 221–22; concept of present as, 199; in the Dardennes' Rosetta and La Promesse, 165, 179; "digging a hole," 48; falling man figure and, 86; in Gaitskill's Two Girls, Fat and Thin, 152; in Gibson's Pattern Recognition, 85; in Johnson's "Exchange Value," 38–39; meanings of, 4–5, 199; the ordinary as impasse shaped by crisis, 8; political, affective paradoxes of, 263; precarity and, 199–200; and production of the present, 4; in Ryman's Was, 45; as "soul-lack" or "soul-delay" in Gibson's Pattern Recognition, 82; in Varda's The Gleaners and I, 295n26; in Whitehead's The Intuitionist, 92

impassivity: Ashbery and, 273n20; in Cantet's Human Resources, 212; in Cantet's Time Out, 220; cruel optimism and, 5; slow death and, 117

impersonality: attachment and, 125–26, 127–28; in the Dardennes' Le Fils, 288n3; defined, 159; in Gaitskill's Two Girls, Fat and Thin, 137, 143, 151–52; as optimistic concept, 159

indirection, 25–26

individuality: as contrary form, 125; Gaitskill's Two Girls, Fat and Thin and, 149–50; psychoanalysis and, 145

infantile dependency, 182–83

informal economy: in Cantet's Time Out, 214–15; in the Dardennes' Rosetta and La Promesse, 163, 173, 178–79

inheritance, 41–42, 174

inoperative community, 254, 300n48

instability: and precarity under neoliberalism, 192–93, 196; sex and, 146–47

instrumental vs. loving persona, 181

insult in Gibson's Pattern Recognition, 85

intellectual subjectivity and composure, 144–46

intelligence, affective, 73, 77, 157

interference: with feedback loops, 249; noise as, 232; Surveillance Camera Players and performance of, 242

interiority, 124, 155–56

interruption: in Ashbery's untitled poem, 30, 32–36; glitches, 198, 253; obesity, lateral agency, and self-interruption, 114–17; self-interruption in Gaitskill's Two Girls, Fat and Thin, 136

intersubjectivity: in Ashbery's untitled poem, 33; Johnson's "apostrophe" and, 25–27; proximity vs., 37. See also intimacy

intimacy: in Ashbery's untitled poem, 32–33; in Gaitskill's Two Girls, Fat and intimacy (continued)

    Thin, 129–30; in Gibson's *Pattern Recognition*, 78; "normal," 286n19; normative, in the Dardennes' *Rosetta* and *La Promesse*, 174–75; in Ryman's *Was*, 45

intuition: Gibson's *Pattern Recognition*, 69–70, 76–79; meaning of, 52–53; Whitehead's *The Intuitionist*, 69–76, 87–93; "women's," 70; as zone of inference, 79

The Intuitionist (Whitehead), 69–76, 87–93

Iraq War, 233–38

irony in Cantet's *Human Resources*, 202–3

"I've Got You Under My Skin" (Nyong'o), 247

Jacobsen, Michael, 110–11

Jameson, Fredric, 20, 65, 67, 270n9, 291n21

JFK, Jr. (Slater), 249–53, 251

Johnson, Barbara, 25–27

Johnson, Charles, 36–43

Johnson, Liza, 232, 255–58

jokes, in Whitehead's *The Intuitionist*, 74

justice and injustice, attachment to regimes of, 184–85

Katrina and postcatastrophe, 255–58

Kehr, Dave, 289n5

Kennedy, Carolyn Bessette, 252

Kennedy, John F., Jr., 252

Klein, Melanie, 27, 259

Klein, Richard, 280n26, 284n63

knowledge and intellect: AIDS and knowledge sharing, 57; Phillips on composure, 144–46; smartness in Gaitskill's *Two Girls, Fat and Thin*, 138–46

Kristeva, Julia, 287n23

Labio, Catherine, 289n7

labor: in Cantet's *Human Resources*, 204–10; in Cantet's *Time Out*, 212–20; child labor, 164; in the Dardennes' *Rosetta* and *La Promesse*, 163–64, 178–79; destruction of work, 193; flexible, 193, 200–202; gendered division of, 154–55, 174; immaterial, 197; in Johnson's *South of Ten*, 255–57; obesity and, 108–9; psychological discourse in evaluation of work, 217–18; of social mourning, 187–88; thirty-five hour work week in France, 202–3, 207; worker revolts, 291n22. See also precarity

Laclau, Ernesto, 98

lag: in Ashbery's untitled poem, 28; attachment and, 125; in Gibson's *Pattern Recognition*, 82; soul lag or lack, 76, 82. See also *Nachträglichkeit* or *après-coup*

The Land of Artistic Expression (Slater), 253–55, 254

lateral agency, 114–17

lateral politics, 261–63

Lefebvre, Henri, 8–9, 63, 198

Lehrer, Riva, 264, 265–67

"Let's Move" initiative, 280n25

Leys, Ruth, 276n36

life and living: aesthetic problem equated with, 202; in Bordowitz's *Habit*, 57; eating and, 117; Foucault on sovereignty and biopower, 97; in Sontag's "The Way We Live Now," 59

lifeworld, 185, 291n20

living-on, 41, 180

Lloyd, David, 290n18

loneliness, 82, 142–44

love: in the Dardennes' *Rosetta* and *La Promesse*, 174–75, 180–88; feminist perspective on, 181; instrumental vs. loving persona, 181; in Whitehead's *The Intuitionist*, 90

Lukács, Georg, 65

lying, 188, 214–15

Lyotard, Jean-François, 285n2, 300n43

Madansky, Cynthia, 232, 233–38
Las Madres de la Playa de Mayo (Mothers of the Plaza de Mayo), Argentina, 229
maieutic listening, 224
malnutrition, 106–7, 113, 283n53
managerial affect, ideology of, 218
managerial labor. See precarity
The Man in the Grey Flannel Suit (Johnson), 217–18
manners, 172, 294n19
Marcuse, Hebert, 10
Marx, Karl, 30–31, 108, 285n2
Marxism, cultural, 63–69
Massumi, Brian, 5, 14, 69, 270n7
masturbation, in Gaitskill's Two Girls, Fat and Thin, 136–37
Matter and Memory (Bergson), 52
Mbembe, Achille, 96, 97, 169, 291n20
McCain, John, 224, 296n1
melodrama: Gaitskill's Two Girls, Fat and Thin and, 157–58; moral valuation of noise and, 230–31; soundtrack and, 34, 157
memory and intuition, 52
metaformal genre in Ryman's Was, 44–45
method acting, 215, 218
Migration magazine, 289n4
Mill, John Stuart, 124
Milton, John, 273n20
misrecognition: in Gaitskill's Two Girls, Fat and Thin, 127; poetics of, 122, 159; tragicomedy of intersubjective misrecognition, 26
Moore, Alan, 290n18
morbidity, 114, 278n19
Moten, Fred, 86
mourning, social, 187–88
Muñoz, José Esteban, 13

Nabokov, Vladimir, 157
Nachträglichkeit or après-coup, 80–81, 278n17, 286n12, 288n32

nanny state socialism meme, 280n28
National Depression Screening Day, 109
necessity, submission to, 177
negation: defetishizing, 123; Gaitskill's Two Girls, Fat and Thin and, 132–33, 135–36; vocal, 231
Negri, Antonio, 169–70, 193, 301n51
neighbors and neighborhoods: in Ashbery's untitled poem, 30; in Bordowitz's Habit, 60; emergence of figure of neighbor, 272n16; in Johnson's "Exchange Value," 37
neo-anarchism, 301n48
neocommunitarianism, 260
neoliberalism: Augé on the nonplace, 291n19; Cantet's films and, 194–95; CCTV art and, 239; the Dardennes' Rosetta and La Promesse and, 167; democracy and psychoanalysis, 194; freelancers and sovereignty, 76; French thirty-five hour work week and, 202–3, 207; Gaitskill's Two Girls, Fat and Thin and, 154; instability, precarity, and, 192–93; obesity and, 109–10; as world-homogenizing sovereign, 15. See also precarity
nervous systems: as autonomous, 14; in Bordowitz's Habit, 60–61; in Gibson's Pattern Recognition, 77, 79, 83; precarity and, 197; in Whitehead's The Intuitionist, 72, 79
Nestle, Marion, 110–11
new anarchism, 301n51
new normal: in Cantet's Human Resources, 206–11; lateral politics and, 261; the "new abnormal," 297n9; origins of, 296n33
"New Realism," 201, 274n1
9/11: Bradley's The Land of Artistic Expression, 254–55, 254; falling man figure, 85–86; in Gibson's Pattern Recognition, 78, 83–86

noise and silence: ambient citizenship and, 230–31; filters and, 223–26, 296n1; moral valuation of noise, 230–31; overhead politics, 227; performative silence and interference, 231–32; political attachment through transmission of, 224; public sphere theory and hearing, 297n12; silent protest, 228–29, 231, 298n17; Slater's *JFK, Jr.* and *The Land of Artistic Expression*, 249–55, 251, 254; social circulation of noise, 224–26; Surveillance Camera Players (scp), 240–45, 241; UltraRed's *Organizing the Silence*, 245–48, 246; voiceless speech, 242, 298n17. *See also* political desire and the body politic in avant-garde art

nonplaces, 291n19

normativity: affect theory and, 53; aspirational, in the Dardennes' *Rosetta* and *La Promesse*, 169–71; fraying of norms, 196; health as side effect of, 106; news 24/7 and postnormativity, 225; new normal in Cantet's *Human Resources*, 206–11; postnormative life in Cantet's *Time Out*, 215; privilege vs., 167; proximate, in the Dardennes' *Rosetta* and *La Promesse*, 174–80; simulacrum of normalcy in the Dardennes' *Rosetta* and *La Promesse*, 172–73

nostalgia and rest in the Dardennes' *Rosetta* and *La Promesse*, 180

Nyong'o, Tavia, 247

Obama, Barack, 228

Obama, Michelle, 103

obesity: corporations, capital, and, 104–5, 108, 111–12; depression and medicalization of, 109–10; in Gaitskill's *Two Girls, Fat and Thin*, 128, 142–43; "globesity," 99–100, 277n11; history of dynamic anxiety, 107–8; lateral agency, 114–17; "morbidly obese," 113; nutritional pedagogy and the French fry, 279n24;

paranoia and biopower, 105–6; race, poverty, and, 112–14; as resistance, 281n35; slow-death crisis-scandal management, 102–6; statistics and measurements, 106, 112, 282n45; structural or impersonal etiologies, 110–11; the underfed and, 106–7, 113, 283n53

objects of desire: as clusters of promises, 23–24; in the Dardennes' *La Promesse*, 166; as transformational environment, 184

object/thing distinction, eventilization and, 275n13

The Office (bbc), 290n18

Oliver, J. Eric, 280n26

"On Composure" (Phillips), 144–46

"On His Blindness" (Milton), 273n20

optimism: affective structure of, 2; in Ashbery's untitled poem, 34; children and, 171; critical theory and, 121; definitions of, 1–2, 14; "healing," 92; objects of attachment and, 23–24; "stupid," 126. *See also* cruel optimism

the ordinary and the everyday: centrality of everyday life, 67; crisis ordinariness, 10, 117, 169; in the Dardennes' *Rosetta* and *La Promesse*, 169–70; disorganized by capitalism, 8–9; everyday life theory, 8, 68–69, 291n19; as impasse shaped by crisis, 8; new ordinary, 262–63; the nonplace and, 291n19; sex and, 146–47; slow death and, 102

Organizing the Silence (UltraRed), 232, 245–48, 246

Palin, Sarah, 224, 296n1

Papadopoulos, Dimitris, 197

paranoia, obesity and, 105

Partnership for a Healthier America, 103

paternalism, in Cantet's *Human Resources*, 204–12

pathocartography, 60

pathogeography, 88–89, 275n12

Patten, Mary, 275n12

Pattern Recognition (Gibson), 69–70, 76–79, 82–87, 153, 275n19

Pentecost, Claire, 55, 61, 61, 118

periodization in Whitehead's *The Intuitionist*, 80

Personal Responsibility in Food Consumption Act (2005), 102, 279n23

perturbation, 6, 278n17

Peter Pan (Barrie), 141–42

Phillips, Adam, 81, 144–46, 194

phrase, concept of, 285n2

"plane of immanence," 60, 274n9

planetary petty bourgeois (PPB), 191–94, 221

play: in the Dardennes' *Rosetta* and *La Promesse*, 170–71; in Johnson's *South of Ten*, 258

political depression, 259–61

political desire and the body politic in avant-garde art: body as political problem, 267; CCTV art and the Surveillance Camera Players (SCP), 238–45, 241; filters and the circulation of noise, 223–26, 296n1; Johnson's *South of Ten*, 255–58, 256, 258; Madansky's *The PSA Project*, 232, 233–38, 234, 235, 236, 299n22; overheard politics, 226–27; political attachment, solidarity, and cruel optimism, 227–28; political depression, cruel optimism, and lateral politics, 259–63; politics vs. the political, 225–26, 252; Slater's *JFK, Jr.* and *The Land of Artistic Expression*, 249–55, 251, 254; thematic overview, 228–33; UltraRed's *Organizing the Silence*, 232, 245–48, 246

political economy in Johnson's "Exchange Value," 37–43

political feeling statements, 247

The Political Unconscious (Jameson), 65, 67

Pollan, Michael, 279n24

Pollard, Jonathan, 76

post-Fordism in the Dardennes' *Rosetta* and *La Promesse*, 171–80

postmodernism, Jameson on shift to, 65

Postone, Moishe, 64

the "post-traumatic," 54

Potamianou, Anna, 13–14, 259

poverty: Declaration of the World Food Summit on, 282n44; in Johnson's "Exchange Value," 41; Marx on private property and, 31; obesity, hunger, and, 107, 112–13, 283n57; social mourning amid, 187–88. *See also* precarity

PPB (planetary petty bourgeois), 191–94, 221

preaching to the choir, 238

Precarias de la Deriva ("The Precarious Adrift"), 193

precariat class, 192, 195, 222

Precarious movement, 193

precarity: adaptation, the precariat, and the historical present in Cantet's films, 194–96; bibliography for, 293n1; in Cantet's *Human Resources*, 191–92, 202–12; in Cantet's *Time Out*, 191–92, 212–22; capitalist time challenged by anti-precarity activists, 294n14; Cinema of Precarity, 201–2, 212; *Droits Devants*, 293n5; entrepreneurial, 76; global movement of the precarious, 270n2; meaning of, 192, 293n7; *précarité* and *précarisation*, 200–201; proprioceptive history of, 196–98; thematic overview, 191–94, 198–200; in Whitehead's *The Intuitionist*, 89

"Precarity: A Savage Journey to the Heart of Embodied Capitalism" (Tsianos and Papadopoulos), 196–97

the present: in Bordowitz's *Habit*, 62–63; in Cantet's *Human Resources*, 210–12; in Cantet's *Time Out*, 221–22; in the Dardennes' *Rosetta* and *La Promesse*, 179; emergency as genre of, 294n14; the eye the present (continued)

and, 236; in Gaitskill's *Two Girls, Fat and Thin*, 157–59; in Gibson's *Pattern Recognition*, 77–81, 92; hope as solution for, 13–14; impasses and production of, 4; lateral politics and, 261; memory and, 52; perceived affectively, 4; precarity and, 192, 199–201; as process of emergence, 7; Stern's "the present moment," 271n1; thick (Harootunian), 59, 68; weight of, 29; in Whitehead's *The Intuitionist*, 75, 79–81, 92. *See also* historical present; impasse; time and temporality

presentism, 4, 68

private property, 30–31, 274n3

Probyn, Elspeth, 284n63

projection, in Johnson's "Apostrophe, Animation, and Abortion," 26–27

La Promesse (Dardenne & Dardenne). *See Rosetta* and *La Promesse*

The Promise of Happiness (Ahmed), 12–13

proprioception: anonymity and, 72; cruel optimism and, 20; dressage and, 63; precarity and, 196–98, 201, 212; security camera aesthetics and, 244

protest, silent, 228–29, 231, 298n17. *See also* political desire and the body politic in avant-garde art

proximity and proximate normativity in the Dardennes' *Rosetta* and *La Promesse*, 174–80

The PSA Project (Madansky), 232–38, 234, 235, 236, 299n22

psychoanalysis, 180–86, 194

psychogeography, 275n12

psychological discourse in evaluation of work, 217–18

psychological prophylaxis (Gibson's *Pattern Recognition*), 77, 83

psychology and class, 155–56

public/private zoning in Ashbery's untitled poem, 33, 36

public service announcements, 233–38, 299n23

public spheres: as affect worlds, 226; hearing and public sphere theory, 297n12; intimate publics, 226–28; precarious, 195–203; public sphere ethics in Cantet's *Human Resources*, 207

queerness: in Ashbery's untitled poem, 32, 34; "families we choose," 176, 290n17; Gaitskill's *Two Girls, Fat and Thin* and, 131, 154–55; interiority and, 125; Sedgwick on, 123

Queer Optimism (Snediker), 12

queer phenomenology, 197–98

race: Johnson's *South of Ten* and post-catastrophe, 257; obesity and, 112–14; Whitehead's *The Intuitionist* and white supremacy, 71–75, 88–90; whiteness in the Dardennes' *Rosetta* and *La Promesse*, 170

Rainer, Yvonne, 55, 56

Rancière, Jacques, 5, 194, 225, 260

rape. *See* sexual violence and rape

reading, in Gaitskill's *Two Girls, Fat and Thin*, 124–26, 148–49

realism: affective, 11, 26, 30, 52–54; French "New Realism," 201, 274n1

recessive action, 86

reciprocity: in Cantet's *Time Out*, 221–22; in the Dardennes' *Rosetta* and *La Promesse*, 168, 175–78, 185

recognition: compassionate, 182; in the Dardennes' *Rosetta* and *La Promesse*, 185; exchange value of, 43; misrecognition, 26, 122, 127, 159

rehabituation, 12, 17, 53–57

religion, 32, 89

"Remembering the Historical Present" (Harootunian), 67–68

reparative criticism, 123–24

repetition: *après coup* and, 288n32; in the Dardennes' *Rosetta* and *La Promesse*, 188; in Gaitskill's *Two Girls, Fat and Thin* and, 136, 137–39; in situation tragedy, 177–78

resonance to one side, in Gaitskill's *Two Girls, Fat and Thin*, 127

Ressources humaines (Human Resources) (Cantet), 191–92, 194–96, 202–12

rest, 180, 214

revolutionary consciousness, 169–70

Rhythmanalysis (Lefebvre), 63, 198

Ricco, John, 34

ritual, 61–62

Roethke, Theodore, 273n20

Rohy, Valerie, 66

Roitman, Janet, 169

romance novels, 148–50

Romand, Jean-Claude, 214

Rosetta and *La Promesse* (Dardenne & Dardenne), social attachment in: children and premature adulthood, 173–74; endings of, 175–78; ordinariness and aspirational normativity, 169–71; post-Fordist citizenship and bargaining, 171–73; proximate normativity, 174–80; psychoanalytic reading and infantile dependency, 180–86; rest imagined nostalgically, 180; Rubin's temporality and Waquant's social mourning, 186–89; sex traffic in *La Promesse*, 288n4; thematic overview, 161–69; working families as sites of production, 178–79

Rosetta Plan (Belgium), 163, 288n1

Rubin, Lillian, 186–87

Ryman, Geoff, 44–48

Satcher, David, 107–8

scavenging, 237, 257–58

Schmitt, Carl, 96

Scott, A. O., 66, 295n30

Screaming Man figure, 90–91

secret life, in Cantet's *Time Out*, 213–14

security: precarity and erosion of, 193; security state, 240–44; surveillance and society of control, 239–40. *See also* precarity

Sedgwick, Eve, 27, 122–26, 158, 259, 262, 287n30

self-annihilation, 133, 136, 159

self-awareness, liberal cultivation of, 124

self-extension: future anteriority of subjects, 99, 277n10; in Gibson's *Pattern Recognition*, 77; interruption and, 116–17

self-understanding, 117, 146

Sennet, Richard, 193

senses: in Ashbery's untitled poem, 31–34; atrophied, 245; Marx on, 31; "war on terror" and, 243

Serres, Michel, 224

sex traffic in the Dardennes' *La Promesse*, 288n4

sexuality: in Ashbery's untitled poem, 32, 136–37; in Cantet's *Time Out*, 220; in the Dardennes' *Rosetta* and *La Promesse*, 176–77; enigma of sexual attachment, 138–39; Foucauldian, 226, 247, 297n10; in Gaitskill's *Two Girls, Fat and Thin*, 133, 140, 146–52; Sedgwick on, 123; in Whitehead's *The Intuitionist*, 89–90

sexual violence and rape: in Gaitskill's *Two Girls, Fat and Thin*, 129–32, 150–52; in Whitehead's *The Intuitionist*, 87–88

shame: in Cantet's *Human Resources*, 207–9; in Cantet's *Time Out*, 214; obesity and, 115; presumed as primary sexual affect, 287n30; Sedgwick's deshaming of fantasmatic attachment, 122–23

silence. *See* noise and silence

singularity: Bordowitz's *Habit* and the singularity of the present, 55; in Gibson's *Pattern Recognition*, 83–84, 91–92; in Johnson's "Exchange Value," 42–43;

singularity (continued)
Massumi on, 270n7; in Whitehead's The
Intuitionists, 91–92
situation: defined, 5–6, 195; events vs., 5;
historical present as, 195–96, 212
situation comedy, 5–6, 176–78, 195
situation tragedy: the Dardennes' Rosetta
and La Promesse as, 177; defined, 176;
genres of aesthetic embarrassment,
290n18; the nonplace and, 291n19;
situation comedy vs., 6, 176–77
slapstick, 244
slow death: Baudrillard on, 119; crisis
rhetoric of, 101–2; defined, 102; event
vs. environment, 100–101; morbidity
and, 114, 278n19; obesity and, 102; self-
interruption and, 117; sovereignty and,
95–100
slow food movement, 115, 285n64
s/m, in Gaitskill's Two Girls, Fat and Thin,
151–52
Snediker, Michael, 12
social attachment at the economic bottom. See Rosetta and La Promesse
social capital, 104, 280n29
social mourning, labor of, 187–88
solidarity and political attachment, 227–
28, 238
Sontag, Susan, 57–59
"soul-lack" or "soul-delay," 82
sound and soundtrack: in Bordowitz's
Habit, 63; in Cantet's Time Out, 214; in
Gaitskill's Two Girls, Fat and Thin, 157;
home/hymn/hum in Ashbery's untitled
poem, 33–36; in Madansky's The PSA
Project, 236–37; maieutic listening, 224;
in melodrama, 34; public sphere theory
and hearing, 297n12; "soundtrack of
our lives," 34–35; voiceless speech, 242,
298n17. See also noise and silence
South of Ten (Johnson), 255–58, 256, 258
sovereignty: freelancers and, 76; as inade-

quate concept, 97–98; infantile dependency and, 182; insult and, 85; in Johnson's "Exchange Value," 42–43; mimetic
concept of, 96–97; nonmimetic concept of, 98–99; Pentecost's "Appetites/
Sovereignty," 118; security state and,
242–43; slow death and, 95–100. See also
anonymity
Spivak, Gayatri, 86, 174
the state and the body politic. See political desire and the body politic in avant-
garde art
Steedman, Carolyn, 155–56, 292n38
Stern, Daniel, 271n1
Stewart, Kathleen, 8, 69, 76
The Structural Transformation of the Public
Sphere (Habermas), 33–34
"structure of feeling," 65
"stupid optimism," 126
The Sturdy Oak (Jordan), 229
subjective privacy and propertied privacy,
274n3
submission: Gaitskill's Two Girls, Fat and
Thin and, 148–49; to necessity in the
Dardennes' Rosetta and La Promesse and,
177–78; surrender vs., 271n1
subordination: and appearance of affects,
158–59; attachment to, in the Dardennes' Rosetta and La Promesse, 180–86;
infantile dependency and, 182–84;
as subjectifying vs. desubjectifying,
287n23; UltraRed's Organizing the Silence
and, 247
substitutes and substitution, 42, 46–47
suburbanism, 29–30
Sullum, Jacob, 280n28
supermodernity, 291n19
surrender vs. submission, 271n1
Surveillance Camera Players (SCP), 240–
45, 241
suspense of character, 289n5
suspicion, hermeneutics of, 123

symptom: as case, 284n61; composure and the lie of, 145; trauma and, 80–81

Taussig, Michael, 8, 60
teleopoiesis, 86
testimony, in UltraRed's *Organizing the Silence* and, 247
thirty-five hour work week in France, 202–3, 207
Thompson, Tommy, 107
Thrift, Nigel, 8, 68
time and temporality: belatedness, 294n14; in Cantet's *Time Out*, 213; crisis time in Bordowitz's *Habit*, 57; eating and, 115–16; environment and, 101, 278n18; Gaitskill's *Two Girls, Fat and Thin* and, 158; global crisis time, 59; not-stopping, 169; working-class attachment and, 186
Time Out (Cantet), 191–92, 194–96, 212–22
torture, 90, 243–44
tragicomedy, 244–45
trauma: crisis ordinariness vs., 10, 81–82; cultural theory and Caruth model, 80–81, 276n33; in Gaitskill's *Two Girls, Fat and Thin*, 126–27, 137–38, 142, 148, 150–52, 155; as genre for viewing historical present, 9–10; *Lifetime* channel movies and, 237; mimetic and anti-mimetic symptom, 276n36; *Nachträglichkeit* or *après-coup* and, 80–81, 278n17, 286n12, 288n32; 9/11 as, 83–86, 254–55; in Ryman's *Was*, 44–48; as style(s) for managing being overwhelmed, 81; in Whitehead's *The Intuitionist* and Gibson's *Pattern Recognition*, 73–74, 77–93. *See also* crisis or catastrophe
trauma theory, 10, 54
travelogue, 60
trending, 255
Tsianos, Vassilis, 197
Two Girls, Fat and Thin (Gaitskill): case

study genre and, 129–33; ending of, 152–58; food and eating, 133–38; sex and romance, 146–52; smartness, intellection, and composure, 138–46; thematic overview, 126–29

UltraRed, 232, 245–48, 246
unoriginality and sex, 147
"unthought known," 138, 155
upward mobility: the Dardennes' *Rosetta* and *La Promesse* and, 179; flexibility and, 201; and hating of the false self, 217; impasse in Cantet's *Human Resources* and, 204–12; in Johnson's "Exchange Value," 41–42; lateral mobility and, 222; value of lateral freedoms and creativity vs., 193
utopia: Gaitskill's *Two Girls, Fat and Thin* and, 139–40; the nearly utopian in the Dardennes' *Rosetta* and *La Promesse*, 163–64; Whitehead's *The Intuitionist*, 70, 74–76, 87, 90

Valverde, Marianna, 115
Varda, Agnes, 200, 294n26
V for Vendetta (Lloyd), 290n18
violence, "deferred," 88, 91
violence, sexual. *See* sexual violence and rape
violence of the state, and death, 96
Vogler, Candace, 286n19
voiceless speech, 242, 298n17
voters, self-disenfranchisement of, 285n66
vulnerability: in Gaitskill's *Two Girls, Fat and Thin*, 130; precarity and, 194, 196

Wacquant, Loïc, 187–88, 293n5
war, 233–38
Warner, Michael, 297nn12–13
"war on terror," 243
Was (Ryman), 44–48
"The Way We Live Now" (Sontag), 57–59

"we," 30–32, 58

"weak theory," 262

wealth as change, in Johnson's "Exchange Value," 39–40

We Are Watching You (Surveillance Camera Players), 240–45, 241

Weston, Kath, 290n17

"'What Angel Would Hear Me?'" (Benjamin), 272n6

"What is a Minor Literature?" (Deleuze and Guattari), 48

Whitehead, Colson, 69–76, 87–93

white supremacy in Whitehead's The Intuitionist, 71–74, 88–90

will: "anti-will," 277n12; interruptions of, 116–17

Williams, Patricia, 277n12, 291n20

Williams, Raymond, 7, 15, 65

Winnicott, Donald, 184

The Wizard of Oz (Baum), 44–48

Woolf, Virginia, 32, 273n21

working class. See class; Rosetta and La Promesse

World Food Summit, 110, 282n44

"zero-point" in Whitehead's The Intuitionist, 72

Žižek, Slavoj, 14, 30, 64, 263, 301n51

"zone of indifference" (Agamben), 279n21

Zorach, Rebecca, 275n12

LAUREN BERLANT is the George M. Pullman
Professor of English at the University of Chicago.
She is the author of *The Female Complaint: The
Unfinished Business of Sentimentality in American Culture*
(2008), *The Queen of America Goes to Washington City:
Essays on Sex and Citizenship* (1997), and *The Anatomy of
National Fantasy: Hawthorne, Utopia, and Everyday Life*
(1991).

. . .

Library of Congress Cataloging-in-Publication Data
Berlant, Lauren Gail, 1957–
Cruel optimism / Lauren Berlant.
p. cm.
Includes bibliographical references and index.
ISBN 978-0-8223-5097-2 (cloth : alk. paper)
ISBN 978-0-8223-5111-5 (pbk. : alk. paper)
1. United States—Social conditions—1980–   2. Popular
culture—United States.   3. Optimism—United States.
4. Progress.   I. Title.
HN59.2.B464 2011
302.23′4097309045—dc23
2011021902